The Tarot Decoded: Raziel'

MW00647658

Table of Contents

Introduction

Pamela Colman "Pixie" Smith

Pamela Colman "Pixie" Smith circa 1912

We are most familiar with the Rider-Waite tarot deck in the English-speaking world, where it was the first deck illustrated by Pamela Colman Smith, specifically for esoteric uses. Most modern tarot readers refer to this deck as the Rider-Waite-Smith tarot deck giving credit to Pamela Smith. This tarot deck included the illustrated Minor Arcana, filled with rich symbolism for esoteric and divinatory use. It was first published in 1909 alongside a book called "The Pictorial Key to the Tarot", written by Arthur Edward Waite, which provided the interpretations that many of us are familiar with today.

Both Arthur Waite and Pamela Colman Smith were members of the Golden Dawn, a metaphysical society whose philosophy included tarot within a larger framework of esoteric concepts, the

Rider-Waite deck was intentionally drawn to avoid strong Astrological and Kabbalistic associations since it was meant to be introduced to the mass market. Instead, the imagery was created from a series of visions that Smith received (Lon Milo DuQuette, "Understanding Aleister Crowley's Thoth Tarot"), and ironically the Astrology and Kabbalah associations were concealed within Smith's illustrations as she channeled her work. These hidden mysteries present themselves to the adept with the eyes to see. Real eyes will realize.

Pamela Colman Smith was known for going into a trance and channeling drawings while listening to music, many years before the surrealists experimented with automatism in art.

Smith was a woman defined by spiritual duality. Initially a member of the Hermetic Order of the Golden Dawn—a collective dedicated to the exploration and study of metaphysics and the occult—she later converted to Catholicism.

Pamela Colman Smith and Arthur Edward Waite became friends around 1901 after meeting as members of the Order of the Golden Dawn. They both craved a deeper understanding of mysticism and the occult. Although both eventually left the order, the two remained friends and continued to explore the symbolism and history of the occult. When Waite discovered the medieval predecessor to tarot during research and decided to create a modern edition, Smith was the only person he felt could help him actualize his vision. In Waite's autobiography, he refers to Smith as: "A Most imaginative and abnormally psychic artist." With Waite's guidance, Smith conjured the Major and Minor Arcana and illustrated the Rider-Waite cards, creating what became one of the most famous tarot decks in the Western world.

Within the tarot community, Smith's contribution has become more widely known. Practitioners and querents (those who are asking questions) have found solace in her story.

In 1909, Waite paid Smith a flat fee for illustrating his Tarot deck. He chose her for the job because of her talent, their common membership in the Golden Dawn, and because he believed her clairvoyant abilities would help her perceive the higher mystical truths he was attempting to convey with his deck. She not only didn't benefit financially from the deck, but the publisher's name was put on the deck instead of hers. Recently, the tarot community has been correcting this injustice by referring to the deck as the Rider Waite Smith(RWS) or Waite-Smith (WS). Waite also commissioned her because she took less than what other artists wanted for the commission. He tricked her into taking the flat rate commission with a hidden addendum that forfeits her rights to royalties. This all done under the guise that the deck would be classified as nonprofit and/or limited production.

It was common practice for women to be less recognized for their contributions during those times in history; men published all the works. This may have been another example where a humble woman gets herself involved with a businessman and opportunist.

It is time to give credit where credit is due, and give her the admiration she deserves; to give Pamela Smith her rightful place in history as a great mystic and contributor to spiritual knowledge. Recognize the genius of her illustrations as seen through the various Astrology, Kabbalah, Gematria, Gnosticism, and Egyptian mythology that can be symbolized by a myriad of things from Judaism to Catholicism, from allegory to sigils. No man nor woman could have drawn this artwork without the help from the divine, conjuring the multidimensional symbology of the Hermetic universe.

I feel that when Smith illustrated the tarot deck, she channeled the archangel Raziel, whose name means 'secrets of God.' The angel Raziel influenced and communicated to Smith through divine revelation and inspiration the mysteries and wisdom of the spiritual laws of nature and life on earth, including the knowledge of the planets, stars and the spiritual laws of creation. Raziel is the angel depicted in the Lovers card, who is seen teaching Adam and Eve all God's secrets. Raziel gave Adam a book called the Sefer Raziel HaMalakh aka 'the book of Raziel the angel', containing the knowledge of the power of speech, the power of thoughts and the power of a person's soul within the confines of the physical body and this physical world, basically teaching the knowledge with which one can harmonize physical and spiritual existence in this physical world. This book was given to Enoch, and then to Noah, and then to Abraham, and then to King Solomon, and eventually this wisdom was channeled through Pamela Smith as she illustrated the tarot deck.

Just as Smith received divine inspiration from Raziel, I too was able to tune in to the frequency of Raziel who revealed to me the deep mysteries and secrets concealed within Pamela Smith's tarot card illustrations. Raziel inspired Smith on the illustration, and I experienced an awakening, as if a veil had been lifted, and afterward felt like an adept revealing the knowledge of the wisdom hidden within the artwork. It was through divine inspiration that I was revealed the language of the symbols. It was a flood of information downloaded all at once. I knew I had to write everything down, and compile all the many tarot secrets into one book. I always felt like something big was going to happen to me once I turned 40 years old, and this is when I experienced this awakening of tarot knowledge. I feel as though I was remembering all these things from my past life. Although, my entire life I have felt 'woke', and have always been drawn to such esoteric things. Beginning around the age of 27 is when I really started to dive into the Kabbalah and the esoteric studies, such as Hermetics. Now, 15 years later, I get to share my wisdom.

A.E. Waite wrote a book "The Pictorial Key to the Tarot" with his own descriptions of Smith's cards, but his interpretations do not match up with the hidden mysteries and secrets hidden within the symbols. It is as if Waite was trying hard to make up descriptions of Smith's illustrations, describing each card vaguely and with imprecise obscurity. Waite was a member of the Hermetic Order of the Golden Dawn, a secret society dedicated to the preservation of occult knowledge. It held the belief that only people who had been members and studied for many years would be 'elevated' enough to be able to receive the most inner teachings, among those teachings, the 'full' meaning of the tarot cards. When this book was written in 1911, public knowledge of the tarot had just started to grow, and there were many charlatans who were using the cards for dubious reasons. To a large extent, this book was written to denounce all of the 'spurious' meanings that had become associated with the cards. Unfortunately, because so much of the real meanings were limited to those who had advanced in the Order, Waite is not very open in sharing those meanings with outsiders. The result is that you get a lot of what the cards AREN'T, but not very much of what the cards ARE.

What you do get within his book, "The Pictorial Key", is a fairly detailed history of the cards and background on early interpretations of the cards. He provides enough divinatory meanings and a couple of spreads that you could use this book to learn the cards and (sort of) how to use them, but his book is really of more interest to the serious student of the Tarot who is looking for historic insights and history.

Smith's voice and vision was not heard, and Waite took the limelight and the credit. The true meanings concealed within the tarot were never given the chance to be known. He even wrote a book describing Pamela Smith's art as if it were his own inspired work.

It is now time for the world to know the real original Raziel tarot secrets that are hidden in plain sight. The world is now ready to absorb this deep wisdom that has been hidden for so many years.

The world is currently experiencing a time of awakening. The curtain is being pulled, and truths that were once hidden are now being revealed. The veil has been lifted. The world is spiritually ready and also in desperate need to know of these Kabbalistic tools and how to (in a practical way) use these tools which have been concealed within the tarot for far too long.

This book pulls back the curtain and reveals the Rider-Waite (Smith) tarot secrets, and will explain the meanings of the symbols, in depth explanations of the Torah analogy, uncovers the Jewish holiday associations, delve into the symbolic language, unveils the gematria (Hebrew numerology), bring to light the spiritual meanings of the Hebrew letters, disclose the locations of the two keys that are used for manifesting wishes, and decodes the ancient SATOR Square. This book includes full detailed descriptions for all 78 tarot cards. Furthermore, this book includes Paths to Enlightenment for each zodiac sign, integrating astrology with the tarot. This book will thoroughly explain the Tarot's Kabbalistic system of reading the cards.

Thanks to the Stuart Kaplan's edited volume "Pamela Colman Smith: The Untold Story" (U.S. Games Systems), written by Mary K Greer, Elizabeth Foley O'Connor, and Melinda Boyd Parsons, details about Pamela Colman Smith are finally available to the general public. Through essays and full-color reproductions of her art, the book presents the first extensive study of her life. It explores her childhood in Jamaica, her involvement in English women's suffrage, and her presence in literary circles that included the Yeats family, and not to mention her vast, diverse artistic output. The book reveals a complex, talented woman whose efforts to overcome patriarchal structures in the 20th century are strikingly relevant in the 21st.

Chapter 1

The Legend of Archangel Raziel

Raziel is the archangel of clairvoyance, spiritual understanding and in reclaiming your power. Raziel is a keeper of the mysteries of life. Connecting with Raziel can help enlighten you to greater knowledge and understanding of many of the subtle workings of creation so you can see beyond the veil and understand that truth is much different than it often appears to us in physical reality. Raziel can also help you understand esoteric spiritual ideas and apply them in practical ways. He knows all the energies and how to use and manipulate them for various purposes. Call on Raziel to soul travel in your dreams. He helps us to perform astral travel successfully. He teaches esoteric subjects and helps develop the wisdom within you. Raziel helps with past-life regression and can help you access wisdom and release blocks from your previous incarnations. He offers guidance regarding all metaphysical practices, including: astrology, alchemy, astral travel, chakras, crystals, dream work, numerology, psychic development, Reiki, and shamanism. He is also the archangel of law makers and lawyers.

His name means, 'secrets of God.' The archangel Raziel played a major role in early Jewish mystical tradition. His name is first mentioned in the Book of Enoch, composed sometime before the Common Era (C.E.). Raziel first revealed his 'secrets of God' to Adam and Eve in the garden of Eden shortly after they partook of the forbidden fruit from the Tree of Knowledge of Good and Evil. This particular scene is illustrated in the Lovers card where Raziel is pictured having a bright glowing yellow halo converged with the yellow sun directly behind his head. Raziel is depicted here wearing his signature gray robe, which gives the impression to whirl as if made of fluid. Depicted behind Raziel is Mount Horeb, the mountain where Raziel was known to appear daily.

The Targum Ecclesiastes, which is part of the rabbinical commentaries known as the Midrash, says in chapter 10 verse 20 that Raziel announced divine secrets orally in ancient times: "Each day the angel Raziel makes proclamations on Mount Horeb, from heaven, of the secrets of men to all that dwell upon the earth, and his voice resounds throughout the world." Raziel is depicted hovering over this mountain in the Lovers card with a large sun behind him. Horeb, thought to mean glowing/heat, with reference to the Sun, and considered to be the Mountain of the Sun.

Those who practice Kabbalah, believe that Raziel reveals the divine wisdom that the Torah contains. People sometimes ask for Raziel's help to hear God's guidance more clearly, gain deeper spiritual insights, understand esoteric information, as well as pursue clairvoyance, alchemy and divine magic. Raziel oversees life's mysteries and can help you understand it all. Call on him to increase claircognizance—your innate ability to psychically know. He can remove the blocks to your spiritual gifts, clearing the way for profound psychic perception and instant manifestation. Call on Raziel to unlock your divine potential and abilities. Being the angel who knows the secrets of the universe, he can help you understand high-level metaphysical lore. He can help you decode the true meaning of religious scripture, doctrine and symbols. Call on him to increase the power of ceremonies and rituals. Raziel sits among the highest class of archangels with Michael, Raphael, and Gabriel.

The archangel Raziel was the transmitter of secrets and preserved this wisdom of the knowledge of the universe into a book, the Book of Raziel (Sefer Raziel HaMalakh), known as a book of 'magic.' According to some legends, this 'book' was originally inscribed on a sapphire stone. The Book of Raziel disclosed everything from the astrology of the planets to the creative life energy. It described birth, death, reincarnation of the soul, and other occult subjects. The archangel explained that the contents of the book contained all things worth knowing that can be learnt, and all mysteries, and it teaches also how to call upon the angels and make them appear before men, and answer all their questions. The Book of Raziel is called the first book ever written since Adam was the first human to possess its contents, according to Judaic legends.

According to the legend, Raziel gave Adam the Sefer Raziel HaMalakh after Adam and Eve were expelled from the garden of Eden as punishment for eating of the Tree of Knowledge. Other angels were upset that Raziel had given them the book, however, so they cast it into the ocean. Eventually, the book washed ashore, and the prophet Enoch found it and added some of his own knowledge before he was transformed into the archangel Metatron. The Sefer Raziel HaMalakh, sometimes written HaMalach, then passed on to the archangel Raphael, Noah, Abraham, and King Solomon.

Adam, in his prayer to God, apologized for listening to his wife Eve, who was deceived by the serpent into eating from the Tree of Knowledge. According to the book, God sent the highest of the angels, Raziel, to teach Adam the spiritual laws of nature and life on earth, including the knowledge of the planets, stars and the spiritual laws of creation. The Sefer Raziel HaMalakh explains divine secrets about both celestial and earthly knowledge.

The Zohar, the holy book of the mystical branch of Judaism known as Kabbalah, says that Raziel is the angel in charge of Chokmah (wisdom). Jewish tradition says that Raziel stood so close to God's throne that he could hear everything God said; then Raziel wrote God's secret insights about the universe down in his book. Raziel began the book by stating: "Blessed are the wise by the mysteries coming from the wisdom." Some of the insights that Raziel included in the book are that creative energy begins with thoughts in the spiritual realm and then leads to words and actions in the physical realm.

The angel Raziel also taught Adam the knowledge of the power of speech, the power of thoughts and the power of a person's soul within the confines of the physical body and this physical world, basically teaching the knowledge with which one can harmonize physical and spiritual existence in this physical world. The angel Raziel teaches the power of speech, the energy contained within the 22 letters of the Hebrew alphabet, their combinations and meanings of names.

Raziel is the master of transforming knowledge into wisdom. He teaches us that the eternal divine creative life energy of this earth is love, as well as reveals the many spiritual laws of 'change.' When asked upon, Raziel will surround your being and remove blockages from within you so you reach your full potential and glory. Raziel supports you to break free from the hindering energies. This is the true essence of Raziel's system of tarot, to shed off layers of ego and find your soul's true desire, and then manifest it to achieve fulfillment and enjoy prosperity in your life. Raziel will assist you to find your shine.

He rules the planet Neptune. He has been depicted with sky-blue or gray colored wings. He is one of the cherubim, known as the Sentinel of Innovation and the Monarchy of Pure Inspirations. Cherubs are seen throughout the tarot and each time symbolize Raziel. These cherubs are always gray in color, and the color gray whenever seen throughout the tarot will reflect upon an aspect of wisdom. Again, Raziel is the ruling archangel of the sefirah Chokmah, which means wisdom, is associated with the color gray, and also ruled by Neptune.

Additionally, this archangel symbolically appears in the form of fish, representing the fluidity of divine communications, situations of divine emotional importance, and the surreal world of dreams. This fish symbology appears several times throughout the tarot. For example, in the Queen of Cups card on her gray throne there is a cherub holding a fish in his hand as he blesses it.

He is usually seen with a bright yellow halo vibrating around his head. His aura holds all the colors of the rainbow like a beautiful prism of light. The rainbow is another symbol for Raziel, which is seen in the 10 of Cups card. This particular card corresponds with joy, celebration and pure bliss. Legend has it that a person will see shiny sparks of rainbow colors in the presence of Raziel.

Raziel is associated with the number 13. Interesting to point out is that there are 13 grapes on Eve's tail in the Devil card. It is believed by the Kabbalist Sages that the forbidden fruit in the garden of Eden was a grape. These 13 grapes directly relate to and are associated with the 13 Attributes of God's Mercy. After Adam and Eve ate the forbidden fruit from the Tree of Knowledge, God cast them out of the garden. But God was quick to forgive Adam and Eve of their original sin and He sent Raziel to teach and to guide them in the world outside the garden. This is a display of God offering love and mercy no matter how hard we fall. Moreover, the Hebrew word for love is ahava, with a numerical value of 13. Echad, the Hebrew word for one also has a numerical value of 13. Raziel teaches Adam and Eve how to reconnect and become one with the Creator by atoning (at-one-ing) for their sins, thereby opening up their hearts and embracing love. God's Divine Name Yahweh, YHVH, has a numerical value of 26. Subsequently, 13+13 = 26, and therefore God is one; God is love, one love.

Raziel holds the keys to unlocking your memories that are stored in your deep subconscious. Seen throughout the tarot are pomegranates, and each time represent the act of unlocking one's memory. Pomegranates are known for helping improve and stabilize cognitive memory and has proven to help with Alzheimer patients. When cut in half, all the many little seeds inside the fruit look like a brain. Raziel helps you connect to your past as well as your past lives, helping to remove blockages from past karma that effect you in this life—Jewish mystics refer to this correcting of one's karmic baggage as Tikkun. It was believed in ancient times that each pomegranate contained within it exactly 613 seeds. Which is interesting because there are exactly 613 commandments inside the Torah. Remembering and following these commandments will help a person in their Tikkun process. What's more, Raziel's name has a gematria (Hebrew numerology) value of 248, which is the same amount of 'to do' commandments. That being said, the 613 commandments are split up in two groups: there are a set of 248 commandments that one must follow, and the remaining 365 are forbidden. Raziel connects us to the wisdom advising what appropriate actions to take in order for us to work on our personal Tikkuns. Remove your blockages from within so you reach your full potential and glory.

Raziel is known for bringing light into the darkness, which is the spiritual alchemy practiced by the magician in the Magician tarot card. The Magician is holding a lit candle in his hand, drawing the light from above and bringing it down into the physical realm. If you look closely, you will notice that the Magician and the angel in the Lovers card are the same person.Worth noting here is that the figure-eight 'infinity' symbol above the Magician's head is a known symbol for Raziel as well, representing the infinite existence of our souls, alluding to the patterns and cycles a soul will experience during its progression. And just as Enoch was once a man who was later transformed into archangel Metatron, the Magician was exalted and transformed into archangel Raziel.

Developing a connection with Raziel can help you to uncover new spiritual insights, develop your psychic abilities, remove blockages, increase your creativity, and tune in to Divine magic and manifestation. You can do anything you so desire. You need to believe that you can. Anything is possible.

Raziel's 7 rules for Law of Attraction:

1. Focus on what you want, not on what you don't want.
2. Expect the best and you will get the best.
3. Never mind 'what is', imagine it the way you want it to be.
4. Notice and appreciate every little good thing in your life.
5. Change your beliefs to reshape your reality.
6. Focus on possibilities and not limitations.
7. Practice Gratitude like a religion.

In his book, Raziel reveals two magic amulets. One is for attracting prosperity and success in business, while the other amulet helps ward off negativity brought upon by the 'evil eye.' The amulet for prosperity serves a very similar purpose as the tarot, as far as manifesting wishes and also how it helps one align with their life-purpose. When an individual is in line with their destiny's path, life seems to flow much easier and the sooner they receive the fulfillment promised to them.

Below is Raziel's amulet for prosperity. The picture below is taken from the Sefer Raziel HaMalakh, The book of the angel Raziel, taken from the manuscript written by an anonymous author in the Middle Ages.

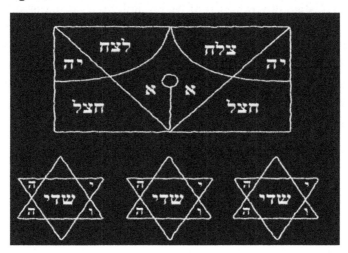

The amulet displays a magic square on top, and depicted below the square are three Stars of Saturn.

The square consists of Hebrew letter combinations that spell the word tsalach, meaning to prosper, be profitable. The word is seen arranged here in many different ways and in different orders, but all reflect the same prosper energy. Also found here are the letters that spell out the name of God, Yah. And located in the center are two Alephs. When you begin to decipher this square, you will realize how it is similar to the way the tarot is set up as well as is geared to help one succeed. For instance, in the center of this square is a diamond, and inside this diamond is a stick with a small circle on top. This circle coincides with the third eye, and when you concentrate on this point you will stimulate the third eye and attract prosperity into your life.

Likewise, the three Stars of Saturn (or Stars of David) below also connect to the third eye. Whereas, each individual has three eyes. For instance, there is the right eye, which sees positive potential, the left eye which gathers a deeper understanding of the negative traits, and lastly, the third eye that sees into the spirit of all things.

When we open the third eye, we are able to tap into the spiritual and draw down desire into the physical. The more layers of ego that we shed the more Light we are able to hold in our vessel. Each day we are bombarded with negativity. Raziel created a protective sigil or amulet to ward off the negative judgements of others to protect from the 'evil eye', and at the same time can be utilized to cleanse and strengthen your third eye, which activates your intuitive powers. Pictured here is this protective amulet, which acts as protection from 'evil eye.'

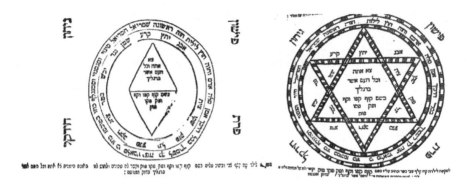

Pictured on the left is an earlier version of the amulet. You will notice the diamond in the middle. The amulet on the right has the same Hebrew letters but made with the six-pointed star. Although, both protect from the evil eye just the same.

In this book, I will explain in depth how these Raziel amulets are precursors to the tarot and to the tarot system as a whole, as well as how they correspond to the tarot's true purpose. Although the tarot can be used to help one obtain clarity in all aspects of their life, including relationships as well as self-reflection, it essentially is a tool that helps one shed layers of their ego and correct their karmic-baggage. As one sheds layers of their ego they become more in tune with their soul's purpose. The tarot offers the keys to align one with their predestined path—a path that leads them to obtaining their promised fulfillment. This and more will all be revealed in the following pages.

Chapter 2

The Secret Connection Shared Between
the Star, Moon, and Sun

THE STAR.   THE MOON.   THE SUN.

We begin to unravel the mysteries first by dissecting the Moon card, which is about obtaining a certain level of spiritual truth and enlightenment. The Moon card holds within it the concept, purpose and theme of the tarot, eloquently illustrated in rich allegory.

Few know or ever realize that the Hermit is the face on the moon. Just as odd, there just so happens to be sun rays surrounding this moon. It must seem strange for there to be sun rays around the moon, but once you grasp the secret hidden in plain sight it will all make sense—and then you will never be able to un-see it.

What we have depicted here are the Moon and the Sun joined as one. This union refers to a time period when the two connect and sync up, as well as reset their conjunction to Earth cycles.

To begin understanding, you must first grasp the concept of their cycles. Beginning with the Sun and its solar month, which is 30–31 days and a solar year consisting of 365 days. Then take the Moon with its lunar month from New Moon to New Moon (The lunar cycle or phase.) and it is 29.5 days, which adds to 354 days (29.5 days times 12 lunar months). This is short 11 days according to the solar calendar. Therefore, in just a matter of 3 solar years, there will be one lunar month difference in pattern as it gets drifted from the normal seasons with wrong observance.

354 days times 3 Lunar years = 1062 days
365 times 3 Solar years = 1095 days

The significance is especially related with farming in ancient times by Egyptians and Chinese, so they started to add a Leap Month every 3 years to compensate the problem and to avoid drift from solar calendar and seasons to which the celebrations and festivities are coordinated.

By doing 11 times, the cycle is completed as 33 Solar years finish and then 33 years is the time which by default gets the sync up of the lunar and solar cycle calendars—11×3 = 33. If you count carefully, you will notice that there are exactly 32 rays surrounding the moon. Then count the Hermit as being a ray himself (a personification), making it a total of 33 rays.

The Hermit card is assigned to the Hebrew letter Yod, which looks like a small fiery flame. You will notice that there are exactly 15 yellow Yod's floating in the sky just below the moon in the Moon tarot card. The Hermit is a personification of the letter Yod. Yod is the spark of fiery energy present in all God's Creation. Yod was present in the Big Bang when God said "Let there be light". Yod was the light, and this is the same light that shines from our sun.

The 32 sun rays around the moon directly relate to the 32 paths on the Kabbalah Tree of Life, which is essentially the path to spiritual enlightenment.

The 15 Yod's directly below the moon's rays are significant as well. Counting the Yod's throughout the tarot always reveals deeper esoteric understanding. Let's take in account that there are 15 Yod's in this card, and also that this card is Roman numeral 18, which gives us 18+15 = 33. So, this reveals to us that there are now two different connections to the number 33 on this card. They are the pair of 33's which coincide with both the lunar and solar cycles.

The Moon card being Roman numeral 18 is significant as well. For instance, when reducing the number 18 you get 1+8 = 9, which is associated with the 9th sefirah, Yesod. Yesod is ruled by the Moon. Coincidentally, the astronomical body and the tarot card of the same name. Yesod is known for holding hidden secrets yet to be unveiled. This Yesod-Moon connection alone is enough to spark interest into any student of the tarot, causing them to dig deeper into their studies.

Essentially, the Moon card is about understanding the duality of the soul, and achieving a higher level of awareness, arriving at the realization that the soul is a union of both the wild wolf and the domesticated dog. Mankind is a combination of dualities; masculine-feminine, fire-water, positive-negative, yin-yang, Sun-Moon.

Worth mentioning here is the much spiritual importance of the number 33. We see it throughout the tarot symbolized by the serpent aka the kundalini, which is a Hinduism meditation practice based on a concept in Śhaiva Tantra, where it is believed to be a force or power associated with the divine feminine where a person raises their soul's vibration through opening up the seven chakras from the base of their spine leading up to the third eye, connecting them to their higher-self. Interesting to note that there are 33 vertebrae in the human spinal column, spiritually referred to as the Jacob's ladder, which is an allegory that represents the path toward ascension of one's consciousness.

This allegory can be seen here in the Moon card with the crawfish crawling out of the astral waters and into the world where it begins its life's journey on the path toward enlightenment, which leads through the pillars. A person crosses over from the world of the known over to the valley of the unknown. At the end of its journey, the crawfish will eventually reach the Moon, and just as the Hermit did before him, the crawfish will obtain spiritual enlightenment. This crawfish will eventually one day evolve to having the 32 rays surround his head and he will transcend up to and become the 33rd ray of light, evolving into the new face on the Moon.

This spiritual evolution is also known has having obtained Christ Consciousness; becoming 'at one' with God. Christ died at the age of 33, and 3 days later he was born again. This is the concept behind the syncing of the Sun and the Moon cycles. They have returned back to the same position as when they started. They are reset and 'reborn', so to speak. At this level of enlightenment, a person is 'at one' with what the Kabbalists refer to as the Light of the Creator, the Source, the Higher-Self.

With further contemplation you will notice that the Moon card contains within it the tarot's three astronomical sources of light, which include the Sun, the Moon, and the Stars (represented here by the 15 Yod's that float in the night sky). Let us count these objects to find additional esoteric significance. For instance, there is the Moon that is united with the Sun, and then count the 32 rays around the Sun, and then the 15 Yod's, and lastly, we consider the Roman numeral of the card, which is 18. This gives us 1 Moon + 32 sun rays + 15 Yod's +18 (the card's Roman numeral, XVIII) which equals 67. The number 67 just so happens to be the Hebrew gematria value for the word Binah, meaning understanding. According to the Bahir, the mystical book of the 1st century, Binah is 'intuitive understanding', or 'contemplation.' It is likened to a 'palace of mirrors' that reflects the pure point of light of Chokmah, wisdom, increasing and multiplying it in an infinite variety of ways. In this sense, it is the 'quarry', which is carved out by the light of wisdom. It is the womb, which gives shape to the Spirit of God. We connect to the Source of God's Divine Light by raising our soul's vibration and elevating our chakras, as we ascend up the 33 vertebrae of our spinal column. It is at this point where we reach the spiritual level of Binah, in which we open the third eye and cross through the portal (her womb) that leads us to the upper astral worlds of consciousness.

These three cards are all sources of light. The Star, the Moon, and the Sun all provide light to our world in their own way. The speed of light is approximately 186,000 miles per sec. At the earth's surface, the nominal value of the solar constant is 137 mW/cm2. The solar constant is the rate at which energy reaches the earth's surface from the sun. This 137 mill watts per square centimeter value corresponds to high noon with the sun directly overhead giving direct light. Also interesting, number 137 is the Hebrew numerical value for the word Kabbalah, which means 'to receive.' And what do we receive? The Light. This is a clue that it takes only the speed of light in order to connect to the light within Kabbalah.

Another connection to the number 186 is found within these three cards. First, add up the Roman numerals on each card. The Star is number 17, the Moon is number 18 and the Sun is number 19, which equal the sum of 54. Then we count all the light sources in each card. The 8 eight-pointed stars in the Star card equal 64 rays. There are 21 sun rays in the Sun card. The Moon card has 32 rays emitting from the moon. And then there are the 15 Yods, which are fiery flames, located directly below the moon's rays. All these add up to being 132 sources of light plus the sum of all three tarot cards that contain the light sources, which is 54, equaling a grand total of 186 (132+54); the speed of light.

Furthermore, Yod's throughout the tarot always are significant. Counting the Yod's grants a deeper understanding and important insight into the hidden mysteries concealed within each card. The Hebrew letter Yod means Hand. Yod is considered the starting point of the presence of God in all things. Yod is the spark of the spirit in everything. Considering this one could say God has His hand in everything. There is a total of 78 Yod's hidden throughout the tarot, which coincidentally is the
exact number of cards in the tarot deck.

Ace of Cups….…....26 Yod's
Tower….………….22
Moon….………….15
Ace of Wands….…8
Ace of Swords….…6

A total of 77 Yod's.

So, where is the final Yod? Yod is the Hebrew letter associated with the Hermit. He is the personification of Yod. And he holds the final hidden Yod to be unveiled. Now, with the Hermit added to the tarot's Yod's, we get a total of 78.

Yod means hand and it is just as important to count the hands as it is to count the Yod's. Hands contain fingers, and fingers are known as digits. The digits add up to a certain value, and that value connects us to a deeper understanding of the hidden mysteries. There are exactly 186 hands in the tarot deck, (which of course includes only the human-like hands of the humans, angels and God's). In the Major Arcana cards there are a total of 26 hands that are depicted holding a tool of some kind. This is the same as well for the Minor Arcana cards that also have a total of 26 hands holding a tool of some sort. This is significant because the numerical value of YHVH is 26. So out of the 186 hands, 26 of them are holding a type of tool (26 hands in the Minor Arcana and 26 hands in the Major Arcana). This is a clue that by applying your hands on the tarot cards they are to be used as a tool connecting you to the Light of God the Creator (at the speed of light).

Chapter 3

The Tarot Grid and the 10 of Pentacles Card are Guides

The Tarot Grid along with the 10 of Pentacles lay down the Tarot's Foundation. The Waite-Smith tarot deck contains within it two map keys that act as guides for understanding how the entire Kabbalistic system of tarot concealed within this deck is formulated—laying down the fundamentals that serve its foundation. These guides hold the true purpose of the tarot, which includes self-reflection, overcoming ego, and reaching self-enlightenment by working on yourself. The tarot can advise us through relationships we have with our friends, family, co-workers, lovers and most importantly ourselves.

The first reference guide is the map key found within the 10 of Pentacles Card. Illustrated on this card are ten pentacles arranged in the Kabbalah Tree of Life formation. Each of these ten pentacles represents and corresponds with each of the ten sefirot on the Tree.

The second tarot guide is a grid made from all of the tarot cards; all except for the Court cards, which I will explain why this is later on. I coined this grid the Tarot Grid, and it consist of 62 cards total, excluding the 16 court cards which are grouped in their own separate category and serve their own individual yet important purpose; functioning differently than the other 'numbered' cards. This grid is created when you arrange the 62 numbered-cards in order ascending from the least to highest value in rows from left to right.

Starting at the top with the Minor Arcana, the Grid begins with the Aces and leads through to the 10's; going from left to right. This arrangement is done within the first four rows, grouping each of the four tarot suits at the top of the Grid above the Majors. The suited cards are arranged by the value of their particular suit, from least to greatest value. This tier arrangement leads downward from the Wands to the Pentacles, although the suits' values ascend as they lead to the suit of Pentacles. Therefore, the ascending order from least to greatest value is: Wands, Cups, Swords, and then Pentacles, respectively. Directly below the Minor Arcana we begin with the 22 cards of the Major Arcana in this same 'ascending in card value' order, beginning with the Magician, numbered 1, leading through to the Wheel of

Fortune card, which is numbered 10. The following row leads off with the Justice card, numbered 11, and ends with the Sun, numbered 19. This leaves you with two remaining cards; the Judgment and the World cards, which are placed on the bottom row. The Judgment card is set at the bottom of the second column, the column associated with the 2's, because Judgment is numbered 20, and when reduced in the numerological way the number 20 becomes 2+0 = 2. Numerology does not deal with double digits, so we reduce the double digit down to a single digit in this manner. The World card is numbered 21, and when reduced becomes 2+1 = 3, so it is placed at the bottom of the third column.

Pictured here are examples of the 10 of Pentacles card and the Tarot Grid for reference.

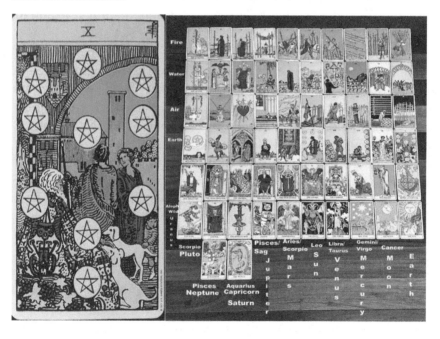

Please note: The Fool card is sort of a 'wild' card in regards that it can be placed in more than one spot on the Tarot Grid. Let me explain why. The Fool is assigned to the Hebrew letter Aleph, which is the first letter in the Hebrew alphabet. The Fool card is placed at the beginning of a cycle or journey. Kabbalah teaches that when one journey ends another one begins, as symbolized by the Ouroboros aka the snake eating its own tail, signifying infinity and the birth-death cycle. Therefore, the Fool can be placed either before the Ace of Wands or after the World card on the Grid, acting as a bridge (or link) between the two cards. For instance, when one cycle ends a new one begins. Relatively speaking, the Fool could show up anywhere on the Grid. The Fool is number zero, which is a 360° circle, and it can appear anywhere on the wheel (aka rota) of the tarot, as the tarot moves around the zodiac wheel, aka the mazzaroth.

Although, the Fool's journey is traveled along the path of the 62 cards on the Grid from top to bottom and then around again, it is ideal for the Fool card to be placed at either the beginning or at the end of a cycle when the card shows up in a tarot reading.

Learning these two map keys will bring you closer to comprehending the Hermetic-Kabbalistic system ingrained within the Waite-Smith tarot deck.

Allow me to further explain the 10 of Pentacles card by first describing how it can be considered a map key referencing the ten sefirot. By understanding the reasoning for why the ten pentacles are placed in their current positions on the 10 of Pentacles card will help you understand the spiritual influences for each of the ten sefirot. Taking this into account, this Kabbalistic system can be applied towards understanding all the 78 cards, because every card is structured in this same manner. The ten sefirot which form the Kabbalah Tree of Life is the foundation for which the tarot system is built upon. Taking this into consideration, you will come to realize that every card in the deck is illustrated over an invisible Tree of Life. As you begin to understand this Kabbalistic system, you will soon begin to understand the language of the tarot's symbols. It might also be noted that the symbols, Roman numerals, and Hebrew letters interconnected within the tarot all contain a certain level of energy. Energy is essentially the language of the tarot, and it can be understood more than words.

The 10 of Pentacles Card:

This card has its ten pentacles arranged in a Tree of Life formation, positioned with accordance to the Kabbalah, and aligns perfectly with specific objects illustrated on this card, which are either in close proximity with or actually touching these particular objects. These illustrated objects contain clues that reveal deeper hidden meaning for each one of the corresponding sefirot-pentacle connections. For example, the 9th pentacle located at Yesod (near the old man's hands) is touching the head of a hidden dog, who is wearing a similar looking robe just as the old man is wearing, which camouflages the dog.

Yesod is associated with the moon, and the moon always reveals secrets which are hidden in plain sight. After some devoted study, you will come to find that all the number 9 cards, and cards associated with the number 9 (the Hermit and the Moon), have concealed within them a hidden secret waiting to be revealed—by one who has the eyes to see. Much the same as the 9's, every one of these ten pentacles share a connection that reveals a specific sefirah's spiritual influence shared with each of the objects illustrated on this card.

Furthermore, the 10 of Pentacles card contains within it all the wisdom needed for any person to read tarot cards Kabbalistically. For instance, (as explained earlier) each of the ten pentacles is assigned to one of the ten sefirot on the Kabbalah Tree of Life, and each sefirah is associated with a particular planet which rules a particular astrological sign that corresponds to one of the four elements. Knowing the combination of these aspects helps us further understand an individual's unique personality traits. Moreover, the element (i.e., fire or water) associated with the individual's ruling planet, combined with the influence of the planet's matching sefirah, will give way to a broader understanding of the four main aspects of the individual: the physical, emotional, spiritual, and the mental. Taking this into account, realize that every tarot card's illustration is structured and designed over an invisible Tree of Life formation. This Tree formation adheres to the Kabbalah three-column (aka three pillar) system. This system includes, the left column of severity, the right column of mercy, and lastly, the middle column is considered the column of mildness. Every card is organized in this Kabbalistic manner, just as the 10 of Pentacles card is, where certain objects are placed and arranged in their specific, yet appropriate locations in order to convey deeper hidden meanings that coincide with certain symbols and/or objects in each card. To sum it up, this Tree of Life system is applied to every card in the deck; every illustration aligns with the invisible Tree as it is the foundation for which the tarot is built upon, and therefore every object, (be it person, animal or symbol) is placed in its proper placement.

By knowing of this three-column system and understanding how it can be applied to every card will allow you to further decode the tarot. For instance, objects located on the left side of the card will relate to certain aspects of severity, judgement, as well as coincide with the concept of 'receiving' energy attributed to selfishness. Likewise, objects located on the right side of every card will relate to aspects of mercy, blessings, as well as contain attributes of 'sharing' energy. And finally, objects located in the middle of the card will relate to aspects of mildness and reflect a sustained balance of these two positive-negative energy polarities confined within the left and right columns.

In addition to this, any object located in the center of the card, be it a person or thing, is directly related to and reflects upon the emotional aspect (matters of the heart) portrayed within the card's illustration. Consequently, the center sefirah on the Tree of Life is Tiferet, which is associated with the heart chakra. When applying the 10 of Pentacles card as the map key, you will find in the card's center is a large house, and as the old adage goes, "Home is where the heart is." This is a clue reiterating the method of decoding the tarot. Know that every card will be designed in this similar manner. In every card you will find depicted in the center either a person or an object that will capture and embody the emotional attribute being conveyed.

Tiferet is attributed to the inner sun located at the core of the human soul. According to the Kabbalists, Tiferet encompasses within it all six sefirot located in the middle of the Tree of Life. This includes the six sefirot in between Binah and Yesod: Chesed, Gevurah, Tiferet, Netzah, Hod, and Yesod. These six sefirot are at the heart of the Tree—at its core. Kabbalists refer to this core as the Zeir Anpin. Zeir Anpin comprises the emotional attributes of the Tree. When taken into account the concept of Zeir Anpin, the Kabbalists consider the Tree of Life to actually consist of only five sefirot: Keter, Chokmah, Binah, Tiferet, and Malchut. These five sefirot represent the cornerstone in which the foundation of the Waite-Smith tarot is built upon. Each card adheres to this Kabbalistic system and is structured and mapped out accordingly, in an orderly fashion, which dictates the placements of the symbols, as well as each character and object depicted within each card.

This Zeir Anpin concept works similarly to the way one would apply the 'three-column' system to interpret the tarot. For example, a symbol or object located at the top center of the card, (and at times directly above a person's head), will relate to energy aspects of Keter in relation to its connection to the divine intelligence of the Creator, the Source of godly insights and inspiration. Likewise, any symbol or object located on the right of the card will connect to energy aspects of Chokmah, which connect to aspects of wisdom and portray any merited godly advice. Objects on the left of the card will relate to Binah, connecting to aspects of understanding. Objects in the center of each card correspond to Tiferet, reflecting the emotional aspect related to the heart of the matter. And lastly, objects located at the bottom center of the card relate to Malchut, conveying what is happening in the now, the present moment. This includes spiritual and emotional aspects that are being manifested now in the physical world.

To fully understand the purpose of the 10 of Pentacles card and this Kabbalistic system is vital for one to be able to read the tarot. Each card adheres to this system, setting the foundation for the language of the tarot, which is communicated through the objects and symbols which are placed precisely in their proper locations in each of the card's illustrations.

The Tarot Grid:

We are able to approach the tarot as an oracle, and as we consult with the cards, we receive counsel and advice for solving many of life's mysteries, but most importantly it leads us closer to knowing thyself, offering us guidance on ways to overcome and transform our ego-nature. Each one of us is born into this world with a certain amount of karmic-baggage that we each need to correct. The Kabbalists refer to this correction as our Tikkun, meaning amending, fixing. This baggage is contained in multiple layers of ego, and is linked to and governed by each individual's unique planetary influences. Learning one's personal astrology, and becoming aware of the negative influences effecting their natal chart, as well as any shadow traits tied in with their specific zodiac sign will give them the upper hand as they attempt to overcome their shadow-nature. The tarot can be considered as a tool containing the keys needed for us to correct our individual tikkuns (karmic baggage). Found within the columns of the Tarot Grid are the paths that pave the way for each person's tikkun, meaning correction, fixing. As they follow these paths, they will learn how to overcome their ego, with accordance to their specific zodiac sign. The purpose for these paths is for an individual to connect to astrological as well as practical guidance as they work towards achieving spiritual enlightenment. We can make the world a better place simply by becoming better versions of ourselves. The world becomes better one person at a time.

Besides its connection with astrology, the Tarot Grid also organizes the cards in their proper order, arranging them in an ascending order from least to greatest value deemed by the card's suit and number. Having all the cards displayed this way reveals to us even more hidden secrets, which provides a deeper connection to the Higher-Self and to higher levels of our conscious awareness. I will reveal these secrets momentarily, but first let me explain the Tarot Grid's design. I plan to unravel the tarot's mysteries one step at a time.

Contained within the first four rows of the Tarot Grid are the four elements that each of the suits represent. The Wands represent fire, Cups are water, Swords are air, and Pentacles are associated with earth. It is in this order that they ascend from lowest to highest in value. This ordering of the cards and their values were set by the Hermetic Order of the Golden Dawn, who A. E. Waite and Pamela Colman Smith, the creators of this tarot deck, happened to be members of. The order of the elements coincides with the tetragrammaton, YHVH, the Divine Name of God, Yahweh, where the letter Yod corresponds with fire, Heh with water, Vav with air, and the second Heh corresponds with earth.

Positioned directly below the Minor Arcana are the 22 Major Arcana cards, which do not relate directly to the four elements like the suited cards above them do. Not like the Minors, the Majors deal less with logical and practical matters and more so with the intuitive traits of the right brain. The first row of Majors starts with card number 1 (The Magician) and then leads to number 10 (Wheel of Fortune). Followed by the second row of Majors which includes the cards that are numbered 11-19. Now, we are left with the last two Major Arcana cards remaining: the Judgement card (20), which goes at the bottom of the second column, and the World card (21), which is placed as the last card at the bottom of the third column.

The last two rows of Major Arcana cards, which are numbered 11-21, are aligned under the columns that correspond to the number each card is associated with when reduced in the numerological way, which is to add together each digit of the double-digit number, reducing it to a single digit number. For instance, if the card's Roman numeral is more than 9, add together each digit of the result. For example, $11 = 1+1 = 2$ and number $12 = 1+2 = 3$, and so on.

Furthermore, aligning the cards on the Grid in this way, within these ten columns, reveals the zodiac paths that can be used as a tool and as a guide for one to conquer their ego-nature and obtain spiritual enlightenment. Each zodiac path contains cards that share the same number. For example, all the number 2 cards create a path for Neptune, which rules over Pisces.

The Tarot Grid acts as the reference guide to the zodiac Paths of Enlightenment. Each zodiac path contains the wisdom, advice and practical spiritual guidance needed for one to transform their ego-nature. By following the advice found within each card on any of the given zodiac paths, which are aligned directly with one's astrological sign, a person will be able to elevate their soul's vibration, and correct their tikkun.

The formula for finding a person's astrological path on the Grid is the same for all signs of the zodiac. The first step is to establish what sign the person is born under. Next, figure out the ruling planet for that specific sign. Then connect the number of the sefirah found on the Kabbalah Tree of Life that is associated with that sign's ruling planet. The number of the sefirah is the number of the path found on the Tarot Grid. Let us use the sign of Aries as an example. Aries is ruled by Mars, and Mars is associated with the 5th sefirah on the Tree, Gevurah, which means that all the number 5 cards in the Grid's 5th column form the path that an Aries needs to take in order for them to reach spiritual enlightenment.

The point of reaching enlightenment is to establish a connection with the higher-self, making it possible to obtain the certainty needed to manifest their desires and to turn wishes into reality.

Every individual is governed by three signs of the zodiac: their Sun, their Moon, and their Rising Sign. All of which are important to understanding a person's character and personality traits, as well as flaws. Learning more about your personal astrology is one step closer to knowing thy self, which is essential as you journey along the path towards spiritual enlightenment.

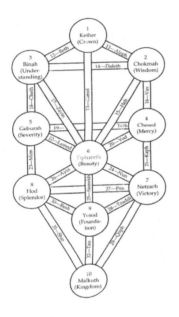

Chapter 4

The Secret Mysteries of the Fool Card Revealed

The Fool can be seen as beginning a new journey, as well as just returning back home from one. He is a ray of sunshine. Do you notice how the stick he is holding is exactly in-line with one of the sun's rays behind his head? This symbolizes that his stick is also a sun ray, and he is wielding it as if he too is a ray of light. The Fool is full of light, love and optimism. Do you see the snow-capped mountains in the background? The Fool is a personification of the sun's light acting as the fiery energy which spans the love that melts the icy mountain tops. As a result, water drains down into the valley—flooding it below. This is why the Fool is walking so close to the ledge without any fear of death. He knows that the waters below will save him if he were to fall. He carries with him a small bag, which is his bag of knowledge. This knowledge is all that he has to begin his journey with. We are born into this world naked, and with no possessions. Although, we do carry within us a spark of Light, and this Light holds within it all the knowledge that we have obtained throughout our past lives. As we journey along our life path, we slowly uncover and reconnect to our past, and awaken who we once were and perhaps who we truly are. The Fool can be seen here as beginning a new cycle or just ending a previous one, and each time is seen carrying with him this bag of knowledge obtained along his journey, or journeys (plural) if referring to each of his previous reincarnations.

The Fool has transformed his wisdom into knowledge. Specifically, knowing how to elevate the heart chakra (the inner sun) in order to overcome all obstacles that life throws at him. This knowledge gives the Fool his great sense of optimism and certainty, knowing that God will always provide. Opening up his heart is the key, and it is how he connects directly to the Creator—the source of the Light. Therefore, the Fool has gained the knowledge that there is 'no-ledge' on the cliff before him. With this knowledge, he knows of no ledge. Thus, he has no fear of any obstacle or challenge that appears before him. Full of heart, blindly optimistic and exceedingly faithful God will provide for him, the Fool enters the world and begins his journey.

Hidden on the Fool's shirt (lower right side) is the Hebrew letter Shin, which looks like a fiery crown. The Shin ‫ש‬ comprises three vertical lines representing three columns. The three lines in the letter Shin can represent the three columns in the Kabbalah Tree of Life, which are the left column of severity, the right column of mercy and the center column known as the column of mildness. Each and every card is structured in this three-column system.

Furthermore, the three-column symbolism is seen throughout the tarot. For instance, the priestess in the High Priestess card sits between two columns. The Hierophant also sits between two columns as well as the prince in the Justice card. Moreover, there are two columns depicted in the Death card, which are the same style as two columns in the Moon card. In the Lovers card, the two trees symbolize the Kabbalistic columns. Likewise, the two trees inside the 9 of Pentacles card also represent the columns.

Correspondingly, the Fool card has hidden within it the letter Shin, which is another representation of this three-column system. The Shin placed on the Fool's shirt, who is located in the center of the card, symbolizes that the Fool is an embodiment of the middle column. The Fool acts as the filament that balances out the left and right column's opposite energy polarities.

Moreover, the letter Shin means tooth, as in the serpent's tooth that bites you with thepoison needed to kill your limiting beliefs as you raise your kundalini as a means to obtain Christ Consciousness.

The three prongs of the letter Shin symbolize three flames. The letter Shin ש is the symbol of fire. This shape is known in many traditions by the trident of Neptune/Poseidon, and the Trishula (three-spear) of Shiva. This is the weapon of the Gods.

Shin also relates to the three primary forces located in the first (top) triangle of the Kabbalah Tree of Life represented by the sefirot Keter, Chokmah, and Binah. In Christianity these three forces are referred to as the Father, Son, and Holy Spirit. Let us remember that in Hinduism, this Trinity or three divine entities, which are all fire, are called Brahma, Vishnu, and Shiva.

Furthermore, the Kabbalistic trinity consist of Male, Female and Central column merged in harmony and synthesized as one. This Kabbalistic trinity can be compared to a light bulb. For instance, both consist of three parts that correspond to three different energy polarities. Whereas, the positive charge of a light bulb would correspond to the right column of mercy. The light bulb's negative charge would correspond to the left column of severity. And lastly, the light bulb's filament can be compared to the middle column that balances out the opposite polarities.

Moving forward, Shin also stands for the word Shaddai, a name for God, meaning Almighty [God]. Traditionally on Jewish holidays, a Kohen (priest) forms the letter Shin with his hands as he recites the Priestly Blessing. In the mid-1960s, actor Leonard Nimoy used a single-handed version of this gesture to create the Vulcan hand salute for his character, Mr. Spock, on Star Trek.

The letter Shin is often inscribed on the case containing a mezuzah—a scroll of parchment with Biblical text written on it. The text contained in the mezuzah is the Shema Yisrael prayer, which calls the Israelites to love their God with all their heart, soul and strength. The mezuzah is situated upon all the door frames in a home or establishment. Sometimes the whole word Shaddai will be written. A person touches the mezuzah each time they enter or exit the house, similar to how the Fool can be seen as either beginning a journey or as returning back home from one.

The Shema Yisrael prayer also commands the Israelites to write God's commandments on their hearts (Deuteronomy 6:6). The shape of the letter Shin mimics the structure of the human heart: the lower, larger left ventricle (which supplies the full body) and the smaller right ventricle (which supplies the lungs) are positioned like the lines of the letter Shin.

A religious significance has been applied to the fact that there are three valleys that comprise the city of Jerusalem's geography: the Valley of Ben Hinnom, Tyropoeon Valley, and Kidron Valley. These valleys converge to also form the shape of the letter Shin, and interestingly enough, the Temple in Jerusalem just so happens to be located where the dagesh (horizontal line) is. This is seen as a fulfillment of passages such as Deuteronomy 16:2 that instructs the Jewish people to celebrate the Pesach at "the place the Lord will choose as a dwelling for his Name".

In the ancient Kabbalistic text, Sefer Yetzirah, the letter Shin is King over Fire, Formed Heaven in the Universe, Hot in the Year, and the Head in the Soul. These aspects are all symbolized in the Fool card. The Fool draws parallel with a ray of sunshine, symbolized by the stick he is wielding which is too a sun ray. Metaphorically, this can be seen as the relationship between the Christ and the Father, where the Sun represents the Father, the Source of the Light. The Fool is the Christ as God (sunlight) incarnate, and they are one.

The Fool card is assigned to the Hebrew letter Aleph, which has a numerical value of 1. The letter Aleph is comprised of three letters in one. There is a Vav in the middle of two Yod's. The individual values for these letters add up to 26. Vav = 6, and each Yod = 10, resulting in 6+10+10 = 26. This is significant because 26 is the same value of the tetragrammaton, YHVH, the holy Four-Letter Name of God, Yahweh. So, Yahweh is within the letter Aleph, which has a numerical value of 1. God is one, three in one.
The Fool is depicted here as being 'at one' with God.

The Fool represents pure Light and unconditional love. The Fool is wearing the Shin on his shirt, and as he returns to the Father, YHVH, he forms the holy name Yeshua, YHShVH. The Fool is a representation of the Shin, and when placed in the middle column or in the middle of the Divine Name of God, YHVH, it forms the holy name Yeshua, meaning salvation. It is the Fool's journey that leads to salvation, and ultimately reunites one with the Higher-Self.

Pictured above on the left is the Hebrew letter Shin. The picture on the right is a zoomed-in photo of the Fool's shirt where there is a hidden Shin drawn on the lower right of the shirt.

Chapter 5

The 10 of Pentacles' Ten Sefirot

Within this chapter is the detailed explanation of each of the Ten Sefirot, and how they coincide with the symbols on the 10 of Pentacles Card.

The 10 of Pentacles card is a key, and also a guide, to the Kabbalistic system of the Tarot. All ten of the pentacles on this card are formed in a Kabbalah Tree of Life formation. Each pentacle represents a sphere, or sefirah, and is associated with that particular energy and its aspects. The placement of the sphere pictured on the 10 of Pentacles card gives us a clue to understanding the aspects of each of the 10 sefirot. Furthermore, each of the sefirot is numbered 1 through 10, and each tarot card as well. Matching the number of the sefirah to the number of the tarot card gives us a deeper look into the esoteric understanding of the messages concealed within each card.

Let's look at the number 9 cards for example. The 9th sefirah on the Tree of Life is Yesod, which is ruled by the moon, and the moon always reveals secrets that are hidden in plain sight. Using this knowledge, we can now look at the 9th sphere (or pentacle) in a new light. The old man in the 10 of Pentacles card is seen here petting one of the two dogs kneeling at his feet. But, if we take a closer look, we see and unveil a hidden third-dog that is wearing a robe similar to the old man's robe, which is difficult to see at first glance. But, if given a second look, you will notice his little nose sticking out, and his little tail wagging in the air. At first, the dog was not visible, and needed to manifest (or unveil) itself. And now that we have seen the hidden dog, he is manifested, and we can no longer un-see him. And that is one of the many lessons of Yesod. All the number 9 cards and cards associated with the number 9 reveal a hidden message for those with eyes to see.

An important thing to mention here is that all the number 10 cards are associated with the sefirah Malchut, which is ruled by Earth, the material realm, also known as the 1% reality that we perceive with our five senses. Malchut is the 'Kingdom' where all things manifest. The proper title of the 10 of Pentacles card is The

Lord of Wealth. It is all about reaping what you sowed and relishing in one's accomplishments. It is about having gratitude for everything you have, and seeing your dreams, wishes and desires come true, and after which being able to share your prosperity with the world and the ones you love. This card is astrologically related to Mercury in Virgo. It contains traits of having great communication with yourself and being open to your imagination and inspiration. Having Mercury in Virgo grants the drive to put ideas into action. This planetary conjunction influences one to pay attention to the details, and enables them to connect the dots in order to achieve a broader and richer understanding of the task at hand.

Each one of the pentacles represents a particular sefirah, and it is touching and/or is positioned perfectly next to a certain object on the card, purposely illustrated in order to reveal deeper insights of this card as well as the tarot system itself.

Let's start with the first sefirah Keter and then work our way down the Tree explaining everything in detail.

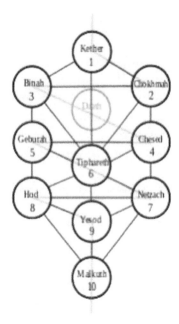

Sefirah #1, Keter: Ruled by Pluto, Associated with the Aces

The pentacle representing Keter is located on the top of the bridge. This is the old man's root desire to create something that will last just as long as this massive and sturdy bridge. It will be here long after the old man dies. The bridge begins at the old man's head (the word Keter means crown) and then extends out above and encompasses everything underneath it, forming a canopy of protection over everything the old man accomplished and achieved. It all started with a simple thought, although a brilliant one. It was all made possible because the old man manifested his desire by bridging is inspired ideas into action, which incidentally bridged the people in his life together.

Sefirah #2, Chokmah: Ruled by Neptune, Associated with the 2's

The pentacle here that represents Chokmah appears as the sun in the sky, shining brightly and providing the Light in the picture. Spiritually speaking, Chokmah provides more so the pure Divine Light of the Creator rather than, say, the light of the sun; the Light from Chokmah carries God's intelligence and provides the conscientiousness enabling one to see things for how they truly are. Chokmah allows you to see both sides of the story or given situation; both the good and the bad. Thus, the duality of things. Also, worth noting here is how Chokmah, meaning wisdom, sits as an authoritative figure on top the right column of mercy.

Sefirah # 3, Binah: Ruled by Saturn, Associated with the 3's

Binah sits directly along the checkered line, receiving a deeper understanding of all things from the 99% realm. She builds and creates the family, as symbolized by the family crest that her pentacle is also touching. Inside the crest is a castle with three red windows. The number 3 connects to Binah and includes aspects of creating and birthing for the betterment of the world. Binah is the motherly energy of the Tree of Life, opposed to Chokmah, who is the father/male energy. Binah builds a house into a home. She is the queen of the castle, and sits as an authoritative figure on top the left column of severity.

Sefirah #4, Chesed: Ruled by Jupiter, Associated with the 4's

This pentacle is located directly underneath Chokmah, symbolizing a 'second sun' in the sky. Chokmah symbolizes the pure Light of the spirit; the astral Light, while Chesed represents physical light. Chesed's pentacle is placed close to the green trees, blessing them with sunlight,which they need in order to grow and live a healthy life. Chesed offers an unconditional love delivered with kindness and mercy, blessing an individual with sustenance, abundance and prosperity.

Sefirah #5, Gevurah: Ruled by Mars, Associated with the 5's

Located on the left side of this card and directly underneath Binah is Gevurah. Portrayed through this card's symbology, Gevurah protects his mother, Binah, as he stands guard on the checkered wall, which separates the astral realm from the material reality. Gevurah's pentacle stands guard at the door; the large door on the bridge, above the old man's head, is the way into Gevurah's emotions only his mother, Binah, ever gets to see. This door leads to the understanding of who Gevurah truly is on the inside. Gevurah has a very big ego and does not allow anyone in. He is always protecting something, albeit his family or his reputation or his sensitive emotions.

Sefirah #6, Tiferet: Ruled by the Sun, Associated with the 6's

This pentacle is placed directly on top of the house located in the direct center of the card, because 'home is where the heart is.' Coincidentally, Tiferet relates to the heart chakra. This house is very large and able to fit the entire family inside comfortably. This house is placed in the center of the picture because this man's family is at the center of the old man's life. His family is his world, and his reason for living. Seeing his family happy brings him joy.

Sefirah #7, Netzah: Ruled by Venus, Associated with the 7's

The beautiful woman with red hair holds this pentacle in her hands. She is very charming, and loves to show off her possessions. She surrounds herself with a man, a dog, and a child, representing she is in harmony with the one's she loves, and the one's she chooses to be around. This includes her family, friends, pets, as well as her worldly possessions. You will notice how she admires her man as she looks at him lovingly. This shows that she is grateful for all that she has been blessed with. By practicing gratitude, she remains focused on her successes rather than past failures. Consequently, this is how she attracts more things into her life to be grateful for.

Sefirah #8, Hod: Ruled by Mercury, Associated with the 8's

Resting next to the old man's head, along the checkered wall that divides imagination from reality, is the pentacle corresponding with Hod. Hod is associated with expressing the splendor of the intellectual mind. This pentacle is touching the astral wall where the old man receives his inspiration, which he utilizes towards creating, building and communicating his ideas in ways that bring more prosperity into his life. The old man acts on his inspiration, drawing forth abundance.

Sefirah #9, Yesod: Ruled by the Moon, Associated with the 9's

The pentacle for Yesod is located on the old man's right arm, which is petting the dog. A closer look will reveal a hidden dog's nose that is touching the pentacle. Yesod is associated with the moon, and the moon always unveils secrets hidden in plain sight. The hidden third-dog is wearing a similar robe as the old man and is difficult to see at first glance. But if you look closely, you can see the dog's nose sticking up and his tail wagging in the air. Yesod reveals deeper understandings for those with eyes to see.

Sefirah #10, Malchut: Ruled by Earth, Associated with the 10's

The 10th and last pentacle, Malchut, is set directly in the middle of where the old man's robe and third-dog's robe touch.

It is difficult to see where the old man and dog are separated, because they appear as being one individual.

With closer examination, you will see that the hidden third-dog has a magic square of Saturn on its head. This is a 3×3 square with 9 segments. The square is located directly in between the pentacles of Yesod and Malchut. Interestingly, the design on the dog's robe is similar to the Kabbalah Tree of Life. Also, the Tree on the dog's robe stems down from the magic square. Thus, the magic square is located at the top of this Tree. Therefore, the magic square being at this particular placement establishes a corresponding connection to the Kabbalah World of Atziluth—the World where Binah resides. This is significant, because Binah is associated with Saturn.

This path is located between Yesod and Malchut, and is known as the 32nd path on the Tree of Life. This is the Tree's final path or branch. Thus, it is assigned to the last letter in the Hebrew alphabet, Tav. Tav means cross or mark, and its Phoenician letter was originally an X or a cross. Hence, the 10 of Pentacles card, which depicts the ten sefirot, being marked with the Roman numeral X. The letter Tav is assigned to the World card, which has a large Laurel wreath illustrated on it. The Laurel wreath represents an award for completion; awarding accomplishment. In addition to this, the wreath is a symbol representing the portal which leads through the mind's eye to the upper worlds of the woke mind. The path of Tav represents the bridge a person must take from Malchut up into Yesod (and vice versa) in order to pass through the portal of the astral realm. This is a spiritual journey from the known into the unknown, so to speak. Tav is the 22nd and final letter in the Hebrew alphabet, assigned to this 32nd path on the Tree of Life, making this card the final destination for desires to arrive at before they manifest into the physical world of Malchut. In other words, Yesod acts as a chute and funnels down desire from the upper worlds into Malchut where such desire is manifested.

   This leads us to transition into discussing the Kabbalah Four Worlds that are associated with the Tree of Life. Predominately, these Four Worlds are, firstly, Atziluth, which includes the top three sefirot, Keter, Chokmah, and Binah. The second of these worlds is Briah, which includes the following three sefirot, Chesed, Gevurah, and Tiferet. Then, there is the world of Yetzirah, which includes the three sefirot Netzah, Hod, and Yesod. And lastly, the fourth and final world is Assiah, which includes the sefirah Malchut.

   When incorporating the Four Worlds into a 10 of Pentacles manifestation reading, know that each of the Worlds corresponds to one of the four senses. Knowing of these aspects can help one interpret a reading more precisely and with more depth. For instance, the world of Atziluth corresponds with sight. Briah corresponds with hearing. Yetzirah corresponds with smell. And lastly, Assiah corresponds with touch. Think of the Tree of Life as a human face where the top tier is associated with the eyes, the following tier with the ears, then the nose, and then the mouth.

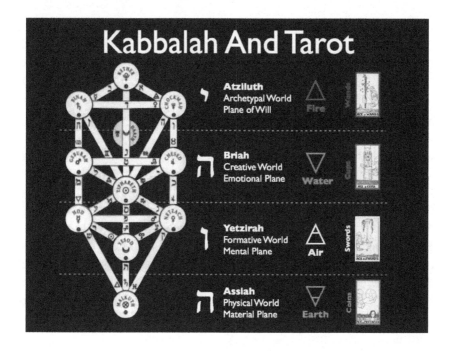

Kabbalah And Tarot

Atziluth
Archetypal World
Plane of Will
Fire
Wands

Briah
Creative World
Emotional Plane
Water
Cups

Yetzirah
Formative World
Mental Plane
Air
Swords

Assiah
Physical World
Material Plane
Earth
Coins

Chapter 6

Decoding the Tarot Grid

The Tarot Grid includes all the Minor and Major Arcana cards, which includes 40 Minors and 22 Majors. Both the numbers 40 and 22 share major significance in Kabbalah. For instance, there are 22 letters in the Hebrew alphabet, and each one of the letters is assigned to one of the 22 Major Arcana cards. The number 40 encompasses a spiritual significance, as well as the sacred gematria value of the Hebrew letter Mem, meaning water, as it relates to spiritual cleansing. For example, in the book of Genesis, the Earth flooded for 40 days and 40 nights. It was a time of cleansing where the entire Earth experienced a large-scale baptism. This concept of spiritual cleansing is relevant each time the number 40 appears throughout the Torah as well as the tarot. The Tarot Grid contains numerous keys concealed within its 62 cards. The combining of certain cards to form paths along the Grid uncovers esoteric mysteries which serve as a medium for enriching one's spirit.

The main path of the Grid begins with the first card at the top and ends with the last card at the bottom. Beginning at the Ace of Wands card, the path trickles downwardly and eventually will end at the World card. By following this path, a person will grow and expand upon their character. Along their journey down this path, they will be faced with life-challenges. Each new challenge will affect one's character differently. These particular situations are depicted in the illustrations on the Minor Arcana and are influenced by certain energy aspects pertaining to each of the individual tarot suits. The tarot suits consist of the four aspects of human life: the physical (Pentacles), mental (Swords), emotional (Cups) and spiritual (Wands) levels of existence. In order to find balance, wholeness and fulfillment in our lives, we need to heal, develop and integrate all four of these aspects within ourselves. From the Ace of Wands to the 10 of Pentacles, a person will have traveled along 40 cards, and this journey requires a relevant amount of time for one to work on their self. By the time one reaches the 10 of Pentacles card they are to be considered cleansed and spiritually ready to begin the transcendence into higher levels of consciousness, transitioning from the Minor Arcana into the Major Arcana. The path along the tarot suits connects a person to the energy of each of the ten sefirot by drawing down the Light of the Creator, which fills our spiritual vessel with the strength needed for our spirit to traverse up through the 22 branches of the Tree of Life that correspond with the 22 Major Arcana. We are able to travel the 22 pathways only as long as we stay connected to the Source of the Light, which is found in the sefirah Keter. Keter is the infinite source, a state of being, the field of possibility. It is the ultimate unseen reality located at the top of the Tree, which is where the roots of the Tree are found drawing down the Light into the vessel. This Light is the energy within the tarot. One's purpose for traveling down the Tarot's path is to obtain Christ Consciousness, and become 'one with God.' Both the tarot and the Torah function similarly in regards to their higher purpose, to connect one with the Light of the Creator.

Along the Tarot Grid's path, one will find life advice, obtain practical knowledge and discover how to manifest prosperity. Although, the spiritual path isn't easy. You will be faced with many challenges that force you to confront your biggest fears. As we follow this path, we find that the biggest obstacle we're faced up against is ourselves. Along the path we discover ourself as we learn to know thy self. The spiritual path can grow taxing. And because we must embark on this journey alone, it seems to defy our character. Although, we are never truly alone as long as we stay connected to the Light of the Creator, and listen to the advice found within the tarot.

You will find that when you add the sum of the Roman numerals of all the cards in the Tarot Grid, you get a total of 451. The number 451 is the gematria value of the name Ishmael, meaning God listens, God hears, (he will) listen to God. This connection reassures us that we are never truly alone on this path as long we maintain a communication with God.

The first card on the Grid is the Ace of Wands, which has a value of 1. The Ace of Wands is considered the root, and the beginning of the tarot. From here the Grid trickles down and ends at the World card. As we now know, when we add up all the cards' Roman numerals from the Ace of Wands to the World card, we get

451. 451 reduces down to 1 (4+5+1 = 10, and when reduced is 1+0 = 1). This numerological equation mirrors the path's concept as well as its purpose, which is to lead one back to the Source, to Keter, the first sefirah, which is represented by the number 1 on the Tree of Life. Therefore, the path begins and ends with 1. Upon the arrival at the end of the path, man becomes 'at one' with God. God is one, and is considered to be the Alpha and the Omega (the first and the last). We see this Alpha-Omega connection within the Fool card, which is assigned to the Hebrew letter Aleph (gematria value of 1) . The Fool card embodies as well as personifies the Light of the tarot. The Light enters the Fool's vessel, giving him the energy needed (breath of life) and the will to begin his journey down the spiritual path. Therefore, the Fool is placed at the beginning of the Grid just before the Ace of Wands, and can also be located at the very end of the Grid as well, just after the World card. The World being the last card on the Grid, coincidentally assigned to the letter Tav, which is the last letter of the alphabet. The Fool binds the end back to the beginning on the tarot wheel; a cycle represented within the Grid. The Light of God that shines within the Fool card is ever present throughout the entire path, from the first card all the way down to the last. "I am the Alpha and the Omega," says the Lord who is God, "He who is and was and is coming, the Almighty." - Revelation 1:8. Likewise, the Fool card can be placed at either the front or at the end of the Grid, as well as any place in between. The Fool card is assigned to the Hebrew letter Aleph, which is typically silent. Also, the Fool is associated with the sefirah Da'at, which is known as the invisible/hidden sphere on the Kabbalah Tree of Life, and referred to as being the seed of the Tree. The initiate who travels along the spiritual path is comparable to a seed, which is planted in the dirt and forced to grow against its nature, up to the surface where it becomes one with the light.

Furthermore, as we continue this path along the Fool's journey, from the Ace of Wands down to the World card, we accumulate the practical knowledge obtained within each of the 62 cards. Consequently, the sum of these 62 cards' Roman numerals is a total of 451, which is (as mentioned earlier) the gematria value for the name Ishmael. As stated in Genesis 17:18-19, God promised Ishmael that he would receive prosperity and success in his lifetime.

The Fool's path along the Tarot Grid can be perceived as one's life journey. Interestingly, Ishmael died at the age of 137 years old (Genesis 25:17), which is significant here because 137 is the gematria value for the word Kabbalah, meaning 'to receive.' The name Ishmael means 'God listens', (he will) listen to God. These gematria connections reveal to us the secret of how to endure the journey; as long as we stay in a constant communication with God, we will receive prosperity and success in our lives.

The number 137 is significant in science as well as in mysticism. 1/137 is the Fine-Structure Constant, which is the measure of the strength of the electromagnetic force that governs how electrically charged elementary particles (e.g., electron, muon) and light (photons) interact. It is the universal force (a dimensionless, "coupling constant") that combines all things together as one. This force is similar to the 'force' referred to in the Star Wars movies. The Kabbalists refer to this force as the Light, the universal God energy, the Source of all Creation. This Light formed matter. This 1/137 Fine-Structure, 'coupling constant' is the force that flows through the Tarot. This force spins the tarot wheel, and allows the end of the Tarot Grid to loop back up and around to the top, back at the beginning to the Ace of Wands card to start the cycle again. Therefore, this electromagnetic force binds the beginning of the Grid's path with its end in a continuous rotating loop. Thus, the Light of Kabbalah, the universal light of the Fine-Structure constant is sealed within the tarot cards. Ergo, the tarot acts a vessel for the Light. As we study and meditate on the tarot, we too can become a vessel, channeling the Light found within it for the sole purpose of passing along our obtained wisdom onto others.

Kabbalists consider human beings as vessels for the Light. We draw down the Light from above and into our vessel and it fills us up, empowers us and it elevates our soul's vibration. The reason

we follow the spiritual path is to raise the life-force (kundalini) energy within us with the intention of opening the third eye. At which point the soul is elevated up into the higher levels of awareness, uniting with Keter and the realm of the Super Conscious aka the Christ Consciousness. The symbol representing this gateway/ portal into the higher realm is the Seal of Saturn, aka Seal of Zazel.

One of the biggest secrets hidden inside the Tarot Grid is that there is a large Seal of Saturn found within the cards' layout. The seal is found by laying out all the tarot cards where you can see them, either on the floor or on a table in the Grid formation.

The seal can be found when you draw a line following the rising and descending numbers of the cards within the Grid. (See picture for reference.)

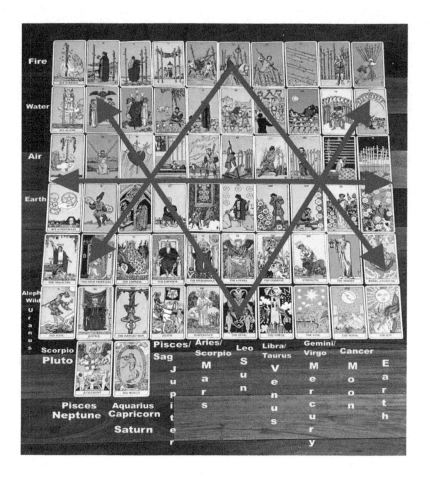

Below is the 3×3 magic square of Saturn. The Seal of Saturn is formed from within this square by following the numbers 1 through 9 in one continuous line, as seen in the picture below.

We discover and uncover the Seal of Saturn hidden within the Tarot Grid firstly by starting at the top of the Grid, and then move down from there. Start with the middle card on the top row, which is the 6 of Wands, and then draw a line in a diagonal motion downward, to the left, down to the High Priestess card. There should now be a straight line connecting the 6 of Wands to the High Priestess. Return back to the starting position, at the 6 of Wands, and from here draw a new line that leads downward, diagonally to the right, from the 6 of Wands all the way to the Wheel of Fortune card. Apply these same steps to the bottom row. Once again, begin with the middle card, which is the Devil card, numeral XV.

Number 15 reduced is 1+5 = 6. Start from the number 6 card on the bottom row (the Devil) which is located directly on the opposite side of the Grid from where we initially started, which was the 6th column with the 6 of Wands on the top row. Then, repeat the same steps that were used for going down the Grid, but this time work your way upward. After completing these steps, you will have two overlapping Vs, where two XXs touch each other forming a ♦ diamond

(or rhombus) in the middle of the Grid. Now draw a line through the two XXs, from one side of the grid to the other, along the top of the cards aligned along the row of Pentacles cards. This line should go straight through the middle of the diamond, and directly through the middle of the Grid, separating the Grid into two halves, with there being three rows above as well as three rows below this line.

When you add up all the numbers of each card located at each of the six points of the seal you get the sum of 45, which is the gematria

(Hebrew numerology) value for both the names of Saturn's 'spirits' known as Zazel and Agiel. These six cards on the seal are the Devil, number 15, the High Priestess, number 2, the Two of Cups, the 6 of Wands, the 10 of Cups, and astly the Wheel of Fortune card, which is number 10—again, all having the sum of 45. (15+2+2+6+10+10 = 45) 45 is also the sum of all the numbers inside the Magic Square of Saturn, which is where the Seal of Saturn originates. Allow me to reiterate that Saturn's magic square is a 3×3 square where each row adds up to 15, and 3×15 = 45. The square includes the numbers 1-9, and when you add the sum of the digits of Saturn's square you get 1+2+3+4+5+6+7+8+9 = 45.

Similar to the Vesica Piscis symbol, the diamond formed in the center of the Seal of Saturn acts as a portal which leads from the astral realm, which the Kabbalists refer to as the 99% reality, into the physical world of matter aka the 1% reality, which is the reality that we perceive with our five senses. This portal acts as a gateway where one is able to draw down a desire from the macrocosm down into the world of the manifest known as the microcosm. It is similar to a womb that's sole purpose is the basis of creation in this universe. It is a doorway that acts as a bridge between spirit and form, matter and anti-matter—the infinite void and all matter.

When studying the planetary magic squares, Saturn is associated with two spirits, Zazel and Agiel. Zazel is known as the Spirit of Saturn, while Agiel is considered the Intelligence of Saturn. Saturn's seal reflects the energy influences of both these spirits. Saturn is the guardian of the threshold between the material and the spiritual worlds; the gateway between eternity and the realm of time and space. Saturn is where the descent into matter begins.

There are three tarot cards that contain a hidden Seal of Saturn aka Seal of Zazel within them: the Hierophant, the 10 of Pentacles, and the Devil card all contain the hidden Seal. These seals in their specific locations on these three cards connect us to much deeper insight and richer understanding of the concealed mysteries within the tarot. I will explain in detail the significance of these particular connections in a later chapter. The thing to focus on now is the Seal's importance to the Waite-Smith tarot deck, and know that it is hidden in more places than one. The Seal of Saturn is the portal to the astral dimension, signified by the number 45, which is prevalent throughout the tarot. Coincidentally, both the names Zazel and Agiel share a Hebrew gematria value of 45. The diamond located in the center of the seal represents the third eye, and when opened one can transverse into higher dimensions of reality between time and space. Within each occurrence of discovering a hidden connection linked to the number 45 within the tarot will always allude to this concept.

The practical reason for why the Seal of Saturn is concealed within the Grid is for the sole basis of protection from Saturn's planetary impact. The seal acts as a protective shield that deflects all of Saturn's negative influences which can include such things as judgment or time restrictions—all the while sealing in the magical essence that Saturn beholds. A magic square, or kamea, is a representation of spiritual forces in a mathematical format. They are typically arranged in such a way that any row is equal to the sum of any column. Each of the seven classical planets have both a Seal and a Kamea, aka magic square. Whereas the kamea sets forces in motion, the seal brings them to a halt. Saturn is known as the lord of time, restriction and karma. Saturn constantly emits waves of solidifying energy down upon us. This low vibrational energy, which is essentially sound waves, delays the process of creation, as well as restricts time in between cause and effect. Saturn governs the time allotted for one to manifest their desires with a blanket of low vibrational egocentric waves that solidify in forms of restriction, frustration, doubt and fear. We experience this illusionary reality created by this energy as karmic life-challenges and daily struggles. The Seal of Saturn acts as a protective shield from that malefic force allowing a tarot practitioner to not be restricted by the time it takes for a desire to manifest itself into reality. They are able to see results very quickly—appearing like magic or a miracle. The tarot has hidden within it the tools and the keys to prosperity that can be used to enrich one's life. With the use of the tarot the Light of Kabbalah is revealed without the restrictions and limitations of the Saturnian influence.

Below is a picture showing the three tarot cards that have a hidden Seal of Saturn within them. Interesting to point out is that the sum of these three cards' Roman numerals equals 30. 30 is the number of years Saturn takes to make its return, known in astrology as the Saturn Return. On the day of one's birth, Saturn is positioned at this point in their birth chart, and begins to retrograde it's influence slowly away, and will not return back for approximately another 30 years. The Hierophant (V), 10 of Pentacles (X), the Devil (15) when added together is 5+10+15 = 30.

The Hierophant is assigned the Hebrew letter Vav, meaning nail. Vav is the nail (or tent peg) that connects a tent to the ground. Vav joins or binds two things together. The Hierophant is depicted as being the middleman connecting the men below to the God above. The Hierophant connects the heavens with the earth, the material with the spiritual, as well as binds the two conscious worlds: the *seen* with the *unseen*.

The Devil card is assigned to the letter Ayin, meaning eye, and relates to the opening of the third eye. By opening the third eye one is able to connect to the upper worlds, and to the higher-state of awareness.

The 10 of Pentacles is considered an 'action' card, and relates to the concept of manifestation. The esoteric title for this card is The Lord of Wealth. It is astrologically associated with Mercury in Virgo, which corresponds with the notion of manifesting brilliant ideas.

The old man in this card draws in inspiration gathered from the imagination of the astral plane, and then formulates those ideas into practical ways of bringing forth prosperity into the real world. Notice the old man sitting close to the checkered wall that divides the two worlds? He is pictured here drawing forth brilliant ideas from the astral realm on the left of the checkered wall and manifesting them into the material world on the right of the wall.

Bear with me as I explain the 10 of Pentacles card and how to uncover its hidden seal. As I mentioned earlier, the 10 of Pentacles card is a map key for the entire tarot system. There being a seal inside the 10 of Pentacles card is a clue that there is also a hidden Seal of Saturn inside the Tarot Grid, and vice versa, because both act as map keys and/or legends for the entire tarot system. Therefore, these two map keys go hand in hand, understanding one leads to the understanding of the other.

The ten pentacles on the 10 of Pentacles card form a Tree of Life diagram. Knowing that this card acts as a map key, this ten-sphere diagram shows us the structure and arrangement for which every tarot card is based upon. Each of the ten pentacles correspond to one of the ten sefirot (spheres) on the Tree of Life. Also know that each object, person, and/or symbol (in this card) next to or touching a particular pentacle reveals a deeper hidden meaning when combined with its particular sefirah (sphere) association.

For an example, let us look at the 9th pentacle on this card, which corresponds with the sefirah Yesod, to get a better understanding. The sefirah Yesod is located on the old man's right hand. Yesod is ruled by the Moon, and the Moon is known to unveil truths that are hidden in plain sight. This 9th pentacle being located on the old man's right hand, the hand associated with sharing and connects to energy influence of the Tree of Life's right column energy, informs us that the old man is offering us a clue. The camouflaged dog, whose nose is touching the 9th pentacle, is depicted with a 3×3 magic square of Saturn upon its head. A dog's eyes are located on the sides of its head, therefore having such a magic square directly in between this dog's two eyes is a clear reference to the third eye, and acknowledges the Third Eye-Seal of Saturn connection. It has now become evident that the old man is signaling to us, discreetly that somewhere hidden within this card is a Seal of Saturn. Perhaps he is giving a nod to the fact, and suggesting that it was with the use of the seal that he was able to manifest the wonderful life portrayed in this card.

Starting from the 9th pentacle we begin to form this seal by drawing a line up to the 5th pentacle. Then once again from the 9th pentacle, draw another line up to the 4th pentacle. These two lines form the bottom 'V' of the seal. In order to create the rest of the seal repeat similar steps as before, but this time start from the top, with the 1st pentacle, which is positioned directly on the opposite side of the 9th pentacle from where we began. So, from the 1st pentacle draw two lines leading down to the 7th and 8th pentacles, thus forming a 'Λ' which overlaps the lower 'V' and creates two XXs with a ♦ (diamond) in the center. Now look closely in the middle of the diamond, and you will see how the castle walls are illustrated in such a way that they form a horizontal straight line that stretches across the entire length of the card. You will notice how this line fits perfectly in between the white and black checkers on the checkered wall which is located directly to the left of the old man's head. This line is placed directly in the middle of the card, and is the final piece to the puzzle needed for creating a complete Seal of Saturn.

The Bible tells us in Thessalonians 5:21, "Test all things; hold fast what is good." Thus, in order to test this new finding, we must test the math. The math never lies. This numerology practice is applicable in both Torah and tarot study. Each Hebrew letter has a numerical value, so by adding the sums and values of words, phrases and verses one can uncover deeper spiritual understanding within the text. Discovering words or phrases that share the same numerical values will reveal even greater significance. This Hebrew numerology practice is called gematria, and is leveraged to disclose more profound spiritual understanding. Hence, Kabbalah is the spirituality of numbers. By utilizing the gematria code of Saturn's Seal found on the 10 of Pentacles card, let's begin by adding the sum of the pentacles' numbers which are used to create the seal. Starting from the top of the seal down to the bottom, the pentacles involved, as they relate to the sefirot, are numbered $1+4+5+7+8+9 = 34$. Are we forgetting one? Kabbalah teaches us that there are actually eleven sefirot on the Tree of Life. The 11th sefirah is the hidden sefirah known as Da'at. Da'at is the seed of the Tree, which encompasses all the knowledge and potential of each sefirot. Da'at is an anagram for DATA, and like DATA, Da'at holds within it the DNA code of the entire Tree. This is the final clue to be unveiled by Yesod, the 9th pentacle, which is to uncover the hidden sefirah Da'at. So, now we add $34+11$, because Da'at is the 11th pentacle, and we get the sum total of 45. And as we have already learned, 45 is the sum of all the numbers in Saturn's magic square.

This is yet another clue, and an important reminder, that we must never forget about Da'at, and to include it whenever we attempt to uncover secrets hidden throughout the tarot, especially secrets associated with the ten sefirot.

As for the other two cards that contain the Seal of Saturn, I will describe those in detail in one or more separate chapters which will have greater relevance to that specific card. For now, I wish to remain on the subject of decoding the Tarot Grid, which shares the closest relationship with the 10 of Pentacles card.

Moving forward, another secret hidden in the Tarot Grid is the precise location of the Prosperity Key, which is a guided meditation used to grant wishes. Whereas the Grid lays out the path for one to take on their spiritual journey towards enlightenment, arming one with practical spiritual tools and life advice, the Prosperity Key acts as a guided meditation. This meditation is a step-by-step key used for manifesting desires—in a practical way, referred to as the 'practical Kabbalah.'

Trace these following steps in order to uncover the Prosperity Key by first locating the middle line of the Seal of Saturn, which is drawn across the suit of pentacles from the Ace to the 10. It is along this middle line where we locate this key that will connect us to prosperity, abundance and worldly desires. It is no coincidence that this path along the suit of pentacles goes straight through the middle of the diamond in Saturn's seal, which represents the third eye. The suit of Pentacles represents the physical and tangible. As we already know, by meditating and opening the third eye we are able to draw down the Light and blessings of prosperity. The next thing to do is to configure the path and/or the chronological steps for this guided meditation. Starting at the Ace of Pentacles card, begin drawing a line outward towards the 10 of Pentacles card—a line which follows the same exact lightning bolt formation/path that is known to pass through the Tree of Life. The lightning bolt represents the Light's path as it travels from Keter down to Malchut, referred to by the Kabbalists as the tzimtzum. In other words, from the Ace of Pentacles to the 10 of Pentacles. Thus, creating a ten-step guided-meditation which corresponds to the Kabbalah Tree of Life. This specific path the tzimtzum lightning bolt travels is one that agrees with both the Kabbalah and Golden Dawn teachings. Likewise, this exact lightning bolt formation is the same as depicted in the Tower card. So, now we follow the path of the lightning bolt as it travels throughout the Tree, which shoots across the middle of the Tarot Grid and directly through the center of

Saturn's seal. This lightning bolt is symbolic of God's Light, and it represents an idea, that spark of electricity, which comes from the brain and travels down our spinal column and then settles in our sexual organs just before manifesting itself into the real world. At which point we transform our ideas into tangible things. This zig-zagging path of the Prosperity key leads from the Ace of Pentacles to the 2 of Swords, to the Empress, to the 4 of Swords, to the Hierophant, to the 6 of Pentacles, to the 7 of Swords, to the Strength card, to the 9 of Pentacles, and ends at the 10 of Pentacles—the 'manifestation' card.

Mentioned earlier, Ishmael's name equals the gematria value of 451, which is the sum of all the cards on the Grid when counting their Roman numerals. God's promise to Ishmael was that he would have prosperity and a life of contempt, and that Ishmael would be protected and blessed throughout his lifetime. Genesis 17:20-21, "As for Ishmael, I have heard you; behold, I will bless him, and will make him fruitful and will multiply him exceedingly". Ishmael's brother Isaac became their Father Abraham's sole heir, although God promised Ishmael that he would raise up a great nation of his own. This 451-connection found here is a code which reveals to us that we, just like Ishmael, also have the power within us to create great things for ourselves. This connection to the name Ishmael, meaning God listens, assures us that God will always listen to us whenever we ask for blessings of prosperity. It is understood God did not simply give Ishmael everything, instead Ishmael had to manifest his own success. God promised Ishmael great things as long as Ishmael took the appropriate actions to do so. Ishmael had to earn his inheritance, so as not to gain a sense of entitlement.

Included within the Prosperity Key is the Empress card who is associated with prosperity. The Empress card can be considered as THE card for prosperity. The 72 Name of God for prosperity just so happens to be the 45th name on the list of 72 names, סאל. Here again we see yet another connection to the number 45.

The Prosperity Key includes ten cards, three of which are Major Arcana cards. This includes the Empress, the Hierophant, and the Strength cards. When we add up the sum of the values of the Hebrew letters assigned to these cards, the result is interesting. For instance, the Empress is assigned to Daleth, which has a value of 4, the Hierophant is assigned to Vav, which has a value of 6, and lastly, the Strength card, which is assigned to Teth, with a value of 9, and by adding the sum of these values we get $4+6+9 = 19$. And we mustn't forget the Da'at, so considering the Da'at we add one more giving us $19+1 = 20$. Remember as you add up the Major Arcana cards in this meditation, just as when deciphering any mysteries involving the ten sefirot, you must not forget the Fool card, which is associated with the hidden 11th sefirah Da'at. The Fool is assigned to the Hebrew letter Aleph which has a numerical value of 1.

Adding the Fool to the other three Majors in the Prosperity Key gives us the number 20. 20 is the gematria value of the Hebrew letter Kaph, meaning palm of hand, which refers to blessings being granted. Think of a High Priest raising his hands and facing his palms to the congregation as he recites the benediction. Priests also place their palms onto people's heads as they receive their blessing. Interesting to note here is that there are now exactly four Major Arcana included in the Prosperity Key once we include the Fool card. There being four of things connects us to the fourth sefirah Chesed, which is associated with blessings of mercy, kindness and good fortune.

The lightning bolt traveling through the Prosperity Key represents the life-force energy that travels along the spinal column aka Jacob's Ladder. This ladder contains 33 steps just as the spinal column has 33 vertebrae, leading from the tail bone up to the skull. The spiritual enlightenment that one experiences occurs in the mind. This enlightening experience involves an ego-death, which releases ego from the vessel making room for the individual to receive more of God's Light. Coincidentally, both the light of the universal force known as the Fine-Structure constant as well as the Light of Kabbalah share the same value of 137. 137 just so happens to be the 33rd prime number. Considering these clues, locate the 33rd card on the Grid from the Ace of Wands at the top which leads to the 3 of Pentacles card. It is interesting to find this card placed in this particular spot because it depicts a man shining a light on a religious text. Let us continue this bread trail by locating the 33rd card from the bottom of the Grid, which is the 10 of Swords. Here we find depicted in this card a man with ten swords stuck in his back that are led directly up his spinal column, aka his Jacob's ladder, or his 33 vertebrae of transcendence. These two cards are very similar in their spiritual message; both dealing with spiritual enlightenment. For instance, in the 3 of Pentacles card you have a man sharing his Light or spiritual knowledge with others, and then at the same time the two others are learning deeper spiritual concepts and being enlightened themselves. These students will now share what they have learned and in turn enlighten others. Religious texts can be read in either two ways, literally or metaphorically. The latter being a way of reading religious texts (e.g., Bible, Torah) in between the lines—in a spiritual way. Most people are never taught the deeper and hidden spiritual meanings behind their religious stories, which are usually encoded in metaphor and allegory. Likewise, the 10 of Swords card metaphorically depicts a man reaching enlightenment after having searched for the deeper hidden mysteries found within himself and deep within his soul—aka soul searching. Knowing thy self can be very enlightening. Some consider it to be the 11th commandment; to know thy self. You will notice on the Tarot Grid that both the 3 of Pentacles and the 10 of Swords cards are located directly on (touching) the median line which is drawn straight through the center of the Seal of Saturn, with the 10 of Swords on top of the line and the 3 of Pentacles just below it. Furthermore, this is the key to understanding the function of the right and left hemispheres of the brain, as it pertains to the Grid. The 3 of Pentacles card being located at the bottom of the median line connects to the right brain traits as it pertains to the awakening of the subconscious mind, stimulated by the Light you reveal to others, either by converting them to think 'outside the box' or by deconstructing their fixed mindsets. All the while the 10 of Swords card connects to the left-brain characteristics such as, thinking analytically, objectively and logically about one's self and one's own behavior. Both cards relate to consciously drawing out the Light from the darkness, which one deals with on a subconscious level, as they consciously and pro-actively improve their character—overcoming ego by implementing shadow work. The 3 of Pentacles pertains to the learning and enlightenment obtained from books, but most importantly being able to see and connect to the deeper spiritual meaning within the text, while the 10 of Pentacles card pertains to shadow work, and the spiritual exercise of getting to know thyself and the act of achieving enlightenment by means of critical self-reflection. All things considered; both these cards reflect a pro-active approach towards spiritual enlightenment.

In order for true spiritual change, one must first grow either unfulfilled or disgusted with the direction their life is heading. This gives them the will to turn their life around and devote themselves to making positive changes and better life choices.

Continuing forward, this lightning bolt represents the spark of energy that occurs when one focuses their intention on balancing the opposing polarities of the brain's two hemispheres. A person must utilize their willpower in order to control certain drives and emotions contained within their psyche. This energy is ever present, although at times we can have either more or less of this energy depending on our emotional state. Retaining this energy depends a lot on how we release it into the world, into our work and onto others. Often, we invest too much of either our time or energy on frivolous things and/or on flaky people, and we gain nothing in return. This energy within us should be cherished. It is the life-force of God within man that can be wielded as a creative force for good. It is concealed within religious texts such as the Torah, and proven to be found ever present in the tarot as well, as revealed here in the Tarot Grid. We are able to connect to this force at any given time and at even given moment. Mankind is able to channel and harness this energy like a conduit. This energy force is all around us, all of the time. How does one explain water to a fish? It is up to each individual to take personal responsibility in maintaining a balance within themselves by controlling their emotions and behaviors.

As demonstrated in the Grid, this energy known as the Light is revealed to us in the beginning and then passes through the cards all the way to the end. Starting at the top with the Ace of Wands, this energy trickles down throughout the Grid all the way to the World card; from the first to the last card. For instance, the first card, the Ace of Wands depicts God's hand igniting the will to receive pleasure, triggered by the 37 rays around God's hand that represent the wisdom of Chokmah—Chokmah having a gematria value of 37. And then we see in the final card, the World card, the World which has the Four Faces of God floating in gray-colored clouds as well as acknowledges the completion of the cycle. The Faces of God gesture for you to pass the torch (the Light) onto others who will follow in your footsteps along the path you paved for them. You will notice the gray-colored objects in this card: the gray clouds as well as the naked maiden clothed in nothing but a gray-colored scarf. Gray is the color that symbolizes Chokmah, meaning wisdom, and therefore wisdom is present in the beginning just as it is at the end of the Grid. One is able to tap into this wisdom as they traverse along the entire tarot cycle, known as the Fool's journey. This example displays the Grid's incorporation of the concept of Alpha and Omega. By making this connection we are able to see how God's Light is ever present all throughout the tarot, just as it is in the Torah.

The Zohar, which is a foundational work in the literature of Jewish mystical thought, breaks up the word 'Chokmah' (numerical value of 37 ordinal, and 73 standard gematria) into the two roots of the word where you have 'Koah', meaning 'potential', and 'Mah', meaning 'what.' When you consider the two root words of Chokmah you get 'Koah Mah', which means "the potential of what is" or "the potential of what is to be."

Once we consider the two styles of gematria (ordinal and standard) for the word Chokmah, we now establish a connection with the number 37 at the beginning of the Grid, with the Ace of Wands, as well as a 73 at the World card. Interestingly, if you were to multiply these two numbers together 37×73 you would get 2,701, which is the gematria value of first verse in the Torah, Genesis 1:1, "In the beginning God created the heavens and the earth." What is neat, once realized here, is that the hand of God is depicted coming out of the 'heavens' in the Ace of Wands card (as He sparks the Light of creation), and then, the final card which happens to be the World card; the word 'world' being synonymous with 'earth', referring back to 'God created the *heavens* and the *earth*.' Another fun thing to add here is that the 22 Major Arcana cards included in the tarot deck are oddly numbered 0-21, and when considering this, we can compare these Majors to the first 21 prime numbers. Coincidentally, the 12th prime is 37, and the 21st prime is 73. This is fascinating, because the 12th Major Arcana card is the Hanged Man who has exactly 37 light rays surrounding his head. And then, the 21st Major Arcana is the World card with all its gray-colored objects that symbolize Chokmah, which has the gematria value of 73. Furthermore, as we decipher the World card we discover some interesting correlations, such as the card's Roman numeral is 21, the Four Faces which correspond to the four fixed signs of the zodiac have a sum of 26 when adding their astrological houses together, the Hebrew letter assigned to the World card is Tav which astrologically corresponds to Saturn who is attributed to YHVH (also represented by the Four Faces) with a numerical value of 26. By adding up these clues you get 73, (21+26+26 = 73). The numbers 37 and 73 are mirrored numbers, just as the 12th and 21st Major Arcana cards' Roman numerals are mirrored numbers. This 'mirroring' is how the Light travels through the Tarot Grid, just as the life-force energy travels up and down the kundalini. Just for fun, let's add the value of the first verse in the Torah, Genesis 1:1, which is 2,701 by its mirrored self. This would appear as 2,701+1,072 = 3773.

This lightning bolt energy travels up and down the chakras like a serpent. Famous philosopher and mystic, Manly P. Hall described this concept eloquently when he said, "Electricity was commonly symbolized by the serpent because of its motion. Electricity passing between the poles of a spark gap is serpentine in its motion. Force projected through atmosphere was called The Great Snake. Being symbolic of universal force, the serpent was emblematic of both good and evil. Force can tear down as rapidly as it can build up. The serpent with its tail in its mouth is the symbol of eternity, for in this position the body of the reptile has neither beginning nor end. The head and tail represent the positive and negative poles of the cosmic life circuit. The initiates of the Mysteries were often referred to as serpents, and their wisdom was considered analogous to the divinely inspired power of the snake."
- Manly P. Hall, The Secret Teachings of All Ages

This energy of the serpentine kundalini ascends from the base of the spine directly up towards the brain. This energy stimulates the brain, allowing the brain to function as an antenna as it attracts brilliant ideas from the upper worlds of the collective unconscious, the Super Conscious. The two hemispheres of the brain work in tandem in the creation and formulation of thoughts and ideas. Scientists still do not know where our thoughts come from. Kabbalists taught that ideas come from the Light. This Light is known as the Fine-Structure constant.

The creation process begins with an idea. Brilliant ideas, not just any idea but brilliant ideas, come from the Light, pass through the third eye and stimulate the back of the head, at which point we decide to consciously make it so, forming the idea into a tangible thing with our hands as we bring forth our thoughts into reality. The Kabbalah 72 Name of God for 'Certainty' is ערי, referring to eye/head/hand. This is how ideas manifest through us; with certainty. With certainty success comes easily, and without certainty our egos tend to get the best of us.

The ego causes us to question our self-worth, have doubts, fears and negative judgments, which prevent and/or delay the brilliant ideas from ever being followed through with. Usually, the first idea that comes to mind is the right one. The first idea is pure and clean before ego has time to corrupt it. When we believe our thoughts to be our own, we forget where they truly come from—they come from the Light. This can cause us to second guess ourselves. If we were to remember that these brilliant ideas come from the Light, then we would have no doubt in them. When we take the Light out of the equation, we allow the ego to corrupt our thoughts. Ego will cause us to over analyze, overthink and judge our ideas as if they are our own. But, if we were to remember that the brilliance comes from the Creator, then we would never judge or second guess these brilliant ideas in the first place. Human beings are merely vessels for the Light of the Creator. The Creator only wants to spread His energy and form life in the material world.

Humans are vessels the Light uses to create and formulate its ideas, which essentially expand, and forever evolve. This is why we need to jump on these ideas as soon as we get them. If we fail to do so, someone else will. Someone else will eventually receive the same idea (which you thought was yours) and manifest it. The Light does not judge, nor does it discriminate. It tosses out ideas just like a farmer would toss out seeds over fertile soil. The Light's sole intention is to share its self. Brilliant ideas are just one aspect of the Light's influence. The Light wishes to grow its ideas and does not care who receives them, just as long as someone, anyone, develops them and makes them so. One should feel blessed when they receive such godly insight and inspiration. It is a rare and remarkable thing to experience such an epiphany. Most people run on auto-pilot, and they have a low-vibrational ego-natured consciousness, which causes them to selfishly concern themselves with their self alone. People such as this would be blessed if they were to only listen to God the Creator, and surrender to His Light, take the "I" out of the equation, drop their ego-driven plans and work for the greater good. Just as the old adage goes, "How do you make God laugh? You make plans". Considering the Law of Attraction where like attracts like, if you were to focus all your energy on positive things, you would only receive positivity in your life. And on the other hand, if you chose to focus all your attention on negativity, then you would receive constant negativity in your life. Energy flows where attention goes. The Light is positive energy. It's the source of unconditional love, joy and happiness. When we connect and surrender to this Light we are connecting to the source of our joy and happiness. Maintaining a connection to the Source makes life calmer, and we begin to feel at ease as we allow ourselves to surrender to the flow of our existence.

To be frank, life is not easy. It takes a consistent and pro-active effort to stay consciously connected to the Light. Overcoming the ego's gravitational weight, which is like an invisible force we can neither see or touch yet are all aware of its presence, as it ceaselessly presses down upon us. It seems as though life is ever so diligently instigating a tactful confiscation of our spirit. We choose to either overcome the ego or we submit to it. It is easy to succumb to this unseen pressure. When we lose ourselves to this egotistic force, we lose our connection to the Light. When we experience a disconnect from the Light we feel as though we are swimming against the current. As soon as we put ourselves above others and focus on our personal needs, focusing on the 'I' instead of the third eye, is when life becomes a struggle and we find ourselves inviting negativity into our lives. You will notice that life becomes less of a struggle when you surrender to the flow and allow the Light to download you its information, delivered to you in the form of brilliance, intelligence, intuition, insight and guidance, which consequently informs and blesses you with vision. The Light guides you towards the next steps you should be taking. Establishing a strong connection to the Light will lead you to feeling fulfilled and guide you spiritually towards achieving your goals without having to compromise your joy, which leads you to live a successful life while doing what you love. Thus, causing you to spread the love which you receive from the Light, paying it forward to others and to the world. This love you feel and the love you share is how the Light works through you in order to expand its life-force energy—by creating such conduits through the medium of vessels that channel its Light. Realize that you are merely a channel for the Light. Think about it. You first receive an idea, and then build upon that idea from previous understanding, and then from there you manifest the idea into something tangible. Basically, creating something out of nothing.

You allow the Light in and then channel it out, which consequently brings feelings of joy, fulfillment and eventually prosperity. Sharing your idea with others with the purpose of improving the lives of others will only attract more positivity into your life. As aresult, people will pay it forward and continue to spread the Light. This process of paying it forward will continue forever. The Light feeds on its own Light, and humans are merely channels to help further expand its own creation. The ego dupes the spirit into partaking in a battle forcing one to exercise their free will to either desire for the self alone or desire for the sake of sharing.

The Light within us has the power to stimulate and strengthen our 6th, intuitive sense. The individual living in a world of negative thought is not conscious of this inner eye. They may occasionally have flashes of intuition or illumination but then fall back into a world of chaos. It takes determination and eternal vigilance to check up on words and thoughts. Thoughts of fear, failure, resentment, and ill-will must be dissolved and dissipated.

Moving forward, there are 86 billion neurons in the human brain. This specific number is significant because 86 just so happens to be the gematria value for the name for God, Elohim. Elohim is usually used in a plural sense, meaning Gods; more than one. This can be comparable to the many neurons of the brain, and can allude to a certain aspect of brain function referring to the concept for when the brain is highly stimulated at a time an individual is connected to their Higher-Self. Also, interesting to point out here is that the gematria sum of all three names of God, YHVH (26), Elohim (86), and Adonai (65) equal a total value of 177. 177 is the gematria value for the phrase 'garden of Eden' which contains the two Trees: Tree of Knowledge and Tree of Life. Bear with me here. The brain acts as an antenna receiving ideas. These ideas stimulate the brain and in return the brain stimulates the two trees within the human body, which coincide with the branches of the arteries and the central nervous system. According to Manly P. Hall, the Tree of Life is associated with the arteries of the heart, while the Tree of Knowledge corresponds to the central nervous system with its branches connected to the brain. The brain receives an idea and then communicates the idea to the body's two trees. Therefore, God (Elohim, 86) communicates with us at the speed of light—186,000 mps.

Mentioned earlier was the significant number 45 and its connection to the tarot system, where 45 is the gematria value for both the names Zazel and Agiel and is the sum of the cards included within the Seal of Saturn, which is located in the center of the Tarot Grid. Keep this in mind when comparing the Grid to the human brain, and the Seal of Saturn to the third eye, which is the connection to God, the Higher-Self. Opening the third eye connects one to Saturn, which is YHVH, Yahweh. Interestingly, when you add the sum of the spelled-out letters of the tetragrammaton, YHVH, או ואה היד הא, the result is 45. Yod (20) + Heh (6) + Vav (13) + Heh (6) = 45.

The name Adam represents man and/or mankind, and man was created in God's image. This concept was portrayed beautifully in the famous Michelangelo painting, The Creation of Adam, where Adam is depicted touching fingers with God. In the painting, God is floating in what appears to be a cloud, but with further contemplation one will see that the cloud is actually a human brain. This alludes to the belief that God is in the mind of man. Man communicates to God, the Higher-self, within his own mind and the voice in his head. It is a coming together of the two hemispheres of the brain and formulating a balance of mind, which results in the opening of the third eye and awaking the 6th sense of intuition. The third eye is symbolized on the Grid as the Seal of Saturn, which has the gematria value of 45. It is the third eye aka pineal gland that acts as a gateway or portal where brilliant ideas and epiphanies are able to enter into the mind of Adam, who's name coincidentally shares the same gematria value of 45. So now we have two 45's: the 45 of Saturn + the 45 of Adam. Saturn is associated with Yahweh/El/Elohim, and is considered God of both the Torah as well as the Tarot. When we add the 45 of Yahweh + the 45 of Adam we get 90. 90 is the value of the Hebrew letter Tzaddi, meaning fish hook, which relates to the practice of meditation, and the concept of attracting, receiving and/or fishing for ideas once we quiet the mind. Moreover, the Hebrew word tzaddik means righteous one. A Tzaddik is known to always be in constant communication with God, where man and God are one. Moses was considered a Tzaddik.

In the Kabbalah 72 names of God, the Name attributed to Certainty ערי which translates as eye, head, hand. This certainty aspect of God is integrated within the Tarot Grid. For instance, the Seal of Saturn represents the *eye*, referring to the third eye, and the Tarot Grid represents the *head* symbolized by the two halves, top-bottom, that coincide with the two hemispheres of the brain, and lastly the *hand* aspect is represented by the Adam (mankind), man who is the tarot practitioner that manifests his ideas with absolute certainty. God has the power to create from His ideas, and Adam (man), who is created in God's image also shares this same power within him; to create something out of nothing.

Achieving absolute certainty can become your superpower. Once achieved, there is nothing that can stop you from obtaining your goals. You would never experience doubt if you knew for certain that everything would work out in the end. Simply knowing that your brilliant ideas come directly from the Light of the Creator should give you all the certainty you need.

Learn to trust your gut instinct and learn to trust the first idea that comes to your mind, especially those rare few that contain the mana needed to ignite the divine spark within you.

The human mind creates its own reality. The last thought a person has, is the one that manifests. Similar to how the child game of "he loves me, he loves me not" plays out, where you pluck the petals of a flower. As the game goes, you pluck the flower's petals, and as you do this recite the phrase "he loves me". You would then pluck the next flower petal as you recite the alternative phrase "he loves me not", and so on continuing to alternate between the two phrases until all the flower petals are plucked. The last phrase spoken determines the outcome of either he loves you or he does not. This is how our brain functions. It believes the last thing we tell it. Like the ancient magic word abracadabra, meaning I will create as I speak. Our words have magic power. We all have the ability to write and/or speak what we wish to manifest onto the material plane. Subsequently, whenever we are either writing or speaking our words, we are in a sense spelling, as in casting a spell. For this reason, be mindful of your thoughts, because they become your words. Becoming mindful of one's thoughts strengthens the sense of discernment required to filter through the endless thoughts that come to mind throughout one's day. With a strong sense of discernment, we can easily recognize a brilliant idea when we receive one. As a result, knowing what we know now about the origin of these rare and brilliant ideas, we are quick to act on them and not second guess their worth.

We live in a world shaped by time and space. Consequently, there is a separation between our desires and the fulfillment that we seek. Obstacles are now free to fill that space. Chaos is able to penetrate that space. The concept of time delays the rewards of our effort. Time creates an opening for problems to appear. In a physical world there is constant friction and barriers every step of the way. By practices of meditation and by working on ourselves we can dissolve ego blockages that appear in the space between cause and effect. Through the practice of meditation, we are able to open the third eye and access higher intelligence. The third eye acts as a gateway, and once opened can grant one the ability to rise above the limitations of time and space. We transcend all physical barriers. We shorten the distance between the goals we set, and our successful attainment of these goals. We dematerialize physical and spiritual obstacles.

A man possesses two aspects to his nature—his soul and his ego. Kabbalists refer to the ego by the code word 'Satan', pronounced Sah-tahn, and referred to as 'The Satan.'

When we behave with ego, we disconnect ourselves from the Source of all spiritual energy. When we subdue our ego, we connect to a realm of Divine energy. This infusion of energy removes chaos and suffering from our life. It tears away fear, doubt, anger and envy from our consciousness. We seal up any openings in our consciousness that might allow negative forces to incite our ego. Our reactive nature is shut down. As we meditate, we arouse the forces of sustenance and financial prosperity. This draws abundance into our lives. It helps remove poverty from the landscape of human civilization. It returns the cells in our body to an embryonic state. They revert back to stem cells. They are purified and revitalized, stimulating healing and igniting the forces of immortality. Meditation retrieves sparks of spiritual Light that dwell within the dark side of our nature. Thus, our ego is weakened and our soul is empowered once more. Hatred is purged from our hearts.

When obstacles confront us, or when doubts consume us, we are often tempted to give up, throw in the towel and say "I cannot go on." The act of persisting onward, when all looks bleak, is where true greatness is found.

Meditation imbues us with the emotional strength to stand after we stumble, to endure when the path is unendurable. We are endowed with the power to finish what we begin, persistence to always follow through, determination to go the distance, and with the tenacity to complete the most difficult tasks.

Personal chaos strikes us because we fail to perceive hidden truths. We do not see the bigger picture. The scope of thinking is limited by our rational, logical minds. Connecting to our sixth sense, and by opening the third eye, we heighten our intuition, we expand our awareness, and we develop deeper insight and evolve clairvoyance. We perceive the end in the beginning.

When we connect to the Light, we then in return share the Light and pass it along to others. As we increase an awareness of the Light of the Creator and its ever presence in the world, darkness and evil are diminished in equal measure.

By meditating and applying the practical guidance found within the tarot cards, the power of renewal and fresh beginnings will arise. Spiritual and emotional baggage is discarded as we begin anew —we grow wiser, more enlightened and more connected to the Light.

I believe it was the archangel Raziel, whose name means 'secrets of God', that revealed the tarot's Divine wisdom. According to the Zohar, Raziel uncovered the deep mysteries of the Torah. The name Raziel has a gematria value of 248, which is the same value for the name Abraham. There are a total of 613 commandments in the Torah and 248 of them are positive, 'to do' commandments. Abraham connects to the 248 do's whereas it was he who began practicing the law of circumcision, and led by example. Revealed to us by Raziel is how we can fix and/or correct the world as well as ourselves by rising above our ego-nature. This correcting of our karmic-baggage is known as Tikkun Olam, meaning repairing of the world, which is a positive 'to do' commandment that once practiced all the other 'to do' commandments emerge and fall into place. There are also 248 words in the Shema Yisrael prayer, which is recited twice a day—once in the morning and again in the evening before bed. The Shema Yisrael is placed inside the mezuzah's in Jewish people's doorways. These mezuzah's usually display a large letter Shin. It is customary to touch the Shin upon entering and exiting the doorway in order to connect one's self to its blessings. Therefore, a Shin is placed in the beginning as well as at the end of the visitor's experience, blessing them the entire time. This concept is represented in the Tarot Grid as well, seen with the Fool who features the letter Shin on the front of his shirt. Like the Shin, we see the Fool at the beginning of the Grid as well as at the end. The Shema Yisrael prayer is in reference to 'listening to god' which is a direct connection to the name Ishmael mentioned earlier, which means God listens, (he will) listen to God. The 248th commandment is about inheritance law, Laws of Inheritance, which is a direct reference to God's promise to Ishmael.

Worth noting here is that the most important commandment (mitzvah) is to love God, and then second is to treat thy neighbor as thy self.

Moving forward, the Seal of Saturn concealed within the center of the Grid is formed with two overlapping V-shaped lines. The points of these Vs are positioned on opposite sides of the Grid, where the Λ pointing upright, and drawn over the Minor arcana, corresponds to the left side of the brain, while the V pointing downward, and drawn over the Major arcana, corresponds with the right side of the brain. The card located at each of these points is a clue to how one can achieve success when utilizing either side of their brain. Furthermore, when looking at the Grid from the left side, (from the side of the Aces), the Grid becomes a map of the brain with the left side of the brain represented by the Minors and the right side of the brain represented by the Majors. These two hemispheres are split directly down the middle, separating the Grid into three rows on the left and three rows on the right, divided evenly by the line drawn through the center of the Seal of Saturn, which runs across the top of each card of the suit of Pentacles.

The downward V's point, which corresponds to the right side of the brain, and is drawn over the Major arcana, is placed over the Devil tarot card which depicts Adam and Eve becoming prosperous in the real world outside the garden of Eden. Adam and Eve can also represent the relationship between the male and female energies. This downward V, which starts at the Devil card, stretches outward and upward to two other significant cards—the 2 of Cups and the 10 of Cups. These two cards, like the Devil card, just so happen to have a man and woman depicted together, bonding in harmony. All three of these cards located at each of the three points of this V directly relate to the right brain's function of communicating emotions and expressing one's self to the outside world. While the left brain deals with our vocabulary's diction, terminology, and literal meanings of the words, the right brain concentrates on the accentuation and the intonation (rise and fall in speaking) of our words. The left brain tells us that we need to take action, while the right brain controls how we go about it. The right brain controls how we ask or demand things that we need from others. This can reflect upon how others judge our character. Our words as well as our behaviors have power and can stay with people for a long time after we leave their presence. How we treat others and how we express ourselves and our emotions displays to the world our character and sets up the platform for others to build our reputation upon. Achieving success in the world depends on our ability to obtain a balance of our male-female, positive-negative, polarities. The level of our balanced or unbalanced emotional state will be displayed to the world and to the people around us by our unconscious behaviors controlled by the subconscious right mind. It is not about *what* we say to others, but more so about *how* we say the things to others that matters most. These unconscious behaviors are so subtle that we don't realize we are doing them, and we will never understand the damage they do to others until the same things are done to us, and that is why we have karma.

By following the same steps used to uncover the connection shared between the cards of the Seal's downward pointing V we can now apply those steps to uncover the upper Λ's deeper meaning, and from here begin to understand the connection the cards of the top Λ share with the functionality of the left brain. At the tip of the Λ's point is the 6 of Wands card. This particular card depicts a successful man being paraded through town as he is honored by his peers. This card being a suit of Wands card reflects personal success and achievement pertaining to the acquiring of knowledge. When you follow this Λ downward to the other connecting cards you will find two cards that are associated with learning, studying and acquiring knowledge, which are the High Priestess and the Wheel of Fortune. The High Priestess card depicts a woman studying the Torah, while the Wheel of Fortune card depicts the Four Faces of God studying books of higher knowledge. Located around the wheel are the letters Rota, meaning wheel, which is an anagram for the word Taro as well as Tora; suggesting that the books the Four Faces are studying are related to either astrology, tarot or Torah knowledge. Hence, the presence of the tetragrammaton, the Holy name of God, YHVH, is placed upon the wheel. The Wheel of Fortune card is associated with Jupiter, who is referred to as the Guru and associated with the obtainment of knowledge.

The Seal of Saturn encompasses the idea of coming together and balancing the two hemispheres of the brain. A well-balanced brain can give way to a powerful sense of discernment utilized to filter the many thoughts that enter the mind—just as the diamond in the rough, one snatches the brilliant from the frivolous. Obtaining a well-balanced mind will bring forth stability in relationships with one's partners, with one's self, and with one's work. Good mental health helps you enjoy life and cope with problems. It offers a feeling of well-being and inner strength.

"If you correct your mind, the rest of your life will fall into place."
- Lao Tzu, Chinese philosopher

Pictured in the graphic design on the next page, to the top left is the concept of the two Keys (guided meditations) and how they coincide with the Tree of Life. Take notice how they are stacked, one upon the other. When applying this concept, the Prosperity Key corresponds with the Tree at the top and the Kundalini Key to the Tree on the bottom. Likewise, the Tree located at the bottom corresponds with the aspects of the subconscious right brain, while the Tree on top associates with the conscious and logical left-brain aspects. In addition to this, the graphic above displays the lightning bolt that travels down the Tree in the exact same way as it does on the Prosperity Key found on the Tarot Grid.

Pictured below is a piece of artwork outlining another example of the two mirrored Trees of Life, one on top of the other.

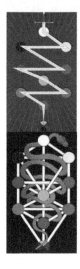 

Notice the All-Seeing Eye symbol in the center mid-point, where the two Trees meet together? This would be where the 'awakening' of the Seal of Saturn would be represented. In the other picture, we see Adam and Eve stacking the two Trees on top of each other, combining them together as one.

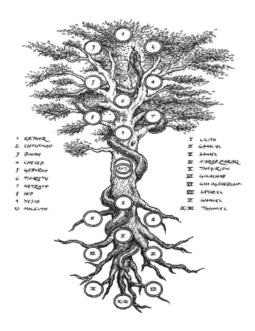

1 KETHER
2 CHOCKMAH
3 BINAH
4 CHESED
5 GEBURAH
6 TIPARETH
7 NETZACH
8 HOD
9 YESOD
10 MALKUTH

I LILITH
II GAMLIEL
III SAMAEL
IV A'ARAB ZARAQ
V THAGIRION
VI GOLACHAB
VII GHA'AGSHEBLAH
VIII SATARIEL
IX GAMLIEL
X/XI THAUMIEL

The idea of there being two Trees, one on top of the other, parallels the concept conveyed earlier regarding the contrasting functionalities of the right and left-brain hemispheres, as well as how they coincide to the two trees found within the human body. These two Trees within the human body include the central nervous system, which stems out from the eyes and brain, and the system of arteries that branch out from the heart.

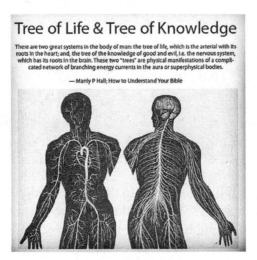

As far as the two hemispheres of the brain are concerned, the left brain is connected to the heart and arteries, while the right brain is connected to the eyes and nervous system. While the heart desires you to take action, the brain tells you how you will go about doing, and in what specific way you will take a particular action. For instance, your heart may desire to feel respected by your peers. This leads the brain to decide to either earn or demand that certain amount of respect the heart desires.

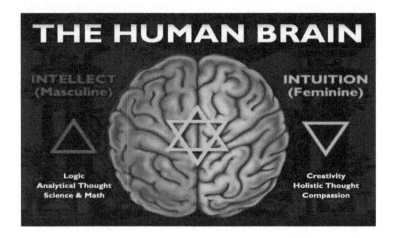

THE HUMAN BRAIN

INTELLECT
(Masculine)

INTUITION
(Feminine)

Logic
Analytical Thought
Science & Math

Creativity
Holistic Thought
Compassion

This balancing of the heart and mind brings us back to the Seal of Saturn and the two spirits associated with it, Zazel and Agiel, which both have a gematria value of 45. These two spirits of Saturn incorporate specific spiritual influences that harmonize with the two hemispheres of the brain, therefore influencing one of the two Trees that exist within the body. They encompass the yin and yang aspect of man. Zazel is comparable to the emotional characteristics of Saturn, while Agiel corresponds with Saturn's intellect. Kabbalistically, this can be expressed when comparing Adam to the mind of man, and Mah to the heart of man. Coincidentally, both the names Adam and Mah share a similar gematria value of 45 just as the names Zazel and Agiel do. Seen symbolized here, we can consider Adam to be analogous with Agiel who coincides with the intellect, while the Mah is related to the emotional characteristic of Zazel. Therefore, Zazel is considered to be emotional, right brain, yin, negative polarity, relating to the Mah/heart, while Agiel is associated with the intellect, left brain, yang, positive polarity, and has to do with the Adam/Mind.

What is Mah, exactly? The Hebrew word Mah literally means 'what', or 'of what.' It is a healthy desire to know. The desire to gain intelligence is what makes the human unique in comparison to the animal kingdom. When we use reason and logic, we draw down a constructive way of interacting with the world around us. By using intelligence, we harness the potential of the universe and curate it for a higher purpose.

The word Mah involves the inspiring of intelligent deliberation from the Divine source as well as from within our souls in order to create positive change in the world. The Mah ignites the will to receive, and the Adam deliberates on how to go about it.

Metaphorically speaking, the splitting of the two hemispheres of the brain, as demonstrated within the Tarot Grid, is comparable to the Exodus story when Moses splits the Red Sea. The concept of formulating a balanced mind in order to regulate the energy flow, by dividing the brain into two hemispheres and allowing the energy to pass through the middle section, known as the corpus callosum, is the secret to miracle making. Fundamentally, this is mind over matter. We all have this superpower within us. It is essential we understand this in order for us to gain absolute certainty that we do indeed possess this power. We need to come to realize that we are the creators of our own reality. When confronted by our personal 'Red Sea' we must first go inward in order to get balanced and centered before we can evaluate the reality of the situation, and then take action based on our own wisdom. It all begins and ends in the mind. What you give power to, has power over you, if you allow it. When you can't control what's happening, challenge yourself to control the way you respond to what's happening. That's where your power is.

In the Exodus story, Moses leads the Jewish people out of Egypt and into the wilderness as they flee from enslavement. The Egyptians chase the Jewish people to the Red Sea. Feeling as though they are trapped, Moses calls out to God and asks for help, which God oddly responds back to Moses saying, "Why do you cry out to me?" - Exodus 14:15. In other words, God says, "Why do you ask me for help?" Implying that they had the power within themselves this entire time to create their own miracles without the help from God. At this point in the story, of all things, God says to Moses, "Why do you cry out to me? Speak to the Children of Israel and let them travel." Other translations say, "Speak unto the Children of Israel that they go forward." In other words, God says, "Stop looking to me for the answers. Get moving! Take action!"

This may seem an odd response to the Israelite's pleas for help, especially when they appear stuck between a huge sea and an army, but it's actually a great piece of advice. For those of us who feel fear at any time, we need to do as Moses and adhere to the steps for focusing the mind's attention: stop, look, listen. Instead of panicking,

Moses chose to pause for a brief moment and take in a deep breath. He was quick to center himself and not succumb to fear.

Fear is the worry for what will occur in the future, whereas Moses consciously placed himself back in the moment and did what he could do with what he had at the present time. Moses' back was to the wall, so to speak, and he had nowhere to go and no means of defending his people. He could have given up, but instead Moses chose to surrender to the voice of God and he did the unthinkable, he led the Jewish people into the sea. When confronted with challenges it is easy to be overcome with worry, doubt and fear.

Our mind can race with anxious thoughts. This is when we must press the pause button and take a beat. We must learn to regain control and calm the mind. Only a quiet mind is able to hear the Holy Spirit's still small voice. In times of stillness, the Spirit will speak to the soul. This balance and coming together of spirit and soul is represented in the Seal of Saturn where the two spirits of Saturn aka the two angels/angles of Saturn's Seal, Zazel and Agiel, become one. Zazel represents the soul of Saturn, while Agiel represents the spirit of Saturn. Agiel is associated with the intelligence of the mind, which is linked to the spirit, while Zazel is associated with the emotional aspect of the heart, and correlates to the soul of Saturn.

Pictured on the following page is the Egyptian take on this concept, where there is both Horus and Set riding on what appears to be a raft. This raft is split into two halves, with Horus and Set standing together as one in the middle. This pictographic can be perceived metaphorically as the two opposing energy polarities coming together as one as they travel across the Red Sea. Notice how there are three serpents on either side of the boat? These correspond to the two hemispheres of the brain. The combining together of the polarities of Horus-Set, Light-Darkness, Positive-Negative, Masculine-Feminine, is depicted in the middle of the six serpents as they part their 'Red Sea.' You will notice that the Tarot Grid is also split into two halves, with there being three rows of cards above and three rows of cards below, splitdown the middle by the median line that goes directly across and through the center of the Seal of Saturn. This median line represents the coming together of the two halves and forming a balance of the two energies, thereby obtaining a balanced mind. For good measure, this concept parallels the

Kabbalists' interpretation of the ark, and the importance of building one's spiritual ark. For instance, an entire sea of water cannot sink a ship unless it gets inside the ship. Similarly, the negativity of the world can't put you down unless you allow it to get inside you.

Pictured here is Horus on the left and Thoth on the right. Horus symbolizing the Sun, while Thoth is associated with the Moon. They are depicted as coming together in harmony.

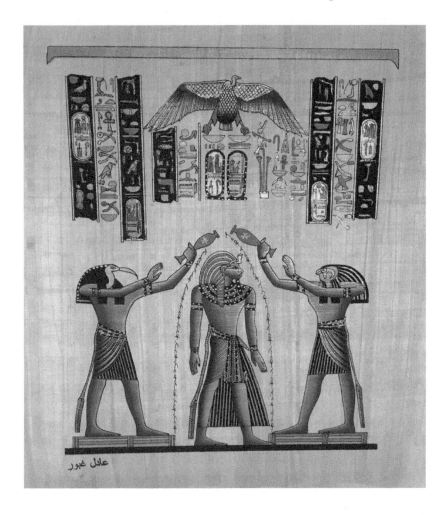

Pictured above is Thoth on the left and Horus to the right standing together in unison as they anoint the Pharaoh. This symbolism agrees with the Kabbalistic three-column system, as well as corresponds to the Masonic pillars, which involves a positive pillar on the right, a negative pillar on the left, and a neutral pillar in the center. Traditionally, the initiate would stand in as the center, neutral pillar, and act as the filament balancing the energy polarities.

Depicted here is Horus on the right representing the positive charge, and Thoth on the left representing the negative polarity.

Spirit is that which inspires us; lifts us up. Spirit is exciting, and gives meaning to life and what we do—spirit drives us to reach our goals. It is our inhalation. Spirit is the deep longing for purpose; it can pick us up and move us thousands of miles away from our front door and comfortable bed. Pilgrims are moved by spirit. Spirit has its negative aspects too, and can be crushed when faced with rejection. Spirit can be too analytical, clinical, and aloof from feelings and from others.

Soul is found in the bonding with nature. It is being with others, communicating, belonging and living with our daily dramas. Soul is baking bread, cooking meals and growing closer with others.

Soul is deep, while spirit is broad. Soul is our exhalation. Soul is antecedent to meaning, and can be considered life in its primal expression. Spirit is enriched by ideas, whereas soul is nourished through rituals, such as family gatherings during birthdays or holidays where we rekindle bonds once shared.

God is consciousness, and through the duality nature of His Light, God expresses Himself through man. God created man so that He may express Himself to creation and the universe. The Light of God the Creator can be measured at 1/137. This Light known as the Fine-Structure constant is the same light that powers our Sun. The measurement of direct sunlight received to an object on Earth from the Sun (a direct sun ray) is known as the solar constant. At the earth's surface, the nominal value of the solar constant is 137 mW/cm 2. The solar constant is the rate at which energy reaches the Earth's surface from the Sun. This 137 mill/watts per square centimeter value corresponds to high noon with the Sun directly overhead giving direct light. 137 just so happens to be the Hebrew gematria value for the word Kabbalah, which means 'to receive.' And what do we receive? The Light. The 1/137 Fine-Structure constant shoots through to the Sun. Therefore, the Sun becomes a vessel for the Light. The Sun then shoots its light and shares it with the other planets in the solar system, and grants life on Earth. The Hebrew word for Sun is Shemesh, which is very similar to the Hebrew word for servant, shamash. The Sun can be seen as a servant for the Light, aka a vessel for the Light.

This light is the source of all energy on the earth. Each living organism shares the energy it receives similar to how photosynthesis works. For instance, sunlight energizes plants' chlorophyll which in turn stimulates the circulation of hemoglobin in blood cells when that plant is consumed by either a human or animal. Coincidentally, both chlorophyll and hemoglobin have exactly 137 molecules each—and both share similar functions. Both receive energy and turn it into sharable energy making it possible for life on earth to continue. For example, photosynthesis helps a plant create glucose which it can then feed on and turn into reusable energy, sustaining its own survival. Hemoglobin produces oxygen in red blood cells which then deliver the oxygen throughout the body, insuring life longevity. Plants exhale oxygen and humans breathe it in, complimenting each other. This may be why plants were created first, before humans in the garden of Eden. Humans are similar to plants in the fact that they have the two 'Trees' within their organic structure. Fundamentally, all living organisms on the face of the earth can be considered as vessels for the Creator's Light that receive Light in order to share it with other vessels. This is how the Light continues on—ever expanding and evolving.

The system designed within the matrix is a Satanic system where every living organism must feed on another living organism in order to survive. Life feeds on life. Or rather, Light feeds on Light. This is why the Light creates vessels, so it can store its energy, and feed on it at a later time when its hungry for more. Similar to how a plant feeds off the reserved glucose it creates through photosynthesis in order to survive. Or how mammals store unused calories in their fat cells. Furthermore, the oxygen we breathe rusts the iron in our blood which causes our skin to wrinkle and organs to fail as we live out a slow death. Our days are numbered and it is important that we spread as much Light as we possibly can, leaving behind a legacy that will inspire others to want to become extraordinary channels of Light and a force for good.

Essentially, the Tarot Grid is a map key of the joining of the dual-polar forces of creation coming together in harmonic balance. Only through this balance does the Creative Force enable creation once again, just as in male-female reproduction. "The All is the mind. The universe is mental. As above, so below. As below, so above." -The Kybalion

The singularity (Source Creation) divides itself into duality (dual forces of nature—Male/Female, Sun/Moon, As Above/So Below, Fire-Air/Water-Earth, Yin/Yang, Blade/Chalice, Left/Right

Brain Hemispheres, etc.) in order to be able to observe and experience itself. When it realizes itself and comes back into Divine Union, Hermetic Marriage, and balance that returning back to singularity enables the creative process of multiplicity to occur again. Only when the one becomes two and the two become one can the one become two yet again. All progression, all evolution, all creation, and all awakening occur as through the process of balancing the dual forces into harmony and oneness.

Thus far, we have uncovered and decoded the entire Tarot Grid, right? Or is there one more final clue in front of us, staring us in the face? We have uncovered the two Trees, the Seal of Saturn, as well as the Prosperity Key. But there is one more secret to reveal.

The Kabbalah Tree of Life consists of 32 Paths of Wisdom. This includes the 10 sefirot, which mark the first ten paths and form the shape of the Tree's layout. In between these 10 sefirot are 22 branches that form connecting paths which are placed throughout the entire length of the Tree. Therefore, forming 32 paths in total. This being said, the Prosperity Key coincides with the 10 sefirot on the Grid that follow the path of the tzimtzum lightning bolt. Now we must count all the branches located on the Grid, which are the lines that connect each of the significant points of the esoteric symbols (found on the Tarot Grid). With further examination, you will see that there are the 10 cards included in the Prosperity Key, which coincide with the 10 sefirot. Then, the 8 connecting lines in between these ten cards. And lastly, consider the 4 lines that form the two Xs of Saturn's seal. This gives us the numbers 10+8+4, which equal 22. The number 22 issignificant here, because it is the exact number of Major Arcana in the tarot deck. This is the clue that leads us to discovering the other key, the Kundalini Key, which is another guided meditation that works in tandem with the Prosperity Key.

Thus far we have discovered the Prosperity Key which is used as a means to manifest wishes by utilizing the tools of the practical Kabbalah. Next, we will uncover the Kundalini Key that is utilized to raise one's soul vibration, which is essential for one to connect to the Higher-Self, and to the source of their desire.

The next clue towards decoding the Kundalini Key is found in the Tower card, which is the card that directly reflects the 22 branches of the Tree of Life, which are represented on the card as the 22 Yod's. This discovery of the 22 lines found on the Grid leads us further down the rabbit hole, as we follow the bread crumbs. Learning how to find and decode the Kundalini Key will be explained in much detail in Chapter 19: The Two Keys Hidden within the Tarot.

Chapter 7

The Seal of Saturn Hidden within the Hierophant Card

The Hierophant sits upon the platform, which can be seen as the foundation the tarot is built upon. With closer examination you will see that his platform is a large carpeted box, which is truly a treasure chest. And the Hierophant holds the keys to unlock it. Locked inside the treasure chest is one's wishes and desires. The Hierophant is the middleman between you and your fulfillment.

The Hierophant is Saint Peter, who was the first Pope, given the
Godly right to rule over the church and its people once Jesus returned
back to the Father in heaven. Jesus gave Peter the keys to the
kingdom of heaven, where Peter acted as the one who bound heaven
and earth, and united the two together as one, as stated in Matthew
16:19, "I will give you the keys of the kingdom of heaven; whatever
you bind on earth will be bound in heaven, and whatever you loose
on earth will be loosed in heaven."

The Seal of Saturn is the door, the gateway to your desire. The
diamond in the middle of the seal acts as the keyhole in which the
Hierophant's keys unlock. The Hierophant helps you draw down
your desire from the astral where you then manifest it in the physical.
On the Kabbalah Tree of Life this would be seen as the bridge,
Yesod, which ultimately connects Binah to Malchut, where Binah is
Saturn and Malchut is the material world. Yesod is the chute the
Light travels through from the upper worlds down into Malchut.

Moreover, extending the concept of Yesod to another area:
The seven days of creation are parallel to the seven lower sefirot
starting with Chesed and working its way down to Malchut. The
sixth day of the week, Friday, is parallel to this sixth (lower) sefirah
of Yesod.

It was on the sixth day that God created Adam (mankind).
"So God created man in his *own* image, in the image of God created
he him; male and female created he them." - Genesis 1:27 In
Hebrew, the word Adam means man, as in mankind, and has a
numerical value of 45.

Interestingly, when you spell out the Divine Name of God,

YHVH, (yod-heh-vav-heh), it too has a numerical value of 45, ואו הא
יוד הא. The Seal of Saturn found on the Tarot Grid, when you add the
sum of its six points, also has a sum of 45. Now, with the Seal of
Saturn revealed on the Hierophant card, you see the six points
created by the seal with the Yod's (Y's and hands) and with the
Vav's and the Waw. It was on Friday, the sixth day that God created
the human being in His own image, and gave man the power within
himself to create something out of nothing. Just as Yesod, the sixth
lower sefirah associated with the sixth day, encompasses the attribute
that 'unites heaven with earth', it is mankind who has it within him
the power to transition the spiritual and Divine onto the material
world. The word yesod means foundation, and knowing that you
have the power within to create miracles and prosperity in your life
is the foundation that the tarot is based upon.

You have within you the keys to the kingdom. Each of the 78
tarot cards hold within them a key to unblock one's ego, which opens
one up to receiving more Light, and it is this Light that is the source
to all your happiness and joy. This connection to the Light is one's
connection to God's intelligence, and to the Higher-Self. Taking this
into account, the tarot is the Yesod, it is the Vav that unites heaven
with earth. The tarot acts as a tool for us to overcome our ego-nature
and it connects us to the Source, from which we gather our brilliant
ideas and then manifest them in order to enjoy a life full of
prosperity and abundance. This fulfillment is achieved essentially by
creating something out of nothing.

There are many clues hidden in plain sight on this card for us
to follow in order to reveal Saturn's seal. The first clue being the
Hierophant's crown. The Hierophant wears the Pope's triple crown,
known also to be worn by Hermes Trismegistus. This crown having
exactly 15 spikes is a clue that there is a hidden Seal of Saturn
somewhere within this card. The number 15 is significant here,
because it's one of the numbers associated with Saturn's magic
square.

Both the numbers 15 and 45 (both being magic numbers of
Saturn) are seen throughout the Rider-Waite (Smith) tarot deck, and
each time connect to Saturn's influence in some way. The Seal of
Saturn aka Seal of Zazel is found within the magic square of Saturn;
a 3×3 square which includes the numbers1-9 in rows and in columns
that all add up to 15, and the total sum of all the numbers inside the

square equals 45. ($1+2+3+4+5+6+7+8+9 = 45$)

For the next clue we look at the 'W' at the top of the Hierophant's crown. The W is the Hebrew letter Waw or Vav, and has a numerical value of 6. This letter is pronounced either way, Vav or Waw, depending on if the person was from either an Arabic origin using the Waw or an Ashkenazi origin using Vav. Either way you pronounce it, the letter has the same meaning, which is hook, tent peg, nail. The Vav looks like a nail ו. Similar to the nails the Romans used to crucify Jesus Christ upon the cross. Jesus' name Yeshua means salvation. The nail (or Vav) here can relate metaphorically to salvation—as in salvation from ignorance. These two men in this card approach the Hierophant seeking to learn the secret occult mysteries hidden within the Church's scriptures, and to connect them to a higher state of spiritual awareness. Christ offered himself voluntarily to be sacrificed upon the cross. Likewise, these men here voluntarily approach the Hierophant. They humble themselves before the Hierophant and ask for spiritual guidance. The Hierophant is depicted here as blessing these men with knowledge of the secret occult mysteries that will tear down their old belief system. These men sacrifice up their old limiting beliefs, elevate their consciousness and cross over into the world of the unknown. Once they embark on this spiritual journey (their ascension) they will no longer be the same. They will have matured and have disassociated themselves from who they once were on a conscious and spiritual level. Just as Jesus on the cross whose soul left his body; His soul ascended and was united with the Father. The Father representing the sefirah Keter, residing in the realm of Atziluth; the realm of pure deity and divinity; the source of God's intelligence. We have to climb to the top of the Tree of Life to see Keter. Keter, meaning crown, represented here by the Hierophant's triple crown, symbolizing him as being thrice great. Through meditation, we climb through different ecstasies and go and talk to our own particular Hierophant. It is not possible to see our own Keter without having also died ourselves (in ourselves, psychologically). We have to eliminate a lot of ego for this privilege. The doorway into Keter is located at Binah. The Hierophant connects man to the Source, by bridging Malchut with Binah, leading one up and through the doorway into where one's joy and happiness reside. Thus, the

Hierophant acts as the bridge binding heaven and earth, like the peg that connects the tent to the ground.

The next clue is located on the treasure chest where you will find two keys formed in the shape of the letter Vav. This 'V' is the next clue leading closer to discovering the hidden seal.

From the points of the Vav and Waw draw lines connecting them to the Yod's. The Hebrew letter Yod means hand, and is represented with the letter Y. So, from the Vav of the keys draw lines upward connecting to the Hierophant's hands. Then, from the Waw on the crown draw lines downward connecting to the yellow Ys (Yod's) on the two men's shirts. The overlapping Vs form two XXs that create a diamond in the center, which is essentially Saturn's Seal.

Yod's throughout the tarot carry great value, and reveal deeper hidden mysteries that always convey something significant. For example, the 26 Hebrew letter Yod's ' depicted as water droplets in the Ace of Cups card, or the 22 fiery Yod's falling from the tower in the Tower card. These numbers are significant, because 26 is the Hebrew gematria value of the Divine Name YHVH, and 22 is the number of letters in the Hebrew alphabet. The Hebrew letter Yod looks like a fiery flame, and Yod's are considered to be the fire at the beginning of all creation. Yod is the first letter in the Divine Four-Letter Name of God, YHVH. In the Jewish mystical tradition, Yod represents a mere dot, a divine point of energy. Since Yod is used to form all the other Hebrew letters, and since God uses the letters as building blocks of creation, Yod indicates God's omnipresence.

Yod has a numerical value of 10. By adding the values of each of the three points of the three V's created within this card we uncover deeper understanding of the spiritual connection concealed here. For instance, the top Λ's points include the letter W on the crown plus the two yellow Ys on the men's shirts, which gives us $6+10+10 = 26$. And then the bottom V formed by the Hierophant's keys plus the Hierophant's two hands (aka Yod's) gives us $6+10+10 = 26$. And finally, notice that the Hierophant's two keys each have an X on them? And the keys form a V (Vav)? The letter X is Roman numeral 10. Therefore, you have Vav, 6, plus the two Xs, which results in $6+10+10 = 26$. As mentioned earlier, 26 is the Hebrew gematria value for YHVH. Taking this into account, there are now three sets of 26s on this card, giving us $26+26+26 = 78$. Which it just so happens to be there are exactly 78 cards in the tarot deck.

Combining all these clues together reveals to us that each card within the tarot holds within it a key which can connect us to God, the Higher-Self, and each card's key helps us conquer the ego. Consequently, by shedding off layers of ego we elevate our soul's vibration, ascend up the chakras of our kundalini, and open up our third eye, where we obtain higher states of consciousness and spiritual awareness. Each card contains within it a key to unlock this portal of the third eye, which is represented by the diamond in the center of the Seal of Saturn. When opening this portal, we elevate to the higher-self and obtain Christ Consciousness. It is at this high state of awareness when we tap into the Source of God's intelligence, where we receive godly insight and understanding. This is this first step towards obtaining a salvation from ignorance, by opening up the mind we can broaden our awareness and begin seeing things in the 'big picture.'

Interesting to note is that there are three actual Vav's in this card. There is the Vav as the V of the card's Roman numeral, the Vav W on the crown, and then the Vav the two keys form on the treasure chest. Each Vav having a numerical value of 6, resulting in 6+6+6 = 18. 18 is the gematria value of the word Chai, meaning life, as in the phrase "L'chaim!", meaning To life! This is the final clue here that sums up the entire message of the Hierophant card, which is that life should be worth living and enjoyed, and that we have within us the power to create prosperity and abundance in our lives. Furthermore, Vav is a picture of a man. Since Vav represents the number six, it has long been associated as the number of man in the Jewish tradition. For instance, man was created on the sixth day, man works for six days, there are six millennia before the coming of the Mashiach, and finally, the 'beast' is identified as the 'number of a man' – 666 (Rev 13:18).

All the answers our within us and we can access this knowledge by opening the third eye and connecting to the Source of the divine truth. Matthew 16:19 "I will give you the keys of the kingdom of heaven; whatever you bind on earth will be bound in heaven, and whatever you loose on earth will be loosed in heaven." We must desire knowledge and transform knowledge into wisdom. And we will be able to take this knowledge with us into the next life. These "keys to the kingdom" refer to a resource of information and knowledge, the possession of which gives the possessor access to power.

"My brain is only a receiver, in the Universe there is a core from which we obtain knowledge, strength and inspiration. I have not penetrated into the secrets of this core, but I know that it exists."
- Nikola Tesla

Chapter 8

The Seals of Saturn Hidden within the Tarot

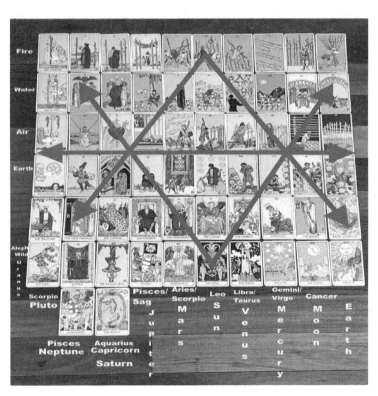

93

Pictured below is Saturn's magic square, revealing the Seal of Saturn.

Have you ever laid out all the tarot cards on the floor or on a table? I have made a Tarot Grid that includes all the Minor and Major Arcana, (excluding the Court Cards). It is in this Grid where you find the first Seal of Saturn, which leads one to believe there are more seals hidden throughout the tarot.

This Grid contains the 40 Minor Arcana and each of the 22 Major Arcana cards. The number 40 as well as 22 are very significant in Kabbalah. For example, there are 22 letters in the Hebrew alphabet. In relation to this, each Major Arcana card's illustration portrays the spiritual aspect of the corresponding Hebrew letter it is assigned to. The number 40 is significant, because it is the numerical value for the Hebrew letter Mem, meaning water, relating to the concept and timing of spiritual cleansing. For instance, in the book of Genesis, the earth flooded for 40 days and 40 nights. This was a time period when the earth experienced a large-scale baptism.

The Tarot Grid arranges the 62 'numbered' cards in their proper order, by starting at the top and working its way down, it begins with the least valued to the highest valued card, all according to the value of each card's number and suit. This specific order that is based on each card's value is in direct accordance with the system set aside by the Order of the Golden Dawn, who follow a system based off of the Western Hermetic Kabbalah. Consequently, the creators of the Rider-Waite (Smith) tarot deck happened to be members of the Golden Dawn Society.

The tarot suits are arranged in an order that coincides with the tetragrammaton, also known as the Four-Letter Name of God in Hebrew, YHVH (Yahweh). Each of the four letters of YHVH are

associated with the four elements: fire, water, air and earth—
specifically, in this order. In addition to this, each tarot suit coincides
with one of the four elements as well, which also follow this same
order. For instance, Wands correspond with fire, Cups with water,
Swords with air, and Pentacles with earth. And it is in this particular
order the cards are arranged on the Grid, working their way down
through the four suits, in their proper order from least to greatest
value. Located directly below the 'suited' cards of the Minor Arcana
are the 22 Major Arcana, which are arranged in order according to
the value of their Roman numerals, positioned from 0-21.

As revealed here now, the Seal of Saturn is hidden within the
Tarot Grid. The seal can be found when you draw a line following
the rising and descending numbers on the cards. Look at the picture
on the previous page for reference.

Starting from the middle card on the top row, #6 (6 of
Wands), and then moving down to the next row diagonally to the #5,
then #4, #3, and ending at the High Priestess card that is assigned to
Roman numeral 2. From here, return to the starting point at the top of
the Grid going back to the 6 of Wands, and then work your way
downward diagonally this time in the opposite direction from the #6
down to the #7, then #8, #9, and ending on the Wheel of Fortune
card, which is assigned to Roman numeral 10. Repeat this formula
just as before, but this time start from the bottom of the Grid,
beginning with the Devil card assigned to Roman numeral 15. The
number 15 when reduced is $1+5 = 6$, which mirrors the starting point
at the top of the Grid. So, starting from the Devil card, repeat the
same steps as before that were used going down the Grid, but this
time you will be working your way upward in the opposite direction.
After having completed these steps, you will have formed two
overlapping Vs, which form two XXs touching each other, and create
a diamond (or rhombus) in the center. To complete Saturn's seal,
draw a line directly through the middle of the two Xs, from one side
of the Grid to the other. This line should pass straight through the
diamond, and as a consequence will form a median-line that divides
the Tarot Grid into two halves, with there being three rows above the
line and three rows below it.

When you add up the numbers of each card included in the
Grid's Seal, which are located at each of the Seal's six points, you
get the sum of 45. 45 just so happens to be the numerical value for

the Hebrew name Zazel, known to be the Spirit of Saturn. Likewise, the Intelligence of Saturn is Agiel, and shares the same numerical value of 45. The six points on the Seal add up to 45, and the cards included are: the Devil #15, High Priestess #2, Two of Cups #2, 6 of Wands #6, 10 of Cups #10, and lastly the Wheel of Fortune #10. Therefore, this gives you 15+2+2+6+10+10 = 45. Furthermore, 45 is also the sum of all the numbers inside the Magic Square of Saturn.

There are three tarot cards that contain a hidden Seal of Saturn within them, and they are: the Hierophant, the Devil, and the 10 of Pentacles. These Seals, which are placed in specific and significant locations on these particular cards, reveal deeper insight into the mysteries that have been concealed within the tarot for far too long.

The Seal's purpose is to provide protection from Saturn's malefic influence, while simultaneously sealing in its magical essence. Saturn is associated with ruling over time, restriction and karma. Saturn constantly emits dulling waves of energy that slow down the time between cause and effect, interrupting the manifestation process by wearing away at us with harsh judgment, restriction, frustration, doubt, and fear. The Seal of Saturn acts as a protective shield from the planet's malefic force allowing a practitioner of the tarot to not be restricted by the time it takes for a desire to manifest itself into reality. They are able to see results very quickly—like magic. In addition to these Seals, the tarot also contains other similar planetary applications. Some of which involve a specific combination of cards which act as keys to specifically help one manifest prosperity.

Moreover, the Tarot Grid holds the map key which pin-points

where to find one's Path of Enlightenment based on their zodiac sign. These 'paths' are located on each of the Grid's columns that lead down from the top to the bottom of the Grid, and lay out the path to enlightenment for each zodiac sign. Each path incorporates wisdom and practical advice that will help guide an individual with the insight they need in order for them to begin working on themselves in hopes of transforming their ego-nature. The formula for finding one's correct path works the same for all the signs of the Zodiac. The first step is to establish what sign the individual is born under. And yet, everyone is governed by three signs: their Sun, Moon, and Ascendant. All three signs are important to learn and work together to influence our personality and shape our character. It is important to understand all three in order to truly know thy self. Once a specific sign is established, figure out the ruling planet for that sign. After which, find the corresponding sefirah on the Kabbalah Tree of Life attributed to that particular planet. Consequently, the number of the sefirah is the number of the path found on the Tarot Grid. Let's use Aries for example. Aries is ruled by Mars which is associated with the 5th sefirah Gevurah, and therefore all the #5 cards located on the 5th column will forge the path that an Aries needs to take in order for them to reach spiritual enlightenment.

Getting to know your three signs and then applying the path to enlightenment formula to each one of them will elevate your awareness and soul vibration as you strive to better yourself. It will help you gain a deeper and more well-rounded understanding of your unique personality, as well as uncover aspects of your shadow-nature.

The point of reaching enlightenment is to establish a connection with the higher-self, aligning you with your destiny, giving you a sense of purpose and direction, feeling you with the confidence needed to reach your goals and make your dreams come true. The Key to Prosperity is hidden in the center of the Tarot Grid, found within the cards that are placed along the median-line which passes straight through the Seal of Saturn's diamond. Before disclosing the exact location of this Key and its purpose, I must first explain the significance of the diamond (or rhombus) formed within the Seal of Saturn. You must first be able to comprehend the significant relevance of it as it pertains to occult magick, and ultimately wish-making.

Similar to the Vesica Piscis, the diamond (rhombus) is a portal/gateway through which one traverses back and forth between the 3rd and 4th dimensions, and from which one brings forth their desire from the astral realm of the 99% reality over into the 1% physical reality—thematerial world. Another way of putting it, it's a gateway where desire from the macrocosm is drawn down into the microcosm, where we manifest it into the material world of matter. It is a womb that's main purpose and energy is the basis of creation in this universe. It is a doorway that acts as a bridge between spirit and form, matter and anti-matter, the infinite void and all matter.

This diamond in the center of the Seal looks similar to a key hole or an eye, and thereby is attributed to the third eye. Subsequently, the Seal of Saturn rules over the sefirah Binah, which corresponds with the third eye. Not to mention, the Devil card associated with Capricorn, who is ruled by Saturn, just so happens to be assigned to the Hebrew letter Ayin, meaning eye. Through its esoteric symbolism, the Devil card's illustration portrays the empowerment obtained when activating the third eye. The letter Ayin ע looks similar to the Latin letter Y. It is said that the letter Ayin has two eyes located at each of its top two points, or Y tips.

the evil eye עַיִן הָרַע   *the good eye* עַיִן טוֹבָה

the will

The right eye sees positive potential, while the left eye sees negative judgements. If you were to place two mirrored images of Ayin side by side, it would form the letter Shin ש, which looks similar to the letter W. This Shin created by the two mirrored Ayin's corresponds with the third eye, and it is this third eye that sees the spirit.

When placing a mirror over these three particular tarot cards, which all contain a hidden Seal of Saturn in them, it reveals deeper hidden meaning. For instance, in the Devil card the Devil is seen raising his right hand and forming the gesture of the El Shaddai displayed by priests during the Birkat Kohanim. This hand gesture usually involves the use of two hands, which together form the letter Shin. Hence, Shin for Shaddai, meaning Almighty [God].

For this reason, when using a mirror, we are able to display a mirror image of the Devil's hand, which then forms the gesture used for the 'raising of the hands' Priestly Blessing referred to as the Birkat Kohanim, which is properly made with two hands instead of one. Traditionally, the priests blessed the people every morning after the sacrifice at the temple. Today, it is offered during Jewish holidays. Although, many synagogues and Christian churches end their service with this blessing as a benediction.

This blessing is found in Numbers 6:24-26, "The Lord blesses you and keeps you; the Lord shines his face upon you and is gracious to you; the Lord lifts up his face upon you and gives you his peace."

With further examination of the picture above, you will see that the mirror image creates a heart-shape above the Devil's hands. This is significant, because the letter Shin is attributed to the heart. Furthermore, it is revealed in the Devil card that one must raise their kundalini energy in order to activate the third eye, which is only made possible after having first opened up one's heart. Moreover, the Devil card is assigned to Roman numeral XV (15). When reduced, 15 becomes 1+5 = 6. The number 6 coincides with the 6th sefirah Tiferet, which is ruled by the Sun, and attributed to the inner sun and heart chakra. Thus, by opening up one's heart is key to opening up the third eye, and this is when the connection to the Christ

Consciousness is achieved.

Jesus, Yeshua corresponds with the letter Shin. For instance, when the Shin is placed inside the middle of the tetragrammaton, YHVH, it forms the name Yeshua (YHShVH).

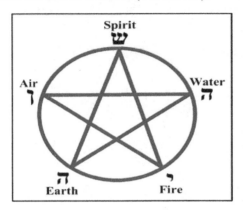

From this picture above, you can see that Shin coincides with spirit. As mentioned earlier, the three eyes of Ayin are as follows: the right eye sees positive potential, the left eye sees negative judgment, and the third eye that sees spirit coincides with the concealed Shin.

The Judgement card is assigned to the letter Shin, and the spiritual meaning of Shin is portrayed within this card's illustration. For instance, depicted in this card is the angel Gabriel who is waking up the dead out from their coffins and delivers to them good, heart-warming news—she offers them a chance at redemption and eternal salvation. The name Yeshua means salvation. The people were dead inside (inside their hearts), and Gabriel delivered to them the good news that Jesus was going to be crucified on the cross the following day, and that he would die for their sins, which meant they could now have eternal life, and thus another chance to repent for their sins before they died. This was the good news attributed to Good Friday; this news caused the people to be overwhelmed with joy and it melted their hardened hearts. This is symbolized here by the snow-tipped mountains melting, and this causes the valley below the mountains to flood. The flood waters rising contribute to the coffins rising up above the ground and floating away.

This 'melting' of the heart allows one to flow along the kundalini stream as they ascend up the chakras towards the third eye.

Pictured here is an esoteric depiction of Hermes Trismegistus, conveying Hermetic principles through the language of symbolism. His body and arms form the Seal of Saturn, with its diamond in the center. You will notice the mirrored image displaying the opposites of night and day. With further examination, you will notice that Hermes has one of his eyes shut while the other is opened, which further reinstates the third eye symbolism, and the attempt to obtain deeper esoteric knowledge by becoming in-tune with the spirit. In the center of the Seal, inside the diamond, is the same crusader's cross depicted in the Judgement card—a card pertaining directly to Christ and the Sacred Heart. It relates to the concept of opening up one's heart as the means to connect to the Father, which is achieved after having activated one's third eye.

Achieving this connection to the Source allows you to rise above the ego and float on a higher plain of conscious awareness.

This Ancient Egyptian pictograph portrays the concept just mentioned. If you pay closer attention to the shape formed by Horus's and Set's arms, you will see the resemblance of the Hebrew letter Shin. But what is more, is that each pair of arms is shaped similar to an Ayin—mirroring each other. Their arms and heads come together and form a Shin.

These mirrored Ayins forming a Shin create a pictograph of what appears to be a boat or an ark. This boat will allow one to float above their ego-nature. Also, this boat resembles an eye with a pupil in the center. This pupil has the crown on top, suggesting enlightenment.

Let's take this mirror concept one step further, and build upon what has been presented thus far—it has been showed the letter

Ayin, meaning eye, is assigned to the Devil card, which has hidden within it a Seal of Saturn, and this seal's diamond is considered to be a gateway into the third eye awareness. Time now to apply what we know so far about the esoteric symbols on the Devil card and use them towards the discovery of new hidden secrets found with a mirror. With this in mind, place a mirror directly along the horizontal line that passes through the middle of the diamond, and in doing so will reveal more hidden mysteries.

Pictured below is the hidden eye found within the Devil card, located in the center.

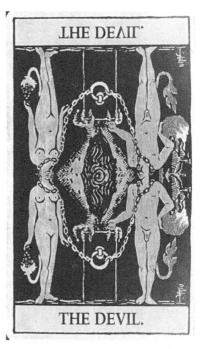

There are three cards which have the hidden Seal of Saturn on them. By applying this mirror method, we will be able to reveal all three eyes hidden inside the center of the diamond of each card's seal.

The Hierophant, the Devil, and the 10 of Pentacles cards all contain a hidden Seal of Saturn.

The hidden eye surrounded with light rays found within the Hierophant card, located directly in the middle of the card.

The hidden eye found within the 10 of Pentacles card when the two heads in the middle merge as one.

The purpose of activating the third eye is to free the mind. Ayin has a numerical value of 70. Each of these three cards have an eye concealed within them, which gives us 70×3 = 210. The number 210 is very significant here, because it is the exact number of years the Jews were enslaved in Egypt, which ultimately is a metaphor for mental slavery. If we take responsibility for our own actions and repent of our sins, we are able to open up and purify our hearts, thus allowing the kundalini life-force to rise within our vessel and activate the third eye. This activation connects us to our salvation— a salvation from ignorance.

Our third eye is connected to the 4th dimension. It enables us to perceive other dimensions and realities. It is an ancient biological device made of stardust that assists in navigating our dreams in our ethereal body, that guides us towards the reality of time travel, telepathy, intuition and other psychic abilities.

Another religious theory suggest that the pineal gland is our true inner Church or place of Connection and Worship. In the Christian religion there is a Bible verse that states, "The light of the body is the eye; if therefore thine eye be single, thy whole body shall be full of light." - Matthew 6:22. This verse can be interpreted as relating to the soul of the third eye.

In closing, there is yet another secret to reveal regarding the method of using a mirror, found when placing a mirror vertically over these three cards. By doing so, it forms a pair of identical images that when placed next to each other disclose deeper hidden understanding each card possesses, and also exposes how all three cards forge together to convey one combined philosophy. So far, you have been shown the hidden 'all-seeing' eye when the mirror is placed horizontally over the card, but allow me to reveal the secrets shown when the mirror is placed over these cards vertically.

Eyes are accredited as being twins, similarly to the way the Gemini twins are symbolized, where one is good and the other evil. Whereas, one eye sees the positive, while the other sees the negative. This aspect of duality hidden within these cards can be brought to light when utilizing this mirror method.

With a mirror placed vertically down the middle of the card, the Hierophant reveals a pair of twins looking up in hopes to see the positive, represented by the Hierophant's two hands aimed upward with each having two fingers pointing towards God. This hand gesture is symbolic of Jesus' divine nature, being both Divine and human at the same time. When using this mirror method with the Devil card, it reveals two Eve's who are both turning their heads and looking away from the raised hands that form the El Shaddai hand-gesture with fear of receiving any negative repercussions. And lastly, the mirror image applied to the 10 of Pentacles displays two 'twin' old men gazing upon the Philosopher's Stone, which is attributed to the Pineal Gland aka the third eye, which enables one to see into the spirit once it is activated.

THE HIER ЯƎIH ƎHT

THE II ƎHT

As you examine these cards closer, you will notice the wording for two of the card's titles have been altered after adding its mirror image. For instance, the Hierophant has been changed to 'The Hier' similar to the term heir, referring to the Adam's in the card. Adam is the Hebrew word for man, and can refer to mankind. In the scriptures, the righteous are promised that they will become heirs to all that God has. Another thing to take into account, according to Hermeticism, the male is considered to correspond to the positive polarity, and therefore the Adam's in the Hierophant card convey this particular polarity aspect. Alternatively, the female Eve's depicted in the Devil card encompass the negative polarity. You will notice the Devil card's title has now been altered to say 'The Ⅱ', which is the astrological symbol for Gemini, and represents the twins. Adam and Eve can be considered as being twins, because Eve was created from Adam's rib, and therefore from the same DNA. Eve was created by God to be Adam's soulmate, and "they shall be one flesh" (Genesis 2:24). Furthermore, Eve having been created from Adam's rib, is considered to be Adam's clone or homunculus. Interesting to mention here is that Eve bore 20 sets of twins in her lifetime. What is more, is the Hierophant card depicting the set of Adam's is assigned to Roman numeral V, and the Devil card depicting the set of Eve's is assigned to Roman numeral XV, which gives us $5+15 = 20$—the exact number of twin-sets Adam and Eve bore.

Moving forward, the Devil card is covered in a mostly black color scheme, and thereby shares an affinity with the dark twin, who sees the negative. The Devil card is also attributed to the sefirah Tiferet, which coincides with the heart chakra. Jeremiah 17:9, "The heart is deceitful above all things, and desperately wicked: who can know it?"

And in the 10 of Pentacles card, we have the two old men depicted as seeing eye to eye with one another, just as the twoAyin's gaze upon each other in the mirror, reflecting upon each other's philosophies and understanding. Here, the old man can be seen as looking into the mirror and reflecting upon his own spirit, coming to realize deeper understanding of all things in general after some time spent in deep thought. The title of this card has been un-altered, and remains the original Roman numeral X. In the Hebrew alphabet, the X is associated with Tav, meaning cross. The ancient symbol for Tav was an X. This is significant, because Tav also happens to mean truth. Therefore, the two old men in the 10 of Pentacles card are portrayed here as searching for their inner truth.

The blue sapphire stone the two old men gaze upon represents the Philosopher's Stone, which is attributed to the Pineal Gland aka the third eye. When speaking of the Stone in a physical sense, the most commonly mentioned properties are the ability to transmute base metals into gold or silver, and the ability to heal all forms of illness and prolong the life of any person who consumes a small part of the philosopher's stone diluted in wine. Other mentioned properties include: creation of perpetually burning lamps, transmutation of common crystals into precious stones and diamonds, reviving of dead plants, creation of flexible or malleable glass, or the creation of a clone or homunculus, which refers to the creation of a 'mini-me' of one's self, similar to a golem. This cloning aspect parallels the concept of twins portrayed within these three cards.

Legend says Raziel wrote his book, the Sefer Raziel HaMalakh on sapphire tablets. According to rabbinical Judaism, from the Midrash and the Talmud, God wrote the first set of ten commandments on sapphire tablets. According to Exodus 24:10, "and they saw the God of Israel. There was under his feet as it were a pavement of sapphire stone, like the very heaven for clearness." (ESV) The Talmud also claims that the emerald tablets of Thoth were actually made of sapphire.

The Hierophant helps one see the positive.

The Devil suggests you refrain from focusing on the negative, and to atone for your sins.

The 10 of Pentacles reinstates the importance of looking within.

Psalm 118:22-23

"The Stone which the builders refused is become the head stone of the corner. This is the Lord's doing; it is marvelous in our eyes."

The moment we close our eyes and open up our heart is when we connect to the spirit. This concept is put into practice when you place two Ayin's together, mirroring each other to form a Shin. This Shin is attributed to the third eye. This level of awareness obtained is considered the Christ Consciousness, which allows one to rise above the ego, permitting one to be *in* the world but not *of* the world. As you view the world of chaos from above, you are able to see the big picture. From this point of view, you realize there is order in the chaos, and everything happens for a reason.

Below is an amulet created by archangel Raziel to help one defend themselves against the Evil Eye, and deflect the critical judgements of others. Inadvertently, it allows you to see the positive within yourself, and therefore clears out any negativity you are holding within you.

Picture of the amulet taken from the Sefer Raziel HaMalakh, the Book of Raziel the Angel.

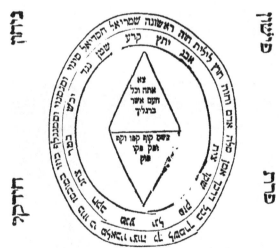

The method of using a mirror to reveal hidden secrets within certain illustrations also applies to the U.S. $2 dollar bill. Check out the $2 bill below which contains a hidden owl. The owl is named Moloch, and is the same infamous owl displayed in the Bohemian Grove. Moloch can be traced back to biblical times. Moreover, the owl was placed on ancient Greek coins as well.

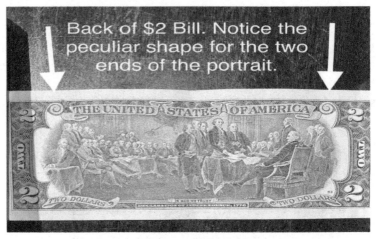

Below is a pictograph depicting Adam and Eve with flames over their hearts that have an eye on them—Twin Flames. Thus, the heart is the key to bringing the two eyes together as one as the way to activate the third eye. This is how you raise the kundalini, and obtain higher awareness.

Depicted in the middle of this Tree of Life are the two intertwined kundalini serpents, which appear as the two strands of DNA. According to Kabbalah, the root of the Tree is located at the top. Therefore, one must gather the seed of desire from the top and draw it down to the bottom, where it manifests. This considered, the pictograph above portrays the wish-making formula. Allow me to explain.

Notice, there is an eye in the direct center that separates the two portions of the kundalini serpents, where the top half is the kundalini serpents being activated by joining Adam and Eve's two eyes together as one. The bottom half is the kundalini serpent passing through the ten sefirot on the Kabbalah Tree of Life. The two halves portrayed here coincide with the two Keys which are hidden within the RWS tarot deck. These Keys, once activated, enable one to manifest their desires, create prosperity and abundance.

"What we see depends mainly on what we look for." - John Donne

"The light of the body is the eye: if therefore thine eye be single, thy whole body shall be full of light." - Matthew 6:22

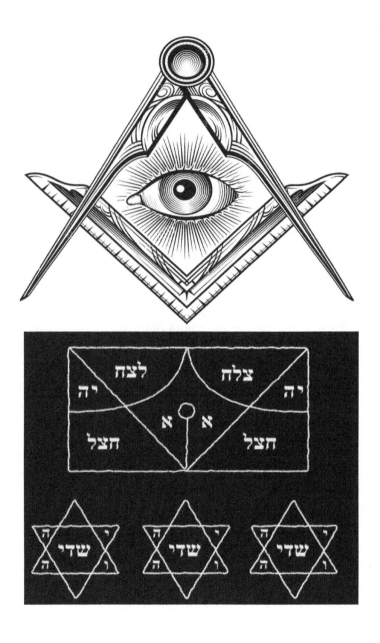

Chapter 9

The Adam and Eve Allegory

This allegory is conveyed with three cards: the Lovers, the Devil, and the Tower, involving the wisdom of archangel Raziel.

There is a Kabbalistic allegory hidden within these three cards; an origin story for the tarot's wisdom. These three cards depict Adam and Eve as they travel along the path of enlightenment that leads to the spiritual transformation all initiates must experience at some point along the path of their own spiritual awakening.

Adam and Eve begin their journey in the Lovers card, where they are seen in the garden of Eden being taught life's mysteries and of God's secrets by the archangel Raziel. Students and readers of the tarot will argue that the angel in the Lovers card is Raphael, but he is indeed Raziel—a fact that will be brought to light within this chapter.

God banishes Adam and Eve from the garden soon after they partake from the Tree of Knowledge of Good and Evil, but He is quick to forgive them and show mercy. God sends His angel Raziel to teach Adam and Eve life's mysteries, so they will be able to prosper in the world outside of the garden. These three tarot cards foretell the story and explain through symbols, numbers, Hebrew letters, and through inspired illustration the secrets and mysteries that Raziel revealed to Adam and Eve, who practiced this knowledge in order for them to achieve prosperity and abundance in their lives.

Their story is told in these three tarot cards and arranged in chronological order according to the card's Roman numerals from least to greatest value beginning with the Lovers card, number VI, then the Devil card, number XV, and lastly the Tower card, number XVI. These three Roman numerals add up to the sum of 37, which is the Hebrew ordinal gematria value of the sefirah Chokmah, meaning wisdom. Coincidentally, the ruling archangel of Chokmah just so happens to be Raziel. Also, interesting to note is that the name Raziel means 'secrets of God', which hits on the fact that Raziel reveals God's secrets to Adam and Eve—secrets that are concealed within the esoteric symbolism of these three cards.

This allegory begins to unfold in the Lovers card when Raziel reveals to Adam and Eve the true origin of their divine nature, and he shows them how they can take back their power by utilizing free will. Raziel teaches them of their God-given power of how to manifest desire into reality. Raziel ignites a spark within them; a will to receive.

In the next card, the Devil card, Adam and Eve are seen applying this new knowledge and taking upon the responsibility of creating their own wealth, serenity, prosperity and abundance for themselves in the new world outside the garden. Yes, they are chained to the black box, which represents the Saturn matrix reality of the material world in which we exist, but those chains are tied very loosely and it is easy for them to break free. Adam and Eve understand how to be *in* the world but not be a part *of* the world. They understand the science of spirituality and are able to manipulate and control the energy polarities within the matrix, as well as within themselves. They understand the dualities of both the positive and negative forces that bind everything—as above, so below. They comprehend the concept of the ego, and how this invisible force is constantly pressing down on us forever attempting to solidify our spirit. This negative, invisible, egoistic force is what the Kabbalists refer to as the Adversary, the Satan, who controls the material world, referred to by the Kabbalists as the 1% reality. Adam and Eve are blessed with the knowledge of how to combat this adversary and not allow themselves to be chained and enslaved to the egoism of the material world.

The final card, the Tower, shows Adam and Eve being knocked off the tower by the strike of a large lightning bolt. They elevated their soul's vibration, their life-force energy, up the tower which is symbolic of the kundalini (one's Jacob's ladder), in order to obtain a union with the higher-power. Their souls ascend upwards through their chakras from the base chakra all the way up to the crown chakra. And once their crown chakra aka the sefirah Keter, meaning crown, is opened they will be able to perceive a higher reality using their third eye, enabling them to see into the spirit of all things. At this state of conscious awareness, one is able to communicate with God the Creator, the source of the Divine Light, where they receive Divine inspiration, revealing insightful messages and epiphanies. This connection with God is symbolized by the large lightning bolt striking the tower. This bolt of energy blesses Adam and Eve with a glimpse of the 'big picture' and a new way of seeing the world. After the tower is struck, they both fall to the ground where they spiritually and emotionally disconnect and dissociate from who they used to be, and detach from narrow minded or limiting beliefs they once thought were true. The fall symbolizes the disconnection from their mental slavery. Their eyes are now open, and their mindsets have expanded. They are transformed for the better after having experienced this spiritual awakening and shift in consciousness—proceeding an ego death.

Notice that the Adam and Eve characters depicted in the Tower card have been knocked off their balance? They are pictured falling down onto opposite sides of the tower from where they initially began in this three-card allegory. You will recall, in both the Lovers and the Devil cards, Eve is positioned on the left side while Adam is located on the right. And now, in the Tower card, they are both seen falling down on opposite sides from their original starting positions in the two previous cards. The tower can be seen symbolically as the Kabbalistic Tree of Life that Adam and Eve ascended. After having reached the highest sefirah, Keter, they were knocked off and had to start over—though portrayed in a positive sense. Whereas, they were struck with spiritual enlightenment, having had an eye-opening experience accompanied by a moment of clarity. Once again, they will have to build up their kundalini's (aka their spiritual towers), but this time with a new conscious awareness; armed with a stronger spirit, an enriched willpower and new sense of purpose.

This is the allegory in a nutshell, albeit there are so many more mysteries hidden in plain sight within these three cards, which I plan to reveal in depth throughout the length of this chapter, further connecting these cards on a much deeper level by combining esoteric wisdom, Hermetic knowledge and Jewish mysticism. In order to grasp this knowledge of how these three cards cohere to each other, and conjoin as one, we must begin by interpreting and analyzing each of these three cards, one at a time, before we are able to fully comprehend the big picture of it all.

As I stated earlier, the Lovers card shows Raziel bestowing Adam and Eve with knowledge. With a privier review, you will realize that Eve is standing (to the left) next to the Tree of Knowledge of Good and Evil. Wrapped around the Tree of

Knowledge is the serpent who has just convinced Eve to eat the fruit from the tree. God commanded Adam and Eve not to eat or touch the fruit for they would die. The serpent spoke to Eve informing her, "you will not die, for the day you eat of it your eyes will be opened and you will be like God, knowing good and evil." - Genesis 3:4-5. Immediately after eating the fruit Eve realizes that the serpent was right about her not dying. Yes, God was angry when he found out they had partaken from the tree and he kicked them out of the garden. But in spite of it all, God was quick to forgive Adam and Eve. Soon after, God sent archangel Raziel to offer them practical life advice and worldly guidance in the form of a user's manual—Raziel gave Adam and Eve a book called the Sefer Raziel HaMalakh, the Book of Raziel the Angel.

Raziel purportedly gave the book to Adam and Eve so the two could find their way back home (so to speak), and help them understand their spiritual nature, thus connecting them to their higher-selves where they could re-establish their spiritual connection with the Creator. The book offered them practical solutions and ways of understanding the world their God had created for them. It features an elaborate angelology, magical uses of the zodiac, gematria, names of God, protective spells, and a method of writing magical healing amulets. In addition to this, the book mentions healing herbs and their practical uses. Eve is seen in the Lovers card looking up to Raziel, representing that she is no longer paying attention to the serpent, and now looks up towards Raziel for guidance. Some scholars see this to be a variant of the story of Prometheus in Greek Mythology.

As it is depicted in the Lovers card, there are four fruits hanging in the Tree of Knowledge. In Judaism, grapes are considered to be the forbidden fruit. Also, the fact that there are four like-objects here links the fruit to the energy aspect of the 4th sefirah on the Kabbalah Tree of Life Chesed, which relates to mercy. This alludes to how Adam and Eve were shown mercy even after they ate the forbidden fruit. Neither Adam nor Eve died, and instead were blessed mercifully with wisdom and knowledge. This is when Adam and Eve experienced a sudden shift in their consciousness, which sparked within them a new sense of spiritual awareness. For the first time they saw the world for how it truly was, as if a veil had been lifted from their eyes.

The serpent here represents the kundalini, and he shows us how we are able to obtain enlightenment by way of gnosis. The kundalini is a Sanskrit word meaning coiled snake. It is an important concept in Saiva Tantra, where it is believed to be a force or power associated with the divine feminine. This energy, when cultivated and awakened through tantric practice, is believed to lead to spiritual liberation. It is a meditation technique to raise your spiritual vibration.

Raziel explained to Adam and Eve what exactly it was the serpent was trying to convey to them, how it was possible for them to elevate their conscious awareness as a way of receiving spiritual enlightenment from within. It is written in the book of Genesis, chapter 3:4-5, "And the serpent said unto the woman, Ye shall not surely die: For God doth know that in the day ye eat thereof, then your eyes shall be opened, and ye shall be as gods, knowing good and evil."

Allegorically, in the Lovers card, Adam is standing next to the Tree of Life with its twelve fiery branches, which represents the twelve signs of the zodiac, understood as being the fiery pulses of life containing the wisdom of all life's lessons and reoccurring cycles. The tree contains the fire of life encompassing excitement, joy, love and big passions. Acquiring knowledge by way of the Gnostic Path can spark the fire of intellectual enlightenment.

Gnostics considered the principal element of salvation to be direct knowledge of the supreme divinity in the form of mystical or esoteric insight.

There is a mountain with a narrow peak pictured in the background of the Lovers card. This is Mount Horeb. In the Targum Ecclesiastes chapter 10:20, it is reported that "each day the angel Raziel, standing on Mount Horeb, proclaims the secrets of men to all mankind". Horeb is thought to mean glowing/heat, which seems to be a reference to the Sun, while Sinai may have derived from the name of Sin, the Mesopotamian deity of the Moon, and thus Sinai and Horeb would be the mountains of the Moon and Sun, respectively.

Thus, Mount Horeb refers to the mountain of the Sun. The sun, in the Lovers card, has exactly 45 sun rays. This number is seen many times throughout the Waite-Smith tarot deck. 45 is a magical number of Saturn. It connects to Saturn's magic square, which is a 3×3 square with each row equaling 15 with numbers 1 through 9, and the total sum of all the digits in the square is a total of 45. The Seal of Saturn found within the square, also known as the Seal of Zazel, acts as a gateway into the astral realm that makes it possible for wishes and desires to manifest faster than usual, bypassing the normal time it takes for those desires to become reality. Furthermore, 45 is the Hebrew gematria value for the name Zazel, who is known as the Spirit of Saturn. Saturn is the guardian of the threshold between the material and the spiritual worlds; the gateway between eternity and the realm of time and space. Saturn is where the descent into matter begins.

These three tarot cards all have a hidden '45' inside of them, which relates to the Seal of Saturn and to the third eye. Raziel reveals to Adam and Eve how to draw down and bring forth their desires from the astral realm and manifest them into the physical realm. As mentioned, the Seal of Saturn is the gateway that allows you to bypass the time that it takes to draw down desire from the astral subconscious reality and manifest that desire into the physical realm. It is essentially the idea of drawing down desire from the macrocosm into the microcosm. And thus, creating something out of nothing.

The second card in this allegory is the Devil card. The Devil sits upon a platform high above Adam and Eve raising his right hand which forms the ancient hand gesture used during the Priestly Blessing (or priestly benediction), which in Hebrew is known as the Birkat Kohanim. This priestly blessing is also known in rabbinic literature as the 'raising of the hands' or rising to the platform or dukhanen, which is Yiddish from the Hebrew word dukhan, meaning platform, because the blessing is given from a raised rostrum or duchanning. This is why the Devil is standing on the black platform in this card. The Priestly Blessing is a Hebrew prayer recited by Kohanim (the Hebrew Priests, descendants of Aaron). The text of the blessing is found in Numbers 6:23-27.

In the 1% (physical) reality a person's perception of what they perceive reality to be is limited, they are only able to perceive reality by using their five senses alone. They are unable to connect to a higher state of awareness, which can only be obtained once the third eye is opened, and thus activating their 6th sense. You will notice in the Devil card that there is an inverted pentagram over the Devil's third eye, and this is a clue that one must meditate on this card to awaken the third eye in order to connect to what they are unable to see and perceive when limiting themselves to their five senses alone.

The Devil's right hand is making the mystical hand gesture, which forms the letter Shin, an emblem for Shaddai, meaning Almighty [God]. The Hebrew word for hand is Yod, and Yod's throughout the tarot always reveal deeper mysteries. According to the Torah, Aaron blessed the people, and YHVH promises that "I will place my name on their hands" (theKohanim's hands) "and bless them" (the Jews receiving the blessing). The Jewish Sages stressed that although the priests are the ones carrying out the blessing, it is not them or the ceremonial practice of raising their hands that results in the blessing, but rather it is God's desire that His blessing should be symbolized by the Kohanim's hands.

The Devil's hand is utilizing his five fingers to relay the esoteric message. Fingers are also known as digits, so we count all the fingers in the entire card. The meaning of the Hebrew letter Yod is hand, and it corresponds numerically to the number 10; the number related to manifesting, and also the total number of digits found on one's hands. Therefore, we count the digits of the hands, connecting us with the Kohanim's blessing and connect us to a deeper understanding of this card's esoteric message. There are 6 human hands (Yod's) making a total of 30 fingers. The Devil's 'bat' feet need to be taken in account as well, because they area part of his body. The bat's feet act and function as the bat's hands, so this makes it eight hands altogether, which makes 8 hands with 5 fingers each, equaling 40 digits altogether.

Many Kohanim make sure to immerse in the mikvah (baptism/cleansing) before the Birkat Kohanim. Interestingly, the number 40 is associated with the time needed for a spiritual mikvah just as the earth was immersed in water during Noah's flood, which happened for 40 days and 40 nights. A mikvah bath or baptism contains a minimum of 40 seah's, which is approximately 120 gallons of water. This is the amount of water needed for a person to fully immerse themselves.

After adding up all the digits on the hands, count the points or *digits* of the pentagram placed over the Devil's third eye and you end up with a total of 45 digits altogether. (40+5 = 45) This is a clue revealing a deeper secret that the Seal of Zazel is hidden inside this card, because the Hebrew gematria value of the name Zazel is 45. 45

is hidden throughout the tarot and always refers to Zazel, the spirit of Saturn. 45 is also the sum of all the digits within Saturn's magic square. The boxy or square-shaped pentagram seen on the Devil's eye is found inside the Magic Square of Saturn. Furthermore, the Devil card, being associated with Capricorn, symbolized by the goat and is ruled by Saturn, further reinstates this card's connection shared with Saturn and the Zazel/Azazel scapegoat that is sacrificed on Yom Kippur. Each point of the pentagram inside Saturn's square is assigned to a digit within the square, specifically in this order: from the 1 to the 4, 4 to the 7, 7 to the 3, 3 to the 2, and then from the 2 back to the 1 as you draw one continuous line to form the pentagram.

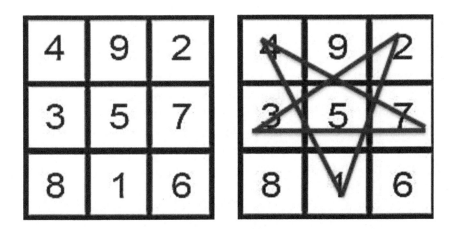

The sum of this pentagram's digits is 18. (1+4+7+3+2, and then add the 1 a second time, in order to complete the full shape of the pentagram.) The Devil card is assigned to the Roman numeral XV tarot card, which gives you 15+18 = 33, the number directly relating to Christ Consciousness; the state of consciousness obtained by opening the third eye. This is the state of consciousness that Jesus was believed to inhabit. It is believed that we can achieve Christ Consciousness through practices such as meditation and by working on ourselves.

The Hebrew letter assigned to the Devil card is Ayin, meaning eye, and has a numerical value of 70. 70 also happens to be the gematria value for the Hebrew word for secret, sod. The word sod's esoteric meaning refers to mysteries given through inspiration and revelation. This clue leads us to believe that in this card there is more than meets the eye. By using this gematria correlation we uncover the secret concealed within this card, which is that the Devil card is associated with a Jewish holiday. This being so, we can safely assume that the other two cards involved in this allegory are also associated with Jewish holidays. How so? This secret was found by following the clue of the Devil's hand gesture, the Shin Shaddai of the Birkat Kohanim, which is only given on Jewish holidays. The Kohen (priest) is the middleman who acts as a channel between God and man, delivering the blessing straight from God to mankind. The priest draws the Light from the 99% astral realm and down into the 1% physical world. The Kohen (priest) stands upon the platform while raising his hands forming the Shin Shaddai for the congregation below. The people were prohibited to look upon the hand gesture. This allowed them to focus more on the act of receiving the blessing. The congregation was told that God's sacred name was displayed upon the hands and faces of the Kohanim priest and that it would 'dim' their eyes if they were to look. It was also out of respect not to look. This is why Adam and Eve are depicted here in this card not looking up at the Devil and avoiding eye contact, which is actually the opposite to how Eve is seen in the Lovers card, where she is seen staring directly up at the angel Raziel—the middleman between God and Eve.

Furthermore, the number 70 coincides with the number of Jewish holidays celebrated throughout the year. The Midrash calculates the 70 holy days as being the 52 Shabbats, 7 days of Passover, 1 day of Shavuot, 1 day of Rosh Hashanah, 1 day of Yom Kippur, and 8 days of Sukkot.

Another interesting connection of the number 70 is found in the Torah when King David mentions, "The span of our life is 70 years, or given the strength, 80 years". This statement refers to honoring the elderly. Old age begins after 70 years old, and those with 'extra strength' reach and surpass the age of 70, and are therefore deserving of honor. Take this into account when understanding the Devil card, which depicts Adam and Eve chained to the world, represented here by the black cube the Devil sits upon. By revealing this hidden esoteric connection between the number 70 and the expected life span of man we are able to uncover the deeper symbolism portrayed within this card, whereas man chained to the cube symbolizes the spiritual enslavement that mankind is forced to endure while under the Devil's (ego) control throughout their expected life span of 70 years.

In the Devil card, there is a pentagram placed directly over the Devil's forehead. Each point of the pentagram corresponds to one of the five elements and to one of the five letters in the Divine name Yeshua, YHShVH.

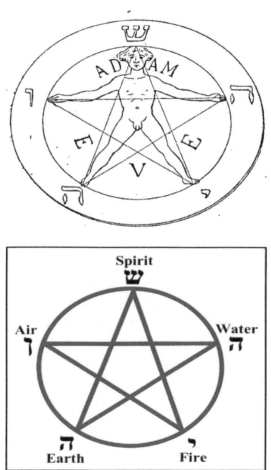

With the pentagram inverted over the Devil's forehead, the letter Shin ש is now laying directly over the Devil's third eye. Shin represents the element of spirit, and we see that the third eye is forming a unity with the spirit of Yeshua (meaning salvation), and connecting to the Christ Consciousness. The remaining points of the pentagram stick out and are able to be seen by Adam and Eve, who are standing below. The four remaining points correspond to the four letters of the ineffable name of God, the tetragrammaton, YHVH, which is prohibited to gaze upon during the Birkat Kohanim. Both Adam and Eve are able to see the Divine Name, but choose not to look out of respect.

The Devil card is associated with Capricorn, which is symbolized by the goat. Capricorn, ruled by Saturn, happens to be associated with Azazel, the Yom Kippur scapegoat. By combining these clues, it hints to us that hidden within this card is a Seal of Azazel, aka Seal of Saturn. Let us look deeper into the spiritual macrocosmic clues that reveal the location of the hidden Seal, which we find by using the sacred gematria (Hebrew numerology) of the Hebrew letters. The Sefer Yetzirah, Book of Creation, written by Abraham, says God created the world in part by using the twenty-two letters of the Hebrew alphabet. The Hebrew letters are fields of consciousness. Each of them is an expression of a unique energy-intelligence, holding specific attributes, and animated by a very powerful spiritual force.

In order to begin, we must first understand the macrocosmic spiritual aspect of the pentagram that is located over the Devil's third eye. The third eye is the portal into the astral macrocosmic realm of the 99% reality. The pentagram represents the microcosmic 1% reality, and because it is inverted it draws down energy from the 99% reality through the portal of the third eye bringing forth desire down into the 1% reality where it manifests. This spiritual-alchemical reaction of drawing down the energies further elevates the crown chakra, and causes it to radiate with God's intelligence. This energy vibration obtained through this meditation connects a person to the Christ Consciousness. This is when the crown chakra, found in a person's head, experiences a state of enlightenment—when a person is 'at one' with the Creator. This state of enlightenment is depicted throughout antiquity as a bright golden halo or nimbus; an aura around the head of saints and holy gurus such as Jesus or Buddha.

The Hebrew letter meaning head is Resh, and it relates to God's intelligence. In a since, man is a beast having primal urges and instincts, albeit with the potential to evolve into an intelligent being.

We now understand and have revealed the significance of the symbolism regarding the Devil's head and how all the heads in this card have the potential to be enlightened after undergoing a third eye activation. So, for now, we draw a line connecting the three 'horned' heads in this card, in order to reveal the hidden Seal of Azazel/Saturn. First, draw a line from Eve's head up to the Devil's head, and another line from the Devil's head down to Adam's head, forming a 'Λ' symbol. Resh has the gematria value of 200. 200 times 3 (heads) equals 600. Now, draw a line connecting the Devil's four 'bat' hands in order to complete the shape of the hidden Seal of Azazel, aka Seal of Zazel or Saturn.

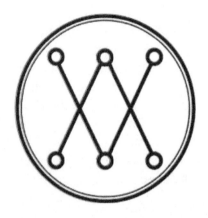

The Devil is a combination of man and beast, and specifically in this case he is part vampire bat. Different from other bats, vampire bats are not blind and can see actually very good. Hence, the association the Devil card has with the Hebrew letter Ayin, meaning eye, to see. Vampire bats are known for attaching themselves to the backs of sleeping goats where they feed on the blood slowly and without the animal ever being aware of it. The Devil technically has four bat hands. He has one bat-hand on each of his two wings, and two bat (hand-like) feet that are the bat's actual hands with five fingers each. By incorporating the Devil's animal parts it connects us to, as well as relates to the beast-like attributes of primal man. The previously drawn lines formed the Seal of Saturn, which acts as a portal that allows us with an evolved conscious state of awareness to reach outside the box, rise above our animal nature, and connect to the higher realms of our spiritual selves.

The Hebrew letter meaning hand is Yod, with a numerical value of 10. Four hands times10 equals 40. The Hebrew letter meaning head is Resh, with a numerical value of 200. Three heads times 200 equals 600. So now we have 600 (sum of the heads) plus 40 (sum of the hands) and we get the total sum of 640. 640 is the numerical value of the Hebrew word tamar, meaning date, as in the type of fruit from a date palm tree. 640 is a significant number in the Torah that relates to the 70 date palms story in Exodus 15:27, which is directly related to the Devil card, which is associated with the Hebrew letter Ayin, which has the numerical value of 70. This goes much deeper and I will explain in full detail near the end of this chapter. There is so much information to be explained here, and it all needs to be spoon fed and be taken with baby steps, and will eventually all come together in the end like the conclusion of a great mystery novel.

After drawing the lines connecting the heads and the hands you should have a large 'XX' shape in the middle of the card, with the two Vs set one on top of the other. Finally, draw a line straight across the Devil's knees, which are sitting perfectly in line with each other. This final line drawn straight through the middle will complete the Seal. You now should have two triangles on top of each other in the middle of the Seal; with one of the triangles pointing upward and sitting on top of a triangle that is inverted, pointing down. These two triangles symbolize the dualistic nature of reality: the macrocosmic 99% reality and the microcosmic 1% reality. The triangle pointing upward represents the macrocosm while the triangle pointing downward represents the microcosm.

Found within this Seal you just made in this card is a kundalini serpent hidden inside the lower triangle, camouflaged as the Devil's phallus. This serpent symbolizes the raising of the kundalini by controlling one's life-force, aka sexual energy, which is located at the base chakra. A person is able to raise their kundalini serpent, ascending it into the upper triangle, which is a representation of the 99% astral realm. The portal by which one accesses this 99% spiritual realm is accessed when the third eye is opened. Remember, that we drew lines connecting all the animal body parts depicted on the Devil card? These lines connected the horned heads with the bat hands, and the line drawn over the goat knees revealed the hidden serpent. This all relates to controlling and having mental power over your animal instincts and sexual drive, in order to ascend up through the kundalini chakras with the sole purpose of activating the third eye. The third eye refers to the gate that leads to the inner realms and spaces of higher consciousness. In spirituality, the third eye often symbolizes a state of enlightenment or the evocation of mental images having deeply personal spiritual or psychological significance.

An interesting thing to expand on here is the deeper esoteric connection the Devil card has with Saturn, its relation to the concept of the matrix reality, and its association with the Archons. The Devil card is number XV in the tarot deck. 15 is the magic number of Tzabaoth (or Yaldabaoth), the Demiurge, who is (according to Gnostic belief) the creator god of the world in which we live—the simulated matrix perceived as reality. He is the head Archon (rulers) and rules over the Archon-angels, or archangels. The Archetypes of the Archangels are placed within the essences of the Major Archana and Minor Archana tarot cards. This Archon-matrix is symbolized by the black box, or cube, the Devil sits upon. This platform (box) is also known as Saturn's cube. Saturn is known as El, Yahweh, Yaldabaoth, the Demiurge, who is the head ruling Archon that chains us down in a prison for our minds. This prison is referred to as the matrix. Yes, our world is a prison, but we can easily take our power back and remove the shackles around our necks, freeing our heads and freeing our minds if we choose to do so. We may be *in* this world, but that does not mean we have to be *of* this world.

Also, another significant thing to mention is that according to Raziel's Tarot Grid, the numerical value of Zazel's Seal, as well as the Hebrew gematria of the word Zazel both equal 45. In the Tarot Grid, 45 is found by adding the sum of all of the cards located at each of the six points of the hidden seal, further reinstating the significance the number 45 shares with the Seal of Zazel, and the important connection it shares with the Waite-Smith tarot. The Divine Four-Letter Name of God, YHVH, Yahweh, when spelled out has a numerical value of 45. This is significant, because Yahweh is associated with Yaldabaoth. Adam, the Hebrew word for man, also shares the numerical value of 45. Therefore, man can become one with God when he activates his third eye.

Moving on to the Tower tarot card, we see Adam and Eve falling to the ground and dropping all of their accumulated knowledge, which was gifted to them by archangel Raziel. Adam and Eve drop exactly 45 pieces of wisdom or ways to connect to God by way of gnosis (knowing), thereby raising their kundalini they ascend up the 'Jacob's ladder.' The tower symbolizes the kundalini, the Kabbalah Tree of Life, as well as the Jacob's ladder, which all essentially relate to the same thing—raising soul vibration, building up confidence and self- esteem. Depicted in the Tower card, we see that Adam and Eve have dropped all their 'tools' to understanding this particular tarot card. These 'tools' are their 45 pieces of wisdom, and this concept of tool can be applied to reading any one of the 78 tarot cards in the deck. These such tools in the Tower card include the Yod's, the crown, the lightning bolt, and the Roman numeral at the top of the card. These tools, and tools similar to these, are used to connect to and understand the tarot on a deeper level. These such symbols are the tools and the language in which the tarot communicates. Let us break down the 45 tools, symbols or pieces of wisdom found in this particular card. First, you have the 22 Yod's, then the crown, which represents Keter, the 1st sefirah on the Kabbalah Tree of Life and counts as 1, then there is the large lightning bolt, which is a big letter W, which can be either Hebrew letter Waw or Vav, and written either with a V or a W depending on the word leaning towards a more Arabic or Ashkenazi pronunciation, and has a Hebrew numerical value of 6, and then there is the tarot card's Roman numeral XVI (16), which all comes to a total sum of 45. (22+1+6+16 = 45)

The number 45 is seen in all three of these cards (Lovers, Devil, and Tower) in some shape or form, connecting them on a deeper mystical level. The connection of these 45's can be found when studying the clues on the surface, but if we look even deeper, we will find that there is yet another number that connects these three cards together, which is the number 15. Both the numbers 15 and 45 are known to be very magical numbers in mysticism.They are both magic numbers of Saturn (the major planetary influence of the tarot) found in Saturn's planetary magic square. The number 15, relating to when the moon is at its fullest, on the 15th of each Lunar month, is the most magical time of the moon's monthly cycle. There happen to be a handful of Jewish holidays that occur on the 15th of the month. Worth mentioning here, is that the Devil in the Devil card is making the sacred hand gesture of the Birkat Kohanim, which is (as mentioned earlier) given only on Jewish holidays. Notice that the Devil card is number XV (15)? You begin to understand that this card being assigned to number 15 is by no mistake. The hand gesture of the Priestly Blessing along with the Roman numeral XV are cluing us in that the Devil card is associated with a Jewish holiday. And when we study deeper into it, we realize all three of these cards are associated with and share a connection with Jewish holidays all occurring on the 15th of the Lunar month—some of which so happen to be exactly 45 days apart from each other.

Worth mentioning here is that the Jewish calendar is a lunisolar calendar which follows cycles of both the moon and the sun opposed to the Gregorian calendar, which only follows the cycle of the sun.

The Lovers card corresponds with the holiday of Tu B'Av aka the 15th day of the Hebrew month Av. The Devil card corresponds with the holiday of Tu BiShvat aka the 15th day of the Hebrew month Shevat. And the Tower card corresponds to the first day of Nisan, the first day of the Hebrew calendar (the original first day of the year, March 21st), which leads up through 15 days towards Pesach, or Passover. Why 15 days later? It ties in with the Exodus story, the great exodus of Egypt. On Rosh Chodesh (the first of the month of Nisan), the children of Israel heard the miracle (from the mouth of God) that they were going to be redeemed on the night of the 15th, later in that very month.

The Devil card is actually associated with two holidays: Tu BiShvat and Yom Kippur.

The Devil card is slightly more complex than the other two tarot cards involved in this allegorical trilogy, mainly because the Devil card contains two polarities and/or ways to see and understand it. It is a mixture of dualities corresponding with the macrocosm and the microcosm aspects of unveiling its hidden secrets, similar to how the Jewish holidays associated with it are revealed.

For example, the Lovers card is associated with Tu B'Av, which is exactly 45 days before Rosh Hashanah (celebrating the creation of the world and the creation of Adam and Eve) followed by the ten days of 'awe' leading up to Yom Kippur, which is associated with the Devil card—the next card in this allegorical trilogy. On the day of Yom Kippur, it is tradition to sacrifice a goat given the name Azazel, known as the 'scapegoat', who takes upon itself all the Jewish peoples' sins for that year. Hence, the Devil in the tarot adorning goat horns. The Devil card is also associated with Tu Bishvat which is celebrated exactly 45 days before the 1st of Nisan, which is the holiday associated with the Tower card. As we progress through these three tarot cards, we also progress through the holidays associated with them. Each of these three holidays correspond with the 15th of their respective months, so we have 15+15+15 equaling 45. Also, remember each of these three cards reveal a hidden connection to 45, so we have 45+45+45 equaling 135. Then add this 135 to 45 (the sum of the three 15's, referring to the 15th day of each month) and you get a total of 180. 180 is significant here because the 15th letter in the Hebrew alphabet is Samekh with a value of 60, and 60×3 (representing the three tarot cards involved) = 180. The root of the word Samekh means 'to lean upon', 'to uphold', 'to support' similar to how a sukkah (shelter) built especially for the holiday of Sukkot would act as a dwelling for God. The Book of Leviticus describes it as a symbolic wilderness shelter, commemorating the time God provided for the Israelites in the wilderness they inhabited after they were freed from slavery in Egypt. Each one of these cards acts as a dwelling that will uphold and support the mystical wisdom of the tarot. The root of Samekh is also found in the Jewish concept of semikhah, the laying on of hands on the head of a sacrificial animal in the blood ritual of the Jewish Temple, relating back to the concept of sacrifice for the redemption of sins that these three cards portray. The letter Samekh has a value of 60, which is the same number of letters found in the Birkat Kohanim, (the Priestly Blessing), given specifically on Jewish holidays, which so happens to contain exactly 15 Hebrew words.

I will explain further in detail along with all the deeper symbolic associations that each of these three cards have with these specific holidays later on in this chapter. The important thing for now is to establish the connection that the holidays have with these three cards.

Starting with the Lovers card, which is associated with the holiday of Tu B'Av, which should not come as too big of a surprise because Tu B'Av is known as the Jewish Valentine's day. It is referred to as being one of the happiest days of the year. In ancient times on Tu B'Av when the moon was full women wishing to marry would wear white dresses (so none would know who was rich or poor) and dance outside Jerusalem's walls in the vineyards while suitors would dance after them. Today in the Jewish world, it is a holiday celebrating the magic of love.

The Mishnah states that, "No days were as festive for Israel as the 15th of Av and YomKippur." (Tractate Ta'anit) Tu B'Av is, according to the Jewish Sages, equivalent to Yom Kippur. And how does this all connect with the Lovers tarot card? Let me first explain the stories in the Torah to gather the reasoning and the connection.

Sages say Yom Kippur symbolizes God's forgiving Israel for the sin of the Golden Calf in the desert, for it was on that day that He finally accepted Moses' plea for forgiveness of the nation, and on that same day Moses came down from the mountain with the new set of tablets.

Just as Yom Kippur symbolizes the atonement for the sin of the Golden Calf, Tu B'Av signifies the atonement for the sin of the Spies, where ten came bearing such negative reports which reduced the entire nation to panic. There were twelve spies, as recorded in the Book of Numbers (chapter 13:1-33), that were a group of Israelite chieftains, one from each of the Twelve Tribes, who were dispatched by Moses to scout out the Land of Canaan for 40 days as a future home for the Israelite people, during the time when the Israelites were in the wilderness following their Exodus from Ancient Egypt. The Spies were supposed to return back to Moses with reports of their findings from foreign lands to let the Israelites know if they found God's 'promised land' where they could settle. Ten of the twelve chieftains told Moses that the land of Canaan was was no good. They lied in order for them to have it all to themselves. As a result of that sin, it was decreed by God that the nation would remain in the desert for 40 years, and that no person 20 or older would be allowed to enter Canaan, known as modern-day Israel. On each Tisha B'Av aka 9th ofAv of those 40 years, those who had reached the age of 60 that year died—15,000 each Tisha B'Av. Tisha B'Av, meaning the 9th of Av, is known to be the most negative day of the year. The 9th of Av commemorates various tragedies that befell the Jewish people throughout history, particularly the destruction of the two temples in 586 BCE and 70 CE. This plague finally ended on Tu B'Av; this plague that had accompanied the Jews in the desert for 40 years ended. That last year, the last 15,000 people got ready to die. God, in His mercy, decided not to have that last group die, considering all the troubles they had gone through. Now, when the 9th of Av approached, all the members of the group got ready to die, but nothing happened. They then decided that they might have been wrong about the date, so they waited another day, and another...

Finally on the 15th of Av, when the full moon appeared, they realized definitely that the 9th of Av had come and gone, and that they were still alive. Then it was clear to them that God's decree was over, and that He had finally forgiven the people for the sin of the Spies.

This is what was meant by the Sages when they said, "No days were as festive for Israel as the 15th of Av and Yom Kippur", for there is no greater joy than having one's sins forgiven; on Yom Kippur for the sin of the Golden Calf and on Tu B'Av for the sin of the Spies.

The scene depicted in the Lovers card portrays what occurred after Adam and Eve ate the forbidden fruit from the Tree of Knowledge of Good and Evil. God was quick to forgive Adam and Eve for eating the forbidden fruit. Shortly after they partook of the fruit, God sent his angel Raziel to teach Adam and Eve all life's secrets and mysteries in order for them to be able to survive a prosperous life in the world outside the garden. Eve is depicted in the Lovers card standing next to the Tree of Knowledge with the serpent wrapped around it. The serpent represents the kundalini chakra system with its relation to how Eve ate the fruit causing her mind to be opened and expand her sense of awareness. Her kundalini was elevated, and she was able to 'see' for the first time, meaning that she now had a new conscious awareness and saw the world for what it truly was. This is the moment she realized that she and Adam were naked. "For God doth know that in the day ye eat thereof, then your eyes shall be opened, and ye shall be as gods, knowing good and evil." - Genesis 3:5.

You will notice there are exactly four fruits inside this Tree of Knowledge. Four like-objects grouped together connects to energy aspects of the 4th sefirah Chesed, meaning mercy. Thus, these four fruits symbolize that God forgave Adam and Eve for eating the forbidden fruit, and they were shown mercy. Interesting to point out here, is that the Hebrew letter meaning serpent is Teth with a numerical value of 9. 9+4 fruits = 13, which directly relates to the 13 Attributes of God's Mercy, as enumerated in the Book of Exodus chapter 34:6–7. Also, worth mentioning here is that archangel Raziel rules over the sefirah Chokmah, meaning wisdom. Chokmah resides on the right column of mercy on the Kabbalah Tree of Life. The gematria value of the word Chokmah is 37. In Genesis chapter 3:3 is when the word Elohim (God) is mentioned for the 37th time. These are all clues revealing that in the Lovers card God is showing Adam and Eve mercy and blessing them with wisdom. The verse taken from Genesis chapter 3:3 is also the first time the serpent speaks to Eve, revealing that the serpent is wise, for no other animal was able to speak in the garden, and the serpent states, "Yea, hath God said, Ye shall not eat of every tree of the garden?", in order to start up a conversation with Eve about how the forbidden fruit will actually not cause her to die.

The four fruits on the Tree of Knowledge are grapes, which further connect to the holiday of Tu B'Av, because the 15th of Av marks the beginning of the grape harvest.

According to a number of Jewish traditions, the forbidden fruit was, in fact, a grape. The Zohar, the Midrash of Bereishit Rabah, the Greek Apocalypse of Baruch, and also Rabbi Meir (Jewish sage of the Mishnah) all point to the fruit of the vine being the delicacy that Adam and Eve found too desirable to pass up.

Archangel Raziel appears to Adam and Eve shortly after they partake of the fruit. Eve is seen here, in the Lovers card, looking up towards the angel Raziel for guidance. Do you notice how she is no longer paying attention to the serpent? Here mind is now opened, and she is hungry for another bite of the fruit, meaning she now has an appetite for knowledge and wisdom. Again, Raziel rules over Chokmah, meaning wisdom. Interesting to note here, if we count all the pieces of Raziel's wisdom symbolized in this card, we get the sum of 70. Let us break it down. There are 4 fruits in the Tree of Knowledge, 12 fiery leaves on the Tree of Life, and then 45 rays around the sun that come to a total sum of 70. 70 is the numerical value for the Hebrew word sod, meaning secret, and Raziel's name means 'secrets of God.' Both Raziel and the serpent revealed secrets to Adam and Eve in the garden.

Raziel is depicted here, in the Lover's card, wearing a gray robe, moreover gray is the color that represents wisdom throughout the tarot. His head is surrounded in a bright yellow aura that appears to converge with the sun. The top of his head is enlightened, and radiating with God's intelligence with his hair depicted as fiery flames. His hands reach out with open palms, as he blesses Adam and Eve with the gift of wisdom, revealing to them all of God's secrets. Raziel is seen coming out of the clouds directly over the peak of Mount Horeb. There are some biblical scholars that argue Horeb is the same mountain as Sinai, but according to the Waite-Smith tarot deck they are two different mountains. In the tarot, the Hermit stands on Mount Sinai, whereas the mountain in the Lovers card represents Mount Horeb. Horeb is thought to mean glowing/heat, which seems to be a reference to the sun, while Sinai may have derived from the name Sin, named after the Mesopotamian moon deity. Kabbalistically, the Lovers card is associated with the sefirah Tiferet, ruled by the Sun. Hence, the large sun (behind Raziel's head) in this card. Subsequently, the Hermit card is associated with the sefirah Yesod, which is ruled by the Moon.

In the Lovers card, Adam is standing next to the Tree of Life that is depicted with twelve fiery branches, which correspond to the twelve signs of the zodiac, taught to Adam by the angel Raziel. The twelve tribes that Moses formed in the desert that dispersed the 144,000 Israelites into twelve groups is an analogy of the twelve signs of the zodiac. Referring back to the ten spies story, there was one chief from each of the twelve tribes that made up a group of twelve tourist that were supposed to find the promised land where the Jewish people would eventually live. The 'promised land' would give the Israelites a new life where they would be metaphorically 'reborn.' This is a metaphor for the zodiac cycle that Raziel taught Adam. It is in this cycle or zodiac wheel where we reincarnate, life after life, progressing through the Zodiac one sign after the other, forever trapped inside an eternal reincarnation loop.

The Lovers card, considered the Jewish Valentine's day, corresponds to the holiday of Tu B'Av, which is exactly 45 days before Rosh Hashanah known as the new year aka head of the year, which leads up to Yom Kippur. This is another connection as of why the Lovers card depicts exactly 45 sun rays around the sun illustrated behind archangel Raziel's head. Yom Kippur is the day on which we are closest to God and to the quintessence of our own souls. It is the Day of Atonement, "For on this day He will forgive you, to purify you, that you be cleansed from all your sins before God", Leviticus 16:30. This is yet another spiritual connection shared between these three tarot cards (the Lovers, Devil, and Tower) all being associated with God's mercy and all portraying an example of God's forgiveness of sins.

Adam and Eve were banished from the Garden of Eden after eating the fruit, and they were tossed into the world of Malchut, the

3rd dimensional physical world. Malchut is the 10th sefirah on the Tree of Life, and refers to the physical world of matter that we perceive with our five senses. Malchut, meaning kingdom, is referred to as the kingdom where all things manifest. For this reason, both Adam and Eve went from the Kingdom of Heaven into the Kingdom of Man. From the Lovers card (Eden) they crossed over into the Devil card (Earth). And the Lord God said, "The man has now become like one of us, knowing good and evil. He must not be allowed to reach out his hand and take also from the tree of life and eat, and live forever". So, the Lord God banished him from the Garden of Eden to work the ground from which he had been taken. (Genesis: Chapter 3) From here, we move forward with the Devil card.

The Devil card is associated with Capricorn, an earth sign, symbolized by the goat. This is one of the reasons why the Devil is depicted with goat horns. Capricorn is ruled by Saturn, symbolized by the color black. Hence, this card's black background. Saturn is also symbolized by the black cube similar to the black cornerstone Adam and Eve are chained to in the Devil card. Saturn is the lord of the matrix, the controlled reality of the material world. Saturn is Yahweh, associated with the tetragrammaton, known as YHVH, which translates as 'God created.' There is a need to emphasize here the certain distinction of what this translation refers to. YHVH is not God the Creator, the source of the Divine Light, instead YHVH is what the Divine Source created, such as the world and all things in it. According to the Gnostics, the creator of this matrix reality is an actual being named Tzabaoth, the Demiurge, aka Saturn, and he is the god in the Hebrew Bible known as Yahweh. And the black box depicted in the Devil card is a symbolic representation of the world in which we exist in—inside the Saturn matrix prison of our existence, trapped inside an eternal reincarnation loop—inside the Saturn cube. Gnostics believe that we (mankind) are eternal soul beings that never die, trapped in an eternal reincarnation loop. God had mercy on us, and He sent Raziel to help guide mankind, so this false reality does not have to be a hell on earth, rather it has the potential to become a Garden of Eden, where all humans live in peace and prosperity, trying to make the best out of a bad situation. To learn more about the Gnostic scriptures, I suggest reading and studying the Nag Hammadi texts. The Nag Hammadi library (also known as the Chenoboskion Manuscripts and the Gnostic Gospels) is a collection of early Christian and Gnostic texts discovered near the Upper Egyptian town of Nag Hammadi in 1945.

The Devil card is a continuation from the Lovers card, and the Tower card continues from where the Devil card leaves off. These three tarot cards combined tell one single story, but each card is its own chapter. Think of the Lovers card as Chapter 1, the Devil card as Chapter 2, and the Tower card as Chapter 3, combined together to tell the tarot's origin story through esoteric symbolism in order to reveal the tarot's purpose—an allegorical trilogy, if you will.

The Devil card relates to aspects of God's mercy, symbolically depicted as the 13 grapes on Eve's tail. These 13 grapes are directly related to the 13 Attributes of Mercy, as enumerated in the Book of Exodus (Exodus 34:6-7). Grapes are a fruit traditionally eaten on the holiday of Tu BiShvat, the New Year for Trees. Grapes are one of the seven fruits the Torah praises on this day, including dates. The other such 'fruits' include wheat, barley, pomegranates, olives, and figs, which are all seen throughout the tarot. The grapes on Eve's tail are grapes that she herself grew/manifested. Although, it was archangel Raziel who was sent by God to teach Eve the knowledge of how to grow the grapes—thereby, being a merciful act of God.

These 13 attributes are the Divine Attributes with which, according to Judaism, God governs the world. The number 13 signifies the infinite. The number 12 signifies constraint and order. For example, the 12 zodiac signs and the 12 months in a year. Above order and control, 13 connotes boundlessness and immeasurability. The fact that there are 13 Attributes of Mercy teaches us that when God shows mercy, He does so without limit. No matter how low we fall, He will come to our aid and forgive us. This was the lesson Raziel taught to Eve in the garden; that God will forgive us when we sin. Living in the material world is a constant battle with the ego, referred to by Kabbalists as the Adversary. Battling the ego is not easy and takes much spiritual work. Knowing that we will be forgiven when we fall gives us the motivation to pick ourselves up whenever we do.

The 13 Attributes of Mercy are based on two verses in Exodus: "The Lord! The Lord! God, Compassionate and Gracious,

Slow to anger and Abundant in Kindness and Truth, Preserver of kindness for thousands of generations, Forgiver of iniquity, willful sin, and error, and Who Cleanses". - Exodus 34:6-7

The Devil card is connected to the holiday of Tu BiShvat, the New Year for Trees. The Torah compares men to being like trees. A tree needs the four basic elements in order to survive: soil, water, air, and fire (sun). Human beings also require the same basic elements. The Devil card essentially is all about man growing spiritually like a tree, elevating his soul from the roots upward and branching out to eventually produce fruit, which can be compared to how a seed level idea or desire has the potential to manifest into reality. Here in the Devil card Adam and Eve are seen starting anew, seeing the world with new eyes and rejuvenating their souls, or 'Trees of Life' found within them, from the roots of their base chakra their soul's vibration ascends up their spine with the purpose of activating the third eye. Ergo, the pentagram over the Devil's third eye symbolism, and the association this card has with the Hebrew letter Ayin, meaning eye, to see. Adam and Eve are 'seeing' for the first time like a baby being birthed into the world out of its mother's womb. Tu BiShvat is considered the birthday for trees. Tu BiShvat is technically the day when trees stop absorbing water from the ground, and instead draw nourishment from their sap. Similar to a tree, Adam and Eve focus on rejuvenating their soul to raise their soul's vibration, with the purpose of activating their third eye in order to draw down desire from the 99% reality, and manifest it into a real tangible thing. Understanding this third eye connection is the key to manifesting their desires in the material world. This concept is essentially the formula used for creating miracles. Inside the soul of every human being is a Tree of Life which, according to the Kabbalists, is a map of the soul. The roots of this Tree are located at the top in Keter, the crown chakra, opposed to a physical tree with its roots in the ground. Keter represents pure nothingness, the Divine Source of all things, and at the same time contains no things. To be connected with Keter is to be in a union with God the Creator, the Light, and pure nothingness. The third eye is the gateway/portal to draw down seeds of desire from the roots of Keter in order to manifest them in the material world. With the knowledge and understanding of this concept, Adam and Eve are able to produce their own sap aka prosperity and abundance.

Mentioned earlier, the Seal of Zazel/Saturn, hidden in the Devil card, reveals the gematria value of 640. 640 is the numerical value of the Hebrew word for date, tamar, which relates to the date palm tree story in the Torah. This particular Torah story reveals the power of trees, which can be compared to how Adam and Eve also share similar spiritual attributes with trees.

Every year, the weekly Torah portion of Beshalach is read in close proximity to the holiday of Tu BiShvat. There are in fact many beautiful and deep allusions to Tu BiShvat (literally, the 15th day of the month of Shevat) in the portion. (The Devil card happens to be the15th tarot card as well, making a further connection.) Some of these illusions relate to the healing power of trees and, on a symbolic level, to the Torah itself, and some relate to the process of rejuvenation that trees undergo in general—and in this season in particular.

As the date palm trees story goes, after experiencing the miraculous salvation at the Red Sea, the Jewish people traveled for three days without water. When they finally discovered water, it was too bitter to drink. God then revealed to Moses a tree, which he threw into the water, causing it to be sweetened. Subsequently, God tells the people that if they listen to His voice, all the diseases of Egypt will not befall them for "I am God that heals you". - Exodus 15:26

Just as the Torah, as well as the Tarot, sweetens reality and has spiritual, psychological, and emotional healing qualities, trees also provide us with physical and psychological succor, offering us healing barks, roots and leaves. Not to mention shade, beauty, and sweet nourishing fruits. Immediately following this episode, the children of Israel traveled and camped in a desert oasis named Elim, where there were twelve springs of water and seventy date palms. (Exodus 15:27) After learning the lesson of the bitter waters the people were given the chance to experience a virtual oasis in the desert that life can become.

70 is the numerical value of the word sod, meaning secret, referring to secrets revealed by way of divine inspiration and through meditation. 70 is also the numerical value of Ayin, the Hebrew letter assigned to the Devil tarot card, meaning eye, relating to the third eye.

Furthermore, the date palm symbolizes the Tzaddik, the righteous person, of whom it is said, "The righteous like the date palm will flourish." (Psalms 92:13) Deep inside their very beings, every person has a spark of the Tzaddik.

It is interesting to note that dates are among the very highest fruits on the glycemic scale, which measures natural sugar content. Dates only grow in hot climates with abundant sun. The process of photosynthesis, by which a plant takes the light of the sun and converts it into energy and eventually fruit, teaches us how we can take the Light of God and transform it deep within us, yield the fruit of inspiration and understanding.

The Hebrew word for date is tamar and has the numerical value of 640, the same numerical value of the Hebrew word for sun, shemesh. When we receive the Light of God and are devoid of ego and ulterior motives, we become transparent vessels that convert the Light into the very blood that flows in our veins. Like a date tree, which is a pure conduit for transforming the sun's energy into unadulterated sweetness, when we are pure, we too can transform the Light of God into inspiration and understanding.

As we begin to understand the many hidden connections within this card, we find that the numerical value for the Seal of Zazel found inside the Devil card is 640, which is the same value for the Hebrew word for date palms, tamar. There were exactly 70 date palm trees; 70 being the numerical value of Ayin, the Hebrew letter assigned to the Devil card. We now are able to comprehend the Devil card's association with the New Year for Trees, Tu BiShvat, meaning the 15th of the month of Shevat, and further understand why the Devil card happens to be the Roman numeral XV (15) card in the tarot deck.

Another subtle connection between the date palms story and Tu BiShvat relates to the underlying spiritual essence of the holiday itself. According to tradition, the sap begins to once again ascend in the trees on Tu BiShvat. This sap is the life-force that culminates in the spring and summer with buds, leaves, and fruit. Therefore, on a symbolic level, Tu BiShvat represents the time when new redemptive energy begins to well up from beneath the surface.

Drinking wine is also central to these holiday festivities. Indeed, the Talmud states that "when wine goes in, the secret comes out." This connection between yayin (wine) and sod (secret) is also reflected in both Hebrew words having the numerical value of 70 (a number also alluded to by the 70 date palms mentioned above.) Delving into the inner dimensions of Torah/Tarot on these holidays, a process aided by the drinking of wine reveals deep concealed secrets and releases redemptive energy into the world, just as the sap rising in the trees on Tu BiShvat culminates in new growth and life.

According to Rabbi Leibel Eiger in his commentary Torat Emet reveals another deep connection between Tu BiShvat and the redemption that occurs in the month of Nisan. The Tower card, the next card to be mentioned with its association with the Jewish holidays, relates directly to the month of Nisan. Rabbi Eiger notes that Tu BiShvat falls 45 days before the new moon of Nisan, that is to say 45 days before the world was actually created, according to the Sages. The 1st of Nisan is the original first day of the new year (March 21st). He explains that the Hebrew word for thought, which is machshavah, can be permuted to read 'thinks of what'; and the word for 'what' (Mah) has the numerical value of 45. Thus, according to Leibel Eiger, on Tu BiShvat, 45 days before the new moon of Nisan, God began to focus His thought on creation. This Divine act of thought (consciousness) parallels the sap rising in the trees in the lower world. And you know now how the number 45 connects to the Seal of Zazel, the gateway (portal) between desire and manifested reality.

Just as one cannot detect from the exterior the sap rising from the roots to the trunk of a tree, so too the arousal of a new spiritual energy on Tu BiShvat is concealed, beginning from the point of pure potential deep inside an individual's soul and slowly ascending till it is fully revealed as a new spiritual energy ready for actualization on Passover, the 15th day of Nisan.

What is more, the Devil card is associated with the month of Capricorn, which is ruled by Saturn. Saturn is also the ruling planet of Aquarius, which rules over the Hebrew month of Shevat.

All three of these tarot cards, the Lovers, the Devil, and the Tower are associated with specific signs of the zodiac, which coincide with these specific holidays that occur within these certain months. For example, the Lovers card is associated with the Sun in Gemini, connecting with the energy influence of the sefirah Tiferet, which is ruled by the Sun, who rules over Leo in the month of Av, thus connecting to the holiday of Tu B'Av. The Devil card is associated with Saturn, who rules over both Capricorn and Aquarius. The goat being the symbol for Capricorn, represented by the Devil having goat horns, connects with the Yom Kippur 'scapegoat' Azazel. The other holiday associated with the Devil card is Tu BiShvat, which occurs in the month of Shevat, corresponding to Aquarius, who is also ruled by Saturn. The Tower card, associated with Mars, who rules over Aries, depicts the 1st of Nisan (March 21st), leading up to the 15th of the month, which is Passover.

Tu B'Av is 45 days before Rosh Hashanah, which begins the ten days of 'awe' leading up to Yom Kippur. Tu BiShvat is 45 days before the 1st of Nisan. These holidays being exactly 45 days apart from each other strengthens the connection that these cards share. Furthermore, each card's holiday is celebrated on the 15th of the month, and 15×3 = 45. Each of the cards has a concealed '45' within it, which further strengthens the deep connection shared by these three cards.

The 3rd and final card in this group is the Tower card, which illustrates the celebration of the 1st of Nisan, considered the beginning of the year for calculating festivals and the reigns of the Kings of Israel. This is why there is a crown on top of the tower, and also why Adam and Eve are wearing festival costumes.

In the Tower card, Adam and Eve are seen falling to the ground and dropping all their accumulated pieces of wisdom that helped lead them up the tower (symbolizing their kundalini). These such 'pieces of wisdom' are the symbols found in this card, such as the Yod's, the crown, the lightning bolt, and the Roman numeral at the top of card. These symbols are all clues to be used as tools in order to read this particular card, as well as any one of the tarot cards in the entire deck for that matter. Found specifically in this card are 22 Yod's, the crown relating to Keter, which is the 1st sefirah and counts as 1, the large lightning bolt that happens to be a W (Waw) with the Hebrew gematria value of 6, and then the card's Roman numeral XVI (16), which equal a total sum of 45 (22+1+6+16 = 45).

Moreover, the Tower card portrays the 1st of Nisan, the New Year for Kings and Festivals, which occurs 45 days after Tu BiShvat. Nisan is ruled by Mars as Aries and symbolized by the Ram. Passover is celebrated in the month of Nisan, where the Jewish people sacrifice either a lamb or a goat, which spiritually connects and coincides with the theme of these three cards, which is ultimately forgiveness.

What is the story behind Passover? Passover commemorates the slavery of the Israelites in Egypt and their ultimate exodus to freedom. This story of redemption from slavery is the master-story of the Jewish People—a story that has shaped Jewish consciousness and values. It is just as relevant today for all humankind as it was 3,400 years ago.

The story harks back to the family of Jacob, who fled their home in Canaan in the face of a terrible famine. They made their way to Egypt where they were welcomed and became a populous people. But when a new king arose in Egypt, he feared the growing Israelite population and enslaved them, a sentence that continued for the next 210 years. Then the God of Israel appeared to a simple shepherd, Moses, in a burning bush, instructing him to go to Egypt and free the slaves.

The story of Passover relates the struggle between God, who demands freedom for the Israelites, and Pharaoh, who symbolizes the hard-hearted forces of tyranny and enslavement. God breaks Pharaoh's spirit by inflicting Egypt with 10 plagues. During the night of the final plague, God 'passed over' and protected the houses of the Israelites, giving the festival its name. Moses led the people of Israel out of Egypt and, with the Egyptian army chasing after them, split the waters of the Red Sea, allowing the Israelites to cross the sea on dry land and escape.

According to Judaism, the main entity of Passover is the sacrificial lamb. The Christian celebration of Good Friday finds its roots in the Jewish feast of Passover, the evening on which Jesus was crucified as the Passover Lamb.

Passover is a holiday of natural regeneration and spiritual renewal, which is another reoccurring theme shared amongst these three tarot cards. There is an established connection with Passover and Yom Kippur both having rituals of sacrificing a goat. The Passover sacrifice, the *pesach*, a symbol of God's power and the ultimate freedom of the Jewish people, invites us to consider the Yom Kippur sacrifice of the Azazel goat in a new light. Azazel acts as the 'scapegoat' taking on all the people's sins for the entire year, and then sent out into the wilderness, never to return. On the Day of Atonement, Yom Kippur, God comes to personally judge the people for their sins throughout the year. This is the reasoning of why the people transfer all their sins over to the scapegoat, so they will be sin free and cleansed before the Lord's judgment. This holiday (Yom Kippur) that celebrates both the rebirth of the natural world and the birth of the Jewish people may indeed offer some clues for understanding the mystery of this ancient Yom Kippur ritual.

Yom Kippur is considered the holiest day of the year, and the day on which people are closest to God. It is the Day of Atonement, "For on this day He will forgive you, to purify you, that you be cleansed from all your sins before God." - Leviticus 16:30

When you add up the Roman numerals assigned to these three cards you get the number 37 (6+15+16 = 37). 37 is the Hebrew gematria value for Chokmah, meaning wisdom. Raziel is the ruling archangel of Chokmah, and has inspired and revealed his wisdom, the secret mysteries of God, towards the creation of these (Waite-Smith) tarot cards. This Adam and Eve analogy is the basis for and the purpose of all the 78 cards in the Waite-Smith tarot deck. The purpose is simple; to shed layers of ego in order to obtain a connection with God, the source of miracles, joy and happiness, drawing forth the power of certainty to make your wishes and desires come true, so you can enjoy a life of prosperity and abundance. The 37th Name, (אני, Hebrew letter combination Aleph/Nun/Yod), of the 72 Names of God happens to be the one that connects to 'Seeing the Big Picture', which is the purpose of these three cards converging together—to reveal archangel Raziel's secrets.

The Lovers card is associated with the Hebrew letter Zayin, meaning sword. It relates to being a weapon of protection used for battling the ego aka adversary. In order to be able to shed, (or in this case with the zayin/sword, slice off), layers of ego you must learn to forgive yourself of past mistakes. Ego can be compared to rust. Nothing can destroy iron, but its own rust can. Likewise, a person can destroy themselves with their own mindset. Take responsibility for your actions and learn to forgive others as well as yourself. Knowing that God will always forgive us makes it that much easier to forgive ourselves no matter how hard we fall. Humans will make mistakes. It is inevitable. This is how we learn. With each mistake we make we learn how to pick ourselves up and move on. And each time we pick ourselves up, we become stronger.

The Devil card is associated with the Hebrew letter Ayin,

meaning eye, to see. We open our third eye and are able to see the world for what it truly is. "The world you are in—is the true hell. The journey to truth itself is what quickens the heart to become lighter. The lighter the heart the purer it is. The purer the heart, the closer to the light it becomes. And the heavier the heart the more chained to this hell it will remain." - Suzy Kassem, an American writer, poet, and philosopher.

The Tower card is associated with the letter Peh, meaning mouth. The voice and the word of God guided the Israelites along the path towards their redemption. "Once we realize that we are being programmed to live our lives along the road of chaos, we can begin to reroute our journey onto a more joyous highway of living. Turn the light on and the curtain of darkness will move to the side, unveiling a wonderful, beautiful world out there." - Kabbalist Rav Berg in "Immortality: The Inevitability of Eternal Life"

The biggest secret Raziel revealed to Adam and Eve was that this world is a prison. He told Adam and Eve the truth, that they were angels just like him but their spirits were trapped in matter (in human form), and also that they had within themselves a spark of the Creator's Light, and held within themselves the power to manifest their desires.

French occult author, Eliphas Levi was adamant about his findings and wrote, "An imprisoned person with no other book than the tarot, if he knew how to use it, could in a few years acquire universal knowledge, and would be able to speak on all subjects with unequalled learning and inexhaustible eloquence."

This picture, taken from the book "Reconditioning the Body to a New Mind" written by Dr. Joe Dispenza, illustrates the concept of the spiritual rejuvenation process.

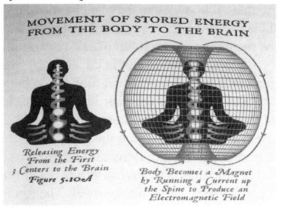

MOVEMENT OF STORED ENERGY FROM THE BODY TO THE BRAIN

Releasing Energy From the First 3 Centers to the Brain
Figure 5.10A

Body Becomes a Magnet by Running a Current up the Spine to Produce an Electromagnetic Field

A person is able to raise their conscious awareness by way of gnosis; by connecting all the dots, comprehending knowledge gained throughout their lifespan, revealing inspiration through self-discovery, all to raise their kundalini, spiritual vibration, and eventually enlighten their crown chakra, all done for the purpose of obtaining Christ Consciousness. Once the vibration is raised a person is able to receive deep insights and unveil hidden secrets through Divine inspiration. These new insights will most likely shatter a person's current limiting beliefs. Aristotle said it perfectly, "The more you know, the more you know you don't know." Just like Adam and Eve in this three-card allegory, where they were on their path to self-discovery, climbed up their spiritual tower, and upon reaching enlightenment at the top is the moment when they were suddenly struck with divine insights that destroyed their foundation, they had built themselves up with—the knowledge they were led to believe as being the ultimate truth. They fell to the ground, dropping all their pieces of wisdom and know-how. They were struck with an epiphany enabling them to see the big picture, which forced them to come face to face with themselves, where they experienced an honest self-realization and self-discovery, seeing things in a new light as they pull aside the curtain to reveal the truth of how wrong they had been about their previous limited beliefs, which they used to hold sacred. But they were quick to forgive themselves, feeling overjoyed and delighted to learn this new truth. This truth set them free, redeeming them and what can be described as a Divine salvation. Seeing the big picture causes them to understand with complete certainty that all knowledge they had learned and wisdom gained through their past experiences up until this point was not in vain because it led them here to this point of self-realization; this moment of clarity. Everything works out in the end.

They began building a new spiritual foundation built upon their new broader understanding and higher level of consciousness. In the Tower card, Adam and Eve are knocked off from the top of the tower and experience a 'fall.' Landing on the ground, having to pick up the pieces and start over—having to rebuild themselves a new tower. Although, this time they will have returned better than before, resulting in them erecting a much stronger tower. Their belief system is ever evolving, and will continue to change and evolve, as they further their search for truth and self-discovery. We keep learning and growing as we progress along the path of self-discovery; the Gnostic path. Everything we learn from social interactions, relationships, and karmic life-situations, are like tiny nuggets of knowledge that we gather along the way, building upon our character, reshaping us and leading us closer to discovering our true selves. No time is wasted on the path to self-discovery. One day we will all look back on our lives and realize that everything worked out in the end. Everything that happened was meant to be and we regret nothing for happening the way that it did; it all led us to where we are supposed to be in this present moment. We never stop learning and growing. The purpose of life is attaining the highest form of knowledge. We are our own saviors, and it is by knowing thyself through self-discovery, Divine Gnosis, that we experience salvation. The Gnostic Path, in essence, is this Path of Initiation—the way to Christ Consciousness.

Gnostics do not look to salvation from sin; rather, they look to salvation from ignorance—the ignorance of spiritual realities. This ignorance will only be revealed through gnosis. Because of the knowledge of humanity's true nature, those who have achieved the gnosis will be upheld from bondage of the earthly existence.

I'd like to conclude by describing in detail the Birkat Kohanim (the Priestly Blessing), the 'raising of the hands' blessing that is gestured with the Devil's right hand as depicted in theDevil tarot card. This blessing is found in the Book of Numbers 6:23-27. This blessing wraps up everything mentioned in this chapter, bringing the lessons and the concepts together within one message.

Traditionally, the priests blessed the people every morning after the sacrifice at the Temple. Today, many synagogues, as well as Christian churches, end their service with this blessing as a benediction.

When recited, the Kohen (priest) raises his hands with the palms facing outward and the thumbs of his outspread hands touching. The four fingers on each hand are split into two sets of two fingers each, thus forming the Hebrew letter Shin, an emblem for Shaddai, meaningAlmighty [God].

Note that the Lord does not command the Kohanim to bless the people using their own words, but rather provides the exact formulation for the blessing, prefacing the instruction with the words: "Thus shall you bless." This reveals that the blessing comes from the Lord Himself, and the priests are but the means for transmitting His gracious will. This is further indicated by the verse that immediately follows the Birkat Kohanim: "So shall they put my name upon the people of Israel, and I will bless them." - Num 6:27

The Birkat Kohanim is exactly 15 Hebrew words, which deepens the connection of the Devil card being assigned the Roman numeral XV, and also very interesting is that the holidays included in these three tarot cards are all celebrated on the 15th of each of the Hebrew months mentioned.

Below is the Birkat Kohanim blessing in Hebrew:

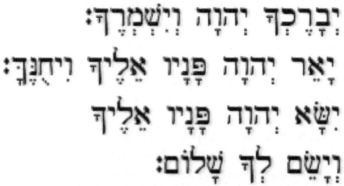

And in closing, I leave you with the English version of this blessing. "Speak to Aaron and his sons, saying, Thus you shall bless the people of Israel: you shall say to them, "The LORD bless you and keep you; the LORD make his face to shine upon you and be gracious to you; the LORD lift up his countenance upon you and give you peace." So shall they put my name upon the people of Israel, and I will bless them."

Chapter 10

How to Read and Interpret Tarot Cards Kabbalistically

Kabbalists consider there to be truly only five sefirot on the Tree of Life. We all know there arc tcn, but what the Kabbalists call the Zeir Anpin, referred to as the emotional core of the Tree, is six sefirot combined as one. These six sefirot include Chesed, Gevurah, Tiferet, Netzah, Hod, and Yesod. This now leaves us with only five sefirot altogether: Keter, Chokmah, Binah, the Zeir Anpin, and Malchut. And it is with these five sefirot that we use to read and interpret every single tarot card in the RWS deck.

Let us use the 5 of Cups card in this exercise:

This is a great card to use as an example of this Kabbalistic tarot reading system (style). And I assure you it is a proven system, and one in which all the other cards abide by.

Each tarot card is drawn upon an invisible Kabbalah Tree of Life formation. This can be easily seen on the 10 of Pentacles card where there are ten pentacles illustrated in a Tree of Life diagram. On account of this, each object touching one of the particular pentacles coincides with that specific corresponding sefirot's energy influence. This works the same for the other tarot cards but in a simpler way because the other cards just deal with five sefirot instead of ten.

Allow me to explain how this five sefirot system applies to every card. Firstly, you will have Keter at the top of the card, which connects to God's energy influence, and will represent the connection the character in the card has with their higher-self. The right side of the card will be associated with Chokmah, and contain blessings of wisdom and advice. The left side of each card connects to the energy of Binah, associated with aspects of receiving with regards to understanding. The bottom of the card connects to Malchut, which is associated with the manifest, and the things that are happening in the now (present time). Last thing to focus on is the person, persons or object placed in the center of the card, which relates to the Zeir Anpin—this is the heart of the card, the emotional connection or aspect. All these sefirot are important to understanding the deeper, and sometimes hidden, meaning each of the illustrations encompass. Therefore, all five sefirot need to be acknowledged and combined together in order to fully interpret the tarot card's illustration.

Let's break down the 5 of Cups card using this Tree of Life system, starting with Keter at the top of the card. There really isn't much here to see. It is just a gray sky. Although, the color gray always represents 'wisdom' throughout the tarot. Interesting to note is that the Hebrew word Chokmah means wisdom, and the color associated with Chokmah is gray. So, a gray-colored sky represents that God is granting His wisdom, and that the picture below depicts a life-lesson about to be learned.

This card depicts a man that is covered up in a black robe/cape, with his head down in dismay and sorrow. He looks over to the house across the river, and he desires to return. He wishes to go back to the life he once knew; his place of stability and comfort. The house is all that he focuses on and he is unable to see a way for him to return. While only focusing on the left side of the card, this man is unable to see any way (the bridge) for him to cross the river in order to get back to his home, aka his comfort zone. He is wearing all black, and the color black always relates to Saturn's influence. Saturn is known as the planet of karma, restriction. In this case, we see that this man is dealing with a karmic life-lesson. Something traumatic happened to him that he had no control of.

Let's look to the left side of this card where we see three cups toppled over. Cups represent emotions, feelings and matters of the heart. Any objects located on the left side of the card will connect to the sefirah Binah, meaning understanding. And encompass aspects of severity. Symbolized with the three cups being knocked over, we see that this man's emotional understanding has been rocked. What he once knew to be true is no longer the case anymore. This is the side of the card that he continues to focus his attention on. He doesn't see beyond the grief. And he chooses to suffer.

If he were to only look to his right, he would see the two cups, which are sitting upright and solid on the ground. These two cups, being located on the right side of the card, connect to Chokmah, meaning wisdom. And also encompass the aspect of merciful blessings. Therefore, these two cups hold helpful advice, and if the man were to turn around and see these two cups, he would be informed of the bridge nearby where he could cross and return back home safely. The suit of Cups represents matters of the heart, and the best way for us to open up our heart is to open up our ears, and allow ourselves to listen to what others have to say. We can always trust other people's advice when they speak from the heart—their words will be truthful, heartfelt and bear no ego.

This man depicted in the center of the card corresponds with the Zeir Anpin, the emotional aspect. You will notice all five cups are located at his feet—at the bottom of the card. This clues us in that he is enduring a test of his emotions in the present time. At the same time, it is apparent that he is detaching emotionally, and closing himself off from the world. This is shown by him choosing to cover himself with the black cape.

The bottom of the card connects to Malchut, meaning kingdom, and is known as the kingdom where all things manifest. As portrayed here through the depicted symbolism, this man is dealing with this emotional life-lesson now at the present moment. Something or someone he once felt an emotional attachment to broke his heart and rocked his understanding of what he thought love was or should be. Perhaps he is the one to blame in this situation? Whichever angle you look at it, he was once emotionally comfortable and now suddenly not.

Whatever happened, happened too fast. And the trauma of it all caused him emotive aftershocks. Now it is hard to stop focusing on it, and it is easy to either blame himself or play the victim. You begin to think of what you should have done or should have said to prevent it from happening in the first place. At this time, it is good to step back and take a look at the situation from an objective perspective. Time now to learn from your past mistakes and promise yourself to never repeat them. Listen to others, and be open to their heartfelt advice as you change yourself for the better, so you can return back to your stable life a changed person who has matured and grown from this situation. No need to return back through the emotional waters. Instead, it is advised to return back over the bridge and return back to a place of stability; having taken the 'high road.'

As you study the cards, you will notice how certain like-objects are grouped together with each other. These like-objects are positioned either on the right of the card or to the left, at the top or on the bottom. Pay attention to this, because the number of similar objects in a group will always correspond to the sefirah with the matching number. For instance, in the 5 of Cups the three cups on the left side of the card connect to the 3rd sefirah on the Tree of Life Binah, just like the two cups located on the right side of the card connect to the 2nd sefirah Chokmah.

The Tree of Life is based on a three-column system, which includes a left, right, and middle column. The left column connects with aspects of receiving, severity as well as understanding. While the right column corresponds with aspects of sharing, blessings of mercy as well as logical wisdom. The middle column is considered the column of mildness, which balances out the energy polarities of the left and right columns; just like the filament in a light bulb. These three columns coincide with the left, right and center of every tarot card. Other cards are not so blatant as the 5 of Cups when applying this Tree of Life system, but do in deed follow suit.

For example, you will see the four cups in a row at the bottom of the 6 of Cups card. The four of things connects to the 4th sefirah Chesed, meaning blessings of loving-kindness and mercy. And since the four cups are located at the bottom of the card, they connect to Malchut, the manifest. So, we see now that the girl in the 6 of Cups card is receiving a blessing of unconditional love at the present moment.

The 6 of Cups card pictured here:

Chapter 11

The Purpose of the 10 of Pentacles Card

The 10 of Pentacles card is a map key and acts as a cipher card for the tarot. The 10 of Pentacles should be considered one of the 'action cards' because it functions in a similar way just as the Pages and the Knights do. The 10 of Pentacles card can be used to reveal what will soon manifest into your life in the present moment.

Whenever this card is drawn it foreshadows something of importance will soon manifest into your life. It is suggested you interpret the next card drawn in its literal meaning, or in its literal context. After the 10 of Pentacles is pulled, the tarot reader will need to draw one more card to see exactly what and how the certain event will unfold. This following card drawn will correspond to one of the ten sefirot on the 10 of Pentacles card, deciphering the manifested outcome.

Furthermore, the 10 of Pentacles is a key to understanding the Kabbalah Tree of Life and the ten sefirot. Each of the ten pentacles on this card coincides with one of the ten sefirot on the Kabbalah Tree of Life, and at the same time corresponds to the object each pentacle is in proximity with or actually touching on this card.

The 10 of Pentacles card's esoteric title is The Lord of Wealth, and it depicts the wealth that the old man has manifested into his reality. This would include his family, friends, pets, large home and estate. Notice how the old man's head is close to the checkered wall? This wall divides the world of imagination from the world of manifested reality. The old man was able to create all this wealth because of his close connection to the astral realm. It was by way of inspiration, intuition and imagination that he was able to create all of this abundance—essentially, creating something out of nothing.

The 10 of Pentacles card is a map key to the Kabbalistic system of the Tarot. All ten of the pentacles on this card are formed in a Kabbalah Tree of Life formation. Each pentacle represents a sphere aka sefirah on the Tree, and is associated with that sefirah's particular energy aspects. The placement of the sefirah, represented here by the pentacle symbol, on the 10 of Pentacles card, gives us a clue to understanding the aspects of each sefirah. Furthermore, each sefirah is numbered 1 through 10, and each tarot card as well. Matching the number of the sefirah to the number of the tarot card reveals what will soon be manifested into your life.

This concept may be better understood if I were to share one or two detailed examples of a specific manifestation reading.

Example #1:

Let's use the Empress card as an example of the 10 of Pentacles manifestation reading. The question from the querent was about finance, and asking what will they soon manifest into their life financially, seeking some guidance and advice.

THE EMPRESS.

Each tarot reading is like an onion with its many layers, and as I describe and reveal each layer, your mind like an onion, will open up and expand, and the dots will eventually connect. Hopefully, the querent will experience a slight shift in their awareness of their own behavior. By the end of this reading, one's mind should be opened and elevated, and able to see the big picture, leading them to better understand what exactly it is they need to do in order to move forward in life.

Please refer to the pictures of these cards to follow along with the descriptions of the symbolism hidden within the illustrations.

So, after first pulling the 10 of Pentacles, the next card I drew was the Empress. Using the 10 of Pentacles as a map key, I am able to see how the Empress card corresponds with a particular pentacle, which represents an energy aspect of the matching sefirah, and will portray to us exactly what will manifest. Furthermore, the 10 of Pentacles signals for us to interpret the next card drawn in its literal context.

For instance, the Empress card is Roman numeral III. All the number 3 cards, and cards associated with number 3, connect to the 3rd pentacle on the 10 of Pentacles card, which corresponds to the sefirah Binah, meaning understanding. Binah is the feminine aspect of God, and she gives birth to all things, including intuitive understanding through contemplation, and literally gives birth to the whole of creation, providing the supernal womb. Do you notice that the Empress is pregnant? This is why she is wearing a loose-fitting gown and is seen here sitting on comfy pillows. There are exactly 40 pomegranates on her gown. The number 40 is significant here because a fetus is inside a mother's womb for 40 weeks before its birth. Notice there is a canal (stream) in the right background of the card? This represents a birth canal.

Notice the six-pointed stars on the Empress's crown? There are exactly 12 six-pointed stars, and $12 \times 6 = 72$. 72 is the Kabbalistic number relating to miracle making—as in the 'miracle' of birth. According to the Kabbalists, Moses engraved the 72 Names of God on his staff, which was used to part the Red Sea—one of the greatest miracles performed in the Torah.

The Empress is depicted here holding onto a golden sceptre in her right hand, which represents her authority and control over the world, and metaphorically her destiny. She has the final say on when it is time to birth something new. This concept of control is symbolized by the wheat crop at the bottom of the card. The Empress has the final say on when it is time to reap the harvest. She planted the seeds and she nurtured the crop, therefore she says when it is time to cut and to gather it.

All the number 3 cards are associated with Binah, who is ruled by Saturn. Saturn is the god of the harvest and agriculture, as well as the lord of time. Saturn is the ruling planet for both Capricorn and Aquarius. Significant here, because Aquarius is symbolized by the water bearer, and babies are birthed out of the womb from their mother's water. Capricorn is represented here as the hard worker who tends to the field, putting their hands into the creation of things and improving life for the betterment of others. So, we have the clues here that lead us to understand that the Empress is a hard worker and she wishes to improve her life as well as the lives of others around her by creating prosperity for all people and things she is involved in —whether it be business, career, charitable work, friends or family. She is the one in control of her prosperity, as well as her destiny.

We now look at one more clue, which is the heart symbol placed at the Empress's side with the astrological symbol for Venus drawn upon it. In Greek mythology, Venus (as Aphrodite) is Saturn's daughter. This being so, the heart represents that Saturn loves his daughter, but because the heart is colored gray, which throughout the tarot always represents wisdom, the Venus symbol being drawn inside the gray heart represents here that Saturn (the Empress as Binah) expresses a tough-love towards his daughter, Venus.

As I stated earlier, there are 40 pomegranates on the Empress's gown. Pomegranates throughout the tarot symbolize memory. Doctors are known to give pomegranate juice to Alzheimer's patients in order to help improve their memory. So, this is another clue that the Empress (Saturn as Binah) does not freely give love unconditionally to her daughter, Venus, because the Empress remembers the past, and she may forgive Venus's past behavior, but she will never forget. The Empress treats everyone like this, and she judges accordingly. She will not enable Venus, or anyone for that matter; she cares too much to spoil them. In addition to this, the Empress does not repeat mistakes. She remembers her mistakes, and learns from them. She is considered a nurturer when it comes to relationships, and how she treats her business, her family, her loved ones, as well as herself.

When it comes to business and relationships, the Empress approaches these things like a Capricorn would attend to a wheat crop throughout the year; nurturing it, looking after it, plowing the field, watering the crops, and planting the seeds during the appropriate times of the year. All this in total control—knowing when to either hold back or when to take action—depending on the circumstances of the current season. This is a gradual process. Only after years of practice and experimentation with the field does the Capricorn know what appropriate actions to take at the correct times of the year; as well as the daily regimens.

The Empress only wants the best for her daughter, Venus, and she wishes to one day be able to show her off and be proud of her. This concept of a child here refers to the development process of anything being taken from its seed level and growing it into something big, where you start with a simple idea and turn it into something that generates a stream of income. The Empress knows that things take time, attention and effort. It is a nurturing process. Like the fetus in the womb during pregnancy being nurtured with its mother's sustenance throughout its 40-week birthing process as it goes through the developmental stages of pregnancy, preparing the fetus to be strong enough and ready to enter the world. And this creation of life is a miracle. The newborn is full of potential and carries within it the power to change the world—hopefully for the better.

As I conclude my interpretation, the answer to the querent's question becomes more direct.

With your finances, remember this analogy and these clues about the Empress and how she handles her life. She is in control of her prosperity. She remembers her past and avoids repeating mistakes in order to improve her future. She continues practicing these new behaviors as they become habit—just the same as one would tend to their crop year after year. The Empress card has a bright yellow background, which always represents a bright future. And know that the Empress is THE symbol for prosperity in the tarot. So, you are guaranteed to have prosperity and abundance in your finances very soon.

We see here, in these cards, that the Empress, like Binah, is about to give birth to a new creation. You should act on your inspiration, especially if this idea has had time to develop and grow in your mind. Now is the time to act, and to no longer wait. The only thing holding you back now from your prosperity is you. Is there a certain thing you are passionate about and don't tell everyone about? Perhaps only your closest friends? Something you have always done since childhood that makes you happy? It is this type of thing that you need to share with the world.

Whatever it is that brings you happiness is sure to bring someone else happiness as well; no matter how silly or lame it may seem. You may think to yourself "there is no way I can make money off of this, there isn't a large enough audience". Nevertheless, you will find that the better the niche, the better chance you have at making a profit. It is now time to remove all doubt and let go of any worries you may have about the future outcome. Now is the prime time to act and give birth to your 'child', which can refer to a business venture that you may have been brainstorming, as well as some niche hobby that you rarely share with anyone. Perhaps this is the nudge you needed, giving you the confidence to begin your side-hustle? This could even refer to you applying for that dream job; the one that you feel unqualified for. Just know that you will be successful at whatever you set out to do—you will reap what you sow. All you need to do now is take the first step, and with a little effort you will soon attract the prosperity which you seek, and you will be blessed with a brighter and more financially secure new year.

Example #2:

Let us look at another example of this type of manifestation reading, one where there is another 'action' card drawn after having first pulled the 10 of Pentacles. So, for example, in a reading when the first card drawn happens to be the 10 of Pentacles you will need to pull one more card to see what will manifest into your life. This has already been explained in the example above with the Empress card, but what happens if the new card drawn after the 10 of Pentacles happens to be a Knight or a Page? What then? At this point you must draw one more card to reveal the climactic outcome gathered from the two previous action cards pulled. Action cards such as Knights and Pages never answer the querent's question completely, so you must keep drawing new cards from the deck until you get either a King, Queen or any one of the Major or Minor Arcana in order to culminate a final answer.

Pictured below is a scenario of a general reading where the Knight of Cups was drawn after the 10 of Pentacles. And thus, one more card needed to be drawn in order to understand the Knight's message, and to reveal what exactly was going to manifest. That final card drawn happened to be the Hierophant.

KNIGHT of CUPS.　THE HIEROPHANT.

All the Knights of the tarot are messengers that deliver a call to action, and this knight in particular delivers an inspired heartfelt message. The following card drawn, the Hierophant, portrays and relays this knight's message. Because this was a general reading, the querent is represented here by the Hierophant, who is a wise man that people approach seeking life advice and spiritual guidance. The Hierophant is the middleman between the people and their higher-selves. The Hierophant holds the keys to occult secrets and mysteries, and he shares his knowledge with those who seek it, but he typically tends to hold back and not reveal too much of his wisdom—only revealing what needs to be heard and understood at the time. He believes some people are not spiritually mature enough to handle such deeper wisdom. With the Knight of Cups drawn before the Hierophant, we may be safe to assume that the Hierophant will experience a change of heart and feel as though he no longer needs to hold back. He is advised now to come out of his shell, his comfort zone, and speak openly as he delivers a heartfelt message.

This reading advises the querent to follow their inspiration confidently, moving ahead with certainty, perhaps zealously, opening themselves up and showing their true self to others. They should no longer hold back what's needed to be said. The querent will begin to speak from their heart as well as their mind, and no longer be afraid to 'get things off their chest.' They will no longer hold back their emotions and feelings. The querent will let people know how they really feel without worrying about what others will think of them. They will allow others to judge them however they wish, as they let their guard down. The Hierophant will have said what needed to be said even if he delivers a hard pill to swallow. He will find the confidence to speak the truth from the heart without regret or remorse—completely unapologetic.

Because the Hierophant card is assigned to the Roman numeral V it corresponds with the 5th pentacle on the 10 of Pentacles card. This pentacle is located on the left side of the card, the second pentacle from the top. This 5th pentacle is located directly on top of the checkered wall which symbolically divides the astral realm from the material realm. Moreover, this 5th pentacle is placed directly above the door on the bridge that has the red windows. This door or gate allows entry into the upper world of Atziluth where Binah, the motherly aspect of God, resides. This pentacle corresponds with the sefirah Gevurah. Gevurah's energy relates to matters of the ego. Gevurah is the watch dog or protector who stands guard over this door, and he does not allow anything or anyone to enter that may harm or pose a threat to his mother, Binah. Gevurah is very protective of his mother. If any harm were to happen to her, it would break his heart. Gevurah sits on the checkered wall that divides the light from the dark—the good ideas from the bad ones. Gevurah acts as the judge with a strong sense of discernment only allowing in those things which are good and would not wreak havoc in the conscious upper world of Atziluth. As Gevurah stands guard over this door, he prevents bad things from exiting as well, which includes negative words and behaviors. And he does this selfishly, not because he worries about how his unruly actions will affect others, but more so worries about the way others will perceive him. He understands the concept of what goes around, comes around so he is mindful. But ultimately, he is more concerned about protecting his own reputation and his fragile ego. Now that we have uncovered the darker side of Gevurah, we can apply this understanding to draw deeper meaning from the Hierophant card.

Moving forward, the Hierophant card shows two men who approach the Hierophant, seeking his guidance. They wish to learn the esoteric mysteries and occult knowledge. The Hierophant, (who represents our querent), may have been holding back before, but now he must learn to say what needs to be said and speak from the heart. The Knight of Cups calls on the Hierophant to speak freely and no longer care about what others will think of him.

Although, it is advised to think before you speak, and make sure your words are truthful. Say what needs to be said, but try to be tactful in your approach. Regardless, it is healthy to tell people what they need to hear. God uses people as his messengers. Therefore, you must become a channel and allow God to speak through you. Say what needs to be heard instead of what you think others wish to hear. Be straight forward and do not sugarcoat it. This all starts with you listening to your inner voice and learning to trust it. Opening the door on the bridge in the 10 of Pentacles is a metaphor for opening your heart. Open the door and allow the spirit into your heart. When you speak from the heart, you speak with truth.

This concludes the example reading. Apparently, a lot of detail can be drawn and interpreted from using just a couple of cards due to the fact each card holds within it so much Kabbalistic wisdom, esoteric and occult knowledge. So much so that it usually takes only one card to answer any and most all tarot questions. Although, once in a while an action card is drawn, which warrants having to pull an additional card. And as a consequence, makes the reading a bit more interesting.

Chapter 12

The System of the Court Cards

The Court Cards are grouped in their own section of the tarot, and function as 'action' cards. With that in mind, the Pages announce change, the Knights deliver a call to action, the Queens receive deeper understandings of the heart, while the Kings offer wisdom gathered from their logical perceptions.

Each tarot suit corresponds to each of the Kabbalah Four Worlds. This applies to the Minors as well as the Court cards. Wands are associated with the world of Atziluth, Cups with Briah, Swords with Yetzirah, and Pentacles with Assiah. The Four Worlds, sometimes counted with a prior stage (Adam Kadmon) to make Five Worlds, are the comprehensive categories of spiritual realms in Kabbalah in the descending chain of existence.

However, the Aces are assigned to the letter Shin, which corresponds to the element spirit, and therefore is associated with the upper realm of the Adam Kadmon. Worth mentioning here is that the Fool card also corresponds with the spiritual energy of the Aces, whereas if you were to examine the illustration closely you will find the letter Shin drawn on the Fool's shirt.

The elemental associations of the Kabbalah Worlds correspond to the five letters in the holy name YHShVH, Yeshua, meaning salvation. The pentagram graphic depicts these elemental associations with their corresponding Hebrew letter in respect to the name Yeshua.

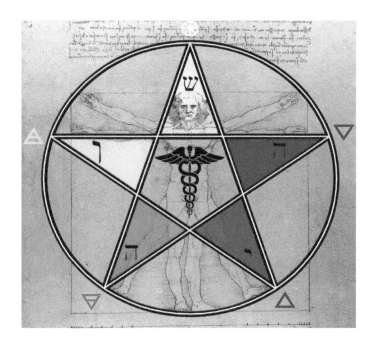

The Holy Name Yeshua, YHShVH

י = Y	Kings	Fire	Chokmah
ה = H	Queens	Water	Binah
שׁ = Sh	Aces	Spirit	Keter
ו = V	Knights	Air	Tiferet
ה = H	Pages	Earth	Malchut

Allow me to explain the functionality of each set of Court Cards, beginning with the Pages.

The Pages:

All Pages correspond to the element of earth, and are directly related to a change that is about to occur in the present time, taking place in the physical reality on the earthly plane of Malchut, which is the Kingdom where all things manifest.

In a tarot reading, the Pages announce a change is coming. Therefore, you must draw one more card to see how exactly this particular change will correspond and effect the interpretation of the following card. This can be considered as approaching the newly drawn card in its 'reversed' meaning or opposite interpretation in accordance to the certain aspect of change announced from the Page. Each Page will relay a different aspect of change that will reverse the context or intention portrayed in the next card that is drawn.

Page of Wands:

The Page of Wands announces a change in one's creative, passionate and ego-driven desire. This particular Page is wearing salamanders on his shirt. Salamanders are known for coming out of hiding whenever there is a heavy rain storm, and then quickly go back into hiding once the rain stops. Salamanders are attracted to the excitement. This is a clue that change of energies is happening now, and that now is the time to ignite your creative idea and/or share your opinion or knowledge of what you feel passionate about. It is your time to shine. Therefore, be ambitious and strive for success. The time is now to show initiative. Notice that there are exactly five leaves on the wand that the page is holding? The number 5 connects to the sefirah Gevurah, which contains attributes of ambition, drive and initiative—matters pertaining to the ego, as well as the Life-Force energy within.

PAGE of WANDS.

Wands represent the element of Fire. Likewise, salamanders are known for being able to walk through fire without getting burnt. Notice that the feather on the page's hat is a red fiery flame? And his boots contain flames as well? This reinstates the fire element connection with the suit of Wands. Also worth mentioning is that this page is standing in the middle of the desert. This is significant here, because deserts throughout the tarot, as well as in the Torah, always represent ego. This ego-driven change can be seen in both a positive or negative polarity, either it creates or consumes, but it essentially is a spark which initiates the will to desire pleasure.

The Page of Wands connects to the World of Emanation, Atziluth, where change is typically triggered by something a person sees. Usually something that entices and intrigues them so much that they too strive to own or obtain a particular object someone else has, as well as begin emulating other people's personality traits they wish they possessed themselves.

Page of Cups:

The Page of Cups announces a change of heart is about to occur. And it is presumably a change for the better. This page is standing on dry land, on a firm foundation, and is seen holding a cup in his hand that has a fish inside of it. The fish was recently swimming in the sea of emotions, and the page kindly scooped the fish out with his cup and brought it safely onto dry land. So, metaphorically speaking, from a place of worry to a place of mental stability. Also, this page is wearing a shirt covered in red flowers, which represents mildness, love and feelings of joy. The fish is no longer in an emotional state, and has become grounded and brought back into reality—down to earth and out of its head, which can be full of anxiety and fear. The sea is deep and corresponds to subconscious feelings and emotions, as well as psychic insights. This sudden change of heart can be brought on either by a message received in a dream or by something someone said. For this reason, it is wise to always remain open to receiving messages from the Universe. The suit of Cups is associated with matters of the heart, and the best way to open up your heart is by opening our ears. People are God's messengers. Always be open and willing to listen to what others have to say, especially when their words come from their heart.

PAGE of CUPS.

The Page of Cups connects to the World of Creation, Briah, associated with the element water. A change in this world is typically triggered by something a person hears from either another person or from the voice within.

Page of Swords:

This page announces that a change of mind is about to occur. The Page of Swords stands on high ground looking over the valley with the wind in his face. This page connects to the World of Formation, Yetzirah, associated with the element air. A change in this world is sometimes altered by something detected by a person's sense of smell. Hence, the reasoning for the wind to be blowing directly in this page's face. The wind brings with it certain aromas that cause the page to reflect upon a past familiarity. This could give way to new insight on something that should be proceeded with caution, like smoke from a fire or a gas leak. On the other hand, this new scent could be an unordinary perfume, leading one to suspect their lover of cheating.

Besides smells, thoughts also come to us unexpectedly and alter our perception of what we initially thought to be true. These types of changes are always positive and lead us towards a greater good.

PAGE of SWORDS.

Do you notice there are exactly ten birds flying in the sky over the page's head? Ten of things connect to the energy aspect of the 10th sefirah Malchut, the kingdom where all things manifest and form. As the receiving sphere of all the other sefirot, Malchut gives tangible form to the other emanations. The page is seen here forming either a new idea or a new hypothesis. Something has triggered a new change of mind and/or has sparked a new curiosity.

Page of Pentacles:

This page announces a change occurring at the present time, dealing with something that is tangible, and has to do with something we all are able to perceive with our five senses—particularly something that exists within the 1% physical reality of the material world. This can include worldly possessions, family, friends, partners, pets, job, career, hobbies, projects, written works, as well as social status and reputation. This particular change may include how others perceive and judge you on your outer appearance. This aspect of change can relate to changes in one's physical health as well.

The Page of Pentacles connects to the World of Substance, Assiah, which relates to the element earth, and corresponds with all things we can touch. Thereby, things that have form.

This concludes the Pages.

We now move forward and begin to describe the Knights.

The Knights:

Each Knight connects to the element air, and corresponds to the sefirah Tiferet, which is the center (core) of the Tree of Life. It is also associated with the heart chakra, and specifically pertains to matters of the heart. Tiferet is said to encompass all the sefirot of Zeir Anpin, a revealed aspect of God in Kabbalah, comprising the emotional sefirot attributes: Chesed, Gevurah, Tiferet, Netzach, Hod, and Yesod. With this considered, all Knights embody the concept of the Hermetic Marriage. Whereas the Knights represent male energy, while their horses represent female energy, and they converge as one. It portrays a union merging between the two opposite polarities. Note that all throughout the tarot horses reflect feminine energy.

Moreover, all Knights in the tarot deliver a call to action, delivering a profound message that rocks one's emotional core. These messages are usually something that a person needs to hear opposed to what they want to hear.

The Knights ignite a desire for one to step out of their comfort zone, and to no longer remain complacent—sparking within them a desire to receive pleasure. The Knights are messengers who announce the time to act is now.

Each 'call to action' is distinctive depending on the particular Knight's suit. The elemental energy influenced by each Knight will place an emphasis on how you should manifest your desire, and at the same time obligates you to take appropriate action towards achieving a goal. For example, the Knight of Wands pushes you to take the first step towards manifesting your brilliant idea, the one you keep putting off. Each tarot card encompasses its own intention consisting of a complexity of polarities. The Knights request you manifest a specific aspect as if it is your new mission. This certain aspect is revealed when you draw the next card.

Knight of Wands:

The suit of Wands represents fire and passion. In correspondence to this, the knight here is seen holding a large wand in his hand just as if it were a large match stick used to ignite the spark of creativity. He awakens a desire to obtain more out of life and to stir excitement. There are exactly five leaves on this wand, which connects to the energy aspect of the 5th sefirah Gevurah—the sefirah associated with ego-driven desires. There are three similar leaves on the horse's strap, which coincide with Binah, meaning understanding. We see here that the knight sees what he likes and is driven to either achieve or obtain this particular thing. The more he researches, learns or gains knowledge of that particular thing he is interested in the more fuel is thrown into his fire (so to speak). Sometimes people get excited about something and they study all about the thing or build an opinion about a certain subject or object, but they never follow through with the idea or project, whatever it is. This knight of wands delivers the message that the time is now to act and to create. It is time now to do something with what you have been excited about. It's time now to stop thinking, and start doing. Take the first step towards your goal.

KNIGHT of WANDS.

This knight adorns salamanders on his shirt. Salamanders are known for coming out of hiding during a heavy rain storm, but then quickly go back into hiding when the rain clears up. Whenever this particular knight is drawn, it is a clue telling you that now is the time for you to begin whatever it is you have been putting off. Most of the time people are in a state of complacency and are comfortable with the way things are going in their life, and they tend to lack a desire for desire. When we feel the creative spark go off (the light bulb) we need to act on it and put those ideas into action. When this knight is drawn, it gives you the extra nudge needed to get the ball rolling. It is time now to be ambitious and show initiative. These such 'windows of opportunity' are rare. You need to act on these feelings fast before the opportunity passes you by. This knight ignites the soul's life-force energy, awakening the desire to create something that aligns with your life's true purpose, leaving you with a sense of fulfillment. Someone wise once told me, "If you are not creating, then you are dying".

Located in this card's background is a desert, and deserts throughout the tarot and in the Torah symbolize the ego. This is because there is no life in the desert, and this being the case, the desert provides a person with the right circumstances and conditions needed for them to get in touch with and connect to their spiritual-self. The desert is a pristine location for one to experience profound spiritual awakenings. Ergo, the brightest Light comes from the darkest of places. The Knight of Wands is depicted here riding a fiery horse, which represents the spark of life, and they are both seen jumping up into the air and out far away from the desert beneath them; metaphorically portrayed here as rising above their ego-inclination. The ego has the power to either lift us up or drag us down.

The ego can be compared to a muscle. A muscle is always eating. If you don't feed it, it will feed on and devour itself. This process is called Catabolysis, where the body catabolizes itself. Catabolysis is a biological process in which the body breaks down fat and muscle tissue in order to stay alive. Catabolysis occurs only when there is no longer any source of protein, carbohydrate or vitamin nourishment feeding all body systems; it is the most severe type of malnutrition. As above, so below. This concept of catabolysis can apply to spiritual development as well. Think of the ego as a muscle in this way, seeing how we must feed it so it doesn't begin eating away at us. This is the concept behind tithing 10%. We give in order to receive, but we only need to give 10%. This 10% can pertain to money or charitable acts, as well as our time. To better understand this concept, consider the symbol for Yin Yang where there are two equal parts of black and white. Have you ever noticed that there are two small dots of opposite colors on each side of the symbol? (A black dot on the white side and a white dot on the black side.) When you understand the concept of the 10% tithe, then you see that the black dot on the white side is not a dot at all; it is a black hole. The white spot was taken out of the white side (Yang) and placed inside the black side (Yin), which gave the 10% from the Yang over to the dark side Yin (ego), which is just the right amount of nourishment that it needs. With further examination, you will realize that the salamanders on the knight's shirt are circle-shaped, and have the left side of them dark while the right side is light, which is the exact same design as the Yin Yang symbol. Therefore, we feed the ego 10% in order to satisfy its hunger, otherwise it will gradually devour our soul just as in catabolysis.

As stated earlier, salamanders only come out of hiding for a short period of time whenever there is a heavy rain storm. They feed on the excitement of it all, and then return back into hiding as soon as the storm stops. For the most part, the weather is calm and it storms only 10% of the time.

Knight of Cups:

This knight is wearing Mercury's wings on his helmet as well as on his shoes. Mercury is the planet of communication, inspiration and quickness—urgency. And as you already know, Cups represent matters of the heart. So, when combining this symbolism together we see that the Knight of Cups is inspired to deliver a heartfelt message that needs   to be heard.

KNIGHT of CUPS.

He is placed before a river and a mountain, symbolizing there are momentous obstacles he must face. No matter how big the obstacle, his message is too important to not deliver, and he cannot allow anything to stand in his way; no matter what.

The knight sits upon a gray horse, and the color gray always represents wisdom throughout the tarot. Wisdom holds in it truth, and truth always has a way of coming out and being heard. The sky in the background is gray as well, further reinstating that truth shall prevail and encompass all.

The knight's shirt is covered in red fish. Red represents passion and drive, while fish represent emotions and feelings. These two symbols when combined symbolize that this knight feels passionately driven to share his message, which contains in it aspects of emotional truths that will rock someone's core; in hopes that the truth will set them free. This truth is symbolized by the knight's armor, which protects him and empowers his sense of zeal.

This knight holds his cup with his right hand. Right hands coincide with the side of our soul that corresponds with sharing and/or giving. This is why we shake hands with our right hand. On the Kabbalah Tree of Life, the right column is the side of blessings, mercy and kindness. It is apparent that the Knight of Cups is truly a knight in shining armor coming to set you free from your emotional bondage.

Knight of Swords:

The suit of Swords represents thoughts and spirit. This particular knight is depicted racing on his horse against the wind and against the odds, (or obstacles in his way), as he delivers his inspired and brilliant idea.

KNIGHT of SWORDS.

This knight is wearing a red cape. And the color red represents ambition, passion and fiery drive. The knight's horse is colored gray, which represents wisdom. Therefore, we see here that the knight is driven to share his newly realized, albeit brilliant idea.

Notice there are two cardinals on the horse's strap. Cardinals have been considered messengers sent by the spirit world for quite literally thousands of years. There being two cardinals connects to the 2nd sefirah Chokmah, meaning wisdom. These cardinals are spiritual messengers that specifically bring newly realized wisdom and insights.

This notion of cardinals being spiritual messengers spreads across a number of different cultures. Wherever these beautiful red songbirds are found, the legend arises. It's therefore not too surprising to see the word 'cardinal' used to signify an important or meaningful object, or relationship. Whether it's cardinal angels, cardinal directions, or cardinal colors, the use of the word denotes something big and noteworthy. This makes it especially appropriate that the word itself contains the Latin root word cardo, which means either an axis or a hinge; a point which everything revolves around or holds all moving parts together. Cardinals are, resultantly, viewed as the revolving point between our world and the spirit world, acting as messengers between the two.

Not only are they spiritual messengers, Cardinals are also a symbol of devotion. The Knight of Swords is full of passionate zeal and devoted to deliver his inspired idea, as if it is a powerful epiphany, and he is determined to act on it and manifest this new idea urgently.

There are four butterflies on the horse's strap, and butterflies throughout the tarot always symbolize manifestation. Taking this into account, a caterpillar must endure a period of solitude before transforming into a butterfly. There are exactly four butterflies, and the number four directly connects to aspects of Jupiter because it rules over the 4th sefirah Chesed, which is attributed to merciful blessings. We see here that the knight has been blessed with a brilliant idea and he is compelled to act on it, and make it so, no matter what obstacle stands in his way.

In the card's background, the clouds in the sky are similar to lightning bolts, and flying in the sky near these clouds is a flock of five birds. Five of things relate directly to the 5th sefirah Gevurah, which corresponds to attributes of the ego, and in this case, it coincides with the aspect of desiring pleasure and fulfillment. This particular idea that has been implanted, and gifted to the knight, has ignited and sparked within him a surge of life-force energy. This has given the knight a new found passion and new sense of purpose; along with new direction. This knight is completely devoted to this new cause.

This feeling, this powerful urge to take action, comes from his heart, and he commits to this new-found passion and allows it to lead him. He feels now that he is serving a higher calling. This concept of heartfelt devotion is symbolized by the small red heart drawn on the horse's head strap.

The knight's horse is jumping up and out of the desert below him. As mentioned, deserts throughout the tarot symbolize aspects of negative ego—deserts being a symbol for complacency as well as spiritual death. This new surge of electricity and excitement is just the thing needed to get this knight up and off his feet.

Knight of Pentacles:

The suit of Pentacles represents practical matters that are down-to-earth. Considering that, pentacles are associated with the element earth and material tangible things. This can include physical health, family, friends, money, and can also relate to how others perceive us, as in our physical appearance as well as our reputation.

KNIGHT of PENTACLES.

The Knight here is seen sitting on a black horse, and black throughout the tarot always connects to Saturn's energy and its planetary influences. Saturn is the god of agriculture, and this is why there is a freshly plowed field depicted in the distance. Saturn is also the lord of time. This gives us a clue that it is time to plant the seeds in the freshly plowed field below.

Moreover, the knight and his horse both adorn white oak

leaves on their heads. White oak is asymbol for rebirth.

The Druids used oak trees in spells for stability, safety, strength and achievement. In North American culture, white oaks are a historical symbol of peace and calmness. Many communities have planted white oak trees to create a calm space and a sense of peace. The white oak often symbolizes serenity.

Metaphorically speaking, when the soil is fertile, it presents a prime time for planting seeds that will birth strong friendships, set up successful careers and positively shift one's lifestyle choices to be geared towards benefiting their long-term health.

The hard work is done and now it is time to simply plant seeds, and watch them grow. Oak trees grow from a tiny acorn seed. Only about 1 in 10, 000 seeds grow into an oak tree, so plant a lot. But know that all big things come from small beginnings.

This concludes the Knights. Proceeding forward, we begin describing the Queens.

The Queens:

The Queens are the archetypes of the feminine energy aspects embraced in each of their particular suits. Kabbalistically, the Queens incorporate the energy aspect of Binah, the 3rd sefirah on the Kabbalah Tree of Life. Generally, they tend to be introverted, passive and idealistically the receivers of their energy. Typically, they are emotionally touched by what they hear, which warms their hearts. Opening up their hearts to new understanding allows them to understand one matter out of another matter—derive one idea from another idea.

The tarot looks upon gender as being more energy based opposed to being biological.

The Kings represent positive charge and correspond with the right column energy on the Kabbalah Tree of Life, which relates to giving, sharing and action, while the Queens are associated with the left column aspects of the Tree, relating to the negative charge, selfishness and passive receiving. Both the Kings and Queens project big personality along with a strong and solid spirit.

Queen of Wands:

This queen is focused on the positive. She gazes out into the future with a positive outlook, and is able to see the good in everything. She holds onto a large sun flower and offers it to others as an attempt to cheer them up and brighten their day.

This queen does have a negative side, but she never allows others to see it. Whenever she has a negative thought, she bites her tongue and keeps her opinion to herself. If she has nothing nice to say, then she doesn't say anything at all. This is symbolized by her wand being placed inside the cement foundation, as opposed to being set on the outside like we see depicted in the King of Wands card. In contrast to this, the King of Wands is considered extraverted and out-spoken, whereas the Queen of Wands is more introverted and reserved. Wands can relate to wisdom and knowledge that is rooted deeply within our belief system and opinions. Through this card's symbolism, we see this queen holding back her opinions and holding back truths that may impact someone negatively. The color gray represents wisdom throughout the tarot, and we see here the gray-colored foundation in which the queen sits upon, which leads to the reasoning for why she places her wand upon this foundation, and inside the cemented area. This reinstates that she is wise and intuitively knows certain unspoken truths about people she cares about. She wishes to keep the peace, and would never use such private information to hurt others. She will not be tempted to use such secrets either to build herself up or for tearing others down —she will refrain from belittling people and/or ruining their reputations. She prides herself in taking the high road.

You will notice the queen has a black cat who sits outside this cement foundation, and this cat guards the queen from any and all negativity that may harm her emotionally. Female black cats are known by the mystics as possessing a negative energy. This energy tends to have a passiveness to it, whereby one must earn the cat's trust, as opposed to a dog that approaches everyone uninhabited and immediately loves them unconditionally. Black cats tend to be drawn to negative energy, and are known to absorb it. This is why they have gotten the bad reputation for being bad luck. It was believed to be a bad omen if a black cat were to cross your path. But on the contrary, since black cats absorb negative energy, they can be considered to be good luck. For instance, they absorb the bad luck around you, and in turn protect you from surrounding negative influences. This is the reasoning of why the Egyptians mummified their cats; to protect themselves from evil entities in the afterlife.

This queen sits mild-mannered in the middle of this card. She corresponds with and represents the middle, central column, on the Tree of Life. Moreover, illustrated on the left side of the card is a desert, symbolizing the Tree's left column of severity, while the right side of the card is depicted as gray land, corresponding with the Tree's right column energy which relates to mercy, and because gray is associated with wisdom, we see symbolized here that the queen is blessed with wisdom and may offer practical advice. Knowing that if she were to focus on the good as well as be grateful for the blessings in her life, opposed to the negativity which is portrayed on the left side of the card, then she will attract more positivity into her life. Deserts throughout the tarot always represent negative ego traits, such as delinquency and spiritual neglect. Nothing is alive in the desert, and it can be considered as a place of spiritual complacency.

The Queen of Wands remains focused on her happy thoughts and ways of creating more joy. You will notice that located behind her head and painted on her throne are two lions who are dancing happily together as though they are celebrating. Two of things (like-objects) connect to the 2nd sefirah Chokmah, meaning wisdom. We see here that the queen is wise to focus her fiery energy, represented by the red lions who both have fiery flames for tails. She focuses on ways to sustain this passionate, fun-loving, energy and harnesses it to create harmony and joy for all. Furthermore, there are three sunflowers depicted on her throne as well. Three of things connect to the 3rd sefirah Binah, meaning understanding. Binah is the feminine aspect of God, which gives birth to all creation. Thus, these three sunflowers represent joy, and the conscious creation of it, to birth joy in others as well as herself. Through this symbolism, we see that the queen is inspired to create joy by creating it within herself and then leading by example with faith that others will also understand the importance of unity in diversity, and then adopt this quality. In addition to this, this queen is wearing a crown which connects to the 1st sefirah Keter, meaning crown. This crown represents her direct connection to Keter, the higher realm where one receives Godly insights and divine inspiration. We see here that the queen's crown is in close proximity to both the lion and sunflower symbols painted on her throne, suggesting these concepts portrayed through the symbolism are revealed to her from the higher-self.

Located on the queen's wand are three leaves, which connect to the 3rd sefirah Binah. Yet again, through symbols we see that the queen absorbs energy and analyzes internally, which builds upon her knowledge base. Like a mother who births a child, she transforms that knowledge into wisdom.

The Queen of Wands wears a necklace around her neck adorning a female lion on it, which hangs over her heart. This signifies that she has a lion's heart. The lion has always been a symbol of courage. The term 'lion-heart' is used for a person who possesses exceptional courage and fortitude. She is a very brave person—a lion-heart means a very fearless person. This queen can deal with any kind of danger or fear because of her resilient optimism.

Queen of Cups:

This queen bottles up her memories, and these memories contain within them her anchored emotions. And these memories are held inside her Holy Grail, which is depicted here as the intricate cup she is holding. This cup is guarded by two cherubim angels. Just like the queen's cup, the Ark of the Covenant was also known to be protected by two cherubim who acted as guardians who protected the contents concealed within the golden chest. In this case the queen's heart is symbolized by the cup, which can be compared to the holy ark.

QUEEN of CUPS.

Inside this cup, the queen's emotions remain bottled up and controlled, giving her the strength to refrain from expressing herself aggressively, or by acting out in a fervid outburst. This queen is a self-contained person. Therefore, she thinks before she speaks. Consciously, she takes a beat and analyzes her feelings before she reacts in any way. Thus, she is considered to have total control over her emotions. Like her cup, (her ark or Holy Grail), she too is a holy vessel, as well as emotionally intelligent. Her soul is deep, with a strong visual memory, enabling her to revive past emotions attached to those memories. Having a strong sense of memory is her superpower, which others see as psychic ability.

This queen sits on her gray-colored throne, and as stated earlier gray represents wisdom throughout the tarot. However, her throne is unique. Whereas, it has a reddish hue added to the gray; red relating to passion, lust, drive, ambition. The mixture of these two colors on her throne (red-gray) symbolizes that she is emotionally intelligent, implying that she thinks before she acts. She is mindful as she pursues any passionate endeavors.

The throne's backrest as well as headrest are colored black;

black being the color which represents Saturn's influence. Saturn embodies a tough-love nature, alluding to this queen's motto that she 'forgives but never forgets.' She does not repeat her past mistakes, especially the ones that hurt her emotionally, thus causing her to be less naive and quicker to avoid drama; knowing that 'if they did it once, they'll do it again.' She is empathetic, enabling her to literally feel everyone else's feelings in the very moment she remembers her own past experiences. By stepping into other people's shoes, she experiences both sides of the story. Thus, seeing past situations in the big picture, as a third-party observer would. Practicing this sense of empathy gives her somewhat of a psychic ability superpower. As she sits at the edge of the Sea of Emotions, she gazes upon her Grail as if it is a crystal ball, visualizing the memories from her past experiences; she is enthralled in the act of feeling her emotions once again. She allows the waves to crash upon her and lets the water douse her and flow threw her, becoming one with the sea, as the rip current pulls her back deep into the undertow of her subconscious mind—a self-inflicted trance state. Although, she must not allow herself to go in too deep and risk drowning. Mark the way she sits in the low-tide water along the edge of the sea. When comparing the water with emotions, notice how she pushes her limits of how much emotion she can handle. She is advised by the three cherubs on her throne to snap out of her trance before it's too late; before the moon rises, effecting the height of the ocean's tide. As a result, the waves will come crashing down on her before she ever realizes it.

The queen's Grail can be compared to a magic crystal ball, but instead of being able to foresee the future, she reflects upon the past. Nevertheless, she predicts the future based on past experiences, knowing that history has a way of repeating itself.

The queen's crown symbolizes her direct connection to Keter, the higher realm of consciousness, from where she receives her divine inspiration and godly insights. Her crown is close in proximity to the cherubs on her throne, establishing her connection as well as communication with the Divine.

Both, the cherubs as well as Keter reside in the upper world of Yitzerah, which just so happens to be the realm that is home to Binah. It is no coincidence that there are exactly three cherubs on the queen's throne, which reflects the energy influence of Binah, the third sefirah on the Kabbalah Tree of Life. This connection incorporates Binah's spiritual relation which the three cherubs embody as they fraternize on the queen's throne.

Cherubs are one of the many symbols for the archangel Raziel and they represent his spiritual influence. Raziel, whose name means 'secrets of God', is associated with revealing God's wisdom. These cherubs, illustrated so close to the queen's crown, symbolize the communicating and sharing of such godly messages and secrets, which reveal pearls of wisdom. Moreover, cherubs symbolize Raziel who is the ruling angel of Chokmah—Chokmah, meaning wisdom. Therefore, each time we see cherubs on a throne we are safe to assume that they are communicating, advising and sharing such godly things.

You will notice there is a cherub at the bottom of the queen's throne holding a fish as he blesses it. The word cherub, plural cherubim, likely borrowed from a derived form of Akkadian: karabu 'to bless' such as karibu 'one who blesses.' Throughout the tarot, fish symbolize emotions and feelings. When interpreting the tarot, fish can symbolize or represent an individual who is currently dealing with this type of inner struggle, i.e., the fish in the Page of Cups card. This cherub is depicted here as blessing the fish as he pulls the fish out of the water. This fish may have had enough swimming in the sea of its own emotions and this cherub was there, sympathetically, to pull the fish out and provide comfort, show grace and offer his blessing. It is easy to get caught up in and over analyze our emotions. We can sink deep and eventually allow ourselves to get sunk down into the emotional abyss where we drown. Sometimes it takes our guardian angel to come rescue us, and pull us up and out of our emotional abyss.

The emotional sea rises just as our blood pressure does, which can cause us to react in a fight or flight behavior. However, the Queen of Cups has control over her emotions and knows when to take a beat and pause to take a breath. Although, she pushes herself and continues to test her limits of just how far deep into her subconscious she can go—a spelunker of the mind, analyzing the heart. Her cherubs bless her with the strength needed to pull herself together and snap out of it—her self-induce hypnotic state.

Finally, yet importantly, the Queen of Cups adorns a necklace that has a shell amulet on it, and it dangles over her heart. This amulet symbolizes the essence of this queen, and reflects the thing she holds close to her heart, which is her core values. This shell holds within it a pearl—a pearl of wisdom. A natural pearl forms when an irritant works its way into a particular species of oyster, mussel or clam. As a defense mechanism, the mollusk secretes a fluid to coat the irritant. Layer upon layer of this coating is deposited on the irritant until a lustrous pearl is formed. This process is similar to how the cherubs protect the queen from emotional irritants. Instead of killing off or getting rid of the 'irritants', the cherubs guide and bless these negative feelings, transforming them into pearls of wisdom that can be later referred back on as having been 'learning experiences.'

The Queen of Cups is essentially the Queen of Hearts, and her Holy Grail is comparable to the Sacred Heart. With further examination you will notice the shape of the Sacred Heart is similar to two astrological symbols for Saturn placed together. The symbol for Saturn looks like the number 5 with a cross on top. Seen pictured here.

When these two symbols are placed together side by side, they form the Sacred Heart.

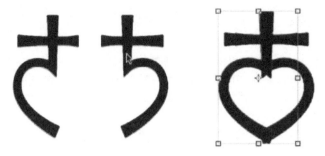

The astrological symbol for Saturn looks like a human ear. When you place two together just as you would two human ears it forms the shape of a heart, and therefore whenever you open up your ears you open up your heart. Jesus said that the only way to the Father was through him. Jesus is the way. Jesus Christ is the Sacred Heart. So, in order to communicate to the Father, to the Higher-Self we must learn to open up our heart.

The Queen of Cups' grail has two cherubs on it, protecting her heart. You will notice how those cherubs, when flipped upside down, are shaped just like the astrological symbol for Saturn. The queen needs to place the two cherubs together in order to unlock her heart. She needs to open her ears and listen to the cherub guardian angels that are trying to help her.

Queen of Swords:

This queen sits high on the mountain peak, overlooking the valley below. Like all tarot Queens, she represents Binah who resides in the upper realm of Atziluth, the realm associated with the sense of sight. You will notice that each of the Queens are depicted focusing intensely at a particular object held in their hands.

The suit of Swords represents thoughts, and we see here the queen holding her sword upright into the air as if it were an antenna, using it to attract inspiration. She sits on the mountain peak high in the air as close as she can to the source of inspiration and Godly insights, known as Keter. As mentioned earlier, Keter, meaning crown, is the 1st sefirah on the Tree of Life, who's connection is symbolized by the queen's crown placed upon her head aka crown chakra. Directly above her crown is a single bird flying over her head which alludes to her connection with Keter, the 1st sefirah. Through the symbolism of the single bird flying directly over the queen's crown we see that the queen has a direct connection with Keter, the source of divine insight and revelation. From the mountain peak the queen is able to oversee her thoughts. With her sword held in the air, she attracts an idea and is able to envision that idea from its beginning seed to its fruition; she is able to see the big picture and the idea's full potential of how it will impact the world as it matures and develops into something great. This queen has the gift of vision; a spiritual discernment—wisdom, understanding and intelligence of the mind. The Queen of Swords lives by the wise words of Loa Tzu (author of the Toa Te Ching), "Watch your thoughts; they become words. Watch your words; they become actions. Watch your actions; they become a habit. Watch your habits; they become your character. Watch your character; it becomes destiny." What we think, we become. She envisions her destiny through inspiration, and then is able to see the idea all the way through, from beginning to end, which is represented by the two moon phases on her throne; the waxing and waning crescent moon phases touching back-to-back looking like butterfly wings—a symbol throughout the tarot signifying transformation and manifestation. She has three butterflies on her throne. Three of things connect to the energy aspect of Binah, meaning understanding, and is associated with the feminine energy of the Tree of Life which relates to birthing/manifesting things. Throughout the tarot, butterflies represent manifestation, and this queen is wise and understands the manifestation process. This process involves meditation as a means to receive intelligent inspirational insights. With her sword held high in the air, like a large antenna, she tunes into the frequency of the Divine. Once she connects to a frequency and tunes in to the inspirations revealed to her, she is able to visualize exactly how her ideas will unfold. You may have noticed this queen is sitting here on the mountain top isolated from everyone. She is like a caterpillar who must endure a period of isolation before transforming into a butterfly.

This queen is lucky, seen here with the wind on her back, and a cherub (guardian angel) by her side. Throughout the tarot, cherubs symbolize archangel Raziel—the one who sits closest to God, and learns all God's secrets. According to the Targum on Ecclesiastes 10:20 (A Targum is a version or a 'translation.'), "Each day the angel Raziel makes proclamations on Mount Horeb, from heaven, of the secrets of men to all that dwell upon the earth, and his voice resounds throughout the world". Taking this into account, the Queen of Swords can be considered to be sitting on top of Mount Horeb, receiving revelation from Raziel. She is considered to be very wise, represented here by her gray-colored robe—gray representing wisdom. Acting as a channel, she receives wisdom from Raziel and is then able to deeply understand past ideas from the understandings of these new ideas received. She points forward as a gesture to march onward with her new ideas. Depicted here with the wind on her back and guided by archangel Raziel, she is a force to be reckoned with, forever evolving her knowledge base, and continually expanding her mind and spirit. She is quick to act on her inspiration as she manifests her ideas.

The Queen of Swords wears a necklace with an amulet dangling over her heart. This amulet's symbol being located directly over the queen's heart represents her core value encompassing the queen's essence. This particular amulet is a large Y, representing the Hebrew letter Yod, signifying that she is the 'heart' of creation.

In Kabbalah, it is considered that all things begin with a thought; an idea. This concept is incorporated with the Yod. Yod shows up in many of the cards such as the Ace of Swords, Ace of Wands, and Ace of Cups, as well as in the Tower card because of its deep symbolic meaning. It symbolizes knowledge from a divine source, but more accurately, divinity. Yod is the building block of all the Hebrew letters. Each letter is compiled of a different formation of Yod's. Yod is the first letter in the tetragrammaton, YHVH, the divine Four-Letter Name of God. Yod is at the beginning of all creation.

Queen of Pentacles:

After some contemplation you will notice this queen is not wearing a necklace. This is significant, because all the other Queens are. This is purposely done to signify that she is not connected to her spiritual side. In the section of her robe over her heart it appears to be a human face located where a necklace would be hanging. This refers to her placing value in other people. She would rather form a bond and/or a trusting relationship with people, offering a trusting give and take relationship where both parties share their advice and practical guidance with each other. Thus, relying on her fellow man instead of forming a communication with the Creator.

QUEEN of PENTACLES.

Just like the other Queens, the Queen of Pentacles is a receiver. She builds upon and takes advantage of the gifts and opportunities that she has been blessed with. This queen in particular can be seen as the most resourceful queen of all. Even when it seems as though she hasn't the resources, she proves to be resourceful, utilizing that which she already has to create abundance.

You will notice depicted on this card is a chuppah that hangs draped above the queen's head. A chuppah is usually hung on the archway that stands over a newlywed couple during their wedding ceremony, and it represents the new house that the newlyweds will live in, as well as the new life they will create together. This queen's chuppah is black compared to the other chuppahs throughout the tarot that are usually colored a vibrant green. The color black represents Saturn's influence. Saturn is the planet that rules over karma and things that take time to develop, as well as governs life-lessons. We see here that the queen has received her house and her life of nobility, and she has taken the time and effort in nurturing it, transforming her house into a home. In addition to this, we see here symbolized in the chuppah's color scheme that this queen has developed and nurtured all that she has across an entire lifespan.

Her success was not obtained overnight. And we can be safe to assume that it wasn't at all easy either. She made the best out of what she had. Whatever you give her, she will make it greater. In the words of Sir William Golding, "If you give a woman groceries, she will give you a meal. If you give her a smile, she will give you her heart. She multiplies and enlarges what is given to her." The Saturn symbolism found in this particular chuppah directly relates to this queen having lived through so much; experiencing many challenges, trials and tribulations. In spite of this, we see the bright yellow sky in the background, which gives us hope that she lives for a brighter day, and she knows how to transform the darkness into light.

The queen's throne is colored black and gray, with an added reddish hue, similar to the color scheme of her chuppah. Knowing that the color gray represents wisdom, we see here that she has learned from all her many life experiences, including passionate relationships and projects that she has put her full heart into, which is represented by the color red. The black suggests that these experiences were karmic life-lessons that were filled with frustration and headache. The symbolism of these two colors mixed in with the decor of the gray throne contribute to the queen's obtainment of knowledge, which she later transforms into wisdom. She builds upon her life experiences and further develops her character. This queen has a cherub resting at the top of her throne behind her head, who whispers words of wisdom and offers up guidance. Although, she may have been stubborn, having to learn things the hard way— having lived and learned. Thus, believing the voice in her head was hers alone, and not her guardian angel.

There are also the heads of a bull and a goat located on her throne, symbolizing the astrological signs of Taurus and Capricorn; both being earth signs (the suit of Pentacles represents the element earth), alluding to the cherub prescribing down-to-earth and practical advice.

The queen's crown has eight red jewels. The number 8 corresponds to the 8th sefirah Hod, meaning splendor and relating to splendor of the mind, associated with intelligence and analytical problem-solving skills. She has been blessed with much opportunity and has not taken that for granted. She has taken advantage of those opportunities, being able to travel and having access to academic study in order to broaden her mind and become an intellectual. Her crown also adorns a red Laurel wreath; a symbol for triumph. In common modern idiomatic usage, it refers to a victory. The expression 'resting on one's laurels' refers to someone relying entirely on long-past successes for continued fame or recognition. This signifies that she respects the good fortune that she has been blessed with, therefore using her royal stature as a force for good, and for the betterment of others.

She is fertile soil, so to speak. Whatever you plant in her, she will grow it into something great. Notice the small rabbit camouflaged in the grass on the right side of this card? Rabbits are a symbol of fertility. This is a female rabbit that will birth new life into the world, bringing joy and beauty. Like this rabbit, the queen will birth children that will someday take her place on the throne. She will nurture and raise these children to grow into strong willed, hard-working, self-driven and independent individuals that follow her example as being a force for good, which is action inspired by a genuine concern for others. When we act with compassion, the seeds we plant today can change the course of our shared tomorrow.

This concludes the Queens. Moving forward, we begin describing the Kings.

The Kings:

The Kings are the archetypes of the mature masculine energy aspect of their particular suit. The Kings embody personality traits of Chokmah, and relate to the energy aspects found on the right column of the Tree of Life corresponding to mercy and kindness. Generally, they tend to be extraverted, proactive and generous with their time and energy. The Kings observe everything. They are watching and learning to gain a logical comprehension for figuring the reasoning behind people's actions. The Kings do not shy away when it comes their time to share the wisdom gathered from their observations.

The King of Wands:

This king is very extroverted as we see symbolized by him placing his wand outside the cement foundation he sits upon. The suit of Wands represents opinions, knowledge and subjects that we feel passionate about—relating to one's deeply rooted belief system in which they build their character upon.

KING of WANDS.

The king placing his wand outside his foundation (his comfort zone) shows that he places his character out there for all to see. There being four leaves on his wand connects it to the sefirah Chesed, meaning mercy. This signifies that the king's opinions are merciful and full of kindness, as well as being supported with ineradicable knowledge. This king adds positivity to the conversation, offering his input and aiding to the situation at hand. He usually has the final say (last word), and determines the final decision on the matter. He speaks softly yet firm, and demands the attention of others. When he speaks, the room becomes silent.

The king's throne is adorned with three salamanders. Groups of three like-objects connects to the energy influence of Binah, meaning understanding. Salamanders are known for coming out of hiding during a heavy rainstorm, but quickly return back into hiding as soon as the rain stops. They are attracted to the excitement. Also, salamanders are known for being able to walk on fire. They are able to endure the heat for a prolonged time before getting burnt. This is the king's understanding obtained by Binah's influence. Let me explain this particular influence. For instance, he is attracted to the fire; to the excitement. Comparably, he can be seen as a fire extinguisher, meaning he will go to wherever there is unrest and he will use his authority to put his foot down and stomp out the fire. He will enter a room and say what needs to be said, and it will end up being the last word on the matter; he will have spoken and therefore it shall be done. When it is all said and done, the dispute will have been settled, and he will then be able to walk away knowing that the issue has been dealt with fairly—leaving with a certainty the fire has been extinguished.

The suit of Wands represents the element fire. This king wears a fiery crown upon his head symbolizing that he is wise and understanding of the fiery energy within—the life-force within us all that can be both creative and destructive. He knows how to control this life-force energy for the greater good.

There are two lions with fiery manes and tails on the king's throne directly behind the king's crown. This represents the connection the symbols share with the king's crown, which is associated with Keter, from where the king receives divine inspiration and revelation. Two like-objects grouped together connect to Chokmah, meaning wisdom. This deepens the connection and reinstates the fact that the king is knowledgeable of the fire element within us, and he knows how to utilize it accordingly.

The King of Wands can be compared to King Solomon, whose name means Sun. Sol-Om-On are three ancient words for the Sun. Sol is Latin for Sun, Om is Hindi Sanskrit for Sun, and On means Sun in Egyptian. Furthermore, the Sun is Leo, the lion, which is a fire sign. Interesting to note here is that the king is wearing a lion-head amulet on his necklace.

Therefore, the King of Wands can be seen as an archetype symbolizing King Solomon. King Solomon was known to be very wise, and famously negotiated the decision to split a baby in two when settling an argument between two mothers. This story is portrayed in 1 Kings 3:16-28. The two women argued who's baby it belonged to. Solomon suggested that the women cut the baby in half so they could both have an equal share of the child. This is when the real mother screamed out in terror for the well-being of her child. She said for Solomon to give the baby to the other woman just as long as he promised not to harm the child. This is when Solomon knew who the real mother was. A mother would not want to hurt her own child. Everyone in Israel was amazed when they heard how Solomon had made his decision. They realized that God had given him wisdom to judge fairly.

The King of Wands is looking to the left of the card, which

The Tarot Decoded

reflects upon his connection to the left-column energy. He is focusing his attention to the left-column of severity on the Tree of Life. This alludes to the idea that the king is attracted to the extreme in his judgments, with the intentions of drawing out the truth in order to fully understand a particular situation. He likes to play with people's egos, knowing just what to say in order to draw an emotional or psychological reaction out of them. Like the salamander playing with fire, the king enjoys the heat, but knows when to stop playing before someone gets burned.

The King of Wands is the executive of the other cards of the same suit, and as such, is charged with making decisions. His ability to be decisive is rooted in two things: First, who he is and what he stands for; the King's core values are centered on firm and unchanging principles. So, when a crisis comes, he does not waver because he has already determined the course he will take. And secondly, the King seasons his decisions with experience. His experiences provide him with practical wisdom: the knowledge of how to do the right thing, at the right time, and for the right reasons.

King of Cups:

The King of Cups can be compared to the biblical King David. Like David, the King of Cups is also attributed to having emotional intelligence. This king is blessed with the ability to perceive, use, understand, manage and handle emotions. People with high emotional intelligence can recognize their own emotions and those of others, use emotional information to guide thinking and behavior, discern between different feelings and label them appropriately, and adjust emotions to adapt to environments. In other words, this king has the cognitive ability that facilitates interpersonal behavior.

206

KING of CUPS.

King David is described as a man after God's own heart (Samuel 13:14, Acts 13:22). Coincidentally, the suit of Cups represents matters of the heart. The King of Cups' throne is depicted floating on top of the sea of emotions, representing the king's control over his emotional state.

David is accredited for writing half the Psalms in the Bible, and although this Psalm 104:26 (KJV) is not attributed to David, it does coincide with this particular tarot card where it states, "There go the ships: there is that leviathan, whom thou hast made to play therein." The leviathan spoken of here refers to a whale, which there just so happens to be a whale illustrated on the left side of this card. The term leviathan is revered as being a large sea monster and can be used to describe a large whale, both of which pose a threat to sailors. Metaphorically, each of us has their own leviathan within us, reflecting upon our shadow-nature. As we try to gain control over our emotions, we may find ourselves vulnerable to triggering certain aspects of our ego, which is when we lose control and lash out in an emotional outburst. We strive to create for ourselves a strong-willed vessel, an ark within ourselves that forms a balanced soul, combining the heart and mind. Although, at times we tend to become overwhelmed with emotion where we either act out with innate anger or in an over-heated, yet heartfelt impulse whenever we feel that our vessels are under attack.

This conscious control of maintaining this inner balance is symbolized by the king's two sceptres, which are placed one on top of the other. The golden sceptre held in the king's left hand represents the king's emotional control, while the gray sceptre engraved on the front of the throne represents the king's control over mind. The merging together of these two polarities form the construct of emotional intelligence. Essentially, this is obtained whenever one unites the male and female energies within themselves. This concept is comparable to the spiritual characteristics symbolized within the Star of David, aka Shield of David. This protective shield defends the king from the leviathan. You will notice that the king's throne is made from the leviathan's whale tale, symbolizing him conquering his ego-nature, considered as the beast within which can easily be triggered if he were to lose focus, and act on his primal urges—whole-heartedly like a buffoon.

The king's shoes are made up of fishes' scales, representing that he is able to breathe under water, and therefore not be succumbed by the emotions of the sea. He adorns a fish charm around his neck, which dangles over his heart. This alludes to the fact that he has a strong sense of empathy as well as compassion, causing him to feel sadness, remorse and regret. Because he is self-aware of his own actions and can feel how his actions affect others, he is mindful with his words and behavior. He feels sorry for causing others pain, and promises himself he will never do it again. He will forgive himself as well as others, but never forget. Thus, he vows to never repeat his mistakes ever again.

Worth mentioning here are the significant numbers related to King David that coincide with this card's spiritual influences. For instance, David was 30 years old when he began his reign as king, his reign lasted for 40 years until he died at age 70. Allow me to explain each example in detail.

The number 30 is significant because it corresponds to Saturn's Return. The Saturn Return is when the planet Saturn comes back to meet your natal Saturn. It takes about 30 years for this slow-mover to return to where it was when you were born. During this time a person is faced with past-life karma, and must overcome a series of tests and is faced with challenges which are later considered life-lessons. As a consequence, these challenges make us stronger.

Furthermore, David reigned for 40 years. The Hebrew letter Mem, meaning water, has a numerical value of 40, and ties in this number to the spiritual cleansing aspect of water.

Moreover, the Hebrew letter Ayin, meaning eye, to see, has a numerical value of 70, which was the age David was when he died. Ayin is a silent letter. It is said that Ayin 'sees' but does not speak, and therefore represents the attitude of humility. On the other hand, Ayin can represent idolatry, which is born out of the heart of envy. When the eye is evil, it can become a slave to the purposes of sin, and impulsiveness. As Rashi said, "The heart and the eyes are the spies to the body: they lead a person to transgress; the eyes see, the heart covets, and the body transgresses." (Bamidbar 15.39)

Described in Samuel 2:11, David coveted another man's wife. As the Bible story goes, King David saw a woman named Bathsheba bathing at night. David was immediately drawn to her, and sent messengers to find out who she was. The messengers returned and told David that she was the wife of Uriah. Despite David knowing that she was married, he sent for her and slept with her. Bathsheba later sends word to David that she was pregnant. This is when David forged a plan to kill off her husband, and set him up to die in an unfair battle.

This story reminds us of how great men who are called by God are still humans and struggle with sin. The cause of all this drama was initially started with David's wandering eye. Giving way to sin hardens the heart, and provokes the departure of the Holy Spirit. Before this drama ensued, David was pure in the eyes of God. At this point in his life, he was at the peak of his political career, and admired as the messiah of his people, having conquered Jerusalem and established it as the kingdom of the Israelite nation. He had overcome Goliath, guarded over his father's flock, as a mighty warrior conquered armies, all while growing spiritually closer to the Creator. But eventually this streak ended as soon as he succumbed to sin. It was his wandering eye that was the death of his pureness. Ergo, dying at the age of 70, (the numerical value of the letter Ayin, meaning eye), he left this world without having a perfect reputation. Jesus, the only person to be mentioned more in the Bible than David, was the only perfect being to ever walk the earth.

David recognized that just as his sin was against God, so it was only God who could cleanse. And so, he pleas for cleansing as stated in Psalm 51:1-2, "Have mercy on me, O God, according to your unfailing love: according to your great compassion blot out my transgressions. Wash away all my iniquity and cleanse me from my sin."

King of Swords:

This king can be compared to Hermes Trismegistus, who was a great priest, philosopher, and king. Hermes Trismegistus is associated with Hermes, Mercury, and Thoth, attributed as being the founder of Hermeticism. He was called Trismegistus because he was known to be 'thrice great', and praised the trinity, saying there is one divine nature in the trinity.

KING of SWORDS.

The suit of Swords represents the element air, represented by the three air signs of the Zodiac: Gemini, Aquarius, and Libra. Incorporated within the tarot, these signs' influences correspond as follows: Gemini is assigned to the Lovers card, Aquarius is assigned to the Star, and lastly, Libra is assigned to the Justice card. Subsequently, the King of Swords comprises all three of these air sign cards' shared zodiac influences. Thus, reflecting this king's thrice greatness.

Further significance is revealed once you add up the sum of these card's Roman numerals. For instance, when you add them all up, you get 34, which just so happens to be the sum of all the numbers included within Jupiter's magic square. Jupiter is the ruling planet of the sefirah Chesed. Within each of these cards we see through symbolism the act of drawing forth a deeper understanding from Binah down into Chesed, from the higher realm of Atziluth down into the world of Briah. Thus, formulating one's understanding of a previous matter to deal with a current matter as a way to create peace and harmony in the current situation or circumstance. This can be seen in one's acts of charity and kindness as they attempt to create the feeling of peace all can harmonize with. Therefore, improving the current environment for the betterment of all. Each air sign card is about connecting to higher understanding by reaching up one's 'sword' to connect to and attract godly insights, and then draw it down into ways of making the world a better place for everyone. Therefore, creating a heaven on earth. This isn't so much about creating something physical as it is more so about creating an emotional feeling, and creating a vibe that brings people together, a sense of warmth, love and hope for a better today, and creating an optimistic outlook for a better tomorrow.

Kabbalistically, this is drawing from the upper world of Atziluth deeper understanding and bringing it down into the realm of Briah, the emotional realm, where people are able to feel a shared sense of calmness and joy in their hearts simultaneously. This feeling can be the result of a charitable act or selfless deed, and can be done with music, words or art which inspires and uplifts others. It is a warmth felt within our bosom uniting people together as one.

The king holds his sword upward towards Binah as he attempts to attract deeper understanding of all things. Depicted over the king's left shoulder, on the right side of the card, are two birds flying in the sky. Two like-objects connect us with the influence of Chokmah, meaning wisdom. These two birds represent the king's connection to Chokmah, as he attracts higher wisdom and godly insights with his sword.

You will notice that the Justice judge also holds a sword high into the air. This reflects the same concept of one's attempt to connect to the upper world of Atziluth, where Chokmah and Binah both reside.

Furthermore, as we look deeper into the symbology of these air sign cards, the Hebrew letter assigned to the Lovers card is Zayin, meaning sword. Spiritually, it refers to being able to attract inspiration, and then once that inspiration is obtained, being able to filter out the bad ideas, thus discerning the good ideas from the bad.

In addition to this, the ruling archangel of Chokmah is Raziel, who just so happens to be the angel depicted in the Lovers card.

Raziel is associated with being Thoth, Hermes/Mercury, as well as Hermes Trismegistus. Raziel's name means 'secrets of God', and we download these secrets whenever we raise up our spiritual swords, similar to an antenna or how an iron rod attracts lightning, and we connect to the frequency of Chokmah.

The scarlet ibis in the Star card is an Egyptian symbol for Thoth. Thoth is attributed with having taught mankind the practice of meditation, which is a predominate theme portrayed in the Star card. For instance, the card is assigned to the Hebrew letter Tzaddi, meaning fish hook. Metaphorically, one is supposed to toss up their fish hook into the astral waters and catch inspiration and godly insight. The virgin, Isis, is portrayed in the Star card doing just that.

The air signs of the zodiac are the thinkers, communicators, and the doers. They are the leaders of society. They have the ability to see a situation from an intellectual perspective without being clouded by emotion. Air signs are all about ideas, achievements and correct information. They are focused on the details. They act on their brilliant ideas and then follow them through.

King of Pentacles:

This king can be compared to king Bacchus, known as the Roman god of wine and viticulture. He was known as the inducer of drunkenness, religious ecstasy, and frenzied states of creativity. Bacchus was a bringer of ecstasies and inducer of frenzied states such as creativity and religious devotion. Also known as Eleutherius, meaning liberator in Greek. Bacchus represented the spontaneous and unrestrained aspects of life. He operated through inducing a state of drunkenness into his vessels. This state freed the inebriated from social conventions and allowed new ways of thinking and acting.

KING of PENTACLES.

Illustrated throughout the King of Pentacles card are plants with ability to induce higher states of consciousness. This includes the poppy flowers on the king's crown, magic mushrooms near the king's throne, and decorative wine grapes embedded in the king's garb.

The god of wine, the great reveler, and the paragon of drunkenness, Bacchus was the deity that bestowed the gifts of inebriation and altered states upon humanity—as well as controlled the growth of grapevines. Bacchus was always depicted as a young man who was usually beardless and often drunk, similar to the king depicted in this card. At times he carried a thyrsus—a staff or wand covered in ivy vines, liken to the golden sceptre held in the King of Pentacles' right hand.

There is an old adage that goes, "When the wine goes in, the secrets come out." Essentially, this was how Bacchus maintained power over others, by knowing everyone's secrets and things they held private. This included the debauchery taking place during the king's hedonistic parties. Bacchus was known to throw lavish parties where everyone was encouraged to get drunk and lose all inhibitions. In this state he believed people opened up to their true selves and spoke truthfully. As the party grew on and as people became drunk on wine, their secrets eventually came out. The king took careful note to all that was said and done in those parties, which was later used as leverage over people as a way of persuading them into doing his bidding. Trading secrets can be currency for gaining power.

On a lighter note, inducing a higher state of conscious-awareness tends to bring people closer together on a soul level, by shedding layers of ego we reveal our true selves. Thereby removing our masks (false fronts), we are able to see each other's truth, and realize that we are all connected as one. This feeling of oneness is achieved when we break down the barriers of our ego identity. Once these false identities are dismantled, we see how much we all have in common with one another. This could have been the king's metaphysical purpose for throwing such hedonistic and overindulgent parties.

The King of Pentacles' throne is adorned by four Taurus bulls, reflecting upon Taurus personality traits of being down-to-earth, as well as indulging in life's greatest pleasures and luxuries, with an outlook on life to be best lived when eating, drinking and being merry. Taurus is straight-forward with an honest approach as a means to clear the air, setting everyone on the same page, and same level of understanding, in order to create harmony and an overall sense of stability.

I will conclude this chapter by explaining how each of the Kings as well as the Queens share a mutual connection with three tarot cards that coincide with zodiac signs of the same element. I will explain how the Kings portray the logical meaning each combination of zodiac sign cards share, while the Queens reflect upon the deeper spiritual understandings concealed within the combination of cards.

Beginning with the Kings:

Each King represents the combination of all three of its zodiac signs that correspond to its specific suit's element. The three cards assigned to each particular element portray the ultimate zodiac personality trait each King embodies.

The **King of Wands**, as portrayed with the three fire-element signs, represents taking appropriate action when the time is right.

The **King of Cups,** reflecting the element water, encompasses the spiritual concept of the Hermetic Marriage, which is the conscious will to balance and combine one's mind (logic) with the matters of their heart (emotions) with the intention of self-mastery, as you grow a thicker skin.

The **King of Swords**, representing the element air, portrays the concept of drawing down deeper understanding from the upper worlds in order to create a sense of peace and harmony felt in the atmosphere. Thus, lightening the mood and uplifting morale.

The **King of Pentacles**, expressing the element earth, draws down secrets from the upper worlds with intentions of manifesting them in the material reality. By providing prosperity and abundance for others one will receive abundance in return as well. When your dreams are based on how you can improve the lives of others, the whole universe conspires to make your dreams come true.

Continuing with the Queens:

While the King cards reflect upon a certain aspect of logical reasoning portrayed within these zodiac card's illustrations, the Queens reflect upon a deeper understanding concealed within each three-card combination that is not so easily detectable. Therefore, we must look deeper under the surface paying closer attention to the smaller, more subtle details.

The **Queen of Wands**, representing the element fire, focuses on the bright side of things as a method for controlling her temper.

The **Queen of Cups**, corresponding with the element water, bottles-up her emotions, concealing them inside her vessel, later to be called upon as a means of emotional protection from any future contingence which could provoke hypersensitivity.

The **Queen of Swords**, reflecting the element air, manifests her inspired ideas, acting on her intuition.

The **Queen of Pentacles**, sharing an infinity with the element earth, finds a way to convert her blessings into something significant; adding long lasting value. For example, turning her house into a home. She practices gratitude like a religion. Therefore, she makes the best out of whatever she has, and can be looked upon as being truly grateful for all the many blessings and opportunities that come her way. Her motto is, "When I don't have the resources, I become resourceful."

Aligning with the Kings and Queens of each tarot suit, based on the four corresponding elements, is a list below describing the cards that are assigned to the zodiac signs in these three-card combinations:

Fire:

Corresponding to Aries, Leo, and Sagittarius, represented by the following tarot cards: The Emperor, Strength, and Temperance, respectively. When placing these cards in a row, in accordance to their Roman numeral values, one can see the King of Wands' connection regarding the control over one's impulses, to wait patiently for opportunity to present itself before taking action. Thus, acting out of logic and reason opposed to overzealous reactiveness. The Queen of Wands remains focused on the positive aspect of a situation as to deviate from impulsive behavior that may cause her to over-react or jump the gun, so to speak.

All three of these cards share the common theme of remaining patient, and advise controlling one's impulsive behavior. This aspect is better understood when incorporating the spiritual meanings of each card's Hebrew letter. For instance, the Emperor is assigned to the letter Heh, meaning window, and refers to one who waits for a window of opportunity to present itself to them. Likewise, the Strength card is assigned to the letter Teth, meaning coiled serpent, who awaits patiently in the shadows for its prey to approach. Unaware of the serpent's presence, the prey walks up to the serpent hiding in the shadows and is suddenly attacked.

Lastly, the Temperance card is assigned to the letter Samekh, meaning prop, prop up, support, and alludes to the concept of creating one's human vessel to be a temple able to hold-in and sustain one's temper.

As you look into the numerology of these cards, you will uncover deeper spiritual significance. For instance, the sum of the Roman numerals gives us 26. The Emperor is IV, the Strength is VIII, and Temperance is XIV, which is 4+8+14 = 26. The number 26 just so happens to be the gematria value for the Divine Name of God, YHVH. Coincidentally, the Four-Letter Name YHVH is written on the angel's robe, (over his heart), in the Temperance card. By controlling one's emotions, one maintains a control over the matters of their heart. As stated in Jeremiah 31:33, "But this is the covenant that I will make with the house of Israel after those days, declares the Lord: I will put my law within them, and I will write it on their hearts. And I will be their God, and they shall be my people."

Water:

Corresponding with Cancer, Scorpio, and Pisces, represented by the following tarot cards: The Chariot, Death, and The Moon, respectively. When this combination of cards is placed in a row, you can see the King of Cups' connection regarding the concept of the

Hermetic Marriage, when the opposite polarities combine; light merges with the dark. As the Queen of Cups gazes upon this bottled-up energy, she analyzes the given situation as an intermediary in order to unveil the truth, revealing light from darkness. One must realize the truth, that in order to move on, you must learn from your mistakes. This is how you grow.

Mistakes are a powerful motivator for change. You can't reach what's in front of you until you let go of what's behind you. Thereby remembering our past mistakes will prevent us from repeating them.

The three cards in this particular combination share a common theme of breaking free from social norms and limited belief systems with an intention to reinvent one's self-identity. In this regard, when we incorporate the spiritual meanings of these cards assigned Hebrew letters, we reveal deeper meaning. For instance, the Chariot card is assigned to the letter Chet, meaning fence, and refers to things such as personal beliefs we keep private, and at the same time create barriers separating people apart from us that don't share similar views. The Chariot is about breaking down these barriers that separate us from each other. Similarly, the Death card is assigned to the letter Nun, meaning fish. And what happens when you try to clutch a fish in your hands? It immediately slips out of your control. This concept coincides with the theme here of breaking free of social norms, and discontinuing outdated systems by refusing to conform. Thus, challenging the status quo. Last of all, we have the Moon card, which is assigned to the letter Qoph, meaning back of head. As you can see, the letter Qoph ק looks like the back of a man's head. The idea being portrayed as that of 'following' after or behind, or to follow in a circuit or cycle. As a word, it is used in scriptures as the word for 'ape', Kuf. Apes are known for mimicking or following what others do. Therefore, the Qoph/Kuf when applied with the Moon card, advises one to follow the path paved by God and the heavens, as opposed to following one's own ego-nature. Just as the wolf and dog (depicted in this card) battle over dominance; if you are not the lead dog, then the scenery never changes.

Air:

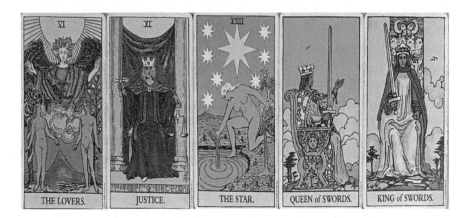

Corresponding with Gemini, Libra, and Aquarius, represented by the following tarot cards: The Lovers, Justice, and The Star, respectively. When this combination of cards is placed in a row, in accordance to their Roman numeral values, one can see the King of Swords' connection of raising up his sword into the heavens as a means to draw down godly insights and deeper understandings for ways to create an atmosphere of peace and harmony. The Queen takes this inspired intuition one step further and forms an action plan in order to manifest these brilliant ideas into something substantial and long lasting.

These three cards combined share a common theme of humbling one's self and asking for help from above. In the Lovers card, Adam and Eve are depicted looking up towards the angel Raziel, humbled when he offers to teach them his wisdom and deliver to them practical guidance from above. The Hebrew letter assigned to this card is Zayin, meaning sword, in reference to how a spiritual sword can cut through man's many thoughts, and can be utilized to discern between the good and the bad ideas. This is why Raziel approaches Adam and Eve after they have eaten from the Tree of Knowledge of Good and Evil, to give them the sword they need to filter out the good from the bad. We continue to see this theme in the Justice card, which is assigned to the letter Lamed, meaning ox goad, which was the shepherd's sharp poker used to authoritatively lead his flock as well as protect them from predators. The letter Lamed happens to be the tallest of all the letters in the alphabet ל, and is shaped similar to the Justice card's knight who sits upon the judge's throne with his sword held high into the air over his right shoulder. Analogously, Lamed reaches high into the heavens and gathers godly insights of how to better protect and guide his 'flock', aka the other twenty-one letters of the Hebrew alphabet. Moving ahead, the Star card is assigned to the letter Tzaddi, meaning fish hook, which refers to the idea of tossing one's spiritual fish hook up into the ether or astral waters in order to attract inspiration. As seen in this card, the virgin is a channel, reaching into the astral waters gathering deeper understanding with the intended purpose of applying such new understanding in ways aimed at changing the world into a better state. Interesting to point out is that the word tzaddik means righteous one, and refers to a person who walks with God. The Tzaddik raises his spiritual sword high into the air forming a direct connection, communicating with the Creator, becoming 'at one' as he 'walks with God.'

As we look further into the numerology of these cards, we uncover deeper spiritual connections. For instance, when you add up these cards' Roman numerals you get the sum of 34. The Lovers card is VI, Justice is XI, and the Star is XVII, which gives us 6+11+17 = 34. The number 34 is significant because it is the number of Jupiter's planetary kamea or magic square. Jupiter was known as the God of the sky, air. He was known by the Romans as the sky father.

Earth:

THE HIEROPHANT. THE HERMIT. THE DEVIL. QUEEN of PENTACLES. KING of PENTACLES.

Corresponding with Taurus, Virgo, and Capricorn, represented by the following tarot cards: The Hierophant, The Hermit, and the Devil, respectively. When these cards are placed in a row, the combination of like-symbols reflects upon the King of Pentacles' spiritual connection relating to drawing down secrets from the upper worlds with the intended purpose of manifesting those ideas into ways of creating prosperity and abundance in the material world.

The Queen builds upon these ideas and applies her resourcefulness in ways that prove to maintain and prolong these such endeavors.

You will notice that all these three cards depict their main character as holding up their right hand towards God. This suggests they are attempting to receive godly insights from above. And you will notice their left hand holding onto a staff, representing their intention to manifest their ideas. All three of these cards contain some sort of connection to the sefirah Yesod, meaning foundation. Yesod is considered to be the chute from which the macrocosmic Light is funneled down, manifesting itself into the microcosmic material world of matter. With this considered, the staffs in these cards can be metaphorically portrayed as being representations of the male phallus.

Also worth noting is that all characters involved here have their right hand raised up towards Binah, meaning understanding, and is associated with Saturn influences. Whereas, Saturn is synonymous with YHVH, Yahweh. For instance, the Hierophant points his two fingers upward, representing he is attempting to connect to God, and receive godly insights and understandings of the esoteric mysteries. Likewise, the Hermit holds up a lantern which has the Star of Saturn aka Star of David inside of it. And lastly, the Devil holds his right hand into the air and forms the sacred hand gesture, which forms the Hebrew letter Shin, referencing Shaddai, (meaning Almighty [God]), known as the Birkat Kohanim blessing aka the Priestly Blessing. This hand gesture is used by the Kohen High Priest as they bless the congregation with God's peace. The High Priest acts as the middleman or channel for God's word as he offers this benediction. The term Birkat Kohanim is known as the 'raising of the hands' blessing, as well as 'raising up the platform.' Hence, the connection here with Yesod, which means foundation—and thus, 'raising up the foundation'.

These three cards share the common theme of manifesting prosperity from the insights they received from above. Viewed in this way, we can see the commonality shared by understanding the spiritual meanings associated with each of these cards assigned Hebrew letters. For instance, the Hierophant is assigned to the letter Vav, meaning tent peg, which reflects the idea of binding and/or connecting two things together as one. Thus, drawing heaven down to earth. Next is the Hermit card, which is assigned to the letter Yod, meaning hand. The Hermit depicted here on top of the mountain is comparable to Moses who climbed Mount Sinai, where he received the ten commandments, which were written by God's own hand. Thereby, God's hand manifested the new law of the land. At last, we have the Devil card assigned to the letter Ayin, meaning eye, and refers to the third eye. The concept portrayed here is for an individual to physically become a channel for the Light of the Creator. Therefore, the Light enters the body through the third eye, where it is then funneled down into the vessel, to later be used as the source of energy needed for the individual to manifest their desires, including their hopes and dreams. Thus, creating a heaven on earth.

Interesting to note is the numerology connection when you add up the sum of these three card's Roman numerals. The Hierophant V, Hermit IX, the Devil XV added together equals the sum of 29 (5+9+15 = 29), which is the number of days in a Lunar month cycle. This is significant here, because the Moon rules over the sefirah Yesod, for which these cards all share a common connection to.

Diving deeper into the gematria of these three cards, another spiritual connection is made. For instance, the Hierophant is assigned to Vav with a value of 6, and the Hermit card is assigned to Yod with a value of 10, and lastly, the Devil card is assigned to Ayin with a value of 70. The sum of these three numbers is 86, which just so happens to be the value for the Holy Name of God, Elohim. Elohim, being synonymous with Saturn, as each card portrays the concept of drawing down insights from Saturn (Elohim/Yahweh)and manifesting them in the material world.

Pictured below is a chart displaying all the tarot cards that are associated with specific zodiac signs.

Chapter 13

The Secret of the Wands

Wands symbolize certain aspects relating to core belief systems, grounded opinions and ideals deeply rooted within an individual's character. Wands correspond with the element fire. This fire energy is what drives us to manifest the things that we are passionate about—things that we spend much time on developing. The more time and energy we put towards our passions, the more knowledgeable we become on that particular subject. In time, we gradually become experts. The knowledge we obtain as we travel along our paths, obtained either from life-lessons or from simple curiosity, builds upon our character and shapes us into the person we believe ourselves to be. We are made up of our values, morals, ethics, as well as the virtues we possess. We are what we know, and what we know to be true.

The wands are like trees, and trees relate to agriculture. The god of agriculture is Saturn, who also happens to be the god of time. By counting the number of branches (on the wands) on each card, we are able to figure out the timing significance associated with each card.

The specific timing portrayed in each card can relate to a handful of different Kabbalistic understandings. While some of the cards relate to either a day or a year's time, other cards will relate to a particular sefirah on the Tree of Life, such as Binah (for example), meaning understanding, advising that it is now time to be more open-minded, and to dig deeper, as well as motivate you to manifest your inspired ideas and to utilize the creative-force within yourself; giving birth to new and better ways for manifesting prosperity and abundance into your life.

A specific example of this timing significance is found in the 7 of Wands card, where there are exactly 20 branches found on its seven wands. 20 is the Hebrew gematria value for the letter Kaph, meaning open palm. This advises a person that the time is now to let go, drop it and stop persisting. This can relate to stubbornness and the need to prove one's self right. Learn to bite your tongue. Say what needs to be said, and then quit talking before you end up lecturing and/or cast your judgments or force your opinions onto others. This unruly behavior is usually followed with something either said or done that you later regret. The 7 of Wands advises one to learn when to say when, to know when enough is enough, and to simply let go.

An open palm will release its grip around the wand, and therefore release its control.

The table below shows the breakdown for each of the cards in the suit of Wands, displaying the number of branches along with the proper timing significance associated with each card.

Wands Card	Number of Branches	Significance
Ace of Wands	3	♣ Corresponding with Binah: birth, creation, understanding
2 of Wands	6	♣ Corresponding with Tiferet: peak level, at one's best, head radiates brilliance
3 of Wands	9	♣ Corresponding with Yesod: unveil the unseen, see what others cannot
4 of Wands	5	♣ Corresponding with Gevurah: healthy ego boost, enhanced confidence
5 of Wands	12	♣ The 12 different signs of the Zodiac, representing differentiating personality types
6 of Wands	12	♣ The 12 months of the year, representing a year's time
7 of Wands	20	♣ The Hebrew gematria value of the letter Kaph, meaning open palm (of hand); time now to release, let go

8 of Wands	24	♣ Referring to the 24 hours in a day, take it one day at a time
9 of Wands	27	♣ Associated with the Lunar Return, which prepares one for their Saturn Return; a time in a person's life where they are faced with an identity crisis
10 of Wands	33	♣ Corresponding to the Christ Consciousness; an elevated spiritual awareness, achieved through practices such as meditation and by working on ourselves

We must consider the suit's four Court cards as well. Keep in mind that the Court cards are categorized separately from the ten pips, but do indeed reveal important significance that should not be overlooked.

Wands' Court Card	Number of Branches	Significance
Page of Wands	5	♣ Connecting to Gevurah: healthy ego boost, sense of drive, ambition, positive change, spark new opinion
Knight of Wands	5	♣ Connecting to Gevurah: healthy ego-boost, desire to rise up and out of complacency, driven, passionate, creative
Queen of Wands	3	♣ Connecting to aspects of Binah: deep contemplation, birthing, develop ideas fully

King of Wands	4	♣ Corresponding with Chesed: merciful kindness, blessing knowledge, bestowing wisdom

We know now that concealed within each one of these cards is a deeper level of understanding revealed to us by simply counting the branches. Knowing this revelation arouses within us a desire to find out more secrets hidden within the suit of Wands. What mysteries could we uncover if we added up all the branches found throughout the entire suit of Wands?

Are there more significant connections to uncover? The answer is yes, and the findings are mind-blowing.

Within the suit of Wands, when we add up the total number of branches found in the pips (Ace through 10), we get 160 branches. 160 is the gematria value for the Hebrew word eyts, meaning tree. When you add the total number of branches found in the court cards, you get 17 branches. 17 is the gematria value of the Hebrew word tov, meaning good.

Combine the two words together and you get 'good tree', which would allude to the Tree of Knowledge of Good and Evil, as well as the Tree of Life. Both trees would be considered here because in Biblical Hebrew the word for tree, eyts, can be used as singular (tree) as well as in a plural sense (trees). The plural form of the word eyts is eytsiym, which always refers to 'wood' in the bible. When you add 160+17 you get 177. 177 is the Hebrew gematria value for the phrase 'garden of Eden.' These gematria connections reveal to us 'the good trees in the garden of Eden.'

The suit of Wands relates to knowledge, as well as the element fire, which coincides with the letter Yod—the Hebrew letter which is present in all creation. The letter Yod looks like a small flame; considered the fire of life or fire of creation. These associations further reinstate the significance that the suit of Wands shares with the two trees in the garden of Eden: the Tree of Knowledge and the Tree of Life.

In the garden of Eden, humans were regarded as the apex of creation. The trees in the garden represent man's potential, bearing fruit containing the sustenance they needed to evolve emotionally, as well as intellectually. God forbid Adam and Eve from partaking the fruit from the Tree of Knowledge. Yet, we all know telling someone "No" is the spark that awakens their desire—it ignites the will to receive. After Adam and Eve ate the forbidden fruit from the Tree of Knowledge their eyes were opened and they had a new broader sense of awareness. Their curiosities were ignited, and they had a thirst for the knowledge of the absolute truth of things. They were now able to experience pleasure, and the new sense of 'knowing' was pleasing to them. Their hearts were overwhelmed with a passion and a new lust for life. This new fire energy stimulated their 'will to receive', consequently ushering in the ability of willpower, which was necessary for them to control these new emotions felt for the first time—as this desire awakened within them.

The Minor Arcana cards in the suit of Wands, from the Ace to the 10, portray the progression of knowledge obtained by a person along their path to enlightenment. These ten cards depict the spiritual path up the Jacob's ladder aka the pathways or branches of the Tree of Life that exists within the human soul. As a person travels along this path, they transform the wisdom they gain into practical knowledge, incessantly broadening their spiritual awareness.

Interesting to note here is the relationship between cause and effect that the Aces share with the 10's in each suit. For instance, the Aces represent the root level (the cause), and the 10's reflect upon the Ace in its manifested form (the effect).

Each of the number 10 tarot cards depict the manifested idea, or concept, that is portrayed in the Aces of their same suit.

For instance, with the suit of Wands, the Ace has 3 branches on its large wand, while the 10 of Wands card has 33 branches. The number 33 connects to the concept of achieving Christ Consciousness. This is the manifested concept portrayed in the Ace of Wands card.

Let me explain. The 3 branches in the Ace of Wands connect to the energy that emanates out from Binah—the feminine creative force of God. The energy of Binah awakens within us the desire to obtain deeper spiritual understanding of all things. This particular Ace represents the root cause of the soul's desire to reach higher levels of awareness—having the will to achieve Christ Consciousness. This higher state of consciousness can be achieved through practices such as meditation and by working on ourselves.

The number 3 goes into 33 eleven times. The 11th sefirah, the hidden sefirah, is known as Da'at, meaning knowledge. Da'at contains within it all the knowledge or DATA held within the 10 sefirot on the Tree of Life. Da'at is considered to be the seed of the Tree. The sefirah Da'at is concealed within the Ace of Wands. Therefore, the path made from the Ace to the 10 is actually eleven steps opposed to ten. As a person progresses up this path, and continues to work on improving themselves, they will gradually elevate their soul's vibration, allowing them to ascend up the different levels of the soul, and climb up the Tree of Life within themselves. As they transverse along this path of cards, they will simultaneously travel through each of the ten sefirot as well. This path truly begins with Da'at, the hidden seed, and ends at the 10 of Wands. The Da'at is associated with the Fool card. The Fool card is placed before the Ace of Wands, acting as the hidden sefirah, the hidden seed beneath the earth which sprouts the root, which is represented in the Ace. By placing the Fool card at the beginning, it technically gives this path of Wands eleven cards.

Depicted in the 10 of Wands card is a man carrying ten wands which represent all the knowledge he acquired from each of the previous ten cards along the path laid out by the suit of Wands. He continues forward onto the next phase of his life, taking with him the knowledge he acquired and applies it towards resolving practical matters in the real world. The 33 branches found in the 10 of Wands card represent the elevated soul as it expands, ascending towards the upper world of Atziluth, at the top of the Tree. This ascension is a return back to the Source, to the World of Causes, and forming a connection with the divine presence of God the Creator in the infinite realm where man becomes one with God—sharing one consciousness.

The cells inside a seed all contain DNA. The code in that DNA tells the seed's cells what to do. When the seed is planted in the ground, its DNA will tell it how to grow into a plant.

There are millions of different species of living creatures on Earth and each one has its own unique DNA code. This concept of DNA can be compared to the concept of Da'at as being the seed containing all the DATA acting as the DNA code for the suit of Wands. This DNA code is concealed within the symbols illustrated on the Ace of Wands card.

Let us decipher the code. Firstly, you will notice that on the Ace there are exactly 37 rays of light surrounding God's hand. 37 is the Hebrew gematria value for Chokmah, meaning wisdom. Furthermore, the Ace also contains 8 Hebrew letter Yod's, which are colored green, and look similar to leaves. The number 8 corresponds with Hod, meaning brilliance of the mind. The 8 Yod's, which look like leaves, plus the wand's 10 leaves, (symbolizing the ten sefirot), equals 18. 18 is the gematria value for the word Chai, meaning life.

Worth mentioning here is that the Zohar, which is a foundational work in the literature of Jewish mystical thought, breaks up the word 'Chokmah' (numerical value of 37-ordinal), into the two roots of the word where you have 'Choah', meaning 'potential', and 'Mah', meaning 'what.' When you consider the two root words of Chokmah you get 'Choah mah', which means 'the potential of what is' or 'the potential of what is to be.'

Let us look at the breakdown of the Ace's DNA code to uncover deeper meaning.

Ace of Wands card consist of:

37 • Light rays that surround God's hand: Chokmah, wisdom

3 • Branches on the wand: Binah, understanding

10 • Leaves on the wand's branches: Ten Sefirot

8 • Yod's floating in the air: Hod, glory, brilliance

18 • Leaves in total when adding the 10 leaves on the wand and the 8 green-leaf Yod's together: Chai/life

When we add the sum of all these significant numbers, we get 37+3+10+8+18 = 76.

76 is the ordinal gematria value of the first word in the Torah, Bereshit בראשית, meaning "In the beginning". Students of the Torah always argue why the Torah does not begin with an Aleph, which is the first letter in the alphabet. Let us consider the Fool card here. The Hebrew letter assigned to the Fool is Aleph, with a value of 1. The Fool card is unique in that it can be placed at the beginning, the middle, or at the end of the Tarot Grid (or tarot wheel). The Fool can be perceived two ways, either it is just beginning a new journey or has returned back from one. As soon as one cycle ends, a new one begins. On the Tarot Grid, the Fool can be placed at the beginning of the Minor Arcana, (before the Ace of Wands) as well as be placed at the junction between the 10 of Pentacles and the Magician, where the Minors transition into the Majors. The Fool can also be placed at the very end of the Major Arcana, following the World card, which is merely the link which leads back to the Ace of Wands; connecting the end of the cycle back to its beginning. At this point, is where the Fool begins another journey; another rotation of the tarot wheel. The Latin word for wheel is rota, and is associated in mysticism as a routine and continuous loop of a specific cycle. For example, a yearly cycle consisting of 365 days, which is one complete Earth rotation around the Sun. The Kabbalists view the Torah as a yearly cycle consisting of reoccurring holy days that merit the opportunity for one to connect spiritually with the Creator. The Tarot can also be seen as such a cycle; a soul cycle depicted allegorically as the Fool's journey traveled along the path to enlightenment.

Aleph, in Jewish mysticism, represents the oneness of God.

The letter can be seen as being composed of an upper Yod, a lower Yod, and a Vav leaning on a diagonal. The upper Yod represents the hidden and ineffable aspects of God while the lower Yod represents God's revelation and presence in the world. The Vav (hook) connects the two realms. Aleph relates to the element air and the Scintillating Intelligence of the path between Keter and Chokmah on the Tree of Life just before this 'intelligence' is implanted in the vessel of Binah. When we add the Aleph (1) of the Fool card, (which is silent), to the beginning of the word Bereshit, concealed within the Ace of Wands card, we get $1+76 = 77$.

This is significant, because 77 is the gematria value for the Hebrew word mazel, meaning luck. We see here, in the beginning of the path of Wands, the gematria connection to mazel (77), and then, found within the final four Court cards, which represent the full expansion of the suit of Wands, we have a combined gematria value of 17, which just so happens to be the value of the word tov. Thus, the two opposite ends of the path, from beginning to end, laid out by the suit of Wands, links the beginning with Mazel, and the end of the path with Tov, as in the phrase "Mazel tov". Mazel tov, meaning good luck, good fortune. This is a clue letting us know that if we follow the advice found along the path of Wands, from the beginning to the end, our lives will be blessed with good fortune.

The original Hebrew word for 'tree' is 'etz' which is spelled and pronounced almost identically as the Hebrew word 'etzah', which means 'advice.'

The suit of Wands is the root of the entire tarot. The Ace of Wands is the first card in the tarot deck. Furthermore, the Ace of Wands is the first card on the Tarot Grid—located at the top left corner. At this location on the Grid, we have established the spiritual and gematria connections shared with the word mazel. Let us look deeper into the meaning of this word. Mazel is the term in Jewish mysticism to describe the root of the soul. The word mazel literally means 'a drip from above' or things that are 'trickling down from above.' The Tarot Grid begins with the Ace of Wands, and from there it flows down, and expands outwardly, forming rows of cards which increase in value as they descend further down the Grid, which flows from the Ace of Wands down to the World card.

Kabbalah teaches that every sefirah contains a whole Tree

inside itself. This concept is represented on the Ace's wand which has ten leaves on its three branches. This wand having three branches is a clue that the suit of Wands is associated with the third sefirah Binah, and the fact that this wand has ten leaves, we can assume that there is a whole Tree of Life to be found within the suit. Because this wand is associated with Binah, we can be sure that each card within the suit of Wands will reveal to us the manifested energy which emanates from Binah, just as fruit grows on a tree's branches.

I mustn't forget to mention the 'mushy' house depicted in the background of the Ace of Wands card. This house is seen as being in an imaginative dream state; merely an idea that is without form. This house represents the spiritual state of Da'at.

After having deciphered this Ace's many symbols, one could fully interpret the meaning this card encompasses. The Ace of Wands is about experiencing an epiphany, which ignites a brilliant idea. The Ace overwhelms you with creative energy, which inspires and motivates you to act upon your ideas. It represents the awakening of desire. It grants the willpower to turn an inspired idea into a reality, and to see things through. This creative force gives you the desire to create a better and more fulfilling life for yourself. It gives you the motivation to work on yourself and build upon your character. This energy allows you to perceive things differently; in a positive light. It represents the moment when a person experiences a mild shift in their awareness, which brings upon an optimistic approach towards problem solving, which is necessary for one to become a master at transforming the wisdom gained from personal experience into practical know-how—being able to understand one matter with the understanding of another matter.

By studying this path of cards, which leads from the Ace of Wands to the 10 of Wands, (which travels through the ten sefirot located on the branches of the Tree of Life), one could gain the spiritual knowledge necessary to conquer their ego-nature. By applying the life advice found within each of the Wands cards a person will be led towards self-improvement and correcting unruly behaviors. When life is approached pro-actively, it proves to be the easier path taken in the long run. It is wise for a person to correct themselves pro-actively before life does it for them. Life has a way of facing us with challenging situations that trigger us and cause us to react negatively. We must be aware of our behaviors as well as our habits, and to quit any habit which does not serve us. The purpose of traveling this path is to grow spiritually, obtain higher levels of awareness, and in the end achieve Christ Consciousness.

The path paved out by the suit of Wands guides us to the deeper understanding of how the wands relate to the trees in the garden of Eden. One could follow this path in order to find their own personal 'Eden' or paradise—in order to obtain a spiritual connection with the higher-self, and raise the awareness and the inner richness which can pass through the mind and the soul only.

Worth mentioning here are the multiple significant gematria connections shared with the Wands and the number 177. Firstly, 177 is the gematria value of the phrase 'garden of Eden'.

177 is also the value of the Hebrew word qoz, meaning walnut. Walnuts are linked with discernment—the particular gift received by Adam and Eve after eating from the Tree of Knowledge of Good and Evil. After which, they were able to discern between the two. The walnut reminds us to use discernment as we navigate through times of challenges, loss and misfortune.

Walnuts were known in ancient times as the 'nut of Jupiter.' Jupiter has always been associated with knowledge; the thirst for knowledge, evolution of knowledge, and expansion of the mind. It is interesting that the structure of a walnut resembles a human brain. In fact, walnuts are considered one of the best foods for brain health and longevity.

The suit of Wands represents the source for all energy, and it symbolizes human willpower—the ability to control one's energy. The Wands advise us of ways to control our impulses and actions; self-control. Interesting to note is that the Hebrew name Uel, meaning the 'will of God' has the gematria value of 177.

Moving forward, the suit of Wands is rooted in the power of 3. The number 3 corresponds to the third sefirah on the Tree of Life, Binah. Binah represents the feminine creative force of God; present in all creation. Binah is the 'will to form.' The number 3 is associated with being the seed level, the root cause of manifested matter. The word Binah, has a gematria value of 67. $67 \times 3 = 201$, which is the value for the Hebrew word Or, meaning light.

Let us look further into the first couple verses of Genesis to deepen our understanding of this gematria connection.

Genesis 1:1-5

In the beginning God created the heavens and the earth.
Now the earth was **formless** and empty, darkness was over the surface of the deep, and the Spirit of God was hovering over the waters.
And God said, "Let there be light," and there was light.
God saw that the light was good, and he separated the light from the darkness.
God called the light "day," and the darkness he called "night." And there was evening, and there was morning—the first day.

We see in these verses that the earth was without form before the light—formless.

Coincidentally, in the third verse it states "And God said, Let there be light", and with the light came creation, forming the structure of time; creating the first day, which divided the light from the darkness; morning and night. From Binah came the light of creation and the will to form.

The light gives matter the will to manifest. The seed, or spark, of light within Binah, who represents the third sefirah, which holds the spiritual power of the number 3, expands outwardly and manifests itself into the 3rd dimension. This light, which contains the creative force of God, continues to add upon itself as it multiplies its greatness for infinity.

Binah takes the original idea and expands and develops it both in breadth and depth. It crystallizes and clarifies the details of the idea.

When God brought forth the light of creation it formed the first day, separating the morning from the night, and creating a sense of time. Binah, who gave birth to the light, is ruled by Saturn. Saturn is the god of agriculture, hence its association with the suit of Wands (trees), but most importantly Saturn is the lord of time. The Hebrew word for day is yom. Yom is not just for day, but for time in general. How yom is translated depends on the context of its use with other words in the sentence around it, depending on its translation and use of hermeneutics. The word day is used somewhat the same way in the English language. For examples, "In my grandfather's day, there were no cellphones" or "In the day of the dinosaurs, plant life was larger." The word yom is used in the name of various Jewish feast days such as, Yom Kippur, the Day of Atonement. Yom is also used in each of the days of the week in the Hebrew calendar, as in Yom Shabbat, meaning 'rest day' aka Saturday. The word yom has several literal definitions. Yom can pertain to a period of light (as contrasted with the period of darkness). It can also be used as a general term for time, or point of time. It can describe the period between sunrise to sunset or sunset to next sunset. It has been used as reference to a 24-hour day, a year, an age, an epoch, as well as a season.

Throughout the suit of Wands, we see the correlation between cause and effect, and how a seed contains the potential of the manifest. The only thing separating the cause from its effect is time. Time permits the development of growth, expansion and evolution, which we see portrayed in the Wands in multiples of 3. For instance, there are exactly 59 wands found throughout the entire suit. $59 \times 3 = 177$, which is the value of the phrase 'garden of Eden.' This reference takes us back to the relationship the Ace of Wands shares with the 10 of Wands card. Let me explain. The Ace being the seed level (the cause), and the 59 wands, which are found throughout the entire suit of Wands, represent the manifested effect. The cause, or seed level of consciousness, symbolized in the Ace is the implantation of desire, arousing a desire for desire. The final card found at the end of this path of Wands, from the cause to its effect, is the 10 of Wands, which represents the Ace's potential in its fully manifested form.

You will notice the Ace has 3 branches on its wand, while the 10 of Wands card contains 33. The multiple of 3 concept is easy to spot here, but what is the connection? We know that 33 divided by 3 equals 11, but what is the significance of the number 11? I will explain. The Ace of Wands contains the seed, Da'at, which grows and expands upon itself, furthering its growth and development as it travels along the path laid out by the suit of Wands' cards. The seed's progression is portrayed in each card, and continues to evolve up into the 10 of Wands card. At this point, the seed could be considered as a fully developed fruit, having grown 10 times its original size. The man in the 10 of Wands card is pictured carrying ten wands in his hands as he marches forward. He is moving onto the final 11th stage of the seed's evolution, where he will reach the 33rd degree. This is the stage where the soul returns back to the Source—where the effect returns back to the World of Causes. The seed of the Tree of Life is known as Da'at; considered the 11th sefirah on the Tree. Concealed within Da'at is the seed containing a spark of God's Light, which implants the seed with the desire and the will to grow, expand and evolve. This evolution process leads the seed back to the source of where it started. Kabbalah teaches that the root of the Tree of Life is located at the top of the Tree; at the sefirah Keter, meaning crown. The seed's path leads down the Tree to the lowest sefirah Malchut, which is the kingdom where all things manifest. From this point, the seed expands, grows and evolves back up the Tree, eventually returning to the source where it becomes one with the Creator. Interesting to note here is that Jesus Christ was 33 years old when he was crucified. On the day of his death, he was reunited with the Father.

The concealed light within Da'at is a spark of the Divine Light, which is present in all creation. It is a spark of the Divine. When you add the sum of the values for the three divine names of God, you get 177. Add the names Elohim (86), Adonai (65), and YHVH (26) which gives you $86+65+26 = 177$. 177, being the value of the phrase 'garden of Eden', connects us to the Kabbalistic concept of Eden, which is that it represents paradise. Kabbalist suggest that this 'paradise' can be reached by obtaining higher levels of awareness. Hence, the 33rd degree, Christ Consciousness.

The ten sefirot are generally divided into two categories: Intellect and Emotions. The category of Intellect includes the three intellectual powers of Chokmah, Binah, and Da'at. The emotive powers are represented by the seven channels of Chesed, Gevurah, Tiferet, Netzach, Hod, Yesod, and Malchut. They are also referred to as the Three Mothers and the Seven Doubles.

The Three Mothers are seen as the source or the root of the other seven sefirot, just as a mother is the source of her offspring. The Three Mothers are the intellectual powers Binah, meaning understanding, Chokmah, meaning wisdom, and Da'at, meaning knowledge. By forming a connection with the Three Mothers one is able to tap into the source of God's intelligence where they can receive Godly insights and deeper understandings that grant them the willpower to transform wisdom into knowledge.

"Knowing yourself is the beginning of all wisdom." - Aristotle

Aristotle's quote is at the core of how to improve and strengthen your willpower. Once we understand the root source of our behaviors, it is easier to work towards our goals.

Most of our choices are made on 'autopilot', without any awareness of what's really driving them or the effects they will have in our lives. So, the first step to changing any behavior is self-awareness. Self-awareness is the ability to recognize what we are doing as we're doing it. Our thought processes, emotions and reasons for acting are an important part of making better choices.

Having the desire to improve yourself and the willpower to see it through will result in you being happier, feeling healthier, more satisfied in your relationships, wealthier and further ahead in your career, and better able to manage stress, deal with conflict and overcome adversity.

Chapter 14

The Secrets Hidden in the 9's

All the number 9 tarot cards and tarot cards associated with the number 9 contain a secret hidden in plain sight waiting to be unveiled by someone with the eyes to see. Real eyes will realize.

The 9th sefirah on the Kabbalah Tree of Life is Yesod, which is associated with the Moon. The light reflected by the Moon unveils secrets and hidden truths about our emotional, shadow-nature.

The light of the Moon unveils hidden secrets and hidden truths.

9 of Wands:

And so, we begin with the 9 of Wands card. Here we see a man holding a wand tightly in his hands as he faces an overwhelming challenge before him, represented here by the eight wands that form an intimidating wall—blocking him from proceeding any further.

Each of the 9 wands has 3 branches, with a total of 27 branches altogether. The number 27 connects us to the Progressed Lunar Return. The Progressed Moon takes 27 years to complete the cycle around the natal chart, and it generally marks an opening of the emotional body that can be exhilarating or painful, depending on the person's natal chart and the way the individual handles challenges. This prepares a person for their Saturn Return. It takes approximately 30 years for Saturn to return and complete its orbit back into your life from the day of your birth. A 'return' happens when any planet completes its entire circuit through the sky and returns to the same place it was at the time of your birth. Saturn Returns rule over growing up, accountability, fears, insecurities, reality, higher self-standards and karma. It can result in an identity crisis where you will have to face your deepest fears. A person begins to feel the energy of Saturn's return as early as the age of 27. Saturn's influence passes through and can be felt until the age of 32. And then, by the age of 33 years old, a person is considered to be 'born again.' They have dealt with past-life karma and are now spiritually ready to begin their new journey. They have reached true mature adulthood. Saturn helps us become stronger.

9 of Cups:

Next, we have the 9 of Cups card. Pictured here is a man sitting proudly in front of a row of nine cups that are displayed neatly on top of a curved shelf. The secret hidden in plain sight here is that the nine cups portray a curved Jewish menorah used during Hanukkah, the festival of lights. The shelf is curved, mimicking the style of menorahs that were made in early times.

The man sitting with his arms folded is known as the shamash, meaning attendant or servant, who lights the candles of the menorah. The shamash is the name given to the ninth candle on the menorah, which is the specific candle used to light all the other eight candles on the menorah, signifying the eight days of Hanukkah. The man pictured here is proud, knowing he was the one that lit all these cups using the light found within himself. Interesting to note here is that the Hebrew word for Sun is shemesh. The shemesh is similar to the shamash because they both serve humanity and sustain life. They both are dependable and can be counted on to do their job, and they both are the source of their own light and are fulfilled when they share their light and provide a reliable source of light for others.

9 of Swords:

The 9 of Swords card shows a man sitting up in his bed with his head in his hands, crying and feeling guilty, which brings upon emotional insecurities. This can also reflect feelings of being victimized. Nine swords line up above his head. Swords represent thoughts, and these nine swords which are lined up in a row above this man (in the air) symbolize the list of thoughts racing through the man's head, which cause him anguish.

The secret hidden in plain sight here is carved in the wooden panel on the base of the bed. Carved in the wood is a picture of a man violently pushing another man to the ground. The man in the bed is wearing white, representing his innocence in the matter. He blames others and plays victim. It doesn't matter if he was the one who did the pushing, or if he was the one who was pushed to the ground in this scenario, in either circumstance he views himself as being the victim. His hair is white, symbolizing his belief in his purity and innocence, but also conveys wisdom. Therefore, the man is wise to think about and rehash the details of the confrontation, making himself a mental list to further analyze the details of what happened.

His blanket is covered with astrological symbols of the zodiac. The zodiac contains all the knowledge of karmic lessons learned along the path of life. He would be wise to comfort himself in such great understanding, and then wake up the following morning with peace of mind. He will have a stronger spirit, which will empower his mood control, and he will no longer find himself lashing out in the future. For having replaying the confrontation in his head, and feeling sorry for his actions, and thinking about what he should have done instead, is a practical form of repentance. Next time, when this or a similar situation happens again, he will do what he would have rather have done instead, and not repeat the past mistake; having truly learned from his life-lesson.

9 of Pentacles:

The next card, the 9 of Pentacles, shows a maiden holding a Peregrine falcon. Falconry being a traditional sport practiced by both men and women. She holds her falcon here waiting for her suitor to arrive. This scene could be symbolically connected to the social event of the Tu B'Av holiday, known as Jewish Valentine's Day where maidens would dance in the vineyard and wait for suitors to approach them, looking for marriage. Falconry was a perfect activity to set up the scenario for courting. These falcons were coined the term 'lovebirds' due to the fact that they brought men and women together.

The suit of Pentacles can relate to friendships and

relationships, such as the relationship and bond this woman and her falcon share. She is depicted here gazing at her Peregrine falcon with love and pride. It takes time, patience and nurturing care to train a falcon obedience, trust and how to hunt. From the look on the woman's face, this falcon appears to have made this maiden feel proud of its accomplishments and growth. The falcon must have come a long way.

The secret hidden in plain sight here is the 40 roses on the maiden's dress. The number 40 is of much significance in Kabbalah, and is seen throughout the tarot as well as the Torah. The number 40 represents a measurement of spiritual timing it takes to cleanse and to purify the soul. This process can be challenging, requires a persistence of will and involves a devotion of your time as well as patience. It takes 40 days for someone to break their old habits and routines and begin a new one. The number 40 represents the time needed for personal growth, transition, change, the concept of renewal or a new beginning. The number 40 has the power to lift a spiritual state. The number 40 connects to the sefirah Binah, which means understanding. According to the Talmud (Avot 5:26), at age 40 a person transitions from one level of wisdom to the next. He reaches the level of Binah, the deeper insight of understanding one matter from another. Binah is connected to the feminine aspect of the Tree of Life. After Moses led the Jewish people for 40 years in the wilderness, he told them, "God has not given you a heart to know, and eyes to see, and ears to hear, until this day" (Deut. 29:3-4). From here we see that it took the Jewish people 40 years before reaching a full level of understanding.

40 signifies the time needed for spiritual cleansing and being ready to receive God's blessings. The 40 roses on this maiden's dress signify that she is open to receive love and is mature enough for marriage. It shows that she is ready and willing to commit to a husband. All the number 9 cards are associated with the sefirah Yesod, which is ruled by the Moon. The Moon relates to aspects of receiving and of passiveness, connecting this card to this woman's situation where she is depicted as waiting in the vineyard for her suitor to approach. It reflects upon trust and faith, just as the maiden trusts in her falcon to return she also places faith in her suitor to arrive.

The Hermit:

In the next card we have the Hermit seen standing on the mountain top. He holds the lantern that guides others up and along the path to enlightenment. He wields a golden staff representing the spiritual knowledge he obtained during his lifetime. The six-pointed star inside his lantern is Saturn's star which holds the spiritual Light and understanding of Binah, which is ruled by Saturn. He has reached enlightenment and has become a channel for the Light. He is the gateway or bridge that creates a union between the astral plane of Yesod and the physical world of Malchut. Yesod is the bridge (or chute) between the infinite potential of procreation that flows into it and its actual manifestation in the progeny of man.

This can be understood by looking at the magic and mathematics of the number 9. When you multiply any number with 9 you always end up with the digital root number 9. For example, $9 \times 2 = 18$, and when reduced is $1+8 = 9$. Or $9 \times 6 = 54$, and then reduced is $5+4 = 9$. Or try a larger number: $9 \times 2,376 = 21,384$, and then reduce this large number by adding its digits $2+1+3+8+4 = 18$, which then further reduces to $1+8 = 9$. The sum of the digits always equal 9. Also, the multiplying of number 9 by continuous numbers will result

in a pyramid formation with numbers getting larger and larger as
they fan out from the top working their way down.

Table 1	Table 2
$1 \times 9 = 9$	$1 \times 9 + 2 = 11$
$12 \times 9 = 108$	$12 \times 9 + 3 = 111$
$123 \times 9 = 1107$	$123 \times 9 + 4 = 1111$
$1234 \times 9 = 11106$	$1234 \times 9 + 5 = 11111$
$12345 \times 9 = 111105$	$12345 \times 9 + 6 = 111111$
$123456 \times 9 = 1111104$	$123456 \times 9 + 7 = 1111111$
$1234567 \times 9 = 11111103$	$1234567 \times 9 + 8 = 11111111$
$12345678 \times 9 = 111111102$	$12345678 \times 9 + 9 = 111111111$
$123456789 \times 9 = 1111111101$	$123456789 \times 9 + 10 = 1111111111$

Sum of digits in
each line equals 9

The sefirah Yesod is the bridge from infinite down into finite. It
funnels down all the other sefirot down into their manifest state.
Yesod is identified in the Torah with tzaddik, meaning the 'righteous
one', and usually associated with a righteous person, which is
symbolized by the Hermit, who is easily comparable to Moses who
was considered to be a Tzaddik. In the very body of the tzaddik,
finite and limited in time and space, God's infinite Light and creative
life-force becomes manifest. The tzaddik creates on the spiritual
plane as well as on the physical plane. This idea can be
conceptualized by the male phallic, symbolized here by the Hermit's
staff, and the procreation process of life-force from within
manifesting in the seed or semen of man. The tzaddik experiences
creation in the inner third eye of his consciousness, in the continual
flow of new insights and true innovations in his spiritual study. He
creates by arousing the souls of his generation to return to the path of
enlightenment and reach unity with the higher-self.

The secret hidden in plain sight here is the evil face on the back of
the Hermit's head. This face appears grumpy, angry, negative and
judgmental. This face represents the Hermit's ego; his adversary.
This adversary is the voice in the back of the Hermit's head telling
him to give up on the people that he is helping. The adversary sits
with his arms crossed, losing his patience with the Hermit, all the

while complaining, bitching, doubting and being pessimistic. The Hermit struggles to keep this negative voice out of his head. The adversary attempts to make the Hermit feel as if he is working towards a lost cause, and that his people are not worth it. The adversary tells the Hermit he should save himself, focus only on himself and move on progressing towards a higher state of enlightenment. But the Hermit knows that by helping others he will in return receive Light and wisdom by helping them establish a union with God the Creator.

The Hermit can be seen here as a representation of Moses standing on top of Mount Sinai, where he receives the Ten Commandments from God. Sinai, referencing Sin, the Mesopotamian deity of the Moon. Mount Sinai, meaning the mountain of the Moon.

As the Exodus story goes, Moses comes down from the mountain with the first set of tablets to find the Jewish people idolizing a golden calf. Moses is infuriated and he breaks the tablets on the ground. The people were obviously not ready and/or worthy to receive God's commandments. God then told Moses to give the people a second chance; to go back up to the top of Mount Sinai, where Moses would have to make a second set of tablets for the Jewish people. This story illustrates Moses' battle with his own ego as he tries to do the right thing as a leader of the Israelite nation. For 40 years, Moses cared for the children of Israel as a nurse carries a baby, fulfilling their every need, and representing them before God, especially when they messed up and incurred His displeasure—which happened all too often. Moses' tenure as leader was punctuated by episodes of rebellion and complaint, but he always ended up giving the Israelites a second chance.

The Moon:

The Moon card is very magical and holds many secrets hidden in plain sight. For instance, the 32 rays located around the Moon. These rays correspond to the 32 paths of wisdom one takes along the Tree of Life on their journey towards spiritual enlightenment. The Hermit is seen here as the face of the Moon with its 32 rays surrounding his head. The 32nd path, which is Tav on the Tree of Life, connects the sefirah Yesod to Malchut. The 32nd branch is the bridge from the infinite potential of the astral plane down into the manifested finite material plane of existence. The enlightened Hermit is connected to and is in union with the Creator's Light and is reflecting (sharing) His Light to the world below.

Pictured below the Hermit is a wolf and a dog. The Hermit shares his Light and wisdom with the wolf, transforming him into a domesticated fun-loving dog. The crawfish coming out of the water represents mankind at their early stage of conscious awareness as they enter the world and begin their spiritual journey. This crawfish resembles the symbol for Cancer (ruled by the Moon), the crab, which portrays the Hermit at the beginning of his journey in search of enlightenment. The Hermit is now at a point where he can guide others, and he becomes the nurturer; and thus, arriving at the end of the cycle. The Hermit sheds light on the path, guiding the crawfish along its journey up through the pillars. These pillars mark the boundaries of the known, a crossroads going from one state of awareness to the next, crossing into the unknown.

With the light of the Moon the Hermit unveils the 15 Yod's floating in the night sky. The number 15 is associated with Saturn. It is one of the magic numbers of Saturn's square, which includes, 3, 9, 15, and 45. When you add the 15 Yod's to the number of the Moon card, Roman numeral XVIII, you get 33 (15+18). 33 represents the connection and union with the Christ Consciousness obtained by a fully enlightened being that has progressed all the way up the Jacob's ladder, or the kundalini, also known as the 33 vertebrae of the spinal column from base chakra up to the crown. When a person is connected to the Christ Consciousness is when they are able to draw energy from Saturn, through the third eye, and make wishes come true— manifest their desires. Furthermore, the number 15 relates to the full moon, because it is the 15th day of the Lunar cycle that the moon is fullest. The fullness of the moon makes it possible to unveil the 15 Yod's hidden in the night sky, which makes it possible to make the connection to the number 33 that relates to Christ Consciousness.

And this concludes the secrets of the 9's. Knowing these hidden mysteries is the key to understanding these cards on a deeper level that will enrich further study and improve tarot card readings.

Chapter 15

The Mystical Number 40: Found Throughout the Tarot

The number 40 reveals great significance any time it is seen throughout the Tarot. Each time connecting to a much deeper understanding of the spiritual messages concealed within the particular card.

There are nine cards in the Rider-Waite-Smith tarot deck that contain hidden and some not so hidden 40's within them. And these nine cards are: the Ace of Cups, 9 of Pentacles, the Death card, the Chariot, the Wheel of Fortune, the Hanged Man, the Hierophant, the Empress, and the Hermit.

Allow me to explain where to locate the example of 40 in each of these cards.

Ace of Cups:
Written on the large cup is the letter M, which is the Hebrew letter Mem, meaning water, and it has a numerical value of 40. This 'M' on the cup is also referring to the Virgin Mary. Depicted here is the white dove representing the holy spirit as it places a communion wafer, representing the body of Christ, into the M-Cup. This cup

represents the vessel (or womb) of Mary. Thus, the Holy Spirit places the spirit of Christ inside Mary's womb, impregnating her. The length of a woman's pregnancy is always considered to be 40 weeks.

9 of Pentacles:
There are exactly 40 flowers on the woman's dress, representing her being both spiritually and physically mature to receive courtship/marriage.

The Death card:
There are four Xs on the horse's strap. The Roman numeral X has a value of 10, where10×4 = 40. This example of 40 refers to the knight arriving at a turning point in his life, and having reached a certain level of spiritual maturity, self-realization.

The Chariot:
There are exactly 40 stars on the chariot's blue canopy, again alluding to spiritual growth and reaching a higher degree of awareness.

The Wheel of Fortune:
There are exactly 40 items found within this card. There are 10 groups of 4 alike pieces of wisdom, which results in 10×4 = 40.

The Hanged Man:
The Hebrew letter associated with this card is Mem, meaning water, with a value of 40.

The Hierophant:
There are four Xs on the Hierophant's platform that he sits upon. Thus, 10×4 = 40.

The Empress:
The Empress's dress adorns 40 pomegranates—alluding to the 40 weeks of the gestational period.

The Hermit:
The Hermit is actually Moses standing on top of Mount Sinai, where he dwelled in the presence of God for 40 days and 40 nights. The 40

days aspect is portrayed in the lighter front side of the Hermit/Moses, while the 40 nights aspect is portrayed on the Hermit's darker back side. Although the Hermit's robe is all the same shade of gray, (the color associated with wisdom), the Hermit's two faces reflect either a light or dark disposition. Have you ever noticed the Hermit has two faces? He has a compassionate face in the front, and at the same time has a displeased face on the back of his head. With thorough examination, you will notice that there is another Hermit located along the Hermit's entire backside. The Hermit's dark side is standing with his arms crossed and his nose in the air. This darker, displeased side expresses Moses having to return back up Mount Sinai after having witnessed the Israelites worshipping the golden calf. As the story goes, Moses came down the mountain after 40 days with the first set of tablets/ten commandments, which were written by the hand of God himself, and saw that the Jewish people were not spiritually ready to receive them, having had built a false idol. At this point, Moses crushed the tablets upon the ground in a mad rage. God then commanded Moses to return back up the mountain for another 40 more days, where he would have to make a new set of tablets on his own. Moses was allowed to return back to his people once they were spiritually ready to receive the new set of tablets.

The letter Mem means water, and all these tarot cards listed above relate to the element water in some way. For instance, the three water signs of the Zodiac are Cancer, Scorpio, and Pisces, which correspond directly to some of these cards. For example, the Chariot is directly associated with the sign of Cancer, the Death card is associated with Scorpio and the Wheel of Fortune is ruled by Jupiter, who rules over Pisces. All the number 9 cards correspond with the Tree of Life's sefirah Yesod, which is ruled by the Moon that rules over Cancer. Therefore, the 9 of Pentacles card as well as the Hermit are influenced by Cancer's energy. Likewise, the Empress who is pregnant sits on a comfy bed of pillows in front of a canal, alluding that her *water* is soon to break out of her birth canal.

Mentioned earlier, the Hanged Man card is assigned to the Hebrew letter Mem, and it bears the healing aspect in which water encompasses. The Ace of Cups bears a similar connection to the healing and cleansing power of water. All four tarot Aces correspond to the Four-Letter Name of God, YHVH, known as the tetragrammaton. For instance, the Ace of Wands connects to Yod (fire), Ace of Cups with Heh (water), Ace of Swords with Vav (air), and lastly, the Ace of Pentacles with the second Heh (earth). Thereby, the Ace of Cups corresponds with the element of water.

As seen specifically in the Hierophant card, and yet similarly in all these cards, the number 40 connects to a certain degree or level of time it takes to reach a spiritual cleansing, which is needed in order for one to receive higher wisdom or desire. The number 40 represents the time it takes to transform your mind, body, spirit and soul. 40 is a significant number seen throughout the tarot, and always associates with reaching a higher level of understanding by way of spiritual growth. 40 is a measurement of time according to its spiritual context, and this particular concept of time is relative.

The number 40 reveals great significance throughout the Tarot, the Torah, the Talmud, and the Bible. The number 40 represents transition or change; the concept of renewal; a new beginning. The number 40 has the power to lift a spiritual state.

According to yogic technology, it takes 40 days to change a habit—to retrain the mental process and nervous system. Practicing anything for at least 40 days allows you the opportunity to incorporate it into your being, turn on, wake up, transform.

In Judaism, when a person becomes ritually impure, he must immerse in a ritual bath, known as a mikvah. The Talmud tells us that a mikvah must be filled with 40 se'ahs (a measurement of water). Immersion in a mikvah is the consummate Jewish symbol of spiritual renewal.

It is no accident that in the story of Noah, the rain poured for 40 days, and submerged the world in water. Just as a person leaves a mikvah pure, so too when the waters of the flood subsided, the world was purified from the licentiousness which had corrupted it in the days of Noah.

Moses was on Mount Sinai for 40 days and came down with the stone tablets. The Jews arrived at Mount Sinai as a nation of Egyptian slaves, but after 40 days they were transformed into God's nation.

According to the Talmud, it takes 40 days for an embryo to be formed in its mother's womb.

In Kabbalah, 40 represents the four sides of the world, each side containing the ten sefirot.

When a rabbinical court finds someone guilty of a crime, the punishment is sometimes lashes, prescribed in the Torah as "forty less one." The purpose is to bring the offender to a point of change, transition and atonement.

There are 40 days between the first day of Elul, when the Jewish people begin to blow the Shofar to prepare for Rosh Hashana, until Yom Kippur, the end of the annual teshuva (repentance) period. These 40 days are the most auspicious time for personal growth and renewal.

According to the Talmud (Avot 5:26), at age 40 a person transitions from one level of wisdom to the next. He reaches the level of Binah—the deeper insight of understanding one matter from another. After Moses led the Jewish people for 40 years in the wilderness, he told them: "God has not given you a heart to know, and eyes to see, and ears to hear, until this day." - Deut. 29:3-4. From here we see that it took the Jewish people 40 years before reaching a full level of understanding.

To conclude, the number 40 is concealed within each of these nine cards. $40 \times 9 = 360$. The number 360 is significant here, because it is the gematria value of the Hebrew letter Shin when it is spelled שׁין.

360 is the total degrees of a circle, and therefore the word Shin reflects upon the concept of spiritual return, as well as change, and becoming well-rounded. Things take time to develop. And knowledge takes time to be fully understood. We grow with experience, which comes with time, and as we continue along our spiritual path our knowledge obtained will eventually transform into wisdom.

The letter Shin means tooth, and as a tooth that bites into something hard and difficult to digest at first, it begins to first chew on it, and slowly transforms it into something softer before it can be swallowed. Once swallowed, we digest it slowly and it gives us sustenance.

Knowledge, just like food, gives us pleasure. Once we get a taste for it, we grow hungry for more. In this cycle of uncovering hidden truths and acquiring deeper understanding of all things, we come full-circle. 360 is the total degrees of a circle, thus the word Shin reflects upon the concept of spiritual return, as well as change, becoming well-rounded. Things take time to develop. It takes time for knowledge to be fully understood, and it takes experience which comes with time for that knowledge to transform itself into wisdom. As mentioned, the letter Shin means tooth, and a tooth will bite into something hard, chew on it, and then slowly transform that certain something into something that can be swallowed. Once swallowed, we then slowly digest it and it gives us sustenance. Knowledge like food gives us pleasure, and we grow hungry for more. In this cycle, we come full-circle. When something 'comes full circle,' it completes a cycle, returns to its beginnings. When a human life has come full circle, it goes from optimism to pessimism and back to optimism again. And yet, with each new beginning, each time we take another bite of our desire, we are not merely starting from scratch, but rather we are starting from experience.

Below is a list of examples of the number 40 found in Judaism and in Christianity.

Judaism:

In the Hebrew Bible, 40 is often used for time periods, 40 days or 40 years, which separate 'two distinct epochs.'

Rain fell for "forty days and forty nights" during the Flood (Genesis 7:4).

Noah waited for forty days after the tops of mountains were seen after the flood, before releasing a raven (Genesis 8:5-7).

Spies were sent by Moses to explore the land of Canaan (promised to the children of Israel) for "forty days" (Numbers 13:2, 25).

The Hebrew people lived in the lands outside of the promised land for "forty years". This period of years represents the time it takes for a new generation to arise (Numbers 32:13).

Several early Hebrew leaders and kings are said to have ruled for "forty years", that is, a generation. Examples include Eli (1 Samuel

4:18), Saul (Acts 13:21), David (2 Samuel 5:4), and Solomon (1 Kings 11:42).

Goliath challenged the Israelites twice a day for forty days before David defeated him (1 Samuel 17:16).

Moses spent three consecutive periods of "forty days and forty nights" on Mount Sinai: He went up on the seventh day of Sivan, after God gave the Torah to the Jewish people, in order to learn the Torah from God, and came down on the seventeenth day of Tammuz, when he saw the Jews worshiping the Golden Calf and broke the tablets (Deuteronomy 9:11). He went up on the eighteenth day of Tammuz to beg forgiveness for the people's sin and came down without God's atonement on the twenty-ninth day of Av (Deuteronomy 9:25). He went up on the first day of Elul and came down on the tenth day of Tishrei, the first YomKippur, with God's atonement (Deuteronomy 10:10).

A mikvah consists of 40 se'ahs (approximately 120 gallons or 454 liters) of water.

The prophet Elijah had to walk 40 days and 40 nights before arriving at Mount Horeb (1 Kings 19:8).

40 lashes are one of the punishments meted out by the Sanhedrin (Deuteronomy 25:3), though in actual practice only 39 lashes were administered.

(Numbers 14:33–34) Alludes to the same with ties to the prophecy in The Book of Daniel. "For forty years—one year for each of the forty days you explored the land—you will suffer for your sins and know what it is like to have me against you."

One of the prerequisites for a man to study Kabbalah is that he is 40 years old.

"The registering of these men was carried on cruelly, zealously, assiduously, from the rising of the sun to its going down, and was not brought to an end in forty days" (3 Maccabees 4:15).

Christianity:

Christianity similarly uses forty to designate important time periods.

Before his temptation, Jesus fasted "forty days and forty nights" in the Judean desert (Matthew 4:2, Mark 1:13, Luke 4:2).

Forty days was the period from the resurrection of Jesus to the ascension of Jesus (Acts 1:3).

Moses' life is divided into three 40-year segments, separated by his growing to adulthood, fleeing from Egypt, and his return to lead his people out (Acts 7:23, 30, 36).

In modern Christian practice, Lent consists of the 40 days preceding Easter. In much of Western Christianity, Sundays are excluded from the count; in Eastern Christianity, Sundays are included.

Chapter 16

Meditational Grounding: To Merge
One's Self with the Tarot

In order to prevent oneself from experiencing an anxiety attack, they are advised to 'ground' themselves. They are supposed to slowly look around their surroundings and exercise their senses one by one while concentrating on their breathing. This will cause them to snap out of their head and come back down to earth, and back to reality.

Experts suggest following six steps to prevent an anxiety attack. The first step is to breathe deeply in through your nose and out through your mouth slowly while concentrating on your breathing. The next step is to slowly look around and find five things you can see. After which, look around slowly and find four things you can touch. Then, look around and find three things you can hear. Then find two things you can smell. And finally, as you look around, connect to one emotion you feel. This is called Grounding, and it can help when you feel like you've gone too far in your head and lost all control of your surroundings.

Grounding will get a person *out* of their head, while Meditational Grounding will get a person *into* their head, with the intention of transporting them into a non-physical realm, where they ground themselves (consciously) into another dimension or conscious state of awareness.

These six steps for grounding fall under the concept of practicing mindfulness. Mindfulness can help ground you in the reality of what's around you. Since panic attacks can cause a feeling of detachment or separation from reality, this can combat your panic attack as it's happening. However, when practicing Meditational Grounding the more mindful one is of the new realm they wish to transport their conscious awareness into the more real and tangible (clearer) that world becomes to them. It only requires a simple shift in consciousness.

Ultimately, the idea is to place yourself, aka ground yourself, into the illustrated world of the tarot.

In order to ground one's self into their physical reality, psychology experts advise a person to focus on the physical sensations they are familiar with, like digging your feet into the ground, or feeling the texture of your jeans on your hands. These specific sensations ground you firmly in reality and give you something objective to focus on. This concept is ideal when applied to the practice of Meditational Grounding for when you wish to truly dive into the tarot.

When attempting to ground yourself into the tarot, find a focus object. Some people find it helpful to find a single object to focus all of their attention on during this grounding meditation. Pick one object in clear sight and consciously note everything about it possible.

For example, you may notice the peculiar way a person places their foot on the ground, and how it's slightly unbalanced. Perhaps a certain leaf stands out amongst the others. Describe the pattern, color, shape and size of the object to yourself. Focus all of your energy on this object, and you will begin to detach from your physical surroundings.

Following these steps will consequently allow one to 'sink' into and/or 'ground' one's self into the card's illustrations on a subconscious level. Opposite of how to deal with a panic attack where you try to get out of your head, you follow these steps in order to delve further inside your head, and into another dimension altogether. Either way you look at it, it is all about shifting your consciousness out of one state and into another. As you transport yourself into the illustrated world of the tarot you will transition your awareness from your physical reality and place your consciousness into the realm created within the tarot card. The deeper you delve into a subconscious and meditative state, the further you ground yourself inside the card.

As you meditate, imagine yourself inside the tarot card as if you are actually there. Slowly look around and acquaint yourself with your new surroundings. As you look in all directions, this new world will gradually develop into something more tangible, just as if you were lucid dreaming. At this point, your mind will be open to receiving deeper understanding, godly insights and inspiration attained with higher levels of awareness, which is needed to unveil the mysteries hidden within the symbols. "Symbolism is the language of the mysteries. By symbols men have ever sought to communicate to each other those thoughts which transcend the limitations of language." - Manly P. Hall

Furthermore, the idea is to focus and connect to the tarot on a deep subconscious level as you submerge yourself and become one with a particular card (or even a combination of cards), and purposely lose grip with the physical reality around you. By using empathy, this can be achieved on an even deeper level. Empathize with the people or the emotional state of the particular situation portrayed within the illustrations. The greater the emotional connection you obtain with a particular card, the more real that illustrated world and the people inside it become to you. Begin practicing this meditation method using just one card, and then as you become more comfortable with it you will eventually develop similar results when using three or more cards at a time.

Follow these steps below to ground yourself into, and merge yourself with a particular tarot card.

To begin, place a single tarot card before you, either in your hand or on a table, somewhere close enough to be able to see all the details of the illustration. Focus on the object in the center of the card. This will usually be a person, but in some cases will be an object or symbol. As you begin to focus your attention on the center of the card, concentrate on your breathing. Breathe in slowly and then breathe out just as slowly. There is no wrong technique to use here, just as long as you remain focused and concentrated on breathing in and out slowly. As you begin to relax and feel your shoulders getting heavier, follow the next 5 steps that will trigger your senses and cause your soul to vibrate on a higher spiritual level which shares an affinity with the energy confined within the tarot's symbology.

Step 1:
As you concentrate on the card, find five things you can see. This can be anything. This can even include the main object in the center of the card that you began focusing on from the start of this meditation. This step may also include you seeing a person, the sky, a flower or even a house.

Step 2:
Find four things you can touch. This step includes things that you would be able to physically touch like a horse or a tree, opposed to the sky, a star or the sun.

Step 3:
Find three things you can hear. As you locate these three things, try to hear the sounds in your head as if you are really there. What would the bird chirping sound like, or the sound of the wind blowing at your back? Or the sound of footsteps in the sand?

Step 4:
Find two things you can smell. Just as in step 3, imagine yourself there inside the card and breathe in through your nose those certain smells that would be unique to the location illustrated on the card. Can you smell the flowers? Can you smell the ocean? What does the air smell like? Does one particular smell trigger a past memory?

Step 5:
Find and connect to one emotion that you feel. Look at the faces of the people as well as the animals in the cards. What expression do they have on their face, and how does it make you feel? Can you empathize with them? Are any of these people or animals in similar situations that you have once been in or have personally experienced before? Are you able to relate to them on an emotional level? Look at the color of the card's background. Is it a bright yellow or is it an ominous black? What emotions do these colors stir up within you?

Once you feel like you are done with this meditation and wish to snap out of it and return back to the real world, simply follow the steps in a retrogressive way. Once again while concentrating on your breathing, wiggle your toes, place your feet into the ground, feel the fabric of your pants, listen to the sounds around you and of your physical environment. And then slowly open your eyes and pin-point an object to focus on. Breathe in and smell your new surroundings, and slowly look around you in order to ground yourself back into your physical real world.

As you concentrate and connect to the cards by practicing this method of meditation, you will be able to see new things and uncover new meanings of the cards on different and deeper levels of understanding.

The many secrets and mysteries concealed within each card are portrayed through a combination of allegory and symbolism, which encompass a multiple of different esoteric understandings needed in order to convey just one spiritual concept depicted within the card's illustration, thus allowing one to comprehend the wisdom of the card's spiritual message based upon their own level of esoteric understanding.

The more your mediate on a card and truly empathize with it by putting your spiritual-self inside the card's 'esoteric-shoes', the more you will see. Each time you will uncover new truths, and each time you will leave with more wisdom than you had to begin with. Once you unveil the secrets hidden in plain sight, you will not be able to un-see them. This new wisdom can be transformed into knowledge, and it is only the knowledge we gather that we are allowed to take with us into the next life.

> The majority believes that everything hard to comprehend must be very profound. This is incorrect. What is hard to understand is what is immature, unclear and often false. The highest wisdom is simple and passes through the brain directly into the heart
>
> — *Viktor Schauberger* —

Chapter 17

The Spiritual Meanings of the Hebrew Letters

Each one of the 22 Major Arcana cards are assigned to one of the 22 Hebrew letters. The spiritual meaning of a particular letter is portrayed within that specific card's illustration for which it is assigned to. In addition to this, descriptions for each card's corresponding Hebrew letter as it's described in Psalm 119 have been included, which is an acrostic poem; the verses of each stanza begin with the same letter of the Hebrew alphabet.

Tarot Card—Hebrew Letter—Spiritual Meaning

#0, Fool—Aleph—Ox, who pushes forward with new beginnings. Aleph draws down heaven into earth and binds the two as one, thus creating heaven on earth.

Psalm 119:1-8,
"Blessed are they whose ways are blameless, who walk according to the Lord. Blessed are they who keep the statutes and seek him with all their heart. They do nothing wrong; they walk in his ways. You have laid down precepts that are to be fully obeyed. Oh, that my ways were steadfast in obeying your decrees! Then I would not be put to shame when I consider all your commands. I will praise you with an upright heart as I learn your righteous laws. I will obey your decrees; do not utterly forsake me."

#1, Magician—Bet—House, referring to the human body as the vessel that houses the soul. The Magician has on his table all the tools needed for him to build a strong vessel within himself, further developing a stronger spirit and will.

Psalm 119:9-16, "How can a young man keep his way pure? By living according to your word. I seek you with all my heart that I might not sin against you. Praise be to you, O Lord; teach me your decrees. With my lips I recount all the laws that come from your mouth. I rejoice in following your statutes as one rejoices in great riches. I meditate on your precepts and consider your ways. I delight in your decrees; I will not neglect your word."

#2, High Priestess—Gimel—Camel, with regards to how a camel rises up, stands up, and takes responsibility and/or rises to the occasion when asked. Camels may seem worthless when sitting on the ground in between jobs but are quick to rise up and become great when needed. The concept of 'rising up' corresponds to the rising up of the soul's kundalini energy, as the life-force energy ascends up the spinal column, which in turn raises one's soul vibration.

Psalm 119:17-24, "Do good to your servant, and I will live; I will obey your word. Open my eyes that I may see wonderful things in your law. I am a stranger on earth; do not hide your commands from me. My soul is consumed with longing for your laws at all times. You rebuke the arrogant, who are cursed and who stray from your commands. Remove from me scorn and contempt, for I keep your statutes. Though rulers sit together and slander me, your servant will meditate on your decrees. Your statutes are my delight; they are my counselors."

#3, Empress—Daleth—Door, alluding to the door of opportunity presenting itself to you, thus bringing you luck of prosperity. Someone will open a door for you, so to speak.

Psalm 119:25-32, "I am laid low in the dust; preserve my life according to your word. I recounted my ways and you answered me; teach me your decrees. Let me understand the teaching of your precepts; then I will meditate on your wonders. My soul is weary with sorrow; strengthen me according to your word. Keep me from deceitful ways; be gracious to me through your law. I have chosen the way of truth; I have set my heart on your laws. I hold fast to your statutes, O Lord; do not let me be put to shame. I run in the path of your commands, for you have set my heart free."

#4, Emperor—Heh—Window, as in actively looking for a window of opportunity, and then jumping on that particular opportunity as soon as it presents itself, without any hesitation. Seize the day.

Psalm 119:33-40, "Teach me, O Lord, to follow your decrees; then I will keep them to the end. Give me understanding, and I will keep your law and obey it with all my heart. Direct me in the path of your commands, for there I find delight. Turn my heart toward your statutes and not toward selfish gain. Turn my eyes away from worthless things; preserve my life according to your word. Fulfill your promise to your servant, so that you may be feared. Take away the disgrace I dread, for your laws are good. How I long for your precepts! Preserve my life in your righteousness."

#5, Hierophant—Vav—Nail, tent peg, to bind or connect, referring to combining heaven with earth, just as a tent peg binds a tent to the ground. Therefore, the Hierophant is the middleman who connects a person on earth to God in heaven. The Hierophant helps people receive the blessings/fulfillment owed to them which are bound in heaven. The Hierophant also helps a person bound things on earth, acting as the authority over legal issues, and such things pertaining to religion, banking and government.

Psalm 119:41-48, "May your unfailing love come to me, O Lord, your salvation according to your promise; then I will answer the one who taunts me, for I trust in your word. Do not snatch the word of truth from my mouth, for I have put my hope in your laws. I will always obey your law, for ever and ever. I will walk about in freedom, for I have sought out your precepts. I will speak of your statutes before kings and I will not be put to shame, for I delight in your commands because I love them. I lift up my hands to your commands, which I love, and I meditate on your decrees."

#6, Lovers—Zayin—Sword, referring to the spiritual sword of discernment that cuts through the good and bad ideas, focusing on the positive thoughts and filtering out the negative ones. The sword grants one the gift of knowing both good and evil, and therefore they are blessed with the wisdom to know the difference.

Psalm 119:49-56, "Remember your word to your servant, for you have given me hope. My comfort in my suffering is this: Your promise preserves my life. The arrogant mock me without restraint, but I do not turn from your law. I remember your ancient laws, O Lord, and I comfort in them. Indignation grips me because of the wicked, who have forsaken your law. Your decrees are the theme of my song wherever I lodge. In the night I remember your name, O Lord, and I will keep your law. This has been my practice: I obey your precepts."

#7, Chariot—Chet—Fence, alluding to things we keep held in private or fenced in, such as secrets and/or secret plans we hold sacred and do not share with others outside our circle of trust. This can relate to like-minded groups such as secret societies, corporate, military, private social groups as well as certain cults. Although, it can simply refer to a yoga group, astrology group or a private gym. Consequently, this card is considered to be the 'secret society' card. The knight depicted here is like a religious zealot or missionary set out to persuade people into following his unique set of ideals, theories and philosophies. On a lighter note, this knight can be perceived as being a life coach, astrologer or spiritual advisor.

Psalm 119:57-64, "You are my portion, O Lord; I have promised to obey your words. I have sought your face with all my heart; be gracious to me according to your promise. I have considered my ways and have turned my steps to your statutes. I will hasten and not delay to obey your commands. Though the wicked bind me with ropes, I will not forget your law. At midnight I rise to give you thanks for your righteous laws. I am a friend to all that fear you, to all that follow your precepts. The earth is filled with your love, O Lord; teach me your decrees."

#8, Strength—Teth—Coiled Serpent, corresponding to the way a serpent waits patiently in the brush, hiding and waiting for its prey to pass close by, and then when the perfect moment presents itself, when the prey is most vulnerable or not paying attention, the serpent strikes. This card is about being patient as well as smart by allowing your desires to come to you. It is advised to remain mindful and watch out for repeating habits. Look for an opening or moment of weakness when your prey or foe is at their most vulnerable. Then strike when the timing is right and catch them red-handed when they repeat the same mistake as before—therefore, catching them with their tail between their legs, just as the lion in the Strength card is depicted.

Psalm 119:65-72, "Do good to your servant according to your word, O Lord. Teach me knowledge and good judgement, for I believe in your commands. Before I was afflicted, I went astray, but now I obey your word. You are good, what you do is good; teach me your decrees. Though the arrogant have smeared me with lies, I keep your precepts with all my heart. Their hearts are callous and unfeeling, but I delight in your law. It was good for me to be afflicted so that I may learn your decrees. The law from your mouth is more precious to me than thousands of pieces of silver and gold."

#9, Hermit—Yod—Hand, as in God's hand which is involved in the process of all creation. God has his hand in all things. Yod looks like a fiery flame, and is seen as such throughout the tarot. It is the 'spark' of the spirit in everything. In the Jewish mystical tradition, Yod represents a mere dot, a divine point of energy. Since Yod is used to form all the other letters, and since God uses the letters as the building blocks of creation, Yod indicates God's omnipresence.

Psalm 119:73-80, "Your hands made me and formed me; give me understanding to learn your commands. May those who fear you rejoice when they see me, for I have put my hope in your word. I know, O Lord, that your laws are righteous, and in faithfulness you have afflicted me. May your unfailing love be my comfort, according to your promise to your servant. Let your compassion come to me that I may live, for your law is my delight. May the arrogant put to shame for wronging me without cause; but I will meditate on your precepts. May those who fear you turn to me, those who understand your statutes. May my heart be blameless toward your decrees, that I may not be put to shame."

#10, Wheel of Fortune—Kaph—Palm of Hand, an open palm offers its help to pick others up, and point them in the right direction. Also, priests raise up their open hands when giving a blessing, as well as lay their palms on an individual's head when receiving their blessing.

Psalm 119:81-88, "My soul faints with longing for your salvation, but I have put my hope in your word. My eyes fail, looking for your promise; I say, "When will you comfort me?" though I am like a wineskin in the smoke, I do not forget your decrees. How long must your servant wait? When will you punish my prosecutors? The arrogant dig pitfalls for me, contrary to your law. All your commands are trustworthy; help me, for men persecute me without cause. They almost wiped me from the earth, but I have not forsaken your precepts. Preserve my life according to your love, and I will obey the statutes of your mouth."

#11, Justice—Lamed—Ox Goad, which is the stick, prod or poker shepherds use to direct or guide their sheep, as well as protect the sheep from predators. Lamed is considered the 'heart' of the Hebrew alphabet due to it being placed directly in the center of the 22 letters. Here in the center, Lamed stands as the tallest of the letters; watching over the others, guiding and protecting them like a shepherd who tends to his flock. Lamed steps up, rises to the challenge and takes the responsibility of being the leader.

Psalm 119:89-96, "Your word, O Lord, is eternal; it stands firm in the heavens. Your faithfulness continues through all generations; you established the earth, and it endures. Your laws endure to this day, for all things serve you. If your law had not been my delight, I would have perished in my affliction. I will never forget your precepts, for by them you have preserved my life. Save me, for I am yours; I have sought out your precepts. The wicked are waiting to destroy me, but I will ponder your statutes. To all perfection I see a limit; but your commands are
boundless."

#12, Hanged Man—Mem—Water, refers to the healing and cleansing aspect of water. Mem has a numerical value of 40, which is significant throughout the Bible, and always corresponds with a time of cleansing and spiritual growth. For instance, the Jewish people escaped slavery in Egypt after asking God for freedom. God promised them a land filled with milk and honey where they could live and prosper freely in peace, and have the opportunity to flourish as a nation—reaching their full potential. They did eventually reach their promised land, but God made them 'earn' it first. The Jewish people were forced to wonder the desert for 40 years, where they were faced with a series of tests, challenges and had to overcome many obstacles. With the many frustrations came times of uncertainty, leading them to lose hope and test their faith in God. Although, after having to endure such hardships, the Jewish people were eventually allowed to settle in the promised land. This 40-year period elicited for them a means to grow spiritually stronger. This is just one example, for there are many other instances where the number 40 shows up. Specifically, in the story of Noah's flood which lasted for 40 days and 40 nights, or when Moses climbed up Mount Sinai to retrieve the ten commandments for a period of 40 days and 40 nights. The number 40 embodies the concept of the transformation process. Whenever you feel crushed, under pressure, pressed or in darkness, you're in a powerful place of transformation. For example, grapes must be crushed to make wine, diamonds form under pressure, olives are pressed to release oil and seeds grow in darkness.

Psalm 119:97-104, "Oh, how I love your law! I meditate on it all day long. Your commands make me wiser than my enemies, for they are ever with me. I have more insight than all my teachers, for I meditate on your statutes. I have more understanding than the elders, for I obey your precepts. I have kept from every evil path so that I might obey your word. I have not departed from your laws, for you yourself have taught me. How sweet are your words to my taste, sweeter than honey to my mouth! I gain understanding from your precepts; therefore, I hate every wrong path."

#13, Death—Nun—Fish, referring to swimming freely. What happens when you try to hold your grasp around a fish? It immediately slips out, escapes and swims away. Likewise, an open and enlightened mind breaks free from the social norms, defies the status quo and refuses to be administered by limiting beliefs, which are proven to be fomented within a fixed mindset. The letter Nun reminds us to think outside the box, open up our minds, as well as open ourselves up to receiving insight, blessings and love from the Creator—by reconnecting to the higher consciousness. The Creator's

Light is limitless, and therefore endless; affirming death is a mere illusion. The only aspect of death portrayed here pertains to ego-death. It is advised to let go of old habits that no longer serve you. Just as a snake sheds its skin, you release all negativity and reconnect to the divine spark of Light within you, reacquainting yourself with your soul's true identity. Therefore, your soul is reborn and you feel as though you are 'born again.'

Psalm 119:105-112, "Your word is a lamp to my feet and a light for my path. I have taken an oath and confirmed it, that I will follow your righteous laws. Though I constantly take my life in my hands, I will not forget your law. The wicked have set a snare for me, but I have not strayed from your precepts. Your statutes are my heritage forever; they are the joy of my heart. My heart is set on keeping your decrees to the very end."

#14, Temperance—Samekh—Prop, prop up, uphold with relation to a dwelling or tent supporting overhead. The idea portrayed here is to create a strong willpower and maintain it within a balanced vessel that gives one the ability to subdue their temper. Become a spiritual alchemist, and combine within you the dualistic energy polarities such as, male-female, drive-emotion, sharing-receiving. The angel depicted in this card is actually two angels united as one: Raphael, who is the sun/male, uniting with Gabriel, who is the moon/female. The polarities unite, combine and merge as one, and in doing so form a purified human vessel that is able to be offered up as a dwelling for God. Thusly, creating a house of God within the human vessel. The body is a temple. Hence, the name of God, YHVH written over this angel's heart. By inviting the Light of the Creator in, God and man become one in the same—embodying the spiritual concept of the letter *Same*-kh. Furthermore, this card is Roman numeral XIV (14), corresponding with the myth of Osiris, whose body was cut up into 14 different pieces, and then scattered all throughout Egypt. It was Isis who eventually found all the scattered body parts and was able to put Osiris back together. In this sense, the Temperance card is about pulling one's self together and defragmenting the soul. In other words, gaining control of one's self by picking up the pieces. After doing so, you can continue along your path and return back to focusing once again on your life-purpose. This is the process required for maintaining one's body as a temple. Know that all things are temporary, and we must continue to cleanse and purify ourselves in order to maintain our temple.

Psalm 119:113-120, "I hate double-minded men, but I love your law. You are my refuge and my shield; I have put my hope in your word. Away from me, you evil doers, that I may keep the commands of my God! Sustain me according to your promise, and I will live; do not let my hopes be dashed. Uphold me, and I will be delivered; I will always have regard for your decrees. You reject all who stray from your decrees, for their deceitfulness is in vain. All the wicked of the earth you discard like dross; therefore, I love your statutes. My flesh trembles in fear of you; I stand in awe of your laws."

#15, Devil—Ayin—Eye, to see, spiritually referring to the third eye and the 6th sense. The third eye is the gateway or portal into the upper realms of consciousness, making it possible for an individual to tune into the spirit. An individual is able to open up their third eye as a way to draw down their desires from the ethereal realm and onto the material plane where they are manifested.

Essentially, it's the practice of using mind over matter, which allows one the will to achieve miraculous results. By using the mind's power to bend the rules of physics and the nature of reality, mind over matter makes it possible to push one's self further physically in a sort of supernatural way either by outrunning danger or by being able to endure physical pain.

Ultimately, the Devil card is about manifesting prosperity in one's life, and obtaining the will and the know-how of just how to go about doing it. In order to create any amount of abundance in one's life, they must first learn to rise above their ego-nature. A person must overcome self-doubt, fear, victim consciousness and the overall sense of lack, accomplished by re-establishing a connection to the Creator; to the Source of one's happiness and joy. In addition to this, one will learn to adopt the mindset of 'being *in* the world, but not *of* the world.' It is with no doubt possible to make your life heaven on earth, and not have to succumb to the evil of the world, and therefore allowing it to affect your personal happiness.

The third eye is your Pineal Gland located deep in the middle of your brain. To activate this gland, spend more time alone, in silence, watch your thoughts where they are going, don't gossip or get reactive, walk away from violence or revenge, don't judge others for what you judge you become, eat as much organic food as possible, and mainly drink pure uncontaminated waters. The word 'mem-ory' has its etymology steeped in Jewish meanings, it's a compound word comprised of the two words: Mem, meaning water, and Ori, meaning light. Therefore, it has a neat association to liquid Light. Thus, when activated it ignites the plasma of creation and your soul vibrates in-tune with the frequency of nature and all existence. You re-Mem-ber and reconnect with your inner Light. As you remember who you are on the soul level it will enable you to see beyond the veil, and you will elevate your spiritual awareness above the 3rd dimensional plane of existence and connect to your 6th sense.

Psalm 119:121-128, "I have done what is righteous and just; do not leave me to my oppressors. Ensure your servant's well-being; let not the arrogant oppress me. My eyes fail, looking for your salvation, looking for your righteous promise. Deal with your servant according to your love and teach me your decrees. I am your servant; give me discernment that I may understand your statutes. It is time for you to act, O Lord; your law is being broken. Because I love your commands more than gold, more than pure gold, and because I consider all your precepts right, I hate every wrong path."

#16, Tower—Peh—Mouth, pertaining to the things we say (to others as well as ourselves) having a certain degree of power. Our words, as well as our thoughts, have power. So be mindful of your thoughts and your words. Speaking positively will build up your spiritual tower, whereas speaking negatively will destroy it. Peh advises us to keep our plans to ourselves. No one cares about your self-esteem, but you. The idea is to refrain from sharing your plans and come off as boasting in order to attract attention. Rather, use your self-esteem as fuel to help drive yourself towards achieving your goals. When you seek attention you lose your creativity, and it can diminish your self-esteem. Likewise, avoid the habit of seeking approval from others, because it becomes exhausting as well as drains your spiritual tower.

This card is associated with the first Passover, when the Jewish people formulated a plan of escape from their bondage in Egypt. Their plan proved to be successful because no one shared it with anyone else outside of their private homes. The letter Peh is unique because it has a letter Bet hidden inside of it. Bet, meaning house, and Peh, meaning mouth, suggests that things spoken of privately in the home tend to be shared in public. This concept can also refer to one keeping their thoughts private as well. Our private thoughts have a way of being made public. Peh encompasses the old adage "loose lips sink ships". People tend to spill the beans, so to speak. Bearing this in mind, it is advised to keep one's thoughts and words positive. It can take several years to build up a strong relationship, and only an instant, with the wrong words spoken, that bond can be ruined forever.

Psalm 119:129-136, "Your statutes are wonderful; therefore, I obey them. The unfolding of your words gives light; it gives understanding to the simple. I open my mouth and pant, longing for your commands. Turn to me and have mercy on me, as you always do to those who love your name. Direct my footsteps according to your word; let no sin rule over me. Redeem me from the oppression of men, that I may obey your precepts. Make your face shine upon your servant and teach me your decrees. Streams of tears flow from my eyes, for your law is not obeyed."

#17, Star—Tzaddi—Fish Hook, alludes to the spiritual fish hook that gets tossed up into the astral waters of the ethereal realm in an attempt to catch brilliant ideas, and with hope of catching an epiphany. This can only be done while in a meditative state. A Tzaddik is a righteous person, and one who is in constant communication with God. Moses was considered to be a Tzaddik.

The famous quote applies here, "Give a man a fish and he will not go hungry that day, but teach a man to fish, and he will never go hungry again." There is a scarlet ibis depicted in this card sitting in the tree. The scarlet ibis was known to be an Egyptian symbol for Thoth. Thoth is the Virgin Isis' mentor, who teaches her how to meditate. According to legend, Thoth is the one who taught mankind the practice of meditation. Thoth is known as Mercury/Hermes. On the

Tree of Life, Thoth is associated with Hod, the 8th sefirah related to brilliance and glory of the mind, as well as being associated with communication. The connection to Hod is represented in the Star card with the eight, 8-pointed stars. The big yellow star symbolizes the bright and brilliant epiphany caught by Isis with her 'fish hook'.

Psalm 119:137-144, "Righteous are you, O Lord, and your laws are right. The statutes you have laid down are righteous; they are fully trustworthy. My zeal wears me out, for my enemies ignore your words. Your promises have been thoroughly tested, and your servant loves them. Though I am lowly and despised, I do not forget your precepts. Your righteousness is everlasting and your law is true. Trouble and distress have come upon me, but your commands are my delight. Your statutes are forever right; give me understanding that I may live."

#18, Moon—Qoph/Kuf—Back of Head, by consciously stimulating the back of the head (cerebellum) to utilize one's cognitive mind as a means to obtain control of their own destiny. As an individual begins to develop a strong sense of self-awareness they cease following others, and strive to become their own person. They either become the leader of the pack or venture off as a lone wolf. There are two dogs depicted in the Moon card—a wolf and a dog. As the old saying goes, "If you're not the lead dog, then the scenery never changes."

Moreover, the word used in the Torah for ape is Kuf. And what do apes do? They mimic, as in monkey see, monkey do. Portrayed within the Moon card is the idea of Kuf arriving at a spiritual crossroads, coming to a fork in their life-path when they are faced with the decision to either continue their life as it is now, as a follower, or become the lead dog who takes control of its own destiny.

Psalm 119:145-152, "I call with all my heart; answer me, O Lord, and I will obey your decrees. I call out to you; save me and I will keep your statutes. I rise before dawn and cry for help; I have put my hope in your word. My eyes stay open through the watches of the night, that I may meditate on your promises. Hear my voice in accordance with your love; preserve my life, O Lord, according to your laws. Those who devise wicked schemes are near, but they are far from your law. Yet you are near, O Lord, and all your commands are true. Long ago I learned from your statutes that you established them to last forever."

#19, Sun—Resh—Head, and refers to intelligence, brilliance and radiance, when one's head is radiating at its peak level. This is when a person feels at their best, and at their smartest; a phase in their life when the timing of things seems to be on point, giving one the sense that the world revolves around them. This is when one experiences that 'in the zone' feeling. When a person's inner sun is radiating, they feel in love—in love with themselves, with everyone and with life in general. With this new sense of confidence, you show up and feel present—you don't shy away nor hesitate to rise to the occasion. You become more dependable and reliable, and you genuinely find joy when serving others. You spread unconditional love. Feeling as though you have nothing to hide, you are surely free. You are bursting with Light and joy.

When your thoughts are radiating brilliance, you see things in the 'big picture.' With greater awareness, you learn from past mistakes and come to realize that everything that happened in the past had happened for a reason; a divine purpose. You realize in this 'ah ha' moment that by overcoming certain challenges it led you to the point of where you are now in your life. You are who you are now and you are where you are now in life because of it; you come to realize you have been guided by something greater than yourself all along, and you are grateful. You feel loved and you feel special, and worthy of receiving that love. Arriving at this spiritually uplifting point of your life is truly an incredible feat. You feel the miraculousness of the Universe, and how it guides you every step of the way. Everything has its timing, and God's omnipresence continually pushes us closer to achieving our destiny as we travel along our individual life paths. In each of our heads, we are all considered to be the center of our own galaxy.

Psalm 119:153-160, "Look upon my suffering and deliver me, for I have not forgotten your law. Defend my cause and redeem me;

preserve my life according to your promise. Salvation is far from the wicked, for they do not seek your decrees. Your compassion is great, O Lord; preserve my life according to your laws. Many are the foes who persecute me, but I have not turned from your statutes. I look on the faithless with loathing, for they do not obey your word. See how I love your precepts; preserve my life, O Lord, according to your love. All your words are true; all your righteous laws are eternal."

#20, Judgement—Sin/Shin—Tooth, relating to something hard that grinds and breaks down another similarly hard object down into something smaller and softer. For instance, a tooth can be considered a tool that chews on something hard and breaks it down in order to soften it before it can be swallowed, such as a piece of meat or a vegetable. We chew on food before swallowing it, and then it breaks down in the stomach where it is turned into fuel, giving the body nourishment. At times, truth can be a hard pill to swallow, but we find ourselves able to digest it after taking the time to chew on it first. The majority of the time, these newly realized truths turn out to be blessings in disguise. This card is about redemption, granting someone the opportunity to repent for their sins, and a chance to say they are sorry. Both the letter Shin and the Judgement card reflect a second chance at life, as well as a second chance at love. Either by apologizing or by redeeming ourselves we can reunite the bond that was broken. The truth will set us free. Sometimes we suffer because we don't have all the facts and we create our own story, which tends to burn bridges. However, if we were to learn the truth, we would most likely be able to redeem or rekindle the damaged relationship.

Furthermore, the letter Shin is depicted as a fiery flame consisting of three flames or candles of the same candelabra. Shin connects to the fiery energy of creation, relating to blessings granted at the beginning of all creation. Shin also corresponds to the blessings received in the end, when receiving closure at the conclusion of a cycle or phase of a relationship. In this sense, Shin transitions relationships in a positive way, moving out of one state and into the other. Shin positively returns the vibe of a relationship back to how it was felt in the beginning. The word Shin when spelled out has a numerical value of 360, שין, and therefore represents the concept of arriving at or coming to full-circle.

Psalm 119:161-168, "Rulers persecute me without cause, but my heart trembles at your word. I rejoice in your promise like one who finds great spoil. I hate and abhor falsehood but I love your law. Seven times a day I praise you for your righteous laws. Great peace have they who love your law, and nothing can make them stumble. I wait for your salvation, O Lord, and I follow your commands. I obey your statutes, for I love them greatly. I obey your precepts and your statutes, for all my ways are known to you."

#21, World—Tav—Cross, sign of the cross, which in ancient times was written as an X. Tav also means truth and mark, as in leaving your mark of truth behind for others to follow in your footsteps. The idea is for you to pass on the torch and leave your legacy behind for the generations to come. The World card is about raising the bar and setting the new standard, and then passing the torch onto others who will follow in your example. The World card as well as the letter Tav refer to leaving something behind better than when you found it. The World card is the last and final card in the deck, referring to the end of a phase. Or quite literally, the end of the world. Biblically speaking, the end of the world is called the apocalypse, which literally means 'the uncovering', and alludes to the uncovering of hidden and/or forgotten truths. Once these truths are revealed, it sets a new standard and a new set of rules, which evolve the world into a new age or era that improves upon the past. Thus, evolving the consciousness of the world into a higher vibrational state of awareness and enlightenment.

Psalm 119:169-176, "May my cry come before you, O Lord; give me understanding according to your word. May my supplication come before you; deliver me according to your promise. May my lips overflow with praise, for you teach me your decrees. May my tongue sing of your word, for all your commands are righteous. May your hand be ready to help me, for I have chosen your precepts. I long for your salvation, O Lord, and your law is my delight. Let me live that I may praise you, and may your laws sustain me. I have strayed like a lost sheep. Seek your servant, for I have not forgotten your commands."

Chapter 18

The 32 Paths of Wisdom
with their Correlation to the Arcana

Intertwined within the Kabbalah Tree of Life are 32 Paths of
Wisdom. The first 10 of these paths are marked by the 10 sefirot (or
spheres) which form the shape of the Tree's layout. The following 22
paths are the interconnecting branches located in between each of the
10 spheres. It just so happens that the tarot's 22 Major Arcana
correspond with these 22 branches.

     Listed here in this chapter are brief descriptions explaining
the energy aspects for each of the 22 Major Arcana. Each card's
illustration reflects upon the combined energy influences that each
pair of connecting sefirot contain. These 32 paths coincide with
Athanasius Kircher's Tree of Life system, which was introduced in his
1652 work, the Oedipus Aegyptiacus. It is Kircher's Tree of Life that
is adopted by the Golden Dawn Society and then applied to the Rider-
Waite tarot deck.

     Kabbalists consider the Tree of Life to be a map of the soul.
This Tree contains 10 sefirot that form a vessel for the Light to enter.
By practicing meditation and by working on ourselves, it is possible
to activate these sefirot as a way to release certain ego-blockages
within us, which is crucial for clearing space within your vessel in
order to draw down the Light from above. This concept is similar to
how one would pour liquid into a glass. Whereas the liquid, which
represents the Light, enters from the top of the glass and rises up;
filling the glass up to the brim.

     The glass in this analogy represents the human body. It is our
responsibility to transform our ego-nature in order for us to allow the
Light in. The act of clearing out ego-blockages and activating the
sefirot is all done through the first 10 paths. The following 22 paths, or
branches, become activated as the liquid pours down into the vessel
from above, and activates each branch on its way down to the base of
the Tree.

     And this describes the Tree's energy flow. You now
understand that the Light, the life-force energy, is drawn down from
above and into the vessel twice. The first time is to activate the 10

spheres in order to clear out ego from the vessel, and the second time is to fill up the volume of the vessel with the life-force energy, referred to as the Light. Like shining a flashlight into a dark tunnel, the light will diminish the darkness.

Here is a list of the 32 paths arranged in accordance to the energy flow as the Light travels down into the vessel and traverses along the branches of the Tree. The first step is to activate the 10 sefirot as a means of clearing away all ego-blockages, and thus forming a fit and uncontaminated vessel.

1. Keter
2. Chokmah
3. Binah
4. Chesed
5. Gevurah
6. Tiferet
7. Netzah
8. Hod
9. Yesod
10. Malchut

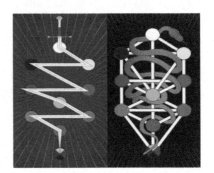

Once the vessel is prepped and sterilized, one is able to begin drawing down the Light from above. Buddha was asked, "What have you gained from meditation?" He replied, "Nothing!" Then he continued, "However, let me tell you what I have lost: anger, anxiety, depression, insecurity, and fear of old age and death."

11. Aleph-Fool
12. Bet-Magician
13. Gimel-High Priestess
14. Daleth-Empress
15. Heh-Emperor
16. Vav-Hierophant
17. Zayin-Lovers
18. Cheth-Chariot
19. Teth-Strength
20. Yod-Hermit
21. Kaph-Wheel of Fortune
22. Lamed-Justice
23. Mem-Hanged Man
24. Nun-Death
25. Samekh-Temperance
26. Ayin-Devil
27. Peh-Tower
28. Tzaddi-Star
29. Qoph-Moon
30. Resh-Sun
31. Shin-Judgement
32. Tav-World

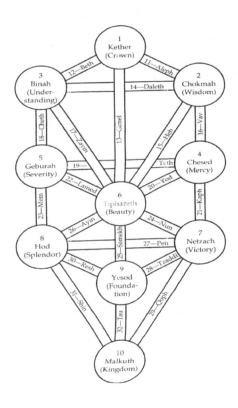

Below are the 22 Branches of the Major Arcana with explanations for each branch's consciousness connection:

11. Fool:

Connecting Keter with Chokmah—Bringing forth knowledge gained from past life, encompassed within the Creator's Light, in an optimistic attempt to obtain wisdom of both good and bad. Whole-heartedly pursuing one's healthy curiosity to know the 'what' of all things.

12. Magician:

Connecting Keter with Binah—Bringing forth the practical tools obtained from past-life and adapting them in order to gain a deeper understanding of all things. Thus, being able to understand one matter by applying the understandings of another matter.

281

13. High Priestess:
Connecting Tiferet with Keter—Opening up the heart as a means to purify and cleanse the soul through the act of forgiveness, with intentions of connecting to the Light of the Creator.

14. Empress:
Connecting Chokmah with Binah—Merging wisdom with understanding to birth prosperity.

15. Emperor:
Connecting Tiferet with Chokmah—Pursing your passions and going after your big dreams, not letting anything get in your way. Willing to take risks, knowing that mistakes will be made, with the intention of learning from those mistakes. Having the willful drive to follow your heart with blind optimism.

16. Hierophant:
Connecting Chokmah with Chesed—Humbling yourself, asking for guidance and blessings from either a mentor or a person in a seat of authority, who will offer to you their wisdom which can be transformed into useful practical knowledge.

17. Lovers:
Connecting Tiferet with Binah—Igniting the spark of desire to obtain deeper understanding, begin to open up your heart and ears to godly insight. Be willing to learn, as well as develop a healthy sense of curiosity. Obtain knowledge of the difference between good and bad. Crave the guidance of a mentor who holds pearls of wisdom and is willing to share their keys to prosperity with you.

18. Chariot:
Connecting Gevurah with Binah—Desire to obtain deeper insight of the occult and esoteric, knowing that in this reality there is more than meets the eye. Embodying a rich zealousness to learn and to truly understand the deeper mysteries of the world in order to reach higher levels of spiritual awareness that will quench the thirst for one's need to know. Such secret wisdom and esoteric study are not acquired in vain. Once understood, such esoteric mysteries are meant to be shared with the world, and such ideas will gradually shift the

consciousness of the collective towards a spiritual evolution, eventually making the world a better place.

19. Strength:

Connecting Chesed with Gevurah—Patience is a virtue. One must practice restriction and utilize willpower to win control over their impulses. Good things come to those who wait. Sit back and hold tight as you observe certain habits and routines. This allows you time to pin-point certain weaknesses and vulnerabilities. This observation done in stillness blesses one with the knowledge of when and how to make their attack—knowing exactly when to plant seeds and when to take specific actions toward achieving their goals.

20. Hermit:

Connecting Tiferet with Chesed—Practicing compassion and empathy for those who do not agree with you. You may find them unable to comprehend the advice you bestow upon them, because they are not yet mentally mature enough to absorb such things. Practicing compassion will allow you to give others a second chance.

21. Wheel of Fortune:

Connecting Chesed with Netzah—Blessed with the good fortune of having someone who has 'been there, done that' reach out their hand and offer you help. They notice that you are new to your surroundings and a bit inexperienced, so they show you kindness, compassion and offer guidance; show you the ropes. They point you in the right direction.

22. Justice:

Connecting Tiferet with Gevurah—Stepping up to take responsibility. Willing to do whatever it takes to protect and look after your loved ones. Having the initiative to become a compassionate, and big-hearted leader, who is willing to make personal sacrifices as a means of achieving equal justice for those he is responsible for.

23. Hanged Man:

Connecting Hod with Gevurah—Be careful what you wish for. Once we begin taking the appropriate actions toward manifesting our goals is when life places obstacles and challenges in our way. We continue to experience this restriction as we work to transform our dreams into reality. God wants to give us everything we desire, and He does, but He delivers our desires wrapped in filthy ego-soaked packages. It is then our responsibility to unwrap these dark packages and unbox the Light concealed within them. God always grants our wishes, but we must first have to earn them before we can receive. We must endure challenges, overcome obstacles, and deal with everyday frustrations and annoyances as a means to earn our fulfillment. It is crucial to remain focused on the end result; the idea, concept or the happy thought which embodies your wish in its manifested state. You must learn to utilize analytical problem-solving skills to overcome the day to day challenges you will be faced with. Endure to the end by focalizing your mind on the prize, and on the fulfillment you will attain. Do not focus on what you will have to give up, instead fantasize on what you will gain. Most times, it is the 'why' that is so important to keep focused on. The reason why we get up every day and do what needs to be done in order to reach our goal is what truly motivates us. What is your 'why'? For some, it's simply to be free.

24. Death:

Connecting Tiferet with Netzah—Love conquers all. Learn to reach a compromise and put aside your differences for the greater good. The ego makes us want to hold onto the past and continue holding onto grudges, resentments and disputes. Time to let go of the past so you can move on. You cannot reach what's in front of you until you let go of what's behind you. For some, this can reflect in an exhaustive ego-death. Ego-death is a complete loss of self-identity. May you have the courage to break the patterns in your life that are no longer serving you. This includes limiting beliefs and a fixed mindset. By practicing meditation and working on ourselves we are able to recognize and take responsibility for the flaws of our ego-nature. Some refer to this as 'shadow work.' Shadow work is the process of exploring your inner darkness or 'shadow self.' Shadow work uncovers every part of you that has been disowned, repressed and rejected. It is one of the most authentic paths to enlightenment. You no longer identify with your own consciousness, and thus become one with all.

25. Temperance:

Connecting Tiferet with Yesod—Put into practice the concept of the Hermetic Marriage by combining the energies of the Sun with that of the Moon existing within the human vessel. This is the marriage of the body and the spirit for the mutual development of each other. In man, this takes place when the heart and mind form a union, and when the male and female energy polarities combine into one, and also when the positive and negative poles unite. In the Gospel of Thomas it states, "When you make the two into one, and when you make the inner as the outer, and the upper as the lower, and when you make male and female into a single one, so that the male shall not be male, and the female shall not be female: then you will enter the kingdom." The 'at oneness', wholeness, holiness is achieved through the practice of this spiritual alchemy.

26. Devil:

Connecting Tiferet with Hod—Having a desire for desire, and sparking the ambitious energy needed to propel you towards becoming self-motivated and driven, putting your brilliant ideas into action to manifest prosperity. You don't get what you wish for. You get what you work for. As we strive towards manifesting our goals, we are constantly bombarded by challenges, frustrations and obstacles. It seems that as soon as we make a conscious decision to act on our ideas, we feel the static of ego restricting us from our desire. It takes a strong spirit to rise above the ego's gravitational force that blankets us, it is a negative weight that we all feel constantly pressing down upon us. It seems as soon as we begin pursuing our desires, we are immediately thrown into situations where we feel the weight of the world upon our shoulders, and the gradual pressure that ensues. We cannot control others or the things that happen to us. We can only control the way we respond to what's happening. That's where our power is.

27. Tower:

Connecting Netzah with Hod—Building up one's self-esteem by keeping things private. It seems that as soon as we tell others of our plans of how we will manifest our ideas, when we boast, is the moment when we let out our steam. Actions speak louder than words. People respect your accomplishments when they see your results, not when you talk about your plans to obtain them. No one cares about your self-esteem, but you. Yes, it is important to have desires and strive to achieve success, but also just as important to keep those things which are private, such as your plans, to yourself. Otherwise, you will lose the mental/spiritual energy you very much need in order to reach your goals. When you seek attention, you lose your creativity. In addition to this, it is equally important to refrain from sharing private information with others who do not need to know. This may include secrets or things that are considered to be sacred. Furthermore, we must remain mindful of our thoughts, because our thoughts become our words. And those words have the power to either build up or destroy the things we hold sacred. For instance, it may take a year or two to build up a strong trusting friendship, but in only an instant, with the wrong words being said, the friendship can be completely ruined. In spite of this, know that you can always start over. And looking on the bright side of things, this time you will not be having to start from scratch, but from experience.

28. Star:

Connecting Yesod with Netzah—Practicing meditation as a means to soul search, which in turn raises your soul's vibration, as you obtain a higher sense of self-awareness. In the same degree, forming a bond and communication with your higher-self. Meditation helps you search for the answers within. This can be done alone, and in certain circumstances is best with a mentor or spiritual practitioner who is able to walk you through a guided meditation. Guided meditations can target specific negative emotions that may be attached to memories that anchor down in one's soul and tend to wreak havoc on their subconscious, similarly to how a cancer effects the cells around it. The longer it stays in there, the more damage it can cause. Time to set aside your ego and open yourself up to personal transformation. Be open to change, and willing to receive help from either a mentor or the Higher-Self. By unblocking each of the seven chakras, you release the negative feelings of fear, shame, guilt, grief, lies, illusion and attachment.

Living only in the physical, mental and emotional realm makes energy limited. Tap into the spiritual dimension and the energy is limitless. "We are stars wrapped in skin. The Light you have been seeking has always been within." - Rumi

29. Moon:

Connecting Netzah with Malchut—Learning to transform your ego-nature, and gain control over primal instincts and impulsiveness. Thus, obtaining maturity and willpower. Before the age of 27, each person must deal with past-life karma, aka past-life baggage. Before reaching true adulthood, you will find yourself attracting the same types of personalities into your life, and you will continue to face the same kinds of challenges. Time and time again, with one dilemma after the other, we are faced with similar challenging situations where we find ourselves placed, yet again, in similar circumstances all for the divine purpose of us to learn who we are and who we are not. Once we turn 27 years old, we experience our Lunar Return, which is a period of our life where we go through an identity crisis. This Lunar Return prepares us spiritually for our Saturn Return, which we experience around the age of 32. Hence, the 32 rays around the moon in this card. The Saturn Return ends once a person reaches the age of 33; it is at this point they are considered to be truly an adult, and deemed 'born again', having had dealt with all past-life karma before this Saturn Return phase. Now, at the age of 33, a person has a chance at redemption and can start over, repent from past mistakes and move forward with their life. Having transformed from their immature, wilder and more selfish mentality, into a more kind-hearted, considerate and well-behaved individual. It is about learning to transform the wild wolf personality into that of a domesticated dog characteristic. Incidentally, depicted on this card is a wolf and a dog about to embark on their life path. Within each of us are these opposing personality types, one being wild natured while the other domesticated, and they are at battle with each other. One is pride, greed, anger, jealousy, hate and resentment. The other is love, happiness, humility, faith, hope and courage. The personality that will win is the one that you feed.

30. Sun:

Connecting Hod with Yesod—Being able to freely radiate your true self. Becoming the source of your own happiness, and in doing so you spread joy to others. It wasn't easy getting to this point of spiritual enlightenment. It was only achieved after a long and challenging time, having endured numerous karmic life-lessons faced upon you, which you ended up learning from. And now you are able to look back at your past and see how far you have come, and realize how much you have grown. You are finally able to let go of any and all attachments, and to feel 'at one' with everything. Living ego-free is living free to just be. With much time spent working on yourself, you eventually get to a point in your life where you learn to truly love yourself. You reach a point where you're able to see the big picture, and realize that everything that happened to you had happened for a reason. And you would not be the same person which you have grown to become now, and you wouldn't be able to appreciate the blessings bestowed upon you now, if everything that had happened to you had happened any other way then it did. You begin to unveil (reveal) the deeper meaning or hidden truth that it was all meant to be. You come to realize now that the Universe was guiding you in the right direction the entire time. It was leading you towards your dreams, and pushing you to accomplish your goals. You come to the realization that you were the only thing slowing you down or keeping you from reaching your goals in the past, and now going forward you remain mindful of how you choose to react in similar situations. You are now able to see in the big picture of it all how everything that had happened had happened for a reason—perhaps a divine purpose. Once you come to this realization, you feel the need to give back and to help others reach the same enlightenment. You do this in your work and also in your relationships. "It's how we give back to the world that shapes our life, defines us as humans, and builds joy from within." - Karen Berg, an author and founder of the Kabbalah Centre International

31. Judgement:
Connecting Malchut with Hod—When we are told of new information that goes against what we have previously been led to believe was true it can be (at first) difficult to digest. We are taken unawares, as higher truths are brought to light. It takes us a minute to figure out that the revelation of higher truth is actually a good thing. At first, when we hear good news, we don't immediately understand

its significance. Maybe this is due to us having lost hope of ever hearing good news, especially after experiencing a tragedy or loss. We may find ourselves to be in such an emotional state where we choose to suffer, shutdown and distance ourselves from the outside world. Taking this in consideration, when we first hear good news, it takes a moment for us to digest the information and for it to sink in. This pertains to learning of new truthful information, pertaining to (but not limited to) new rights, protections, new freedoms, as well as receiving a much-owed apology, a debt being redeemed to you, or hearing that you have been given a second chance at redemption— offering you a chance to make amends and repent for a past mistake. Hearing the truth is always good, although at first it can be a hard pill to swallow, in the sense that it can catch you off guard. It is advised to chew on it, think carefully about what it means to you, before you undermine any decision or future action. Truth is shared from the heart. Once shared with others, it enters their ears, and is felt in their heart. It is the truth that melts the heart. And the truth sets us free. It releases the ego-blockages that surround our heart chakra so we may clear out our vessel and make room for the Light to enter.

32. World:

Connecting Malchut with Yesod—Leaving your mark on the world, done by unveiling new truths and new discoveries that change the world for the better. It is the legacy you leave behind that enables you to pass along the torch onto others who will follow in your footsteps and continue to make the world a better place. Biblically, the 'end of the world' is known as the apocalypse, which literally translates as 'the uncovering', relating to the uncovering of truth.

The truth will set us free, as well as permit us to progress forward in the right direction. Moreover, truth will set us free from ignorance, whereas we obtain salvation from ignorance. Ignorance is slavery, and knowledge is freedom. Those who have achieved gnosis will be upheld from bondage of the earthly existence. "The spiritual journey does not consist of arriving at a new destination where a person gains what he did not have. It consists in the dissipation of one's own ignorance concerning oneself and life, and the gradual growth of that understanding which begins the spiritual awakening. The finding of God is a coming to one's self." - Aldous Huxley, philosopher

Chapter 19

The Two Keys Hidden within the Tarot

Found on the Hierophant card are two keys, which are located and displayed on the Hierophant's platform. These two keys are the only 'keys' symbol in the entire Rider-Waite (Smith) tarot deck, and because of this, they hold a great importance that should not be overlooked. Essentially, these keys unlock one's desires. The platform he sits upon can be looked at as being somewhat of a treasure chest, and his keys unlock it. The Hierophant acts as the bridge or middleman between you and that which you desire. He will help you manifest such desires, and make your wishes come true.

These two Keys are hidden within the tarot deck. One is found in the center of the Tarot Grid and the other is found within the Major Arcana cards. The Key found inside the Tarot Grid holds the secret to manifesting wishes, and I refer to it as the Prosperity Key. It utilizes a more practical approach towards manifesting. The Key hidden within the Major Arcana holds a secret (a guided meditation) to raising the kundalini, otherwise known as a person's chakra system, that starts at the base of the spine, leading up to the third eye, elevating the soul's vibration as the energy ascends, eventually connecting a person to their higher-self. As one raises their spiritual awareness and begin working on themselves, they gradually shed off layers of limiting beliefs and eventually let go of their previously held identity, thus reaching enlightenment.

It is imperative to note that the Kundalini Key must be used **first** before using the Prosperity Key. The kundalini must first be elevated in order for a person to be able to connect to the Source, where their desire is located, and from where such desire can be accessed and drawn down into the manifest. In other words, the tarot practitioner must first raise their vibration and consciousness in order to reach the meditative state needed to be able to draw down their desire and manifest it into their reality.

Moving forward, it is important to know that both these two Keys consist of ten cards each and coincide with the ten sefirot on the Kabbalah Tree of Life. Each card within these Keys shares a specific energy aspect with one of the Tree's sefirot relating to

Kabbalistic wisdom and/or planetary influences.

For instance, the first Key, the Kundalini Key, which includes only Major Arcana cards, places ten cards in a precise order, all aligning with the ten sefirot on the Tree of Life, and in accordance with their specific planetary influences. While the Prosperity Key's ten cards align with the tzimtzum lightning bolt found within the Tarot Grid, which is also based on the energy influences of the ten sefirot, but in a more practical sense.

In order for you to understand these concepts better, allow me to first explain the Kundalini Key in detail. This Key starts out with the Judgement card, placing it in the #1 position in the ten-card layout, at Keter, which is the first sefirah of the ten. Both Keter and the Judgement card coincide with Pluto. This method of placement sets in motion the entire key's layout, which reflects upon the planetary correspondences shared between the tarot and the Tree of Life's ten sefirot. Moving forward, the second card in this layout is the Hanged Man located at Chokmah, associated with Neptune. And then, The World card at Binah, associated with Saturn. Followed by the Wheel of Fortune at Chesed, which is associated with Jupiter. Then, The Tower at Gevurah, being associated with Mars. Next is The Sun card at Tiferet, which is associated with the Sun. The Justice card is placed at Netzah, which is associated with Venus. Temperance is placed at Hod, which is associated with Mercury. The Devil card is placed at Yesod, reflecting aspects of the Moon's influence, connecting to the idea of how the moon unveils secrets which are hidden in plain sight, as well as how the full moon grants us the opportunity to tap into the magic of the astral plane. And lastly, we complete this layout with The Star card located at Malchut, because both are associated with Earth. These ten Major Arcana form the Kundalini Key, which is a key to raise your consciousness, and your chakras in order to connect to the higher-self, where self-awareness, enlightenment and a connection to the Source can be obtained. Further explanation for each of these planetary connections will be revealed momentarily. But first, I must explain certain esoteric and Kabbalistic concepts that led me to formulate these tarot card connections. Bear with me as I unravel this puzzle in the simplest way possible, so that you too may be able to decipher all of this yourself when attempting to follow the same steps.

What's interesting about the Tree of Life is that it has its roots at the top of the Tree, and draws down its energy from the Source, from Keter and into the human vessel. Subsequently, the Kundalini Key shares an accord with this concept. For instance, the Key starts out at Keter with the Judgement card and from here leads down and traverses throughout all the sefirot, eventually ending at the Star card in Malchut—at the base of the Tree. Upon reaching Malchut, this life-force (Light, energy) forms in the shape of the vessel, thus stimulating the sefirot and giving structure to the Tree of Life within, creating a map of the soul. At this point, all ten sefirot are stimulated, and vibrating on a higher frequency. Once the sefirot are charged, the ego-blockages surrounding them are released. The vessel has now cleared the space needed in order for the Light to be drawn down into it once again. And thus, the vessel has now transformed into becoming a pure channel for the Light. As the Light enters the vessel from above, it stimulates the Tree's 22 branches as it traverses down along through each of the sefirot once again. Picture a dirty wine glass as the human vessel. The Light, like water, enters the glass and cleanses it, preparing it for the wine to be poured in. The Light, visualized now as being water, pours down into the glass and transforms itself into wine as the vessel fills up.

From the Tree of Life diagram, we can see that there are 10 spheres (aka sefirot), with nine spheres above and one at the very furthest point below. The last sphere corresponds to the earth, the material world of Malchut, a dimension which has no Light of its own. Above Malchut, beyond the upper nine spheres, is the endless infinite Light-force of the Creator—a force of goodness and love unfathomable and incomprehensible to the finite mind. The upper nine spheres are emanations full of the Creator's Light—the highest levels of pure energy.

Descending from energy to matter, from above downward, each level becomes denser until we reach the realm of physicality, or the world of matter. One above Malchut is the level of Yesod, which is the funnel that gathers the Light from the upper spheres of pure energy and releases it to Malchut. Yesod is like a straw. The suction that pulls all the Light from the upper dimensions through Yesod to Malchut is created by the consciousness of humanity. We draw all that Light down through the spiritual structure into the physical dimension with our desire. As we draw to us that which we desire, if our desire is clear and tuned to Light, we draw Light and are the cause for illuminating this world.

This process creates the Tree's energy flow and its sustaining current. Similar to how a sugar maple tree goes through its yearly cycle of drawing in water from its roots, drawing in sustenance (minerals and nutrients), eventually producing its own sap that is transported up the tree from its roots to its leaves. This process occurs yearly as winter turns into spring. And when the sap runs dry the process starts over again; every year. This concept of rejuvenation can be seen metaphorically in the Kundalini Key's card layout, where The Star card (at Malchut) depicts the virgin Isis who acts as a pure channel for the Light as she draws in the energy from the astral waters and fills her vessel (metaphorical human vessel), which gives her the sustenance she needs to elevate her soul's vibration. This energy ascends up the Tree of Life within the human soul, like a flash of lightning, to the Judgement card located at Keter, where we see the people rising up and out of their coffins; awakening and returning back to life. These people rise and rejoice with a new breath of life, just as the water from the roots of the maple tree transform into the sweet sap. Notice how the coffins are floating in water? This is the melted ice from the snowy mountain tops seen in the background of the card. When compared to the sugar maple, this card can be seen as portraying the end of the winter cycle when the days are getting longer and winter is turning into spring. The sun is melted the snow and flooded the valley below, causing the coffins to rise up from the ground.

The Major Arcana cards included in the Kundalini Key are arranged in a perfect order that corresponds to the particular planet assigned to each of the spheres on the Tree of Life. Learning each card's planetary association is key to understanding the reasoning for the card placements involved here. These important connections will be explained in each of the steps below. Knowing these planetary connections is the glue that holds this Key together, and the cornerstone to understanding the significance herein.

The Kundalini Key:

Beginning at the root of the Tree of Life is the sefirah Keter, which represents the Source of the pure Divine Light, pure nothingness, and the intelligence of the Creator—the realm of pure potential. It is here where we find the first card, Judgement.

Judgement:
The first card in the Kundalini Key, the Judgement card is placed at Keter, representing the soul's desire, and contains the intention for using this Key. Depicted in this card is the archangel Gabriel, who is blowing her trumpet, and grabbing the people's attention just before delivering to them a warm and heartfelt message. The message is something that gives the people reason to rejoice and to wake up and rise up out of their coffins of limitation. It is a powerful message that sparks life into them, giving them reason to live, and offer them hope. Gabriel informs the people that Christ will sacrifice himself on the cross the following day, which offers them a chance at redemption, and an opportunity for them to repent for their sins. Because of Christ's sacrifice, they can now be saved. Gabriel's trumpet creates a specific sound able to raise their consciousness and elevate their spiritual vibration with its angelic frequency. Each chakra has its own unique tone. And as we recreate those tones within us, we begin to raise our chakras and elevate our kundalini's spiritual vibration. As a consequence of this, we align (harmonize) with the same frequency as the Creator.

These people pictured in the Judgement card, with their hands raised upward, are reaching out and connecting to God, their source of joy and happiness. By tapping into the Source, the Light, one is able to receive epiphany, godly insight, intuition and clarity of gnosis. Thus, achieving wisdom from the Higher-Self. As portrayed here, the people are colored gray, and gray throughout the tarot always connects to and represents wisdom. Therefore, it is the wisdom they have obtained, and the newly learned truth that sets them free.

The Hebrew letter assigned to this card is Shin, meaning tooth. Comparable to the kundalini serpent's poisoned tooth. It's the serpent's tooth you must get bitten with in order to kill off the personality you once identified yourself with. Essentially, referring to an ego-death, which is needed before one can be unified with the cosmic-consciousness. This letter looks like a crown, which just so happens to be the meaning of the Hebrew word Keter.

Heart-warming messages are not all easy to digest at first. They seem to catch us unaware, usually coming from out of nowhere. When we first hear it, truth is not always easy to understand. We are caught off-guard, causing us to question our beliefs. For some, truth can be a hard pill to swallow. The letter Shin advises us to chew on it. The longer we chew on it, the easier it is for us to swallow, digest and understand. Truth will set you free, but only if you allow it to by welcoming it into your heart.

Moreover, Shin is the middle letter in the Divine name of God, Yeshua, meaning salvation. The Four-Letter Name of God, known as the tetragrammaton, is YHVH, and once the letter Shin is added into the middle, the five letters form the name YHShVH, the name of Christ, Yeshua. Both the Judgement card and the letter Shin connect us to the energy of the Christ Consciousness, which connects us to the All Knowing where we gain salvation from ignorance. The letter Shin is shaped like a tooth, and can be seen as a crown with fiery flames, similar to a three-candled candelabra. Also, interesting to note is that the letter's shape mimics the structure of the human heart. As portrayed in the Judgement card, it is the warming of the heart that melts the ice-capped mountains, which floods the valley below and causes the coffins to rise up from the ground.

Some may not realize it, but there is a hidden letter Shin on the Fool card, located on the bottom right of the Fool's shirt. The Fool card is assigned to the Hebrew letter Aleph, the first letter in the Hebrew alphabet. The Hebrew word for fire is Aleph Shin, and for this reason it is now apparent why the Fool has a fire within him, and he begins his journey full of heart and drive, like a ray of sunlight. The staff the Fool is carrying is directly in-line with one of the Sun's rays behind his head, representing that the Fool himself is also a sun ray. The Fool shoots out, springs forward and lights up the world, unconditionally sharing his light with all.

Furthermore, this gives suggestion to the energy of Jesus Christ, and to the concept of Christ Consciousness. The addition of Shin to YHVH yields YHShVH, which can refer to the Christ manifested.

The letter Shin is often inscribed on the case containing a mezuzah, a scroll of parchment with Biblical text written on it. The text contained in the mezuzah is the Shema Yisrael prayer, which calls the Israelites to love their God with all their heart, soul, and strength. The mezuzah is situated upon all the door frames in a home or establishment. The Shema Yisrael prayer also commands the Israelites to write God's commandments on their hearts (Deut. 6:6); the shape of the letter Shin mimics the structure of the human heart: the lower, larger left ventricle (which supplies the full body) and the smaller right ventricle (which supplies the lungs) are positioned like the lines of the letter Shin. The mezuzah blesses one as they enter through the doorway and also as they leave. This concept is embedded within the Fool who can be seen in two ways: one where he is starting out on a new journey, or another scenario where he is seen upon his arrival as he returns back home from one. Because of this, the Fool is assigned the Roman numeral zero, which is a 360° circle. Interesting to point out is that the word Shin when spelled out equals a gematria value of 360, שׁין, alluding to the idea of how one , returns after a long spiritual journey full-circle and unites 'as one' with the Source. Thus, becoming 'at one' with the Creator, just as Jesus Christ was united with the Father upon his crucifixion.

The Judgement card is associated with the planet Pluto. Pluto is the ruling planet over Keter, further reinstating the deeper connection that it has to its position at the top #1 placement of the Kundalini Key. The Judgement card placed at Keter represents the desire to obtain Christ Consciousnesses, achieved after elevating the kundalini. Thereby, connecting one to the endless realm where they unite with the Source, the Divine Light.

Hanged Man:
The Key's second card is the Hanged Man, positioned at the 2nd sefirah Chokmah. Both the Hanged Man and Chokmah are associated with the planet Neptune.

The Hanged Man is assigned to the Hebrew letter Mem, meaning water, and has the numerical value of 40. The number 40 has great significance in the Kabbalah. It relates to a certain level of consciousness obtained when a person begins to understand deeper spiritual concepts. Containing spiritual aspects of water, 40 reflects upon the relevant period of time needed for one's spiritual cleansing. This cleansing concept parallels the flood story in the Book of Genesis when the earth flooded for 40 days and 40 nights. According to the story, the waters covered the entire face of the earth, just as if it had experienced a large-scale baptism.

Depicted within this card, the man is seen hanging from a tree, upside down. Oddly, there are rays of enlightenment surrounding his head—37 to be exact. The number 37 is significant in the tarot, as well as Kabbalah, because it is the same gematria value for the word Chokmah. Interesting due to the fact that this card is placed at Chokmah in this Key. Chokmah means wisdom. Therefore, what we see portrayed here is this man having to endure a learning experience, or life-lesson; albeit one dealt with trial and error.

Notice the tree this man is hanging from is in the shape of the letter T? This represents the Hebrew letter Tav, which is related to truth, as well as being associated with Saturn. Thusly, the man is uncovering truths about himself, and learning life-lessons, as he endures Saturn's karmic influences. Saturn being the planet of karma, frustration and restriction, teaches us life-lessons.

But Saturn is not wholly maleficent. Saturn is also the planet that grants wishes. The challenges and obstacles Saturn faces you with are meant to help you learn how to overcome weaknesses, thus making you a stronger person in every sense of the word. Saturn wants you to receive whatever you desire, but you must earn it first. We see here portrayed through symbolism, the Hanged Man radiating a brilliant idea and wishing to manifest it. Although, before his wish is granted, he must first submit to a series of Saturn's tests. As the old adage goes, "Be careful what you wish for."

The idea of learning how to surrender to the voice of God, and to the will of the Creator, is symbolized by the shape of the Hanged Man's arms and legs. With closer examination, you will notice that the man forms an alchemical symbol for sulfur, which is symbolic of the human soul in spiritual alchemy. The Hanged Man's soul is represented here as being at peace. He has learned to float on top of the water (so to speak) by surrendering to life's flow, which leads him closer to fulfilling his wish. By working towards his goal little by little each day, he remains within this flow and builds a momentum. With time, all the challenges, frustrations and obstacles he is faced with along the way won't seem so bad. Nothing can crush his soul. Instead of struggling to tread water, he learns to float. He allows the tide of the subconscious, which is now connected to the Light, to take him in its flow. He learns to let go and surrender.

The Hanged Man card is about realizing how the wish-making process works, and accepting the challenges that come your way. Know that we receive everything we ever ask for, but it is up to us to overcome the life-challenges thrown at us in order for us to earn our desire. This prevents us from gaining a sense of entitlement. By remaining focused on the reason of why you wish to achieve the intended goal will be the fuel needed to endure the many inconveniences experienced along the way.

The World:
The third card included in this Key is The World. It is placed in the 3rd positioned with the sefirah Binah. The World card and Binah are both assigned to the planet Saturn.

The World card is associated with accomplishing a strong sense of certainty, and obtaining a higher degree of self-realization. The large Laurel wreath symbolizes an award given once a person graduates from the higher degree of understanding. The wreath can also symbolize a womb which gives birth to a new phase or new beginning; a new chapter in one's life. This womb can also represent the opening of a portal into the astral realm, allowing one to draw down the seed of their desire from the macrocosm with the intention of manifesting it in the material world.

The World card is assigned to the Hebrew letter Tav, which means truth, as well as cross, sign or mark of the cross. This can relate to the portal that our desire *crosses over* into the material realm. Interesting to note is that a folded up cross forms a cube, resembling the six-sided cube of Saturn. Like opening a gift-box, the cube unfolds and offers up its prize. Big dreams take big imagination. You must truly think outside the box. Tav is the last letter in the alphabet. Bearing that in mind, the World card being assigned to the letter Tav alludes to the idea of 'the end of the world', which Biblically is associated with the apocalypse. The word apocalypse literally means 'the uncovering', and relates to the uncovering of hidden truths. This being said, it is imperative to search within your own soul and uncover hidden truths. Try to find the real reason for why you desire a certain goal. For example, a person's 'why' may include freedom. Freedom can be a primary motivator, both professionally and personally. The World card placed at Binah is about crossing through the portal and into the realm of endless possibilities.

Wheel of Fortune:
The fourth card on the Key is The Wheel of Fortune, connected to Jupiter and assigned to the sefirah Chesed. Jupiter is known as The Guru and teaches mental powers, oneness, and science of Light.

This card has a big wheel illustrated on it and in the center of the wheel is a large X, which is the planetary seal for Jupiter. This sigil is designed in such manner that its traced lines touch every number or unit square of that planet's kamea (magic square). It symbolizes the governing force of the planet.

Pictured here is the 4×4 magic square of Jupiter.

THE *KAMEA* OF JUPITER
& PLANETARY SIGILS

4	14	15	1
9	7	6	12
5	11	10	8
16	2	3	13

- Each row and column contains 4 numbers
- The square contains 16 numbers from 1 to 16
- Each row, column and diagonal adds up to 34.
- All of the numbers in the square add up to 136

The planetary symbol for Jupiter looks like the number 4. Jupiter is connected to the number 4 and that is why the symbols on this card are in groups of fours. Firstly, there are the four alchemical symbols which form a cross at the four points of direction: North, East, South, and West shown overlapping the large cross of Jupiter's sigil in the center of the wheel. Next, there are the four alchemicals on the cross: mercury, sulphur, water, and salt. Then you have the four letters of the word TAROT, which can be spelled backward and forward as TORA and/or ROTA, surrounding the wheel. There is also the tetragrammaton placed alongside the word tarot. The tetragrammaton being the Divine Four-Letter Name of God, YHVH. And then, located at each of the four corners are the four fixed faces of God, which are associated with the four fixed signs of the zodiac, and they are from clockwise, starting from the left and then going to the right: the man who is Aquarius, the eagle is Scorpio, the lion is Leo, and the bull is Taurus. The four books that each of the four faces of God are holding relate to the Old Testament's four main sections: the Pentateuch, the Former Prophets (or Historical Books), the Writings, and the Latter Prophets.

The energy and influence of Jupiter is one of mercy, blessings, divine guidance, and most importantly gifts of knowledge. According to Hindu teachings, Jupiter is a Brahmin and a teacher of deities considered a devata, here 'devata' means whose mind is always in ascending mode. Here in the Wheel of Fortune card Jupiter gives the knowledge of how your mind can go in ascending mode. This is why the four faces in each corner are studying books. The word Tora, which means 'the law', is found written around the wheel, as well as the tetragrammaton, which translates as 'God created.' Initiates study the world that God created and see how it and everything in it is all made of the same essence, and realize that everything is connected. As above, so below. Such things as well as the yearly seasons and cycles are learnt from studying the Torah.

Another group of four found on the Wheel of Fortune card are the alchemical symbols connected to the four phases a soul cycles through towards enlightenment. For instance, to the left of the center wheel is the serpent. Serpents throughout the tarot always relate to and symbolize the kundalini. The kundalini here is a clue that we can raise our kundalini chakras by way of gnosis. Obtaining gnosis gets the wheels turning inside of us and elevates our vibration as we ascend up towards the crown chakra, where we reach enlightenment, obtain a broader sense of spiritual awareness and open up the third eye. The Wheel of Fortune card is all about raising your kundalini by way of gnosis and opening your third eye. This is the way to elevate your consciousness through the 4th sefirah Chesed, leading you through the Abyss on your way to reaching Binah, which is where the portal (depicted as a wreath in the World card) is located. The wreath being symbolic of the portal to the upper worlds, and a direct connection to Saturn.

The next symbol included in this group is the dog-headed creature hanging on the side of the wheel known as Anubis, who is the Egyptian God that guides the recently deceased souls through the underworld and helps them along their way in the afterlife. The Anubis is seen here guiding your soul upward and ascending up through the chakras of the kundalini.

The next symbol here is the Sphinx, who sits firmly on the top of the wheel. The Sphinx acts as a beacon that guides one's soul in the right direction, similar to how a light house would guide a sailor in the night. At the same time, the Sphinx sets an example for what you should strive to become. The Sphinx is the elevated soul, holding the sword which represents spirit, having the body of a lion representing strong body, and with a human head representing that he has a human soul. The Sphinx is a balanced combination of soul, body, and spirit fixed firmly on the top of the wheel like the North star navigating the way and paving the path for each traveler's journey.

The last one included with these four creatures, or bodies, is You. The self, 'You' are the final piece to the puzzle. In total, there is the Serpent, the Sphinx, the Anubis, and then You. You see, you 'the self' is the mind, the Serpent is the body, the Sphinx is the spirit, and the Anubis is the soul, which are all attributed to the four main aspects of an individual that work together to guide them in the path of life.

Moreover, these four bodies also coincide with the four alchemical properties illustrated on the wheel, which are Mercury (mind), Salt (body), Water (spirit), and Sulphur (soul).

With further examination, you will notice that in the very center of the wheel is a tiny cog which has eight spokes that form eight pie-pieces. The number 8 connects to the sefirah Hod, which is associated with Mercury (Hermes/Thoth). Hod has to do with splendor of the intellectual mind. Hod as Mercury teaches us to pay attention to the small details. We must look further into things in order to grasp deeper insights that may be staring us directly in the face. For instance, the Roman numeral of the card is X with the value of 10. After already seeing that there are objects and symbols in the card that are in groups of fours, we must write them all down and make a list of them in order to get a broader understanding of their significance.

The Roman numeral X at the top of the card lets us know that there are 10 groups of fours. This gives us a total of 40 items. As you know now the significance the number 40 has with the tarot, and in reference to reaching a certain degree of spiritual awareness and understanding.

And these ten groups of four are:

The **Four Faces of God**, which are assigned to the four fixed signs of the zodiac: Aquarius, Scorpio, Taurus, and Leo.

The **Four Bodies**, known as the four main aspects of an individual: the physical body, emotional body, spiritual body, and the mental body. These four bodies are symbolized and associated with the kundalini Serpent, the Anubis, the Sphinx, and the Mind of the tarot practitioner.

The four letters that spell **ROTA**. (wheel)

The four letters that spell **TORA**. (law)

The four letters that spell **TARO**. (wheel of law)

The **Four Alchemical Symbols:** Mercury, Sulphur, Water, and Salt.

The **Four Books** that each of the Four Faces of God are holding. The Old Testament contains four main sections: the Pentateuch, the Former Prophets (or Historical Books), the Writings, and the Latter Prophets.

The **Four Directions** of the cross: North, South, East, and West.

The four letters of the tetragrammaton, **YHVH**. (Yahweh/Yehovah)

The **Four Units** or points of Jupiter's X that correspond to the planetary sigil and the four unit-squares or numbers at each corner of the X in the kamea of Jupiter, also known as its magic square.

This gives us a total of 40 things, (digits, or units) found in this card that make up the whole, and lead us to deeper meaning. The number 40 connects to a certain degree or level of time it takes to reach a spiritual cleansing. The time it takes to transform your mind, body, spirit and soul. 40 is a significant number seen throughout the tarot and always associates with reaching a higher level of understanding by way of spiritual growth. 40 is a measurement of time according to its spiritual context. And this concept of time is relative.

Something else worth mentioning is that 40×34 (the magic number of Jupiter's square) = 1,360. The sum of all the digits in Jupiter's magic square equals 136. So, here we see an even deeper connection to Jupiter and the number 40 and how it all relates as a whole. The knowledge that numbers hold a certain level of consciousness is the basis of the Kabbalah, which is essentially the spirituality of numbers, and this is all encompassed within the wisdom of The Wheel of Fortune card.

"The path isn't a straight line; it's a spiral (or wheel). You continually come back to things you thought you understood and see deeper truths." - Barry H. Gillespie

Something worth mentioning here, as you look for deeper meaning or hidden secrets in this card, is that the numerical value of YHVH is 26 (Yod is 10, Heh is 5, Vav is 6, Heh is 5), which is the same value if you add up the number of the four astrological houses of each of the fixed signs, also known as the Four Faces of God (Yahweh).

Aquarius......11th house
Scorpio.........8th house
Taurus..........2nd house
Leo..............5th house
Total: 26

The point of finding all these hidden things is to obtain a deeper understanding and to gain a broader knowledge base. The knowledge is the connection. Knowledge is the power. And it is through gnosis (knowing) that ignites the energy needed to get the wheel's turning.

The Hebrew letter assigned to this card is Kaph, meaning palm of hand. This relates to a hand offering help to lift you up. Just as Ezekiel was lifted up into heaven, in his vision, by the hand of God where he saw God's Four Faces.

The Tower:
The Tower card is associated with Mars and the sefirah Gevurah, which influences drive and ambition. Gevurah's influence is portrayed in the Tower card with the two people (Adam and Eve)

who are both driven to reach the top of the tower, a metaphor for their 'Jacob's ladder', where they will achieve enlightenment. Once they believe they have reached the top of their tower is the moment they are hit with a bolt of lightning. This causes them to immediately fall back to the ground where they are forced to start over. This scenario is not as bad as it appears. In fact, it's quite the contrary. For instance, the lightning bolt strikes our crown chakra the moment we receive an epiphany. We are granted a brief moment of clarity and understanding. Throughout our lives we search for truth, and there are some things we are led to believe to ring true, and then later as we mature, we find many of our beliefs to be false. These types of realization usually come as a shock, and causes us to reassess our character. But, as a result, our sense of character grows stronger. Now, with a slight shift in consciousness, and by simply changing perception, you can start over. Although, this time you will not be starting over from scratch. This time you will be rebuilding from experience.

The purpose of raising our vibration is to open up our crown chakra. Once opened, we receive new insights that shatter our limiting beliefs. We then take in this new energy and put it into action— manifesting our ideas. This concept is the entire philosophy behind path work and Kabbalistic meditation. In Kabbalah, there are 32 paths on the Tree of Life. This includes the 22 branches that connect the 10 sefirot, thereby forming the 32 paths. When you begin to raise your spiritual vibration, you must first start at the base of the tree, at Malchut. From here, you draw down the Light from the roots of the Tree, found at Keter, which is the top crown, drawing down Light from the Source and it traverses along the 22 branches. These 22 branches are represented on the Tower card with the 22 yellow Yod's, which are directly associated with the 22 Major Arcana. The flow of energy (the Light) that enters one's Tree of Life, their Tower, is drawn from above as if the human vessel was a large lung. The Light that enters can be compared to oxygen that is drawn into the lungs. The oxygen fills the lung and opens up, clears out the capillaries, and then exhales the waste. Thus, allowing more oxygen to enter and expand and heal. Likewise, the Light first enters the vessel to clear out the ego, which opens up space for more Light to enter. So, the first breath (inhale/exhale) is to clear away ego-blockages surrounding the sefirot, and the second breath stimulates the branches, which ultimately raises the kundalini energy and forms a pure channel for the Light; a sustained circuitry. It is the connection to the Source that supplies one with the breath of life. It is the source of one's joy, fulfillment, and also where one receives epiphanies. Establishing a connection to the Creator's Light creates a circuit of energy that continues to run up and down your core.

It is no coincidence the Tower card is associated with Gevurah. Both are influenced by Mars and both relate to matters of the ego. The Tower card offers us the clues of how to transform our ego by transforming our consciousness to be mindfully aware of how we consciously use our words. For instance, the Tower card is assigned to the Hebrew letter Peh, meaning mouth. Gevurah means strength/severity. Consequently, our words have the strength to either build up or destroy. The secret of the letter Peh is that our words begin as our thoughts, and those thoughts have the power to either build ourselves up or they can tear us down. The Tower being assigned to Peh also advises us to let go of negative ego-blockages, including limiting beliefs, doubt, fear and unworthiness. This includes negative and/or limiting thoughts that hold us back from reaching our full potential, or prevent us from achieving our destiny.

Peh has the gematria value of 80. 80 is the same value of the word Gevurah, and also the same value as the word Mashiach, which means anointed or anointed one. It was used in reference to priests and kings in ancient Israel, who were literally anointed with holy oil, usually when they were set apart to be a religious and/or political leader of the people, as in a consecration or coronation. These were each considered saviors, liberators of the people in some way; known as a Messiah.

The startling revelation of Kabbalah is that each and every person is actually the Messiah. The removal of chaos requires a shift in consciousness, which is symbolized by the lightning bolt striking the tower. The awesome Light of the Creator is then revealed in its full splendor where chaos, the epitome of darkness, simply fades away, for darkness cannot coexist with light.

The Light of the Creator anoints your crown chakra, and as you speak words of strength you begin to rebuild your personal tower (your spirit and soul's vibration) anew.

This metaphor is a hint that we can use our words to build our spirits up by saying positive affirmations and by repeating Kabbalistic prayers, such as the Ana B'Koach. The Ana B'Koach is considered to be the most powerful Kabbalistic prayer, containing 42 words which invoke the energy of the Creator. By saying the words out loud, the Ana B'Koach rejuvenates the soul, magnifying the energy of anything you do throughout your day. The sounds created by verbalizing the words have the power to build up and rejuvenate one's soul vibration. This higher level of soul vibrational frequency connects us to and keeps us in tune with the Source, which attracts more of the same positive 'like' energy that shares an affinity with the Source, and can act as a protective shield against any negative outside forces. Like attracts like. The Law of Attraction. This is how we build up our spiritual towers.

Our words have power. God created the world and the universe with the power of His voice. In the book of Genesis 1:3 it says, "And God **said**, Let there be light". In Genesis 2:7 God creates life with his breath, "And the Lord God formed man of the dust of the ground, and **breathed** into his nostrils the breath of life; and man became a living soul".

Hidden within the letter Peh is the letter Bet, meaning house. The spiritual meaning of this refers to the importance of keeping personal things private. For instance, things that we speak of privately in our homes have a tendency to be said in public. Likewise, the things we think about to ourselves in our heads have a way of slipping out as well. It is important to keep positive thoughts in our heads and to refrain from judging others harshly, because when we allow the wrong or inappropriate things to slip out it has potential to cause chaos if we are not careful. Our thoughts and inner voice become our words, and those words become our behaviors. Others judge our behavior, which will prove to either make or break our reputation. You can say one wrong thing and ruin an entire relationship that took years to build. It is imperative to always speak positively to yourself, and speak in a positive light. Before you speak to others, think to yourself, "Am I adding anything?"

"Do not speak bad of yourself. For the warrior within hears your words and is lessened by them." - Old Japanese Samurai Proverb

The Tower card reminds us that our words have power. Be mindful of both your thoughts and your words, for they have the power to raise your soul's vibration, as well as your spiritual tower.

The Sun:
The Sun card is associated with the Sun and is assigned to the sefirah Tiferet, which is attributed to the inner sun. Like the sun, this card contains aspects of regeneration.

Furthermore, the Sun card is assigned to the Hebrew letter Resh, meaning head. It suggests the idea that this is the highest path of human intelligence. This is the point of the connection to the human intellect. The sun is also the Son (Jesus) who carries on the work of his father (God). Jesus is the spirit manifest. Jesus is the *head* of God's household. And is always depicted with a bright halo or aureole of light surrounding his head. For instance, this symbolism is seen in the tarot's Hanged Man card. The Christ's mind is enlightened with the spirit of God and then he manifests those intellectual ideas into the world, creating miracles and healing the sick. Christ also taught that the kingdom of God is found within. Christ connects to his inner sun, which is the way he connects to his crown chakra; his higher-self, also known as the Father. Jesus said the only way to the Father is through him. Jesus is the way. Jesus is the Sun, the holy heart chakra, which is associated with Tiferet, which encompasses the emotional aspects of the Tree. The sun positioned at Tiferet is a composite of the four elements, the signs of the zodiac, and all the planets. They are all involved under the rulership of the sun, as is symbolized by the hexagram. That figure (the hexagram) means the perfect integration of personality and higher-self. It connects us to our inner-sun as we strive towards obtaining adepthood. This is when our head is enlightened with a new intellectual perception of the higher-self; a complete success on all levels. Meditate on receiving clarification and a deeper understanding of the intelligence of your mind. Search for what you truly desire and allow that to become your happy thought, and focus your intentions on that one thing. That one positive thought will trump all negative thoughts. Intellectualize your desire and why you value it.

Focusing on the end goal will prove to be the energy needed to charge up your inner sun—the reason for rising each day. It will give you a lust for life and sense of purpose. That one single positive thought will allow your core to vibrate radiantly, opening up your heart chakra, which will raise your spiritual vibration as you ascend toward the Crown, the Father; the intellectual mind located in your head. You will feel as if you too, just like a saint painted on a wall or ceiling of a cathedral, have a halo or an aureole surrounding your head (Resh).

The letter Resh has a numerical value of 200, which is directly in the middle of the Hebrew alphabet's numerical system that contains in it numbers valuing 1 to 400. Resh means head and is associated with beginning, i.e., the head of the month or head of the year. The letter Resh is spelled out as the word Rosh as in Rosh Hashanah, the *head* of the year or Jewish new year. Resh is connected to the 'heart' of the first word in the Bible, Be*resh*it, which means "In the beginning." Ergo, the word Resh (head) is found in the middle of the word Bereshit. The other remaining letters form the word Bet, which means house or household. So now we have the word Resh (head) inside the word Bet (house); head of household. The opening word of the Bible points to the head of the household and that is Jesus. Jesus is the head of God's household. The first line in Genesis states, "In the beginning God created the heavens and the earth." Rosh, meaning head, implies intelligence, and thus contains a hidden message that God is intelligence. And that intelligence created all things.

The letter Resh is located towards the end of the alphabet, and then we see the letter in the beginning of the Bible. And then we have the numerical value placing the letter inside the middle of the Hebrew alphabet. All this is a clue that the intelligence of Resh is found throughout as well as in the center of all God's creation. All things spin around it, outwardly from it, and orbiting it, as if it were the Sun.

We have the power to ignite and regenerate our inner-sun by building up a positive ego with a loving heart, improving ourselves so we can achieve our goals, and follow our passions to accomplish what we love, and in return we will improve other people's lives by sharing our success and being an example; paving the way for others. We can accomplish anything that we set our mind to.

Justice:

The Justice card is associated with the sefirah Netzah and is connected to the planet Venus. The Hebrew letter Lamed, meaning ox-goad or staff (used to prick or poke; heard sheep or cattle), and representing authority is assigned to this card. Lamed is related to Libra, an air sign of balance and harmony. Netzah means victory and it too is associated with aspects of balance and harmony. Lamed is located directly in the middle of the Hebrew alphabet and is known as the 'heart' of the alphabet because of its central location. Lamed is the only Hebrew letter that ascends above all the rest. That part that projects above the invisible line of the alphabet is called the Tower in the Air. This represents the power to ascend, the possibility of religare or bind to form a union. This tower in the air, the upper segment of Lamed, is our hope; as represented by or symbolized by the sword in the Justice's hands pointing upward in the air towards Binah. The sword is pointing up directly at Binah and drawing down her energy of understanding, and seeing things in the big picture. Like this sword, Lamed reaches up in hope of the possibility to unite with God, to know God, and to know our Divine source.

The gematria of the letter Lamed is very interesting. Lamed itself represents the value 30, but its constituent parts, Vav (6) and Kaph (20), yield the number 26, which is the number value of the tetragrammaton, YHVH. Since Lamed is the central letter in the alphabet and is raised higher than the rest, it represents YHVH, or the King of Kings.

Elevate your thoughts and expand your mind. Be open. Swords

represent our thoughts, so elevate your thoughts just like Lamed is elevated, and you will connect to god and receive inspiration and deeper insights—see things in the big picture. Lamed oversees all the other letters, so act as if you have authority. Knowing that your thoughts create your behavior, think above the rest and you will behave above the rest.

Temperance:

The Temperance card is connected to the sefirah Hod, which is associated with the planet Mercury. The Hebrew letter assigned to Temperance is Samekh, which means 'to prop up' or support. Samekh relates to a dwelling, as in creating your human vessel as a temple or dwelling for God. We learn here to build up our life-force in order to energize our kundalini, giving us spiritual support—allowing the Light of the Creator to enter and fill our vessel and dwell within us.

The secret of the Temperance card is that the angel depicted in it is a combination of the two archangel's Raphael and Gabriel who are both infused with one another here, and unite as one. They are a perfect union of fire and water. Raphael represents the sun and Gabriel the moon. Kabbalistically, the sun is symbolic of positive male energy having an aspect of sharing/giving, and the moon relates to negative female energy of a more passive and receiving nature. This angel focuses on the energy of magical balance, and controlling the ebb and flow of the mixing the energies of fire and water with each other, back and forth between the two vessels. The angel mixes water (emotions, feelings) into fire (sexual drive, ambition, impulses) and then recycles the fire back into the water. The process involves an inner manipulation of powerful spiritual energies. The sexual energy of a person, known as Life-Force, can be controlled through meditation, elevating their soul's vibration to eventually reaching a spiritual orgasm. The life-force energy can bring both ecstasy and enlightenment. What happens is the establishment of a rhythmic masturbatory motion of inner energy. The mental control of this energy, its conscious manipulation, is symbolized by the interchange of fire and water, depicted by the interchange of fluids between the two vases. The key to this actually simple process is the infinity symbol, the figure eight which Pamela Smith uses above the figure

311

of the Magician or above the virgin's head in the Strength card. It is an ebb and flow which is confined, or is used within very specific perimeters but which is taken in either direction at will. As one changes the rate of vibration of this inner energy, one raises the level of consciousness, i.e., moves from chakra to chakra, or up the branches of the Tree of Life within.

It's all about controlling the inner alchemical process of mixing the energies within. The mental control over the ebb and flow of sexual and emotional energies. Churning the energy back and forth, to and fro, as it creates a stronger vibration empowering the chakras as it ascends up the spinal column (kundalini), rhythmically binding, generating and charging the life-force. The longer you hold it in the more it builds up, and it has the potential to become your superpower; utilizing willpower to exert mind over matter. Your sexual energy and emotions are the fuel needed to power your mind.

The Devil:
The Devil card is assigned to the sefirah Yesod in this key for a handful of different specific reasons. For one, the fact that this card is associated with the holiday of Tu BiShvat, which occurs during a full moon on the 15th day of the month of Shevat. This is significant because, the moon rules over Yesod, and the moon always reveals secrets that are hidden in plain sight.

The biggest secret hidden in this card is that there's a kundalini serpent camouflaged inside the Devil's groin. Also hidden within this card is a concealed Seal of Saturn. Saturn is the God of time, and one of the esoteric titles for the Devil card happens to be 'The Child of the Forces of Time.' The Seal of Saturn is revealed when you draw a line connecting all the figure's heads, and another line connecting all the Devil's hands that coincide with the Birkat Kohanim, Priestly Blessing. This includes the Devil's 'bat' feet as well as 'bat' hand. And lastly this includes the Devil's human hand which forms the Shin Shaddai hand gesture. These lines form two overlapping Vs which form two Xs together side by side (XX), which then creates a diamond in the center of the card; located directly over the Devil's groin. Hidden inside the lower half of this diamond is a serpent substituted in place of the Devil's phallus. One thing about the diamond is that it acts as a portal or gateway from the astral plain into the material world of Malchut. Similar to the womb symbol, the Vesica Piscis, this rhombus/diamond acts as a portal birthing our desire. Such a portal can allow a desire to manifest rather quickly and bypass the restriction of time; manifesting wishes like magic. Yesod provides the bridge into this portal, acting as the chute that funnels desire from Binah down into Malchut, the manifest.

Something interesting to mention here is the significance of drawing the lines that connect the heads and hands making out the Seal of Saturn. The Hebrew letter meaning head is Resh with a value of 200. There are 3 heads depicted in this card, and 3 times 200 equals 600. Now count the number of hands, which includes counting the Devil's 'bat' hands and feet-hands. The Devil is depicted as half man and half animal, which should be taken in account when adding up the number of his bat hands, (which there are 4), and directly relate to his animal nature. This includes his bat hand and his two bat feet that are technically a bat's hands. The Hebrew letter Yod means hand and has a value of 10. 10 times 4 (hands) equals 40. So now we have a total of 640. And then we add the value of the four points of the pentagram, which are associated with YHVH, and have a value of 26, found within the four points of the pentagram, (not including the inverted point located over the Devil's third eye, which represents the convergence of the letter Shin with the third eye). These four points, which stick out from the Devil's head, directly relate to the four elements: fire, water, air, and earth. The 5th point assigned to the Devil's third eye represents spirit and the union the Devil forms with spirit by way of the third eye, thus symbolizing that the combination of head, eye, and spirit are one. Now add up all the numbers and you get $600+40+26 = 666$, which is also the sum of all the numbers in the square of the Sun, which is connected to the sefirah Tiferet, associated with the heart chakra. When the heart chakra is opened it acts as the key that connects one to their crown chakra, Keter, where one obtains Christ Consciousness and experience the 'at oneness' with God. Tiferet (heart chakra) is associated with the Christ within, known as the Sacred Heart. Christ said that the only way to the Father, (crown chakra/Keter), was through him. You must open up your heart in order to open up the third eye and connect to the Higher-Self. So, here we have the secret unveiled that the Devil is both the tempter and the redeemer.

Furthermore, 666 or 6+6+6 = 18, and when reduced 1+8 = 9, which is the number of the sefirah Yesod. What is more, the value of the Magic Square of Saturn is 45. The Seal of Saturn aka Seal of Zazel is found within Saturn's magic square, and the Hebrew gematria value of the word Zazel is 45, and then reduced is 4+5 = 9 (Yesod).

Also, when looking at the Kundalini Key as a whole with all ten cards laid out in their correct positions, the bottom 5 cards, above Malchut, in the astral plane, form an inverted pentagram just the same as the one on the Devil's third eye. This includes the sefirot 9, 8, 7, 5, and 4. When you add up the numbers of the sefirot that correspond to these 5 cards you get 33, which is the number that represents Christ Consciousness. This is because there are 32 paths on the Tree of Life leading up towards Keter, and once past Keter you reach the 33rd degree or level of conscious awareness referred to as the Christ Consciousness. At this level is where a person is truly 'at one' with God.

Yesod is associated with the sex chakra and reproductive organs. Zazel's Seal forms a diamond that is actually two triangles on top of each other. Similar to the Vesica Piscis symbol, the lower triangle pointing downward, known as the feminine triangle, perfectly forms around the Devil's groin area. Here we unveil a hidden serpent phallus. The snake or serpent represents the kundalini, and it being symbolically located here, as the Devil's phallus, we are given a clue that it is his sexual energy which fuels his life-force, which raises the kundalini and opens the third eye. The Devil's third eye has an inverted pentagram over it symbolizing that by opening the third eye one can draw down desire from the macrocosm and manifest it into the microcosm. In other words, manifesting and birthing your thoughts into reality.

The Hebrew letter assigned to the Devil card is Ayin, which means eye. It can also stand for salvation, as in salvation from ignorance once enlightened, which connects to the letter Shin, which has a connection with the name of Christ, Yeshua or YHShVH, meaning salvation as well. The Four-Letter Name of God is YHVH and when you add the letter Shin in the middle you get the Divine name of Christ, Yeshua. Therefore, opening up your third eye allows you to obtain Christ Consciousness and redeem salvation.

Moreover, the numerical value of the letter Ayin is 70. The full spelling of the word Ayin has the value of 130, עין. The pentagram represents the life-force, which is YHVH. YHVH's value is 26, and 26 times 5 (the five points of the pentagram) equals 130, which is the value of the word Ayin, which means salvation. Whereas the name Yeshua, attributed to the pentagram, also means salvation. So, by using your life-force, you are able to open up your third eye where you obtain Christ Consciousness and then are able to connect to and form a union with God's intelligence.

The Devil card contains one of the greatest mysteries of the Kabbalah, which is that the Devil is the necessary means of reaching the Christ Consciousness of Tiferet. The Devil is both the Tempter and the Redeemer.

He is also described as the Prince of the Air, indicating that this energy of meditating in the flow of astral currents, this *Air* is to be understood here at the whole of Yetzirah aka Zeir Anpin, located in

315

the astral plane, which controls the ebb and flow of matter—further reinstating the Devil card's esoteric title 'The Lord of the Gates of Matter.'

May I conclude this card's description by reiterating the intention for its meditation, that Yesod is the gateway from the astral plane down into Malchut. Yesod acts as a funnel that all the conscious energy and life-force flows through from desire into the manifest. That desire is captured through the opening of the third eye—by communicating with the higher-self.

The Star:
The Star card is assigned to the sefirah Malchut and is associated with the Hebrew letter Tzaddi, meaning fish hook. The Tzaddik, meaning righteous one, meditates, frees their mind and casts their metaphorical fish hook up into the astral plane of the subconscious in hopes of catching (receiving/attracting) inspiration and godly insights. They attempt to obtain a deeper core understanding of all things. A Tzaddik is considered one who is in a constant communication with God. Moses was considered a Tzaddik.
The virgin maiden depicted in this card is a pure channel for the Light, seen dipping her vessel into the astral waters and pouring it onto the land to nurture the earth. The virgin symbolizes perfection of the physical form of nature.

To be a Tzaddik is to be on the path of initiation, and one who strives to ascend spiritually. The seven white stars in the background represent the seven chakras of the kundalini, which are illustrated here elevated and vibrating harmoniously, suggesting the virgin has reached this higher level of awareness, where she feels as though she is one with nature.

The Star card is connected astrologically to Aquarius who is the water bearer, which holds relevance to Tzaddi (fish hook). The virgin fishes with her vessel, dipping it into the astral waters.
Coincidentally, Aquarius is attributed to the practice of meditation, which is essentially the main aspect of the Star card. As we meditate, our heads (in a way) are like antennas (or perhaps fish hooks) tuning into, aligning with and sharing an affinity with the frequency of

God's intelligence—we tap into the higher dimensions of the collective unconscious.

The bird in the tree is a scarlet ibis, which has a fish hook for its beak. The ibis represents the Egyptian god Thoth, who is usually depicted has having the head of an ibis. The eight stars in this card connect to the 8th sefirah Hod, which is directly associated with Mercury as Thoth/Hermes. While meditating on this card, strive to be like Thoth, connect to or channel Thoth's energy as you fish, just like the ibis, into the astral waters of the subconscious as well as the collective unconscious. Open-minded, lacking ego, letting go of limiting beliefs and enlightening all the seven chakras in order to elevate your soul's vibration so as to draw down and bring forth prosperity into your life.

A Tzaddik remains in a constant conscious-state of meditation, and is a pure channel for the Light. Their kundalini ascends up the spinal column to Keter where they receive a spark of God's intelligence. And like a bolt of lightning striking a pool of water, the energy of 100% certainty is jolted through the Tzaddik's body, from the righteous one's head down to their feet, into the realm of Malchut. Now they know for sure without a doubt and with 100% certainty what needs to be done in order to manifest those Divine insights they received. As a channel, the Tzaddik receives in order to share. They know that by sharing their Light they will, in return, receive more Light. And they understand the more they give, the more they will receive. This is the secret to having prosperity in the world of Malchut. The Tzaddik is selfless, ego-less, honest, open and always looking for new opportunities to share.

This world is a paradox. In order to receive what you want you must give what you don't have. Although, you get what you give. For example, if you want money, you give someone your time. If you want respect, you give others respect. If you want a job, help others find work. If you want compliments, give others compliments—and so on.

The first Key, the Kundalini Key, reveals the steps of the guided meditation needed in order to raise the chakras and connect to the

Christ Consciousness, the state of mind that vibrates at the same frequency of the one Divine source of pure Light. This higher awareness is needed in order to wield the second key, the Prosperity Key.

Here is a breakdown of the guided meditation for the Kundalini Key in its 10 steps, which work backward from Malchut up to Keter. The paradox concept in practice. As we meditate, we must start at Malchut and work our way up the inner, spiritual, Tree of Life towards Keter, which houses the source of the Light. We work our way from the bottom to the top as we raise the kundalini, while drawing down Light from the upper worlds of Keter.

Step 1: The Star at Malchut:
Become like Thoth and cast your fish hook into the astral waters of the subconscious mind. As you breathe deeply, focus on triggering the initiation of the seven chakras.

Step 2: The Devil at Yesod:
Focus on your sexual energy, life-force, to be the fuel that ignites the spark of energy needed to get the inner wheels (sefirot and chakras) turning. Transform the will to receive pleasure for the self-alone into a positive intention of receiving Light in order to benefit others, thus becoming a channel for the Light.

Step 3: Temperance at Hod:
Control the spiritual-alchemy process; the ebb and flow of sexual drive and emotional feelings, churning around and around in circular spirals and gaining strength, as they pick up momentum, becoming the energy each of the sefirot feeds on for their source of power. Like music that starts out slow and then gradually intensifies as additional instruments join in to create one harmonious and steady rhythm. Visualize how your actions bring joy to others. Feel the warmth that you receive when seeing the happiness, you provide.

Step 4: Justice at Netzah:
Raise your mental sword up high into the air like a lightning rod attracting the electricity, drawing down the intelligence of God, and connecting to, being one with, binding a union with, the Divine

318

Source. Unite your consciousness with the Source existing in the 99% astral realm in order to become a channel for the Source who uses you as a conduit to create more vessels and more channels in the 1% material world.

Step 5: The Sun at Tiferet:
Strive to reach adepthood. Imagine your head enlightened and united with a new intellectual higher-self. Feel your third eye tingle as well as the back of your head—the Occipital Lobe. Your inner Sun will begin to radiate as you become centered.

Step 6: The Tower at Gevurah:
Allow your limiting beliefs to be rocked and challenged. Break free of mental bondage and take back your power. Be open to receiving an epiphany from the still small voice of the Creator, which will bring forth godly insights and guidance; revealing to you the next steps for you to take. Cultivate good thoughts and remain positive. Think of blessings and you will attract blessings. It is encouraged to say a Kabbalistic prayer, such as the Ana B'Koach, or to repeat mantras and/or state positive affirmations.

Step 7: Wheel of Fortune at Chesed:
Connect to and recall your own personal level of gnosis. That knowledge is the source of power needed to kick the process into high gear. By connecting the dots, and discovering new as well as re-establishing previous realizations that you know to be true, and being able to see the big picture, seeing how everything is connected. This will cause sparks to go off, which is just the thing needed to raise the kundalini through the Abyss, to the next level, where the portal to the third eye is located—the World card. Your accumulated learned knowledge is your source of power you plug into in order to get those wheels turning in an ascending mode.

Step 8: The World at Binah:
Focus on the large wreath depicted in this card. The wreath represents the womb, or the portal/gateway, leading to where you plant your seed aka your desire, and also acts as the portal turnstile from which your desire is birthed from. The wreath is symbolic of

the Vesica Piscis as well as the diamond in the Seal of Saturn—it is the third eye, your sixth-sense, the gateway into the astral dimension.

Step 9: The Hanged Man at Chokmah:
"But the attitude of faith is to let go, and become open to truth, whatever it might turn out to be.", Alan Watts. Let go and allow yourself to float as the sea of your subconscious takes you where you need to be. You must surrender to the flow of the current. Focus on the end result and have faith that it will come to pass. Focus on what you will gain instead of what you will have to give up. Envision the end result as if it has already happened. The brain does not know the difference of what is real and what is not. The brain believes that your envisioned imagination is real. Therefore, your dreams become possible to obtain. It is as though you are implanting a memory, and your brain believes it to have already happened. And this is how you plant seeds of prosperity. As long as you put forth action towards achieving your vision, your brain will work effortlessly to connect the cause with the effect. This is the Law of Attraction working in your favor.

This future envisioned goal is promised to you as long as you put forth the effort to earn it. This knowledge of Universal laws and knowing how the 'game' works is the reason the Hanged Man's head is radiating with Light. The man in this card is at ease and is rest assured that his dream will become a reality one day, and this is the 'happy thought' that gives him the strength and serenity to endure any challenges and all obstacles that life places before him.

Step 10: Judgement at Keter:
A calling to you to rise up and embrace a higher level of consciousness for the service of your higher good. You are experiencing a spiritual awakening and realizing that you are destined for so much more. This is your cosmic up-leveling. Time to tune-in to a higher frequency. Let go of your old self and step into this newer version of who you are evolving into, closer to who you really are on a soul level, which is a pure channel of Light for the Creator. Connect to a blend of intuition and intellect. Trust the inspired ideas that you receive, and have absolute certainty that your first thought is the right one.

Knowing that the first idea that pops in your head is given to you directly from the Creator, thus the first idea or thought is pure, having not yet been judged by the ego. "The gift of mental power comes from God, the Divine being, and if we concentrate our minds on that truth, we become in tune with this great power." - Nikola Tesla

Interesting thing to note here is that there is always a hidden sefirah within the Tree of Life known as Da'at. Da'at encompasses all the intelligence of the ten sefirot. If you rearrange the letters, you can get the word DATA; an anagram for Da'at. It is also known as the 11th sefirah. Da'at is associated with Uranus, which corresponds to The Fool card. The Fool, at its core understanding, represents Christ Consciousness.

Another hidden connection here within the Kundalini Key is found when you add up the sum of the Hebrew letters gematria values for the first five cards or steps involved, from Malchut to Tiferet, which adds up to 450. These five cards are at the base of the pentagram, at the beginning, which represents the initiate's desire to have an affinity with the energy of the Seal of Zazel aka the spirit of Saturn whose number is 45, and open or unseal the portal door into the higher dimension. Another way of saying this is, the energy obtained in these first five cards builds up the momentum needed for the soul to ascend through the entire ten steps (ten sefirot) eventually opening the third eye. Moreover, when you consider adding the hidden Da'at from the Fool card, and then adding the Hebrew letter Aleph (assigned to the Fool) to these first 5 cards you get the sum of 451, because Aleph's value is 1. The number 451 is significant, because it is the gematria value for the name Ishmael, which means 'he will listen', 'God listens', 'he will listen to God.' This connection reinstates the concept of silencing yourself in isolated meditation and listening to the still small voice of the spirit. God's promise to Ishmael was to inherit prosperity and abundance, but as long as Ishmael did what he had to do to earn it, and therefore Ishmael never gained a sense of entitlement.

Now that we have established exactly which cards are involved in the Kundalini Key we need to know where and how this Key is found within the tarot. Knowing this will strengthen the connection.

The Kundalini Key is found within the Tower card by counting all the Yod's contained within it. There are 22 Yod's in total and they directly relate to the 22 Major Arcana. The Tower is struck by a large lightning bolt, symbolizing an epiphany received from the initiate's connection to their higher-self. Once you solve the mystery of the 22 Yod's and figure out the secret hidden in plain sight it truly is an "ah ha" moment.

Before diving into this connection with the Yod's I must first explain the concept of the 45 pieces of wisdom inside the Tower card. There are exactly 45 clues or pieces to be used as tools for a person to be able to read any Rider-Waite (Smith) tarot card. For instance, in the Tower card there are 22 Yod's, the large letter W that is the Hebrew letter Waw, or Vav, and has a numerical value of 6, the crown on top of the tower representing the sefirah Keter (1st sefirah) and counts as 1, and then finally the Roman numeral of the card, which is XVI (16). Add up all the pieces to the puzzle and you get 22+6+1+16 = 45. 45 is the numerical value of Zazel, the spirit of Saturn, and also connects this card to Saturn's magic square, which is where the Seal of Zazel/Saturn originates from.

The Tower card is associated with the 1st of Nisan (March 21st), the original first day of the year according to the Hebrew calendar. On the full moon, the 15th day of Nisan, is the holy day of Passover (Pesach). Both the New Year and Passover celebrate rejuvenation and growth, which is the basic concept behind the Kundalini Key.

Going back to the 22 Yod's in the Tower card, which represent the 22 Major Arcana. They are divided into two groups in this card; one on each opposite side of the tower. There are 12 Yod's located on the left of the tower and 10 Yod's located on the right of the tower. This is the first clue as of how we begin grouping the major Arcana cards into two separate groups.

Knowing that the Tower card is associated with the magic square of Saturn is the first lead (or clue) to solving this puzzle. Saturn's square is a 3 by 3 square with rows containing the numbers 1-9. Each row and column adding up to 15. And then 15×3 = 45 (1+2+3+4+5+6+7+8+9 = 45). Now gather all the Major Arcana cards that are numbered 1-9 and place them in three rows of three and use them to recreate the magic square of Saturn. Refer to pictures below.

4	9	2
3	5	7
8	1	6

$$4 + 9 + 2 = 15$$
$$3 + 5 + 7 = 15$$
$$\underline{8 + 1 + 6 = 15}$$
$$15 + 15 + 15 = 45$$

Pictured here is the magic square created with nine tarot cards on the left and the three cipher cards on the right.

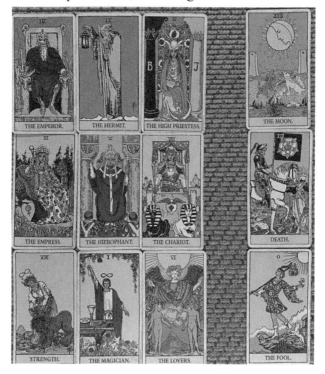

There are three Major Arcana cards that contain a hidden '15' within them. These three cards act as ciphers to let us know that the math is correct for each of these three rows in the square. These three cipher-cards have 'like' or similar symbols that relate to the theme depicted within each of the three cards in each row furthering their connection. This column the three cipher cards form symbolically portrays the Hermetic Marriage of the Moon and the Sun.

This 'marriage' takes place in a man when the heart and the mind are joined in eternal union. It occurs when the positive and negative poles within are united, and from that union is made the Philosopher's Stone. The philosopher's stone, more properly philosophers' stone or stone of the philosophers is a legendary alchemical substance capable of turning base metals such as mercury into gold or silver. Subsequently, each of the three rows inside the magic square depict this concept of Hermetic Marriage in their own unique spiritual-alchemical way.

The cipher card that corresponds to the first row is the Moon card, which has 15 Yod's depicted within it. The Moon card depicts the union of the sun and the moon coming together as one. This symbology coincides with the three cards in the first row. For instance, the Emperor is Aries, which is a fire sign. The first row's third card is the High Priestess, who has water pouring out from her and is covered in moon symbolism. The middle card, the Hermit, acts as the bridge and unites the sun/fire and the moon/water so they can conjoin together as one.

In the second row the cipher card is the Death card, which has Death colored in a black and white color scheme. This scheme portrays the yin-yang duality of nature coming together and joining in marriage. In the Death card, Death is dressed in black armor riding a pale-white horse, and carrying a black and white flag. There are four Xs on the horse's strap, which gives us $4 \times 10 = 40$. 40 is the Kabbalistic number associated with spiritual transformation. Death has confronted his dark side and is ready to have a spiritual balance of yin and yang within, and this is why he presents himself to the Pope, who has the authority to marry royalty. Death is a royal knight carrying the royal flag adorning the Tudor Rose. The black and white combination was a sign of royalty, as seen on the checkered floor of King Solomon's temple. Speaking of royalty, the first card in the second row is the Empress. She is secretly pregnant underneath her gown.

The middle card is the Hierophant, which is the Pope with the authority to marry royalty, who sits before two people wishing to be bound together legally. The third card in this row is the Chariot. The two sphinxes pulling the knight's chariot are colored black and white, and they represent the knight staking his royal claim and his ownership in an authoritative procedure. In this row, the Hierophant is marrying the knight in the Chariot card with the pregnant Empress. The timing is appropriate as seen in the number 40's connection with the Death card, because a pregnancy lasts for 40 weeks before the mother births the baby. These two wished to have the royal wedding before the birth of their child. With further examination, you will notice the Empress's gown has 40 pomegranates on it, and also the Chariot's canopy has 40 stars, which reinstates that these two are emotionally and spiritually ready to form a union.

Lastly, the flag that Death is carrying has a flower (the Tudor Rose) with 10 petals and 5 leaves equaling 15 points altogether, which marks the hidden '15' that further proves the Death cipher-card to be correct.

The third row's cipher card is the Fool. He has the sun directly behind him with exactly 14 rays. The 15th ray is the stick or staff that the Fool is holding in his hand. This stick is directly on the line with one of the sun's rays behind him, which is a clue that his stick is also one of the rays of sunshine to be considered when adding all the sun's rays together, making it a total of 15 sun rays.

The Fool card is all about having the combination of the pureness of the Creator's Lightmerged with the fire, passionate life-force, within. This example of 'marriage' is the theme depicted in the third row. Starting with the Strength card, the innocent and pure virgin is depicted merging with the lion, who represents the element fire. The pureness of the Creators Light merge as one with the fiery sexual/passionate drive. The middle card is the Magician who is wearing a combination of both white and red robes simultaneously symbolizing the union of innocent purity with passionate and fiery creative drive. The Magician reaches up in the air with his righthand to draw down the Light in order to create and to manifest. The third card is the Lovers card where we see Adam and Eve beginning their life together; a combining of Eve's pureness and symbol of virginity, with Adam's fiery drive symbolizing life-force. Notice how the tree behind Adam has fiery flames for its branches? Adam and Eve are seen here joining together as one.

Interesting to note here is that hidden on the Fool's shirt is the Hebrew letter Shin, which looks like a fiery crown. The Shin ש comprises three vertical lines representing three columns. The three lines in the letter Shin can represent the three columns in the Tree of Life in Kabbalah, which are the left column of severity, the right column of kindness, and the center column is known as the column of mildness and mercy. We see this three-column symbolism throughout these tarot cards involved with this Magic Square of Saturn card-layout (spread). There are the columns in the High Priestess card, the columns in the Moon card, the columns behind the Hierophant, and also the columns in the Death card. In the Lovers card the two trees symbolize the two columns. Finally, the Fool card is the final cipher card and contains hidden within it the Shin, which represents the three-column system. Furthermore, when looking at the column of the three cipher cards you will notice that there is the moon on one end and on the other end is the sun, represented by the Fool, and then in the middle is Death, who symbolizes the two dual forces of the Sun and Moon joining together as one. The Shin in the Fool card further reinstates this 3-column system by having the left column of severity represented by the Moon card, joining the right column of kindness, represented by the Fool card, with the middle mild-column, represented by the Death card that synthesizes these three cards into mercy and harmony.

The letter Shin means tooth, as in the serpent's tooth that bites you with the poison needed to kill your limiting beliefs as you raise your kundalini (serpent) opening your third eye a nd obtaining Christ Consciousness. As mentioned earlier, the three prongs of the letter Shin symbolize three flames, and the letter ש (Shin) is the symbol of fire. This shape is known in many traditions by the trident of Neptune/Poseidon, and the Trishula, (three-spear) of Shiva. This is the weapon of the Gods.

Shin is also related with three primary forces, which in the first (top) triangle in the Kabbalah Tree of Life are represented by the sephirot Keter, Chokmah, and Binah, which in Christianity are named Father, Son, and Holy Spirit. Let us remember that in Hinduism, this Trinity or three divine entities, which are fire, are called Brahma, Vishnu, and Shiva. The Kabbalistic trinity consist of Male, Female, and Central column merged in harmony and synthesized as one. This Kabbalistic trinity can be compared to a light bulb where you have the positive charge (right column), negative charge (left column), and the filament (central column).

These 12 tarot cards are all in the correct placements and

positioned perfectly as tested by the math and by the illustrated symbology. Each cipher-card contains a hidden 15, which is the sum of all the numbers from each of the square's three rows. Then you have each cipher-card's '15', so 15×3 equaling 45.

The mystery of the magic square of Saturn made from the twelve Majors was discovered by using the 12 Yod's located on the left side of the tower in the Tower card. The Kundalini Key is found using the remaining 10 Yod's found on the right side of that tower.

The Tower acts as the center column of mildness. The 12 Yod's on the left side of the tower connect to the left column aspects of understanding and receiving. The 10 Yod's on the right of the tower connect to wisdom, and also sharing the knowledge received from the left column, which is in this case, the understanding of Saturn's magic square.

The Kundalini Key's purpose is to open the third eye and to enlighten the crown chakra in order to enter through the Seal of Saturn/Zazel, which acts as the portal into the 99% reality of the astral realm. This is the basic concept—the secret mystery hidden within the Tower tarot card. Seen here below is a picture of the Kundalini Key layout/spread with its ten tarot cards.

You will notice how it is two mirrored pentagrams on top of each other. This mirrored pentagram geometry is found inside the magic square of Jupiter (pictured here). The pentagrams of this Key when flipped on its side will form the Seal of Saturn, which is the two Xs that touch and form a diamond in the middle. This is the 'marriage' of Jupiter with Saturn. This union, and merging of energies, is the essential key to manifesting a desire. In other words, make wishes come true.

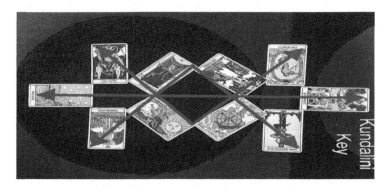

Here is a picture of Jupiter's magic square, and the sacred geometry revealing the mirrored pentagrams in its center.

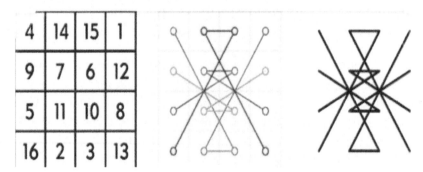

4	14	15	1
9	7	6	12
5	11	10	8
16	2	3	13

These mirrored pentagrams are formed by drawing a line from inside the square, made with one continuous line drawn from the 1 through the number 16.

This same concept of the mirrored pentagrams of Jupiter's square can be applied for the second Key hidden inside the tarot—the Prosperity Key.

The Kundalini Key was found within the Tower card. The Prosperity Key is found hidden within the Tarot Grid directly in the

328

middle and along the line that goes through the center of the concealed Seal of Saturn. The Prosperity Key begins at the Ace of Pentacles and ends at the 10 of Pentacles; the suit of Pentacles being directly related to money, property and prosperity. The ten cards corresponding to this Key relate to the Tree of Life and the ten sefirot, following the path of the tzimtzum lightning bolt. The Key is revealed by following the sefirot down the tree just as energy flows from the Ace of Pentacles to the 10 of Pentacles. This Key starts at the Ace of Pentacles, which corresponds with the 1st sefirah Keter.

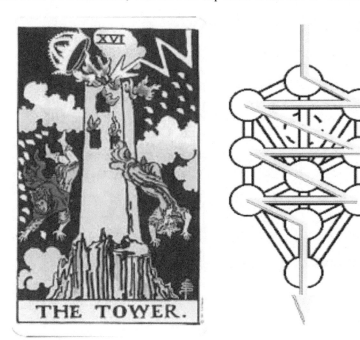

From here, the next card in the Key will correspond with the 2nd sefirah Chokmah, and then to the 3rd sefirah Binah, and so forth leading all the way to the 10 of Pentacles card which coincides with the sefirah Malchut. The energy flows from sefirah to sefirah down the tree like a lightning bolt. This same lightning bolt is found on the Tower card. The Tower card is the cipher-card that is used as reference.

The Prosperity Key follows the path made by the tzimtzum lightning bolt that goes directly through the center of the Seal of Saturn on the Tarot Grid.

The Tarot Decoded

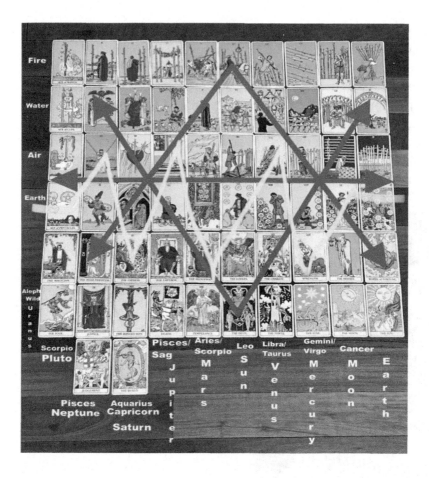

Pictured here is the Prosperity Key with its ten tarot cards for reference.

The Prosperity Key is a step-by-step guided meditation for making wishes come true.

The ten steps involved begin at the sefirah Keter, the 1st sefirah, which is the Ace of Pentacles. The idea is to mentally draw down that wish (desire) and manifest it in the 10th sefirah, the 10 of Pentacles card at the bottom of the Key, Malchut.

The Prosperity Key in 10 steps:

Step 1. Ace of Pentacles:
Have a desire for material happiness, a sincere need or a want. Think of God's hand as it is depicted in the card holding the pentacle as if it were a coin. God is about to place the coin in the slot, which is represented by the whole in the grassy wall. The Ace of Pentacles is associated with the Hebrew letter Heh, meaning window. So, think of it as God placing the coin into the window of opportunity.

Step 2. 2 of Swords:
Meditate and search within in order to pin-point your true desire. Be honest with yourself. The waxing crescent moon is the beginning of the month, and marks the pristine time to plant spiritual seeds. The woman is pictured here with a blindfold covering her eyes with the intention of searching within for answers. Remaining rational, filtering out the bad ideas that don't make logical sense, she confides in the moon to unveil inner truths. She takes advantage of this time at the start of the new month to plant the seeds of her true desire and honest reason for such things. There is no right or wrong, only what feels right for her at this time.

Step 3. The Empress:
Meditate on the 72 Name of God for prosperity (#45 out of the 72 Names, אסל), which will give 'birth' to your wish, drawing down desire from the macrocosm and manifesting it in the microcosm. Utilizing this 72 Name is not necessary, but it will enhance this meditation. The Empress's secret is that she is pregnant, and this is why she is wearing a large and loose-fitting gown. She is associated with the female aspect of God, Binah, who is influenced by Saturn's energy. Therefore, the Empress gives birth to desire; a will to form. For instance, the Empress's crown flaunts 12, six-pointed stars with its 72 points. These symbols divulge the fulfilling of miracles. The six-pointed star is attributed to Saturn, the one who grants wishes. And the number 72 is the Kabbalistic number which is specifically associated with miracle making. It is said that Moses used the power of the 72 Names of God to part the Red Sea. Notice how the Empress has 40 pomegranates on her gown? Pomegranates are associated with memory, as they have medicinal use and are given to Alzheimer patients to improve their memory and cognitive brain function. These 40 pomegranates are a clue that you need to focus and remember what you truly desire as you meditate to gain prosperity. 40 weeks is considered to be the standard gestational period needed for the fetus to fully develop within the womb. With this considered, allow your vision of what you want to fully develop. The clearer your vision, the more attainable your desire will be. To enhance this developmental stage, meditate on the 72 Name for prosperity. Scan your eyes from right to left over the three-letter combination with the intention of drawing forth prosperity. This is all that is required to harness this

energy, although the magnitude of the energy received is powered by the intensity of your will, and gauged by the strength of your intention.

Interesting to note here is that the 72 Name for prosperity is coincidentally the 45th Name, (or three letter combination). It just so happens that 45 is the sum of all the digits, (1-9), in Saturn's magic square. Found within the magic square is the Seal of Zazel, and also interesting to point out here is that the word Zazel has a Hebrew gematria value of 45 as well. The number 45 is significant throughout the tarot, each time it connects to the miracle-making energy of Saturn. Consequently, the Seal of Saturn aka Seal of Zazel forms the shape of a diamond, which looks like an eye and acts as the portal that traverses one's consciousness up and into the sephirah Binah. Ruled by Saturn, Binah corresponds to the third eye and acts as the gateway where one's desires cross over and down into the manifest, and this is when an individual experiences their wish fulfillment.

Step 4. 4 of Swords:
Meditate and focus on your desire just before falling asleep with the intent that your soul will work diligently to obtain what you wish for as you dream. The knight in this card is colored gold and is laying on a golden bed, over a golden sword representing his 'golden' happy thought and desire for prosperity and abundance. Notice in the stained glass window there is a woman bowing down before a Christ-like saint or priest figure, and she is asking him for a blessing. This is an allegory for the thought process going through the knight's head as he meditates. As the knight lays down to rest, he asks the Father to grant him the thing he desires most. The knight can rest assured, knowing that if he asks, he shall receive.

"Ask, and it shall be given you; seek, and ye shall find; knock, and it shall be opened unto you." - Matthew 7:7 (KJV) In John 16:24, Jesus stated, "Ask and you will receive, and your joy will be complete."

Step 5. The Hierophant:
Humble yourself and ask help from the Hierophant for the Keys to

unlock the treasure chest that contains your desire. The chest holds gifts from the higher dimensions. The Hierophant represents your higher power who is able to unbound those gifts promised to you. The Hierophant is associated with Jupiter, which connects to the energy of the mirrored pentagrams in Jupiter's magic square, which is the shape and structure of the Prosperity Key, formed when the Key's ten cards are arranged in their proper layout. As above, so below—what is yours in the astral realm can be yours in the material world as well. Jupiter is associated with the higher mind, spiritual expansion and knowledge. It represents higher religion and philosophy and all philosophical institutions, hence its association with the Hierophant, who is the one with the authoritative power to grant wishes, and to unbound that which is in heaven. The Hierophant blesses you with certainty, assuring you that you will get what you work for. We do not always get what we wish for, but we do always get what we work for. The Hierophant is the middleman who gives you what is owed to you. If you place your desire in the astral, he will draw it down to you. As you strive to achieve your desire, that fulfillment will work its way to you, and eventually the two will meet in the middle. That seed planted in the future will eventually manifest in your present.

Step 6. 6 of Pentacles:

A wish only works when the results are good for everyone. Therefore, it must result in a win-win situation where everyone involved benefits. Everything needs to be fair and balanced with one equal accord. For example, you could not just wish to find a bag of money on the street, because that would mean someone else would be at a loss. They may need that money for something important, such as a life-saving medical treatment. An example of a win-win situation would be if you were to purchase an item from someone, such as a car or house. In this scenario, both parties would leave happy after the transaction was done. The seller would have received the money they had asked for and the buyer gets to acquire their dream house, or dream car.

Step 7. 7 of Swords:

The 4 of Swords card advises to sleep on it. When you wake up the following morning, remember everything from your dreams the night before, and then, write down the things you are excited about. Make a precise list of all the things you want. For instance, let's say you wished for a new house, so write down all the details that excite you about this new house. This may include the overall style of the house, the size of the kitchen, the number of bedrooms, the location, the size of the backyard, etc. Try to be as specific as possible in order to feel that inner spark go off. That spark is the energy needed for your wish to come true. As you write, allow yourself to get out of your comfort zone. Do not let your desires be limited by the costs or by what you think others want. When you feel that spark go off after writing a particular desire, that is your soul communicating with you. That is when you connect to what your soul truly needs. After writing your wish list you may discover one main thing you want that is more important than the rest. After filtering through ideas, you may discover that all you really need is a place to call your own. After manifesting your first wish, it is easier to manifest your second. The first time takes a leap of faith. But once you do, you realize without a doubt that wish making is possible. Seeing is believing. Know that you have the power within yourself to manifest your desires. A spark of the Divine is within each one of us.

Step 8. The Strength Card:

Know that things take time. When you plant seeds, you need to allow them time to grow. Allow your material desires to come to pass in due time. Every type of wish is unique, and the time needed to fulfill certain wishes is relative. Tame the ego by knowing how the game works—things take time. Remain focused on the end result, your wish, and focus on the 'why.' The reason why you want it is the thing that keeps you going. It motivates you to remain persistent. This one positive desire can and will trump all the negative ego-driven thoughts of doubt, fear and unworthiness. Have the strength to endure and remain patient—patience is a virtue. Whatever you put out into the world, including wishes, will always come back to you.

Step 9. 9 of Pentacles:

You are now starting to see small results of your wish coming true. Although they appear as small, remember that results are liken to the rain, meaning that it starts out as a slow sprinkle before a heavy down pour. Remain mild-hearted, and give gratitude for the little accomplishments. This will allow you to stay positive as you endure. Remember to keep your heart open to receive more material blessings. Have an understanding that things take time to come to fruition. And remember, what you put out in the world will always come back to you.

The falcon seen in this card was used for sport in medieval times. Falconry was a sport practiced by nobility, where they trained the birds of prey to hunt. The nobles would train their falcons to hunt for prey and then return back to the owner with the prey in its mouth. Training a falcon to do this took a lot of time and patience, as well as trust. A person had to trust the bird would return. Appreciate the small accomplishments that lead you towards your goal. The falcon was given a small treat or piece of food each time it returned, even though it did not return with a small prey in its mouth, it was still rewarded for returning. These small accomplishments will gradually lead up and grow into the wish (fulfillment) you envisioned.

Interesting to note here is the 40 flowers on the woman's dress. 40 is a significant number in Kabbalah and seen many times throughout the Torah/Bible. The number 40 relates to the time needed for a spiritual cleansing and renewal, and this time is relative. The Hebrew letter Mem, meaning water, has a numerical value of 40, and is associated with a baptism or mikvah. During a mikvah the body is fully emerged in the baptismal waters and comes out clean, (pure), and retains its affinity with the pureness of the Creator. As the old adage goes, "Cleanliness is close to Godliness". The purpose of the mikvah is ritual purity in order for a person to be kosher (fit) and clean to receive God's blessings. In the wish-making process, this pertains to the timing needed for you to shed off certain aspects of your ego, and let go of habits that no longer serve you, and this may even involve breaking ties with people that bring only negativity into your life. You can't reach what is in front of you until you let go of what's behind you. As you release the negativity, you open yourself up to receiving more Light and positivity in your life.

One more thing to point out here is the two trees located on each side of this card. There's a tree located on the far left of this card and another one placed on the far right. These two trees represent the left and right pillars of the Tree of Life: the left pillar of severity and the right pillar of mercy. Whereas, the woman standing in the center of these two pillars would be considered a personification of the third middle pillar of mildness. This is a clue advising you to remain calm and grateful for what you have, and to celebrate the small accomplishments along the way as you work towards achieving your goals. Practicing gratitude will open up and warm your heart as well as relax the soul. This feeling of mildness will merge the left and right polarities. By obtaining balance the soul will begin to harmonize at a higher frequency, and thus raise its spiritual vibration, attracting fulfillment, which shares an affinity with the same frequency of your soul's desire.

Step 10. 10 of Pentacles:

This is the final step, and just as this card paints the picture of a wise man relishing in his wealth, it is also time for you to enjoy your manifested desire. Be comforted, and be grateful you did it. Now is time to celebrate. But overall, you are at peace now, knowing that the power to unlock the door into the higher dimension is real, it's tangible and is yours to utilize whenever, forever. This card's esoteric title is 'The Lord of Wealth.' This card represents prosperity manifested. You are meant to have it all. Life is supposed to be enjoyed. Once we learn the rules to the game, and adapt accordingly, we can create for ourselves a life that has order. It is possible to maintain order out of the chaos.

Interesting to note here is that The Prosperity Key contains only three Major Arcana cards. When you add up the values of each of the Hebrew letters assigned to these Majors you uncover a deeper connection. The sum of the Hebrew letter values for these three cards is 19. Then consider and remember that the Fool card is assigned to the 11th and hidden sefirah of the Key/Tree, known as Da'at. The Hebrew letter assigned to the Fool is Aleph with the value of 1. So, now we have 19+1 = 20, which is the value of the letter Kaph, meaning palm of hand. This is significant, because an open palm refers to the granting of blessings. Open palms are seen throughout the tarot and always represent a blessing being granted and bestowed upon people.

The breakdown of the Major Arcana involved in the Prosperity Key are as follows:

There is the Hierophant card, which is assigned to the letter Vav, with a numerical value of 6. The Strength card, which is assigned to the letter Teth, with a numerical value of 9. The Empress card, which is assigned to the letter Dalet, with a numerical value of 4. And Lastly, the Fool card, which is assigned to the letter Aleph, with a numerical value of 1. So now we have the numbers 6+9+4+1 = 20, which is the Hebrew gematria value of the letter Kaph, meaning palm of hand.

This is a clue reinstating that the Prosperity Key grant's your blessings. The open palm is used by the priest to give you a blessing. Likewise, the open palm is used by a person to receive the blessing as well. Also, there being four Major Arcana cards in this Key (when considering the Fool as the Da'at) connects to the 4 [th] sefirah Chesed, relating to blessings of mercy and kindness.

All the Major Arcana cards' Hebrew letter associations add up to the value of 20, which is Kaph. In Jewish mysticism, the two letters of the word Kaf, כף, are the initial letters of the two Hebrew words Koach, 'potential' and Poel, 'actual', suggesting that Kaf enables the latent power of the spiritual (the potential) to be made actual in the physical. The literal meaning of Kaf is palm, which is considered the location where potential of the Yod (hand) is actualized (interestingly, the gematria for the word Yod is the same for the letter Kaf.) For this reason, we bless children with palms facing them and we envision God as having His palms over us, for this image suggests the calling forth of the latent power of the spirit within for manifestation in the physical world.

Pictured here is the Prosperity Key's card layout which is shaped in the two mirrored pentagrams formation that is similar to the two pentagrams located in the center of Jupiter's magic square—Jupiter being the planet of blessings and good fortune.

Notice that when flipped on its side, the Key will form the Seal of Saturn. This is the same for the Kundalini Key as well.

Ideally, you would have the Prosperity Key placed directly above the Kundalini Key.

This would form a Key corresponding to the human vessel, which leads up through the head, as well as a Key being placed above the head connecting to and residing in the upper realms. As above, so below. The end result of this would have two mirrored Keys stacked on top of each other, where one was placed over the other. This peculiar formation is based on the two mirrored pentagrams found in Jupiter's magic square.

The name Zazel has a gematria value of 45. And since each Key is shaped like a Seal of Zazel, they share a connection to the energy aspect of 45. With the two keys mirroring each other, it gives us 45+45, which equals 90. 90 is the gematria value for the Hebrew letter Tzaddi, meaning fish hook. A Tzaddik, meaning righteous one, is someone who is known to be in a constant state of meditation, a high level of consciousness where they are in a constant communication with God. The Tzaddik always has his fish hook tossed in the astral waters. For example, Moses was known to be a Tzaddik.

Pictured here are the two mirrored Keys, one on top the other, with the Prosperity Key on top and the Kundalini Key on the bottom.

Pictured below is the outlining of the two Seals of Zazel/Agiel, formed by the two Keys.

These two Seals reflect the two ruling spirits of Saturn, Zazel and Agiel. Zazel is known as the darker spirit of Saturn, while Agiel is known as the intelligence (beneficial spirit) of Saturn. Both the names Zazel and Agiel have a gematria value of 45 each. Therefore, 45+45 = 90, the value of Tzaddi, alluding to one evolving into a Tzaddik.

It is the coming together of these two ruling spirits and

energy influences in a sort of Hermetic Marriage, and forming as one, that is the true 'key' to enlightenment. Obtaining a balance of these two opposite polarity aspects, such as the coming together of the two hemispheres of the mind. For instance, the Kundalini Key is associated with Zazel and the right brain (negative, yin polarity) , while the Prosperity Key corresponds with Agiel and the left brain (positive, yang polarity). The Kundalini Key corresponds with intuition and the subconscious, while the Prosperity Key corresponds with practicality and logic. While using the Kundalini Key one meditates and receives, and when using the Prosperity Key, one takes action and utilizes practical steps (practical Kabbalah).

LEFT BRAIN FUNCTIONS   RIGHT BRAIN FUNCTIONS

LEFT BRAIN FUNCTIONS	RIGHT BRAIN FUNCTIONS
Right side of body control	Left side of body control
Number skills	3-D shapes
Math/Scientific skills	Music/Art awareness
Written language	Intuition
Spoken language	Creativity
Objectivity	Imagination
Analytical	Subjectivity
Logic	Synthesizing
Reasoning	Emotion
	Face recognition

Yang		Yin
Masculine		Feminine
Positive		Negative
Summer		Winter
Day	Yang	Night
Light		Dark
Dry		Wet
Hot		Cold
Vibrant		Faded
Solid		Flexibility
Hard	Yin	Softness
Energetic		Calm
Loud		Quiet
Life		Death

Let's test the numbers to insure we found the correct findings for the two Keys.

Beginning with the Kundalini Key, the sum of all the tarot cards included in the Key equals 155. The sum of all the numbers of the cards in the Prosperity Key equals 55. The difference between the two is 100. 100 is the value for the Hebrew letter Qoph, meaning back of head. It is in the back of the head, the Occipital Lobe, where hallucinations, subconscious vision, and the recalling of old memories are stimulated, which would coincide with the concept of the Kundalini Key in the way the Key activates the subconscious mind.

Deeper meaning is revealed when we add the numbers 155+55 together, which gives us 210. The number 210 is significant in the Torah, because it was the number of years the Jewish people spent enslaved in Egypt before escaping their bondage. Metaphorically, this is when the Jewish people freed their minds from mental slavery.

Furthermore, the number 155 is the gematria value for the Hebrew word Qimah, meaning 'to stand', 'to rise up', ascend. This is interesting, because the entire purpose of the Kundalini Key is for the initiate to raise their soul's vibration and to ascend their life-force energy up through the chakras of the kundalini serpent.

In addition to this, the number 55 also shares a similar gematria significance coinciding with the Prosperity Key. It just so happens 55 is the gematria value for the Hebrew word halak, meaning to walk. 'To walk' can be interpreted here just the same as it is described in Deuteronomy 13:4, where it explains the concept of walking before God. It states, "You shall walk after the Lord your God and fear him, and keep his commandments and obey his voice, and you shall serve him and cleave to him." The term mentioned here 'obeying His voice' parallels the 451 Ishmael-connection, whereas Ishmael's name means 'listen to God.' This gematria connection encompasses what has been revealed within this chapter, that one must rise up and walk with God as they travel the path to enlightenment. The connection one obtains by connecting to the Source, the Light, grants them with the power to break free of their mental slavery.

Here is an excerpt taken from the Gnostic Gospel of Thomas,

"But the Master taught that hearing alone was not sufficient. The key was in doing or practice." Thus, if we were to follow the Kabbalistic teachings of Yeshua and put them into practice, and walk the rest of his Halakah (the way to walk according to the law), we will find ourselves on the right path to achieving the Qimah, which is the ascension of one's soul to a higher state of awareness where they stand as one with God, and walk with him—such was the case with Noah, Enoch, and Moses.

Let us break down the number 210 in the numerology method. When reduced, the number 210 becomes $2+1+0 = 3$. Kabbalistically, the number 3 is associated with the 3rd sefirah, Binah, which is ruled by Saturn. So, consequently, we arrive back to where we started, with Saturn.

Pictured here are Adam and Eve standing next to the two Trees in the garden of Eden: the Tree of Life and the Tree of Knowledge. Notice how one is above the other, which the two Keys' mirrored pentagrams are based on, mimicking the same concept, with one on top the other.

The diamond or eye of Saturn's Seal conjoins them together, bringing forth miracles of manifestation—creating something from nothing. And ultimately, making thoughts a reality. And in this sense, each Key can be considered as an 'eye', and then the third eye, the connecting point of the two Keys makes three eyes total.

Whereas the left eye sees the negative, the right eye sees positive, and the third eye sees the spirit. This concept is further explained in much greater depth in Chapter 8: The Seals of Saturn Hidden within the Tarot.

Chapter 20

The Two Keys' Step-By-Step Breakdown

These two Keys provide guided meditations that will help you grant your wishes, goals and desires.

First, the Kundalini Key is used to raise one's soul vibration, then the Prosperity Key is applied to draw down one's desire.

Here is a breakdown of the guided meditation of the Kundalini Key in its 10 steps, which starts from Malchut and ends at Keter. As you meditate, start at Malchut and draw down the Light from Keter, which houses the source of the Light. We work our way from the bottom to the top in order to raise the kundalini, all while simultaneously drawing down the Light from the upper worlds.

Kundalini Key:

Step 1: The Star at Malchut:
Become like Thoth and cast your fish hook into the astral waters of the subconscious mind. As you breathe deeply, focus on triggering the initiation of the seven chakras.

Step 2: The Devil at Yesod:
Focus on your sexual energy, life-force, to be the fuel that ignites the spark of energy needed to get the inner wheels (sefirot/chakras) turning. Transform the will to receive pleasure for the self-alone into a positive intention of receiving Light in order to benefit others, thus becoming a channel for the Light.

Step 3: Temperance at Hod:
Control the spiritual-alchemy process; the ebb and flow of sexual drive and emotional feelings, churning around and around in circular spirals and gaining strength, as they pick up momentum, becoming the energy each of the sefirot feeds on for their source of power. Like music that starts out slow and then gradually intensifies as additional

instruments join in to create one harmonious and steady rhythm. Visualize how your actions bring joy to others. Feel the warmth that you receive when seeing the happiness you provide.

Step 4: Justice at Netzah:

Raise your mental sword up high into the air like a lightning rod attracting the electricity, drawing down the intelligence of God, and connecting to, being one with, binding a union with, the Divine Source. Unite your consciousness with the Source existing in the 99% astral realm in order to become a channel for the Source who uses you as a conduit to create more vessels and more channels in the 1% material world.

Step 5: The Sun at Tiferet:

Strive to reach adepthood. Imagine your head enlightened and united with a new intellectual higher-self. Feel your third eye tingle as well as the back of your head—the Occipital Lobe. Your inner Sun will begin to radiate as you become centered.

Step 6: The Tower at Gevurah:

Allow your limiting beliefs to be rocked and challenged. Break free of mental bondage and take back your power. Be open to receiving an epiphany from the still small voice of the Creator, which will bring forth godly insights and guidance; revealing to you the next steps for you to take. Cultivate good thoughts and remain positive. Think of blessings and you will attract blessings. It is encouraged to say Kabbalistic prayers, such as the Ana B'Koach, to repeat mantras, and to state positive affirmations.

Step 7: Wheel of Fortune at Chesed:

Connect to and recall your own personal level of gnosis. That knowledge is the source of power needed to kick the process into high gear. By connecting the dots, and discovering new as well as re-establishing previous realizations that you know to be true, and being able to see the big picture, seeing how everything is connected. This will cause sparks to go off, which is just the thing needed to raise the kundalini through the Abyss, to the next level, where the portal to the third eye is located—the World card. Your accumulated learned knowledge is your source of power you plug into in order to get those wheels turning in an ascending mode.

Step 8: The World at Binah:
Focus on the large wreath depicted in this card. The wreath represents the womb, or the portal/gateway, leading to where you plant your seed aka your desire, and also acts as the portal turnstile from which your desire is birthed from. The wreath is symbolic of the Vesica Piscis as well as the diamond in the Seal of Zazel—it is the third eye, your sixth-sense, the gateway into the astral dimension.

Step 9: The Hanged Man at Chokmah:
"But the attitude of faith is to let go, and become open to truth, whatever it might turn out to be." - Alan Watts. Let go and allow yourself to float as the sea of your subconscious takes you where you need to be. You must surrender to the flow of the current. Focus on the end result and have faith that it will come to pass. Focus on what you will gain instead of what you will have to give up. Envision the end result as if it has already happened. Your brain does not know the difference of what is real and what is not. Therefore, your brain believes that your envisioned imagination is real and has happened, thus implanting a memory. As long as you put forth action towards achieving your vision, your brain will work effortlessly to connect the cause and the effect. This is the Law of Attraction working in your favor. This future envisioned goal is promised to you as long as you put forth the effort to earn it. This knowledge of Universal laws and knowing how the 'game' works is the reason the Hanged Man's head is radiating with light. The man is at ease and is rest assured that his dream will become a reality one day and this is the 'happy thought' that gives him the strength and serenity to endure any challenges and all obstacles that life places before him.

Step 10: Judgement at Keter:
A calling to you to rise up and embrace a higher level of consciousness for the service of your higher good. You are experiencing a spiritual awakening and realizing that you are destined for so much more. This is your cosmic up-leveling. Time to tune-in to a higher frequency. Let go of your old self and step into this newer version of who you are evolving into, closer to who you really are on a soul level, which is a pure channel of Light for the Creator.

Connect to a blend of intuition and intellect. Trust the inspired ideas that you receive, and have absolute certainty that your first thought is the right one. Knowing that the first idea that pops in your head is given to you directly from the Creator, thus the first idea or thought is pure, having not yet been judged by the ego. "The gift of mental power comes from God, the Divine being, and if we concentrate our minds on that truth, we become in tune with this great power." - Nikola Tesla

Once your soul's vibration is in-tune with a higher frequency, you are able to use the Prosperity Key: a guided meditation to making wishes come true.

The ten steps involved begin at the sefirah Keter, the 1st sefirah, which corresponds to the Ace of Pentacles card. The idea is to mentally draw down that wish (desire) from the 1st sefirah and manifest it in the 10th sefirah, the 10 of Pentacles card at the bottom of the key in Malchut.

The Prosperity Key:

Step 1. Ace of Pentacles:
Have a desire for material happiness, or a need, or a want. Think of God's hand, in the card, holding the pentacle as if it were a coin. God is about to place the coin in the slot, which is the whole in the grassy wall. The Ace of Pentacles is associated with the Hebrew letter Heh, meaning window. So, think of it as God placing the coin into the 'window' of opportunity.

Step 2. 2 of Swords:
Meditate and search within, pin-pointing your true desire. Be honest with yourself. The waxing crescent moon is the beginning of the month, and a time to plant spiritual seeds. The woman has a blindfold covering her eyes in order to look within. She is guided by the moon to see inner truths, and she takes advantage of this time, the beginning of the month, to plant the seeds of her true and honest desires. There is no right or wrong; only what feels right for her at this time.

Step 3. The Empress:

Meditate on the 72 Name of God for prosperity (#45 out of the 72 names, אסל) that will give birth to and create your wish from the macrocosm down into the microcosm. The Empress's secret is that she is pregnant, and this is why she is wearing a large and loose-fitting gown. She is connected to the female aspect of God, Binah, ruled by Saturn. Symbolized by the 12, six-pointed stars with their 72 points, the Empress represents the womb that gives birth to miracles. 72 being the Kabbalistic number associated with miracle making. It is said that Moses used the power of the 72 Names of God to part the Red Sea. Notice how the Empress has 40 pomegranates on her gown? Pomegranates are associated with memory, as they have medicinal use and are given to Alzheimer patients to improve their memory and cognitive brain function. These 40 pomegranates are a clue that you need to continue each day focusing and remembering what you truly desire as you meditate on the 72 Name of God for prosperity (pictured in Additional Charts section). Simply scanning your eyes from right to left over the three-letter combination is all that is needed in order to connect to their energy. The number 40 signifies that one must spend time developing and nurturing their desire in order to birth something great. We do not get what we wish for, but what we plan for.

Interesting to note here is that the 72 Name for prosperity happens to be the 45th name, or three-letter combination. 45 is the sum of all the digits, 1-9, in Saturn's magic square. Found within the magic square is the Seal of Zazel, and neat to point out is that the word Zazel has a Hebrew gematria value of 45. The number 45 is significant throughout the tarot, each time it connects to the miracle-making energy of Saturn. Consequently, the Seal of Zazel forms the shape of a diamond which looks like an eye and acts as the portal up and into the sephirah Binah. Ruled by Saturn, Binah corresponds to the third eye and acts as the gateway where one's brilliant ideas cross over and down into the manifest.

Step 4. 4 of Swords:

Meditate and focus on your wish/desire just before falling asleep with the intent that your soul will work diligently to obtain your wish as you dream. The knight in this card is colored gold and is laying on a golden bed, representing his 'golden' desire for prosperity and abundance. Notice that in the stained glass window is a woman bowing down before a Christ figure and asking for something that will help improve her life. This is an allegory for the thought process going through the knight's head as he meditates on his golden wish, represented here by his golden sword.

Step 5. The Hierophant:
Humble yourself and ask help from the Hierophant for the keys to unlock the treasure chest. The chest holds gifts from a different dimension; from the macrocosm down into the microcosm. The Hierophant represents your higher power, albeit the Pope, God, the Universe, Hermes Trismegistus, the Higher-Self, or what have you. The Hierophant is associated with Jupiter, which connects to the energy of the mirrored pentagrams in Jupiter's magic square, which is the shape and structure of the Prosperity Key formed when the ten cards of the key are in their proper layout. Jupiter is associated with the higher mind, higher education, spiritual expansion, and knowledge. It represents religion and philosophy and all religious and philosophical institutions, hence its association with the Hierophant, who is the one with the power to grant your wish.

Step 6. 6 of Pentacles:
A wish only works when the results are good for everyone; a win-win situation where everyone involved benefits. Everything needs to be fair and balanced with one equal accord.

Step 7. 7 of Swords:
The 4 of Swords advises you to sleep on it. When you wake up the next morning, remember everything from your dream the night before, and write down a list of everything you're still excited about. List your wishes and desires. Be specific of what excites you as a means to ignite joy and giddiness. Write down the things you feel passionate about. You need to feel that inner spark. That spark is the energy needed for it all to come true. As you write, allow yourself to get out of your comfort zone, because when you do you connect to what your soul truly desires. Know that you have the power within yourself to create miracles. A spark of the Divine Light is within all

of us—we simply forgot how to use it.

Step 8. The Strength Card:
Know that things take time. When you plant seeds, you need to allow them time to grow. Allow your material desires to come to pass in due time. Every type of wish is unique, and the time needed to fulfill certain wishes is relative. Tame the ego by knowing how the game works—things take time. Remain focused on the end result; your wish. This one positive desire can and will trump all the negative ego-driven thoughts of doubt, fear and unworthiness. Have the strength to endure and remain patient—patience is a virtue. Whatever you put out into the world, including wishes, will always come back to you eventually.

Step 9. 9 of Pentacles:
You are now starting to see small results of your wish coming true. Although they appear as small, remember that results are liken to the rain, meaning that it starts out as a slow sprinkle before a heavy down pour. Remain mild-hearted, and give gratitude for the little accomplishments. This will allow you to stay positive as you endure, and keep your heart open to receive more material blessings. Have an understanding that things take time to come to fruition. And know that what you put out in the world will always come back to you. The falcon seen in this card was used for sport in medieval times. Falconry was a sport practiced by nobility, where they trained the birds of prey to hunt. The nobles would train their falcons to hunt for prey and then return back to the owner with the prey in its mouth. Training a falcon to do this took a lot of time and patience, as well as trust. A person had to trust the bird would return. Appreciate the small accomplishments that lead you towards your goal. The falcon was given a small treat or piece of food each time it returned, even though it did not return with a small prey in its mouth, it was still rewarded for returning. These small accomplishments will gradually lead up and grow into the wish (end result) you pictured.

Step 10. 10 of Pentacles:
This is the final step, and just as this card paints the picture of a wise

man relishing in his wealth, it is time for you to enjoy your manifested desire, be comforted, and be grateful for the fulfillment you hoped for. You are at peace now, knowing that the key to unlocking the door into the other dimension is real, it's tangible, and is yours to utilize whenever, forever.

The esoteric title for this card is "The Lord of Wealth." This card represents prosperity manifested. You are meant to have it all. Life is supposed to be enjoyed, once we learn the rules to the game, we can create order out of the chaos.

Chapter 21

Applying the Wish-Making Formula
(SATOR Square Decoded)

After having first applied the Kundalini Key, you are then able to access the Prosperity Key, which holds the technology needed for manifesting desires. This wish-making technology is essentially mind over matter. One must learn to free their mind just as the Jewish people freed themselves from mental slavery in Egypt. This Torah analogy demonstrated in the Exodus story contains the mind over matter wish-making code which can be deciphered by using a combination of Kabbalistic wisdom and gematria.

Allow me to explain. The Jews were slaves in Egypt for 210 years. The number 210 is significant here, and it contains the code. For instance, when you add up the card's Roman numerals that are included within both the Kundalini and the Prosperity Keys you end up with the sum of 210. For instance, the Kundalini Key's tarot cards have a sum of 155, while the Prosperity Key's cards have a sum of 55, which is 155+55 = 210 total. Furthermore, when you reduce 210 to a single digit, you get 2+1+0 = 3. The number 3 gives us the connection to the 3rd sefirah Binah, which is associated with Saturn. As we know now, Binah is the connection, the portal to the third eye, connecting one to Saturn's miracle-making energy influence. Therefore, the two tarot Keys when used in tandem have the technology for an individual to free their mind, escape mental slavery, and ultimately achieve mind over matter.

A wish becomes true the moment we feel the spark go off during that initial brief moment when we first receive the vision of us obtaining it. Our destiny is in a gradual and constant attempt to connect with us. What you seek, is seeking you. When such a bright idea like a fantasy, day dream or vision comes to mind, when we envision a clear picture of its fulfillment, and get a glimpse into our soul's true purpose, it ignites a strong desire within us. This vision or epiphany experienced is the Universe calling out to us. In this very instant one's vision is so clear and profound it enables them to see into their destiny's future, from the seed level to its fruition; seeing the big picture. It is in that final fruition stage, when the end result is manifested, this is where our true fulfillment resides; waiting for us.

It is in that imagination place (that metaphysical reality), where we feel at peace, experience joy and connect to feelings of true happiness. It is as though we are implanted with these deeper life-purpose desires as a means to inspire us to want to improve ourselves and our own lives, but it is more so a push for us to improve the world as a whole for the greater good for all. Life has a way of waking us up, and getting us up and out of our complacency.

In that split second, when we receive a vision of our full potential, time stands still. The reason why that moment of epiphany feels so real is because it is. Our destiny is unremittingly calling upon us, and continually gravitating us closer towards our life's purpose. The ego tricks us into believing that these moments of clarity are merely fantasies, and therefore unattainable.

But it is much bigger than that. It is destiny calling. The vision of your potential future fulfillment is what has actually already happened in a previous lifetime, and therefore the life you imagine your future self having already belongs to you. It is a predestined path, agreed upon by you before you entered into this world. In this life, you experience chaos and frustration whenever you resist or go against your predestined path.

In our minds, any future fulfillment we envision has already happened, and therefore already belongs to us. Time, as we experience it, in between cause and effect is an illusion. This envisioned fulfillment implanted through the mind's eye fills us with the same joy we would feel as if we had already received it. This all happens instantly at the speed of light. Like a lightning bolt, this surge of energy shoots through us, and lights a spark within us that ignites our life-force energy, which awakens desire and the will to receive that envisioned fulfillment. Therefore, the cause is seen in the end result, while the effect is seen as the initial idea/vision.

Cause and effect are reversed when perceived in the 3rd dimensional reality within the illusion of time. How we experience this illusion is paradoxical, because there is no space between cause and effect when considered it is all occurring simultaneously. Our lifetimes seem to pass in a blink of an eye. According to our brain we have already obtained our future fulfillment. So, when we work towards obtaining our fulfillment in the present time, we are actually working our way backwards in time to obtain the fulfillment which is assumed to be in the future. And as we work towards obtaining our future fulfillment, our future fulfillment gravitates towards us. In other words, as we work towards fulfilling our destiny, our destiny works its way towards us. We eventually meet in the middle, where we experience the manifestation of our destiny in the present time. In the 3rd dimensional reality experienced in the present time, there appears to be space between cause and effect. This space creates an opening which allows ego to enter and wreak havoc and chaos in our lives. The restriction felt as we work towards our goals can feel as if we are swimming upstream against the current.

Our brains are unable to decipher the difference between what is real and what is imagined. Our brains believe everything we feed it to be true. So, according to the mind, both imagination and reality are real, and both are occurring at the present time. Perhaps the brain functions on multiple dimensions? This may make sense when considering the Fine-Structure constant is what binds the different multiple dimensions together. We humans are soul-beings having a human experience. Our brains are more connected to our spiritual essence than the physical one, although is communicating with the two worlds simultaneously. The brain is not affected by the ego and it does not perceive the illusion of time as we know it. In this life, souls exist trapped inside the human vessel which is trapped within the world. Each individual soul is experiencing yet another incarnation based in the 1% reality controlled by time. We must learn to adapt and endure the slow drawn-out death that is met with restriction, frustration and an overwhelming number of obstacles thrown at us by the ego's negative and unseen, yet ever present gravitational-force. We are promised fulfillment, as though it is the light at the end of the tunnel, only to be obtained after having earned it first. In spite of this harsh reality, we are blessed with the willpower to endure and overcome any obstacles we are faced with. God will never give us anything we cannot handle. The more aware we become of this paradox and the illusion of time, the easier it is for us to 'earn' fulfillment. In time, we grow stronger and more fearless, willing to take on any obstacle or challenge that comes our way. When a person views life as a game, and understands how the game is played, it causes a big shift in their awareness. They no longer feel helpless, adopt victim-consciousness and no longer believe God is out to get them.

We receive our rare and brilliant ideas from the Light, from God.

When you increase your desire to see God's Light in everything, the Light of God draws nearer to you. All things exist in the same time and space. We are capable not only of creation with our hands but instantaneously with our minds. We consist of a transceiver and a resonator. Our minds, our conscious intent, our words and our thoughts transmit and receives harmonic vibrations of Light. All we need is to tap into specific frequencies of the Light and the power of manifestation will resonate within us.

Through the third eye, we are able to envision the totality of an idea from a big picture (third-person) view where we are able to witness the seed of the idea evolve into its full state of fruition. As such, we see the end in the beginning. We first meditate as a means to tap into the Light where we receive insight of the life our future-self has in store for us within the realm of the potential, and we get a glimpse at our predestined fulfillment. Next, as you continue to meditate, visualize yourself actually being there in that future reality. You may experience a tingling sensation as this meditation tends to stimulate the back of one's head (the cerebellum). Once tapped into your full potential, and experiencing the life promised to you, your soul's purpose, you immediately are filled with feelings of joy and happiness. With this excitement and confidence, you are ignited with a passionate desire to put forth the appropriate actions towards creating this future life you have filled with prosperity and abundance.

Epiphany is pure and without ego. Therefore, as soon as we start to take the first step towards manifesting our vision, either by planting seeds or by putting forth the necessary actions, is the moment we are faced with challenges and start to experience certain forms of restriction preventing us from reaching our goals. And this can be so frustrating, because in your mind you already believe you have achieved this fulfillment. Now, when faced with obstacles that challenge you, you may become overwhelmed and feel like giving up. Just know that God wants you to have everything you desire, but you must have to earn it first by having to first endure a series of tests that will prove to challenge your spirit as well as your character. Knowing how the game works, and understanding the rules of engagement, will keep one mindfully aware, and help them maintain emotional intelligence, so they do not succumb to the ego, and such feelings of fear and doubt that tempt one to give up. You will now begin to see the world for how it truly is, and you will adapt to the unseen yet felt energies, and tune into higher frequencies. By tapping into the oneness of everything, you connect to the source of your fulfillment. The best thing one can do to speed up the time between cause and effect is to continually remain connected to the Light. Remain focused on the end result and why you want it. The 'why' attached to the end result is the cause you're fighting for.

This wish-making formula is concealed within the ancient SATOR square, which contains the combination of the words: Sator, Arepo, Tenet, Opera, Rotas. Tenet is, of course, ten running forward and backward, and then joining in the middle. The square is a palindrome. The Sator Square is a two-dimensional word square containing a five-word Latin palindrome. It features in early Christian as well as in magical contexts. The earliest example of the square dates from the ruins of Pompeii, which some scholars attribute to pre-Christian origins, such as Jewish or Mithraic.

S	A	T	O	R
A	R	E	P	O
T	E	N	E	T
O	P	E	R	A
R	O	T	A	S

The Sator square's algorithm functions similarly to the paradoxical wish-making formula implemented in the tarot's two Keys: the Kundalini Key and the Prosperity Key. For instance, one Key helps desire move forward in time while the other pulls fulfillment backwards in time, and eventually both ends of the timeline meet in the middle. This point in the middle refers to the present time when the desire becomes manifested. Both Keys contain 10 cards each, just like the word tenet (*ten*) found inside the middle of the Sator square. Also, interesting to point out is that each Key, when laid out on a table, is formed in the shape of two mirrored pentagrams touching ends with each other, and as a consequence form a Seal of Saturn in the center. Each Key has its own unique purpose, although both work in tandem with each other. For instance, the Kundalini Key raises one's soul vibration which connects them to the Source of their fulfillment, and then that future fulfillment is drawn down into the present by using the Prosperity Key. As an individual works towards their goal, taking the appropriate actions needed, their future fulfillment gravitates backward in time (inversely) towards them.

After applying the two Keys they will eventually connect the cause with the effect at the point in time when the cause and the effect meet in the present moment. This is when one's desire is manifested. The Sator square and the Tarot's two Keys share the same algorithm for wish making. This is how the world works; in paradoxes. The earth is ruled by Saturn, who governs the reality matrix, is the lord over time and fosters the way we perceive cause and effect. As the God of agriculture, Saturn is associated with the Sator square, and is the God of the Tarot as well. Consequently, the inverted pentagrams formed within each tarot Key help draw down desire from Saturn where it is then manifested into the physical world.

Thus far, we have learned the process needed for making wishes come true. First, envision your future fulfillment. Connect to that joy felt when aligned with your life-purpose. Next, begin planting seeds and take the necessary actions towards achieving your purpose. The idea sounds simple, but not so much as in practice. Thankfully, each of the two tarot Keys contain within them 10 steps to follow that will walk you through the practical actions as well as consciousness necessary for manifestation. The Keys act as guided meditations helping an individual connect directly to the source of their fulfillment. In essence, establishing a spiritual connection to the Creator. As long as you stay focused on your goal (the end result), your goal will at the same time continue to work its way back to you —inversely in the time-space continuum. Like a gravitational pull, your goal moves back to you and you meet it in the middle when your wish becomes reality. This algorithm is based in the Law of Attraction, and the code is found within the Sator square, and is unlocked with the tarot's two Keys. Knowing this code and how it can be applied towards wish fulfillment offers an individual the certainty needed to defeat their ego and overcome all the many obstacles they will be confronted with along their path as they strive towards achieving fulfillment. According to the Law of Attraction, like attracts like. Therefore, your mind is considered to be a magnet. Thus, if you think of blessings, you attract blessings. And on the opposite side of the spectrum, if you think of problems, you will attract problems. Thereby, it is advised to always cultivate good thoughts and remain positive.

The Tenet (ten-net) from within the Sator square functions in a similar way when compared to the ten spheres within the Tree of Knowledge, as well as the ten spheres within the Tree of Life. These two Trees, which were first mentioned in the garden of Eden, encompass spiritual aspects that correspond with Kundalini Key and the Prosperity Key, respectively.

Human beings can be considered to incorporate energy aspects of these two Trees as well. For instance, the Tree of Life is considered to exist in the 1% physical reality of the present time. This Tree of Life here coincides with the human body. While the Tree of Knowledge would be associated with higher wisdom and awareness gathered from outside man; from the higher dimensions. Man's connection with the source of higher wisdom is located directly above his head. The human brain connects directly to the 99% reality of the astral plane of existence, as well as the collective unconscious. The higher realms of awareness can be accessed when man opens his third eye, which is the pineal gland located in the rear center of the brain, connecting him to the Higher-Self and to the Super Conscious.

This method for manifesting wishes affirms that the Kundalini Key is to be used first in relation to raising one's kundalini/soul vibration in the present time, after which the Prosperity Key is to be used in order to draw forth the wish envisioned from one's future reality, where it then begins to gravitate its way back to you inversely, just as long as you continue to elevate your kundalini energy while remaining focused on the 'why' all while continuing to take the necessary actions that pull your goal closer to you.

The clue leading us to discovering this wish formula, and also why each Key is assigned to and arranged in these specific card placements, is found within the Tarot Grid. We now know the Prosperity Key is located in the center of the Grid, and that it is formed with the ten cards that line directly along the center of the

Seal of Saturn, which is located directly through the center of the Seal; the portal (diamond) that acts as a gateway into the 99% reality existing in the higher-realms of consciousness.

Worth mentioning here, the Prosperity Key's association with Adam, the first man, who represents mankind, and who just so happens to have an intelligent brain, and therefore contains the third eye. The higher-realms can be accessed when one's third eye is open—thus, the third eye acts as the doorway into the upper worlds. This concept is similarly portrayed in the famous Leonardo Da Vinci painting "The Creation of Adam" where Adam and God are seen touching fingers with each other as God sits in a cloud, covertly shaped like a brain.

Subsequently, it is God who is in Adam's brain. Yet another way of looking at it, God is accessed through Adam's brain—Adam opens the third eye (the 6th sense) as a means to communicate with God.

Moving forward, let me explain how the Kundalini Key, concealed within the Tower card, is found. The hidden clue in the Tower card is shown with the 22 fiery Yod's which are arranged in the precise manner for separating the 22 Major Arcana cards into two groups: an individual group of 12 Major Arcana and a separate group consisting of the other 10 remaining Major Arcana cards. The fact that there are exactly 22 Majors is a clue reinstating that these 22 Yod's coincide with the tarot's Major Arcana. Furthermore, Yod is believed to be at the starting point of all creation, including the 22 Hebrew letters, which directly correspond to the 22 MajorArcana cards.

As we move ahead, let us remember the hidden dog found on the 10 of Pentacles card.

This dog adorns the clue on its back for how to arrange and organize the group of 12 Yod's. Let me explain. There is a magic square of Saturn located on the back of the dog's robe. The magic square of Saturn found here is significant and coincides with the discovery of the hidden Seal of Saturn formed within the ten pentacles on the 10 of Pentacles card. With these 12 Majors, re-create a magic square of Saturn with 9 of the Majors consisting of Roman numerals 1-9 in a 3×3 square, and then use the 3 remaining Majors as the 'cipher' cards. This leaves us with the other group of 10 Yod's, which correspond to the 10 cards used to form the Kundalini Key, which coincidently coincide with the 10 sefirot on the Kabbalah Tree of Life.

The Kundalini Key builds up an individual's spiritual 'tower' allowing one to reach their crown chakra, Kabbalistically referred to as Keter. It is from Keter where we connect upwardly and outwardly into the higher realms of consciousness in an attempt to receive or attract an epiphany. The lightning bolt symbolism in the Tower card represents that jolt of divine insight known as epiphany. This lightning bolt (tzimtzum) is the same as the one which travels along the path of the Prosperity Key on the Tarot Grid. So, at the moment this lightning bolt strikes, we connect to our future potential (at the speed of light) where we are able to plant a seed in the Tree above us located in the upper worlds. With the received epiphany we are able to envision our seed in its full potential, which is ultimately our realized fulfillment.

This epiphany connects us to the Creator, the source of our joy and happiness. This pleasure is the life-force that will spark the lightning into the seed and cause it to grow, and gravitate inversely back towards us, meeting us in the middle at the point where time and space, cause and effect, unite and manifest one's desire— experienced in the present time. Now that you have achieved fulfillment, you may grow prone to repeat this method of connecting to the Source. Being struck by the lightning bolt of epiphany ignites within one's self the 'will to receive' such pleasure again. As you ask, you will receive, and what you seek is seeking you, willing itself back to you, and once again the two timelines will meet in the middle, at which point you experience your manifested fulfillment.

Interesting to note here is that the Hebrew letter assigned to the Tower card is Peh. Peh is a unique letter because it contains a hidden letter Bet inside of it; Bet meaning house and Peh meaning mouth. Thus, our kundalini energy is stored within our house (body) and it can be released out from our mouths. This verbal aspect, in regards to wish-making, can relate to a person stating positive affirmations or by vocalizing certain Kabbalistic prayers, such as the Ana B'Koach. Repeating mantras out loud may also prove to be helpful, as well as speaking positively about yourself and others. By speaking positively, we raise our kundalini energy and open up our spiritual vessel to receiving more Light, and as a consequence it raises our soul's vibration.

This meeting in the middle can be similar to the coming together of two opposing polar energies, and directly associated with the compromise portrayed in the Death card, metaphorically conveyed by the union of the Son and the Father, or as portrayed in the War of the Roses story when the feud between the York's and the Lancaster's was settled through a marriage of the two families. This coming together (reuniting) of opposing energies is also referred to as the Hermetic Marriage, symbolized with the Death card's black and white color scheme. Also, along the spectrum of polar opposites, the Death card is assigned to the Hebrew letter Nun, meaning fish, with reference to the two Pisces fish, where one fish will swim in the astral waters (the future), while the other fish swims in the waters of the earth (the present).

Furthermore, the letter Nun has a numerical value of 50, associated 50% or half of a whole. Thus, each Pisces fish has a value of 50%, so 50%+50% = 100%. The two halves reunite as one. Also, interesting to add is that the Death card is marked with the Roman numeral XIII (13), which is the numerical value for the Hebrew word echad, meaning one. Thus, reinstating how the two polarities unite as one.

The method of using the Kundalini Key can be compared to the way Jesus worked his way back to reuniting with the Father in heaven. For instance, Jesus was 33 years old when he was crucified, and on that day, he was reunited with the Father in heaven. Ascending up these 33 years (or degrees) parallels how the kundalini energy ascends up the 33 vertebrae of one's spinal column leading up to their crown chakra (aka the Father). The Prosperity Key corresponds to the communication one attains with God the Father, whereas the Kundalini Key is utilized as a means for an individual to open up their third eye, connecting them to God the Father, and making it possible for them to establish a connection and a communication with the Creator in a higher state of awareness. Afterwards, the Prosperity Key enables the individual to ask God for a wish, and then draw down that wish and manifest it in the material world.

The two Keys work in tandem in the manner of a palindrome with the purpose of connecting cause and effect in an algorithm that defies space and time. Planting a seed in our future fulfillment can be considered the cause. For instance, after having first envisioned your future fulfillment, then you are struck with the 'will to receive' that fulfillment, thus creating a desire, and therefore the seed planted in the future is the cause. The effect is defined by how an individual motivates themselves to manifest that fulfillment from the implanted seed. The more we strive to receive inspiration, the more epiphanies we will attract. Our vision becomes clearer as our desires align with our destiny. And just as the farmer Arepo mentioned in the Sator square, we too gradually evolve into becoming master seed sowers. The Sator square is a 5×5 square consisting of the words Sator, Arepo, Tenet, Opera, Rotas in a palindrome style.

S	A	T	O	R
A	R	E	P	O
T	E	N	E	T
O	P	E	R	A
R	O	T	A	S

SATOR – seeder, planter, sower, founder, progenitor (usually divine), originator

AREPO – unknown, likely a proper name, either invented, perhaps of Egyptian origin

TENET – (verb) to hold, or he holds, it holds, keeps, comprehends, possesses, masters, preserves

OPERA – work, care, aid, labor, service, effort/trouble, with effort

ROTAS – wheels, (verb) you turn or cause to rotate

One likely translation is:
"The farmer Arepo works wheels (a plough) or uses a plough as he works." Or, alternatively, "The farmer Arepo holds the wheels with effort."

And after considering and comprehending what I mentioned earlier in this chapter, the SATOR Square can now be seen as "Arepo masters the planting of seeds while working within the cycle of time."

Arepo here is a name of a man, and this man can refer to any man, and perhaps to mankind in general. Also, when taking this into account, Arepo could represent Adam, which is the Hebrew word for man.

Deeper spiritual meaning and insight can be drawn from the Sator Square when breaking it down and deciphering it using Ordinal English gematria, as described below.

S	A	T	O	R	73 (19+1+20+15+18 = 73)
A	R	E	P	O	55 (1+18+5+16+15 = 55)
T	E	N	E	T	64 (20+5+14+5+20 = 64)
O	P	E	R	A	55 (15+16+5+18+1 = 55)
R	O	T	A	S	73 (18+15+20+1+19 = 73)

It just so happens that these numbers correspond with significant reoccurring numbers found within the Torah's gematria code, which share the same gematria values of relevant Hebrew terms:

73 is the Hebrew gematria value of Chokmah, meaning wisdom.

55 is the Hebrew gematria value of Halak, meaning 'to walk', associated with the phrase 'to walk with God.'

64 is the Hebrew gematria value of Nebuah, meaning prophecy.

The combination of the values for Chokmah (73) and Nebuah (64) equals 137. The number 137 is significant, because it is the gematria value for the word Kabbalah, meaning 'to receive.' Therefore, in accordance with the Sator square, "When you walk in the wisdom of God, you will receive what has been prophesied (predicted/promised) to you."

Proverbs 28:26 "Whoever trusts in his own mind is a fool, but he who walks in wisdom will be delivered."

The Spirit of Wisdom is an attribute of God. In other words, it's a part of His nature. Much like heat is part of the nature of fire, and it results in a change in the nature of whatever the fire burns, so the wisdom of God is part of His nature, and it changes the nature of the person who walks in it. Your old mindsets, thoughts, attitudes, and habits burn away, and all these become refined in the spiritual fire of His wisdom.

Just like gold refined in a fire, you become a completely different (and much better) person when you walk in the wisdom of God. The wisdom of God is a path that always leads to an abundant life. The more you've been changed by and walk in His wisdom, the more abundance you'll receive and experience in your life.

The importance for making a wish is an attempt to connect one to their soul's purpose—align one's life along the same path as their destiny. "What you seek is seeking you." – Rumi. The more in harmony you are with the flow of your own existence, the more magical life becomes. It is about listening to your intuition, pursuing your dreams, creating your ideal reality and knowing that the things that call to you are calling for a reason. They are part of your purposeful path in this lifetime. Our desires are co-created by the Universe. The things we desire are not that difficult to achieve, if only we are willing to change ourselves. The first thing to change is our consciousness. It is crucial for us to learn how to adapt our intuitive mind into becoming a compass that will lead us to fulfilling our destiny found along our predestined life-path.

Ephesians 2:8–10, which says:
"For by grace you have been saved through faith, and that not of yourselves; it is the gift of God, not of works, lest anyone should

boast. For we are His workmanship, created in Christ Jesus for good works, which God prepared beforehand that we should walk in them."

God wishes for everyone to achieve a fulfilling life here on earth. Everyone is born with certain gifts and special talents, and carry within them a spark of the divine, which ignites within them the willpower and sense of purpose needed to develop their talents and share them with the world. This eventually furthers the evolution process of the world, which is ever changing and evolving. Upon each new reincarnation, you are meant to continue where you left off in your latest attempt at developing specific skills and talents unique to you, which will help the world evolve for the greater good. Within each new reincarnation, you will find yourself continuing to gravitate towards the same interests. What you seek is seeking you. The more in-tune you are with yourself, the quicker you can connect to those natural talents. Through a simple shift in your awareness, you can begin to intuitively look out for signs and pay close attention to gut instincts that guide you towards certain things that will eventually lead you closer to fulfilling your personal destiny. The quicker you are to reconnect to your soul's purpose, the quicker time will seem to pass, and the more fun life will become. Everyone has a flow. You need to find your own flow. Stop resisting, and surrender to your flow.

As I mentioned, the wishes and inner desires you seek now in this life reflect upon things that you have already acquired before in previous lifetimes. These desires are ingrained within your soul, and this is why you keep coming back to them. In order for you to obtain your desire, you must first earn it. This is so you do not get a sense of entitlement. Having earned it will give you a true sense of fulfillment. The quicker you find your flow, and align with your inner truth, the faster you will earn and achieve your promised fulfillment. The truth has never denied the seeker. It is the seeker who has denied the truth. Look within, and don't deny what you see, and don't doubt that you can achieve it. "It is not the possession of truth, but the success which attends the seeking after it, that enriches the seeker and brings happiness." – Max Planck

Chapter 22

Path to Enlightenment Readings,
Combining Tarot and Astrology

Found within the Tarot Grid, using the tarot cards, are astrological paths to enlightenment for all twelve signs of the Zodiac. Included within this chapter are full and in-depth explanations for each sign, including the astrological correlations. The purpose of these readings is to help a person evolve into their full potential as they shed off layers of ego and transcend into a higher conscious state of enlightenment. Also note that while we tend to refer to ourselves as our sun sign, it's just one detail of a natal chart, which is basically a unique snapshot of the sky when you were born. But it's a detail that helps color your core sense of self, identity, personal style, self-esteem and confidence.

Each individual's path to enlightenment will be unique to them, but be that as it may all paths will follow in congruent footsteps where each individual will have to first gather the correct data about their personal astrology, then piece together the meaningful information, after which they will need to organize this information building upon their knowledge base, then apply this knowledge into wisdom as they gain experience. And lastly, as a person self-reflects upon their path taken, having felt as though they have reached their full spiritual-potential, they will have acquired clarity of perception, and will have obtained a higher degree of awareness, thereby achieving enlightenment.

The cards included in each path are laid out accordingly, in an ascending order thus creating the individual zodiac sign's path to enlightenment, which leads from the lowest to highest value card based on specific element associations and the card's Roman numeral. The last and highest valued card reflects the respective sign's fully evolved state, and its highest level of enlightenment that can be reached.

Each individual path will include no less than six cards, consisting of four Minor Arcana cards that correspond to the four tarot suits and at least two Major Arcana cards. This arrangement would appear like so: Card #1 is a Wand, card #2 is a Cup, card #3 is a Sword, card #4 is a Pentacle, followed by card #5 which is a single digit Major Arcana, and lastly, the final card #6 will be a double-digit Major Arcana. This specific ascending order for which the tarot's suits are placed coincides with the tetragrammaton, YHVH. This interrelation was deliberately designed by the creators of the RWS tarot deck, who were members of the Hermetic Order of the Golden Dawn, a secret society devoted to the study and teachings that encompass the Hermetic Qabalah, astrology, occult tarot, and alchemy. The individual suits match up with each letter of the Divine name, YHVH. For Instance, the suit of Wands coincides with Yod, Cups with Heh, Swords with Vav, and Pentacles are associated with the second Heh. For an example, let's lay out the path for Gemini. Gemini is ruled by Mercury, which is the ruling planet of the 8th sefirah on the Kabbalah Tree of Life, Hod. Therefore, the path for Gemini will include all the #8 cards. This particular path will include the 8 of Wands, 8 of Cups, 8 of Swords, 8 of Pentacles, followed by the Strength card, which is Roman numeral VIII, and lastly, the Star card which is numeral XVII placed at the end. Number 17 when reduced down to a single digit becomes $1+7 = 8$. You will come to find these path's arrangements to be very significant, as they pertain to the Tarot Grid, which acts as a reference guide to the entire Rider-Waite (Smith) tarot system. The Grid arranges the Minors according to their specific suit and also to their ascending values, which grow greater as they trickle down the Grid. The Grid places the Majors in a similar fashion according to the value of their card's Roman numeral. Furthermore, the Grid organizes the Minors and Majors into six rows and ten columns, and these ten columns correspond with the planets of the Zodiac.

Each of the four Minor Arcana cards within each path's layout will individually convey a unique astrological influence of their own. In addition, all four cards combined encompass one predominate planetary aspect. In these paths, the four Minors function similarly to the tetragrammaton, YHVH where each letter contains a spiritual attribute of God, and at the same time all four letters together as a whole represent a prevailing aspect of God. For example, let's use Saturn, where each of the Minors included in Saturn's path, which involves all the number 3 cards, will relate to success that is achieved over a long period of time—this is due to

Saturn being the lord of time. Along these paths, from the Wands to the Pentacles you will progress through higher levels of spiritual maturity as you further develop your character. After these four cards, towards the end of the path, is where the Major Arcana cards are placed. The correct order for which they are placed is based on the value of each card's Roman numeral, setting the Major Arcana with the greatest number as the final card. These Majors reflect a particular archetype that sets an example for one to potentially evolve into and hopefully strive to become. Each of these astrological zodiac layouts act as guides, advising an individual on how to grow spiritually throughout their lifetime based on their planetary karma. The signs of the Zodiac are not the cause of our personality traits; they are the effect. These paths to enlightenment offer one the keys needed in order for them to shed off layers of ego and to reveal the Light concealed within themselves.

Picture a lamp sitting in a dark room that has been covered with several layers of lamp shades. These shades represent the layers of ego that surround our vessel. The many shades make it difficult to see the lamp's light, and the room remains dark. But, with the more layers you take off, the more light is revealed, and the brighter the room becomes—you are able to see and connect to the Light source, revealing the real you.

"Only in my pain, did I find my will. Only in my chaos, did I learn to be still. Only in my fear, did I find my might. Only in my darkness, did I see my light." - Unknown

Each Path to Enlightenment reading will include six cards, except for the signs Aquarius and Pisces. These two signs are at the very end of the Zodiac cycle, and because of this they merit special rewards and responsibilities which are attributed to having one more additional card, making it seven cards total for their paths. The reasoning for this will be explained later in this chapter, and will be included within their individual Path to Enlightenment reading.

Each path is found within the Tarot Grid, which has 62 tarot cards laid out in six rows, where the first four rows contain all the cards of the same suit from Ace to 10. These rows descend down the Grid through each of the four suits and lead to the Major Arcana cards that are placed in the two last rows placed at the bottom just below the Minors, with the first row of Majors consisting of cards numbered 1 through 10, followed by the second row of Majors which includes the remaining cards numbered 0 through 19. The last and final two Major Arcana cards are the Judgement card (XX) and the World card (XXI), which are placed on the bottom of the final row. The Judgement card is numbered 20 and is placed under the #2 column. This is because the number 20 when reduced is $2+0 = 2$. The World card is numbered 21, and belongs under the #3 column, because 21 when reduced is $2+1 = 3$. The 2's are associated with Pisces and the 3's with Aquarius, which are the last two signs of the Zodiac and both merit special gifts and responsibilities from Saturn. This will be explained further in detail in these particular Path of Enlightenment readings for both the Aquarius and Pisces signs.

The method used for locating each of these paths works the same way for each and every one of them. In order to find a person's correct path, first determine their astrological sign. Then, determine which planet rules that particular sign. And lastly, establish which sefirah on the Tree of Life is associated with that certain ruling planet. Correspondingly, the sefirah's number connects with the number of the tarot cards on the Grid. As an example, Aries is ruled by the planet Mars, which is associated with the 5th sefirah, Gevurah. After establishing this connection, find the 5th column on the Grid containing all the #5 cards. Here you will find, in order the astrological path to enlightenment for an Aries sign.

To reiterate, all the Path to Enlightenment readings include six cards, starting at Wands, then Cups, then Swords, then Pentacles, and then followed by two Major Arcana cards in their appropriate order from lowest to highest number, respectively. The tarot's suits' value and the order they ascend follows the order of the tetragrammaton, the Divine Four-Letter Name of God, YHVH. Each tarot suit corresponds to the four elements of the tetragrammaton as well, which in their respective order are: Wands/Yod/Fire, Cups/Heh/Water, Swords/Vav/Air, and last but not least Pentacles/Heh/Earth.

As we learn all the zodiac enlightenment paths, which serve as keys and/or formulas that help shed off layers of ego, we inevitably elevate our soul and raise our spiritual vibration which connects us with the higher-self and strengthens our sense of awareness as we transcend into becoming an enlightened individual.

By studying all the paths, even the ones not directly associated with your individual astrological sign, you will gain a deeper understanding of each of the tarot cards and their meanings—full descriptions for each card are included within these zodiac paths, which include all 40 Minor Arcana and all 22 Major Arcana cards.

The tarot deck includes 16 Court cards which are not included in the Tarot Grid. The Court cards are not 'numbered' cards, and they are not associated with astrological influences. For this reason, they are kept separated from the zodiac paths found within the Grid. The Court cards are considered to be 'action' cards and serve a different yet distinct purpose, which is previously explained in Chapter 12: The System of the Court Cards.

Let's explore the individual Paths to Enlightenment by starting at the beginning of the Zodiac, with Aries.

On the next page you will find the path for Aries in Section 1 of this chapter. Going forward, this chapter includes full descriptions for all the 12 houses of the Zodiac in the following 12 sections.

Chapter 22, Section 1: Aries

Astrological House #1, Aries is ruled by Mars and corresponds with Gevurah, the 5th sefirah on the Kabbalah Tree of Life. Aries' path includes all the tarot cards associated with the number 5. In their respective order, this path includes the 5 of Wands, 5 of Cups, 5 of Swords, 5 of Pentacles, The Hierophant, and Temperance cards.

Aries is a fire sign that is all about beginning, having initiative, being impulsive, having lots of energy and being busy with activities. Aries can also be audacious, impatient, imprudent, egocentric and have a selfish approach, and act out in hastiness and recklessness. It is no coincidence that Aries is linked to Gevurah, which translates as strength, and is attributed to aspects of severity, judgement. Gevurah is the essence of judgment and limitation, and corresponds to awe and the element of fire.

Aries energy invites us to step out of the spotlight. Shift your focus away from yourself and turn toward the needs of others. By doing so, we can begin to let go of past mistakes and open up space for deep empathy and selflessness. You can start by asking how you can help.

And one last thing to add, the major life-lesson they need to learn is to complete their tasks.

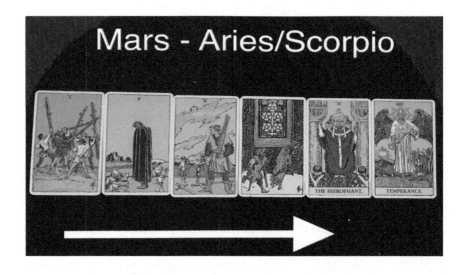

Let's begin Aries' path starting with the 5 of Wands card.

5 of Wands:
Pictured in the 5 of Wands card is a group of men who are all wielding a wand in their hand and battling each other. Each of them is depicted as being dressed differently and having their own individual styles. The suit of Wands represents fire, passion, and opinions. Aries can believe their way to be best. It is easy for an Aries to find themselves butting heads with others' opinions, and they rarely shy away from an argument. Aries are vocal and engaging. They will convince others to join in their creative projects and exciting activities, which may also include spur of the moment adventures, as well as extreme sports. They like to be in control and may come off as a bit bossy causing others to feel timid in voicing their opinion or stand up for themselves. From another angle, this card can reflect upon the inner struggle one has with their own personal beliefs and/or moral values, as well as second guessing decisions made in the past.

The Aries needs to learn that everyone is unique and we all have differentiating beliefs. Develop your own individuality. Focus on your personal growth. Lead by example.

5 of Cups:

Cups throughout the tarot represent feelings, emotions, and matters of the heart. In the 5 of Cups card, we see a person cloaked in a black cape, closed off and isolated to the world.

Three cups have fallen over, representing an unbalance of emotions and a lack of empathy. These three cups being grouped together like this connect us to the third sephirah on the Tree of Life known as Binah, which means understanding. These cups being turned over symbolizes that this person is not willing to listen to others' advice, has become stubborn, and is now trying to figure it all out on their own. This person is internalizing and analyzing themselves to the point of depression. They went from one emotional extreme to the other very quickly. If they were to turn around, they will find two cups sitting upright on the ground behind them. This pair of cups located on the right side of this person corresponds to the second sefirah Chokmah, meaning wisdom. This person would be wise to look at the other side of their situation where they would find the silver lining—a bridge leading him over the water and back to his home; to his comfort zone and place of stability.

This certain emotional aspect is why Aries are so attracted to water signs. Water signs help Aries find the silver lining in all things, and provide them with an emotional bridge leading them back to a life of stability, and comfort just as they once knew it, before they had an emotional temper tantrum most easily triggered by a random and (yet, taken personally) dramatic happenstance.

5 of Swords:

We now move onto the 5 of Swords card. The suit of Swords represents thoughts, spirit, and communication. Here we see a man celebrating a confrontation won with the use of wit and intelligence, causing him to feel over-confident and over-powered. In so doing, he is simply projecting, which causes the other two men to feel those same emotions which he had felt and dealt with recently, as was portrayed in the 5 of Cups card. He is seen now forcing these two men to walk into the sea of emotions just after having broken their spirits. Notice this man is holding two swords in his left hand? Here we see another example of like objects being grouped together. Just like the pair of cups in the previous card, these two swords correspond with the sefirah Chokmah, meaning wisdom. These particular swords being held in this man's left hand, specifically connects to the energy aspect of receiving, as it pertains to receiving wisdom. With this in mind, we can see how the pair of cups from the previous card morphed into these two swords—herein, emotions transformed into wisdom, attained from experience.

We have established that swords represent spirit, thereby, this man's spirit has lifted up and grown stronger as a result of his opening up his heart to other's advice in the last card. The Aries continues his day-to-day routines just as before, but now with a regained sense of self-worth and an additional boost of confidence, and what seems to be for the most part a smooth transition back into his previous comfortable and stable life. However, life has a tricky way of facing us with challenges that push our buttons. It is how we react during these challenging moments that shapes our character. By and by, whenever provoked, Aries prove themselves to be immature when dealing with such things as karmic challenges, irritable agitations, and not to mention human confrontations, as they present themselves. It seems as though the more confidence an Aries has, the easier it is for them to put others down and speak over them. They seem to do this by using words, either directly or indirectly, to put others in their place. They end up lecturing instead of listening, as they feed the need to prove themselves right. They instinctively have a need to argue with others, and are known to stir up an argument just to win one over you. They can be described as being rigid, enforcing obscure unwritten rules such as, "It's the way it's supposed to be."

In the words of the great Chinese philosopher, Lao Tzu—"Be mindful of your thoughts, because they become your words. Be mindful of your words, because they become your actions". Alongside this, understand that the life-lessons you are faced with are meant for you only, gifting you with an opportunity to grow spiritually. It is not your responsibility to preach or enforce wisdom which you acquired from personal experience. You must come to realize that everyone is on their own unique life-path, and everyone has their own karmic-baggage to deal with. No one truly knows the impact their words and actions will have on people or think twice about how they will affect the people around them; not until they, too, just so happen to be on the receiving end of such unruly behavior themselves.

5 of Pentacles:
Pentacles represent material objects and physical things. This includes such things as money, vocation, career, along with relationships and one's health. In addition to this, the suit of Pentacles can also relate to one's reputation. Our reputations are detectable by others and can be easily built up, but just as easily destroyed.

Depicted in this card we see a guy who is walking with crutches and is desperately seeking charity from the woman beside him. Deliberately turning her back on this man, she refuses to help in any way. She refuses to acknowledge the man, appearing to be annoyed with him—having reached her wit's end. What we have displayed here is the Aries repeating their emotional-habit of crippling themselves willfully in a psychological sense, effecting their mental well-being. Due to this, they tend to latch onto others, becoming codependent and rely on others for moral support, to pick them up and out of their tempestuous rut. The Aries goes even as far as physically hurting themselves in an attempt to gain sympathy from others. Once they deceive someone into sympathizing with them, and having earned that person's trust, is when they feel they have out-smarted the other, which places them as the victor. As the victor, they feel they are above you, and now are allowed to talk down to you. At this point, Aries becomes bossy, demanding, and over-controlling. This emotional rollercoaster ride becomes a habit which they have a difficulty breaking free from. If they continue to repeat this cycle, they will never be able to grow spiritually. They will be like the hamster spinning its wheel and getting nowhere, spinning with all its might yet it remains in the same place. If they were to continue this behavior, they would never be able to mature above the level of a teenager.

Without a strong determination and the willpower to change, they will remain codependent on others throughout the course of their lives, though they will never admit it.

Aries needs to learn how to take responsibility, not use others as a means to get ahead, be patient with people, and allow the process of manifestation to evolve organically. If not, this will push people away. It will spoil your job, career, and home-life.

The Hierophant:
Following the 5 of Pentacles is The Hierophant card, which can be perceived as a humbling card. This aspect can be seen here as the two men approach the Hierophant and ask humbly for his guidance and for the granting of blessings. The Hierophant wants nothing more than to grant such wishes and blessings, but one must first ask in order to receive.

The Hierophant is an interpreter of sacred mysteries and arcane principles. He advises us to not take things for face value and urges us to delve deeper, as well as expand our awareness to see things in the big picture. Avoid from being quick to judge, and understand there is always more than meets the eye.

The Hierophant holds the keys to the tarot. The Aries needs to become a humble student of life itself, opposed to them trying to gain control or to conquer the world. They need to learn to open themselves up spiritually, and be willing to learn the sacred mysteries that life is eager to share.

The Hebrew letter assigned to this card is Vav, meaning tent peg, nail. The tent peg is known for binding the tent to the ground. Spiritually, the Vav is known to bind, connect, or join the spiritual world with the physical, and vice versa. It would prove to benefit the Aries to be more like the Vav, and strive to be more in tune with the spiritual, expand their spiritual awareness, and connect to the Higher-Self. When it comes to self-improving, Aries needs to focus more so on themselves rather than trying to change others.

Temperance:

The last and most progressed card in Aries' path is the Temperance card. Temperance depicts the enlightened Aries, who has graduated from the Hierophant's mystery school and has applied the knowledge in practical ways that improve their life and relationships for the better.

Discreetly depicted within this card is a portrayal of the Hermetic Marriage, blending the dualities of nature. For example, the combining of male-female, positive-negative, or fire-water. The angel on this card is actually the combination of two archangels coming together as one, Raphael uniting with Gabriel. Wherein, Raphael represents the male-sun aspect, while Gabriel represents female-moon energy. United as one, they become the master alchemist who manages time with patience, thus allowing the life-forces to mix and flow with each other organically in a natural manner. This sense of control over one's dualistic nature grants them power over their temper. It is essential to learn how to hold in temperamental emotions and bite our words in order to avoid any kind of regretful outburst. Containing one's self and controlling their emotions makes it possible for their fire to mix with their water, wherefore inspiration is allotted the time it needs to communicate with the heart, which as a result gives the ignited impulses the chance to simmer down as they blend and refine themselves, all this occurring simultaneously while you attempt to hold back the urge to act out and cause a scene.

This androgynous angel is the source of its own happiness. This angel represents an independent thinker considered to be self-driven, yet at the same time able to surrender to the natural flow of life's rhythm. This angel seen here having one foot in the water and the other placed on dry land portrays the maintaining of balance of both intuition and ambition, and obtaining the willpower to refrain from acting out in haste and/or without tact. This concept is displayed here as the angel mixes the energies of fire with water in a calm and controlled manner. All the while knowing that the life-force within holds the real power needed to create prosperity and abundance. It is advised to not let go of this life-force until the time is right. The opportune time will present itself. One should surrender to the flow and learn to float with the current, and allow the Universe to lead you, to the doors and open up the windows of opportunity for you. "Things do not always happen the way I would have wanted, and it's best I get used to that." - Paulo Coelho, author of The Alchemist

As you meditate on these cards, think to yourself as you look into your soul, I can feel the sore places where I have been wounded by my ego: worry over what people think about me, needing to be right, angry when things don't go my way. As I let it go and reach for Light on a higher plane, those places in my soul open up. I am free, my ego diminishes and I concentrate on what is really important: love.

"Self-control is strength. Calmness is mastery. You have to get to a point where your mood doesn't shift based on the insignificant actions of someone else. Don't allow others to control the direction of your life. Don't allow your emotions to empower your intelligence." - Morgan Freeman, American actor

Chapter 22, Section 2: Taurus

Astrological House #2, Taurus is ruled by the planet Venus, which is associated with the 7th sefirah Netzah, therefore this path includes all the cards associated with the number 7. And these cards in their respective order are: the 7 of Wands, 7 of Cups, 7 of Swords, 7 of Pentacles, The Chariot, and The Tower.

Taurus is an earth sign that yearns for a stable life. They are ambitious, logical, trustworthy, practical, down-to-earth, organized, and are full of determination. While on the other hand, they can be materialistic, lazy, headstrong, jealous, possessive, self-indulgent, and greedy. In order for Taurus to grow spiritually, they need to avoid being too comfortable to the point of becoming complacent.

Being as how they have a connection to Netzah, meaning victory, Taurus's are naturally headstrong and driven to achieve their goals. They are not ones to easily give up. They are self-motivated, proving they can achieve greatness as they rightfully make their mark, as well as earn respect from their peers.

In addition to what has been stated, stability for a Taurus is maintained after having first put forth the effort. In other words, they work hard so they can play hard. Ideally, the ultimate goal is to create a passive income stream where revenue flows into your account. Initially, you must put forth a significant amount of effort in the beginning before getting the income stream running, but eventually end up having their money work for them. For example, a musician can record a single, and from that hit song is able to live comfortably off the royalties. This passive income concept can also be applied towards real estate, dividend stocks, as well as peer-to-peer lending.

Resist the urge to stay within the realm of comfort and predictability. The energy of Taurus may prompt us to shy away from new ideas, opportunities or people. But this is precisely the time to embrace change and discomfort in order to spark radical transformation. Dare to be uncomfortable. Break out of your box, shake things up, say no to complacency, and say yes to change.

7 of Wands:

In the 7 of Wands card, a man is depicted wearing two different types of shoes, standing off-balance as he tries to obtain some sort of stability on the un-even ground. This struggle to find balance adds to the frustration as he attempts to level out the row of wands set before him. Even though he is faced with a daunting situation, he remains focused on his goal and is driven to complete the task at hand, proving to be victorious in the end.

The suit of Wands relates to opinions, and coincides with the personal knowledge one gains over a lifetime. Wands correspond to agriculture and things that develop over time, such as ideals, ethics, morals. A Taurus can be bull-headed and fixed in their opinion, believing their opinion is better than others. This strong belief in their own opinion makes them even more so apt to convince others into believing it as well. Taurus feels as though they are coming from the right place and are helping, but sometimes people are not mature enough or spiritually ready to change their ways or change their mind, even though the Taurus's new way of doing things proves to be more practical and will end up improving everybody's everyday life.

This brings us to interpret the hidden symbolism concealed within this card, revealing its relation to practical advice that will offer a solution for dealing with these types of situations.

As stated earlier, the suit of Wands is associated with agriculture due to the fact they are trees. Likewise, the god of agriculture is Saturn, who is the lord of time. Thus, every card in the suit of Wands contains a certain aspect of time, relating to either the present moment, a day, or a year's time, depending on the card. The secret to determining the timing aspect of each Wands card is to count the branches on the wands. For instance, there are exactly 20 branches on the seven wands in the 7 of Wands card. The number 20 is significant because it is the gematria value for the Hebrew letter Kaph, meaning palm of hand, open palm. What happens when we open our palm? We immediately let go of our grip. In this case, the man holding his large wand would instantly let go and release his big opinion. By letting go one regains their sense of stability. You re-establish self-respect as soon you realize your opinion and the knowledge it contains is far too great for others to comprehend at the time. You do not allow yourself to stoop down to their level, and once again rise above them. At this time, they are simply not ready, nor or they open to hear what you have to say. The Taurus would be wise to simply let it go and walk away, later to return and try again once the people were ready.

Worth mentioning here is that this card is actually a portrayal of Moses coming down from Mount Sinai with the ten commandments (the new law) in his hands, and attempting to share them with the Israelite nation. Although, at the time the Jewish people were not spiritually ready to receive such powerful knowledge, nor yet open to change. Moses tried to convince them but to no avail. Upon realizing that the people were not yet ready, he broke the tablets upon the ground, metaphorically dropping his opinion and letting it go. Moses then returned back up the mountain to retrieve a new set of tablets, and planned to return back to his people once they were spiritually ready to receive them. Moses remained on Sinai for another 40 days and 40 nights, which Kabbalists consider to be the time needed for spiritual cleansing. The Hebrew letter Mem, meaning water, has a numerical value of 40, thus the number 40 associates with the healing aspect of water, and also the time needed for such a cleanse. Although, this time is relative. You will notice in this card how the Moses character is depicted standing on the cliff over the six wands that are set in the water (aka sea of emotions) below. The wands here represent opinions, significantly smaller than Moses's, symbolizing that they are not yet spiritually mature, and still undergoing the cleansing process. Moses is wise to let go, walk away and return when the time is right.

7 of Cups:

Next, we have the 7 of Cups card. This card depicts a person reminiscing about all the past achievements they have accomplished, stirring up a warm feeling of nostalgia. In addition to this, they think about their future potential and dream of the possibilities. They have in the past and will continue in the future to attach themselves to material objects as a source for their happiness. They are seen now pondering on what future objects they want to obtain. Taurus's approach relationships in a similar manner, treating them as an object and rely on the other person as their source of happiness.

Taurus's have a big desire for the finer things in life, which can include a house, car or job, but at the same time can also include relationships, reaching higher levels of spirituality, and getting close to nature. They seek out these things and consume them as a means to feel good, instead of being the source of their own happiness, and then spreading that happiness to others. Yes, Taurus's are typically fun and cheerful to be around, yet underneath it all, it is really them acting out a selfish desire for everyone to get along so they feel comfortable creating an environment with no contingency.

In social situations one must learn to center themselves. Being centered means we are anchored in both spirit and mind, logic and emotion, physical reality and the ethereal world. Being centered describes being in balance between these two seemingly disparate parts of ourselves. When we are centered, we regain control over behavior and become more in tune with our thoughts. It is important to realize that you cannot control other people or the circumstances around you, you are only able to control how you react to things that happen to you.

You do not need outside sources to be happy. Realize true joy comes from within. We are able to connect to this inner joy once we become centered.

7 of Swords:

Depicted in the 7 of Swords card is a man who is escaping and/or stealing a handful of swords from a desert camp. These swords represent this man's thoughts and ideas. The man's right hand is wrapped around two swords just as someone would grip an ink pen. The symbolism here suggests that this man is acting wisely and writing his ideas down on paper. By writing his ideas down he is able to organize his thoughts, and set his goals accordingly. Thus, providing him with the medium to escape out of his comfort zone and daily routine. As he brainstorms, he will attract inspiration, igniting a desire to achieve more from his life. Writing down one's thoughts is the first step to putting ideas into action.

A Taurus may find themselves stuck in their comfort zone, having allowed fear to keep them holding tightly to old ways of being and thinking.

7 of Pentacles:

Next, is the 7 of Pentacles card that depicts the same man seen in the 7 of Swords, but now portrayed as having lost that thing he had built, or had forged from his idea. You will notice how in the 7 of Pentacles card he is depicted now without wearing his red shoes, which he was previously wearing in the 7 of Swords card. This is significant here because the color red represents drive and passion, which were the specific attributes that lead him towards achieving his goal. Although, seen now in the 7 of Pentacles card, the man is wearing earth-tone-colored shoes, symbolizing that he has lost his passion and has been brought down to earth, so to speak. His esteem bubble has been popped, and he has lost all confidence. It is now evident this man has lost hope in rebuilding what was lost— something he had spent plenty of time working on and striving to perfect. He now judges his work critically and is disappointed that it has lost its appeal.

Pentacles represent material things that we can touch with our hands, such as a job, career, health, and can also reflect upon relationships as well as our reputations. This includes things that we can show off and/or boast about. At this man's feet is a singled-out pentacle, representing a single thought or idea that can help him get it all back. He has recently lost the success he once had, but is blessed with inspiration of how to achieve it again. Taurus is very resourceful and will always find a way to achieve success. But it can be difficult to let go and move onto new projects, jobs or even relationships. Taurus builds a strong emotional bond with whatever they venture into. The idea here is to not give up on the original idea and instead start over from scratch, giving it a second crack at it, albeit this time around with the intentions of rebuilding and improving upon that same original idea. Ensure this time around your project (or relationship) will last as well as develop into something more substantial, maintaining and enduring for the long term. In the beginning, it is easy to get carried away with an idea. We get so riveted with the creative process that we never consider any of the consequences, ensuing rushed planning that attributes to mistakes. However, don't allow this to shatter any faith you had in your brilliant idea. It was indeed brilliant, despite being executed poorly. Give it a second chance, and this next time approach it more logically, as opposed to whole-heartedly.

The Chariot:
Pressing ahead, with The Chariot card. The knight in The Chariot card has applied all that he has learned along his life's journey into achieving great success and being able to conquer the material world. He adorns a 'square' on his chest plate, representing his mastery over the world. The square is an ancient symbol for the world and he 'circles the square' spiritually with esoteric wisdom and by practicing the practical Kabbalah. This knight decorates himself with many esoteric and astrological symbols, displayingboth his esoteric understanding, as well as his devotion to a certain creed or organization.

He flaunts an eight-pointed star on his crown, which represents his high level of intelligence—the number 8 being associated with the sefirah Hod, meaning brilliance of the mind. By utilizing his brilliance, he has been able to overcome challenges by adapting his analytical problem-solving skills towards creating a life for himself that is both secure and stable.

You will notice that there are two sphinxes pulling the knight's chariot. These sphinxes represent the other people chosen (or convinced) by him to help in the endeavor of a greater goal or life purpose, as they share similar like-minded philosophies, and work towards an ultimate agenda.

Correspondingly, the Hebrew letter assigned to The Chariot card is Chet, meaning fence. Its spiritual meaning relates to things we keep fenced in, such as occult or esoteric wisdom, and can also relate to the secret agenda's one has in spreading such sacred knowledge. Secret societies may choose to withhold such knowledge, knowing that sharing such things tend to push others away rather than spark their interest. The Chariot card is covered with many esoteric symbols. For instance, the knight adorns two crescent moons that rest upon each of his shoulders, representing his desire to merit spiritual truths and insight from the Shekinah, the Divine presence of God. He displays several alchemical symbols on his apron. He proudly wears an eight-pointed star on his crown, connecting to Mercury aka Hermes, flaunting his esoteric understanding of the Hermetic occult mysteries and spiritual sciences. With further observation, you will notice there are exactly 40, six-pointed stars on the tapestry which hangs over the top of the chariot. These 40 stars represent the soul's growth and maturity needed to understand the concealed mystical wisdom of Kabbalah. Furthermore, he wields a long staff with a candle at the end in his right hand, which is a tool used for connecting to the higher-self, and to the Light of the Creator. Presented on the front of the chariot is a shield which has a dreidel with wings painted on it. Dreidels are known to only spin for so long. They are merely a temporary enjoyment. Nonetheless, the wings are able to carry the spinning dreidel forever, insomuch where the dreidel would never touch the ground, and remain spinning forever. The idea is to have this dreidel become like the sun disc that is placed in-between these wings, which represents being forever constant and reliable. In order for the dreidel to do this, one must continue spinning it. They must keep constant attention and focus on the certain thing which offers them enjoyment, whatever the dreidel symbolizes to them, thus giving that certain something wings.

The knight fears he could lose the things he has worked so hard for, so he remains focused, maintaining his success so it will continue to last forever. He believes that success is achieved when he is at his best physically as well as spiritually. It is important for him to stay connected to his higher-self—the source of his inspiration for creation. Once he acquires a taste for success, he will then gain the sense of certainty needed in order for him to continue and maintain his successes. He understands that he must continue striving to become better, improving upon what he already knows, and to dig deeper for the purpose of enriching his understanding of life and human nature, with regards to both the material and the spiritual realities that exist simultaneously. It is one's connection to the Source that empowers the life-force within, therefore making it possible to achieve the impossible, and for one to obtain the certainty that they contain the power to ascend mind over matter.

The Tower:
From here, we progress to the final card in Taurus's path, The Tower. Depicted here is the tower having just been struck by lightning, causing a man and a woman to fall out of the tower and onto the rocks below.

The tower represents a particular goal or concept they have been working on, having built it up from scratch over a long period of time, manifesting it from the original idea to its reality. The tower can represent a wide range of things including, but not limited to, a business concept, relationship goals, as well as obtaining a higher level of enlightenment reached only after years of devout spiritual study and ego transformation. Our human spirit is like a tower, that we develop and build up as well. By practicing meditation and working on ourselves we are able to raise our kundalini aka life-force energy within our vessel. This force ascends up from the base of our spinal column to our skull, where we experience the sensation of enlightenment in the crown chakra. Upon achieving this spark of enlightenment, one is able to tap into a new higher-realm of spiritual insight and understanding—obtaining a broader sense of spiritual awareness. With this new awareness comes new 'big picture' realizations and self-reflection. We are then able to realize our wrong doings, and unruly behaviors. From here, we gain wisdom and rise above our limiting beliefs, and shatter our previously fixed mindset. At this point, we experience an "ah ha" moment, and connect to higher truths.

Both the man and woman in this card will have experienced a distinct and personalized spiritual awakening which destroys their tower, and ultimately shatters their belief systems.

They are now forced to pick up the pieces and start over, although they will rise from the ashes stronger and more spiritually mature than ever before.

People tend to believe that material wealth and material objects will bring them happiness. Looking for outside sources blinds one to the truth that such happiness is found from within. Subsequently, the search for inner truth can blind a person as well, because the closer one gets to obtaining such truths, the more so their minds become unwilling to change. Strictly speaking, a person can succumb to a certain agenda and find themselves omitting anything that disagrees with their agenda's reasoning; immediately blocking out or diminishing all outside perspectives.

Over time, we come to realize that money and fame along with material possessions such as a house, a car and business are all temporary things. For this reason, how others perceive our character trumps the way we are judged by either our looks or what we own. The truly important things in life are the relationships we have with ourselves, our family, and our friends. When we open up our hearts and let go of ego, we are able to connect to the people we love on a deeper emotional level, correspondingly sharing our Light with others. The Light felt will be what they remember more so than the fancy gifts you gave them. It is more so about how you make others feel which truly leaves an impact. The Light you have shared, the good things you have done in the world to make it a better place, will last even after you are gone.

These personal connections are what truly matters and what we can take with us on and into the next life. Our relationship with ourself and God (Higher-Self) is eternal. An enlightened Taurus learns to value their connection with the Light more so than an infatuation with material objects.

The Light enters our vessel and raises our vibration, elevating our soul and conscious awareness. This enlightened sense of awareness wakes us up to the fact that life is not about acquiring material things just to quench the need for instant gratification, or to obtain a fading sense of accomplishment. In the long run, having more stuff doesn't matter. It's the impact, the mark that you leave that truly changes the world for the better, and sets an example for others to follow in your footsteps.

Although, this card has many positive traits, it can also be perceived in a negative polarity, whereas the man and woman can be seen as selfishly following their ego-driven desire to obtain enlightenment, as if it were an achievement, comparable to achieving a black belt in karate, for example. They do not understand that to be spiritually enlightened is to maintain a sense of being enlightened, and it's something you grow to become; not something you attain overnight. It takes time and a conscious effort to be able to truly grasp the higher truths in their divine simplicity. Once you see the truth, you can never go back. You can never un-see it. This new shift in awareness, your new 'woke' mindset becomes your essence. Allow me to explain.

The man and woman in The Tower card did the spiritual work required for them to ascend up the 22 branches of the Tree of Life, represented here by the 22 Yod's that float in the air. It was at the top of the tower where they connected to the Source, the crown chakra aka the sefirah Keter, (meaning crown). But with their acquired spiritual knowledge, they had built themselves a spiritual tower of Babel, so to speak. They had treated the achievement of enlightenment just as they would a material object or an award they were wishing to win. Upon reaching enlightenment, their ego stepped in and deceived them into believing that they had done it on their own accord, either with such great tenacity or by having such a high level of confidence in themselves. At this point, they stopped relying on the Light for guidance. They built their tower up to heaven so they could be just as high as God, and then once this higher level was reached, they vainly felt as if they were Gods themselves. Their situation is oddly similar to the old concept, "If you give a man a fish, he will not go hungry that day, but if you teach a man to fish, he will never go hungry again". These people used to be spiritually hungry and they were taught to fish, and now feel like they no longer need the teacher, and they feel like they can continue fishing on their own without any godly help. Although, eventually with time, they will come to find out they need more than just fish to survive this world. They will soon be faced with new challenges that life will throw at them. Today it's fish, tomorrow it's shelter. Nothing lasts forever, and we all experience times of good followed by times of bad. These challenges will seem overwhelming to them now that they have lost their connection to the higher-self and must go at it alone. Without their connection to the crown at the top of the tower, doubts, fears and anxiety will ensue. When we open up our hearts to the Source, to the Light of the Creator, we invite the life-force in, which boosts our tower aka kundalini energy once again. Similar to the old adage, the teacher presents himself when the student is ready. God was always there, they just needed to tap into the Source-energy; the infinite energy which is all around us, all of the time. Once we understand that this is the source and not our own ego is when we begin to build up our spiritual towers within.

The characters in this card will eventually realize the truth that they are merely a vessel, and a channel for the Light. Becoming spiritual isn't about gaining a new personality, getting a new vocabulary or wardrobe, buying crystals or doing yoga. It's about returning to our natural state.

Reaching enlightenment is about preserving a higher sense of awareness so that you can continue realizing new truths and break free from limiting beliefs and a fixed mindset. Once we shatter our beliefs, we must wipe the slate clean and start over. However, don't be afraid to start over again. This time you are not starting from scratch, you're starting from experience.

Resist the urge to stay within the realm of comfort and predictability. The energy of Taurus may prompt us to shy away from new ideas, opportunities, or people. But this is precisely the time to embrace change and discomfort in order to spark radical transformation.

Interesting to note here is that the Hebrew letter assigned to The Tower card is Peh, meaning mouth. The intriguing thing about the letter Peh is that there is a hidden letter Bet inside of it. Bet means house, and can relate here specifically to things that we say in private, in our homes and away from the public. This corresponds to one's spiritual growth and transformation worked on in private, and it is advised to not speak openly or share with others how you are developing spiritually, and avoid bragging about any personal milestones achieved. For instance, when we do decide to speak about our personal spiritual work we are, in reality, either consciously or subconsciously seeking out the approval of others. In this exchange, their approval validates our growth, which consequently exhausts our self-esteem. It is as if the only reason we were working on ourselves is for others to praise us for being a good person. Winning others' approval is like winning a gold star in grade-school or a trophy at the end of a contest, and with each new person you meet they become like a new merit badge you must earn and collect on your sash. Earning others' approval can transform into an addiction, and never be truly fulfilling. It can come to be exhausting participating in a rat race where the award for first place is a pat on the back. And you find yourself doing this with every person you meet; trying to empress them. This approval received from others has a way of diminishing our spiritual towers, as we attempt to raise our spiritual vibration and ascend up through each of the chakras. Holding in this life-force energy gives one the power to build and ascend up their tower, likewise releasing this energy reactively will just as quickly compromise what they have spent so much time and effort building up. Sacred things we keep private and speak of in private have a tendency of coming out publicly if we do not maintain a stable control over our spiritual towers. When we share what is regarded to be private, done with either sarcastic remarks, emotional outburst, or spreading gossip, it has the power to destroy anything we have spent time building. This includes our relationships, friendships, careers, as well as our reputations. It can take years to build a strong friendship, and in only an instant, with the wrong words spoken, can that friendship be destroyed forever.

A Taurus must continue to be mindfully aware of the caliber of their spiritual tower while at the same time remaining mindful of their thoughts, on the grounds that those thoughts have the power to diminish one's spirit, clouding one's judgement and sense of discernment.

The higher the caliber of one's tower, the easier it is for them to lose control over their emotions and act out impulsively. With this power comes great responsibility. You see, our thoughts become our words, and then those words have the power to either build up or destroy the things we care the most about. Behaving reactively releases our light, permitting ego to enter. With the greater amount of light that escapes our vessel, there is a potential for a greater amount of ego to enter. This is why it is so important to be mindful when our spirit feels at its strongest, because this is when we have the greatest potential to cause the most havoc, both to ourselves and to those we love. Having a strong willpower is key to maintaining a stable spiritual tower, granting us with stability in our relationships, friendships and careers.

When you decide to change, do it for you and not for the approval of others. "Self-control is strength. Calmness is mastery. You have to get to a point where your mood doesn't shift based on the insignificant actions of someone else. Don't allow others to control the direction of your life. Don't allow your emotions to overpower your intelligence." – Morgan Freeman, actor

Time now to break out of your shell. Say no to complacency, and yes to change. And only do so for yourself, and your own peace of mind. Your value does not decrease based on someone's inability to see your worth.

As you meditate on these cards, say to yourself, I clearly see my personal limitations. Looking into the past, I notice all of the instances when ego has kept me imprisoned, holding me back from true joy and fulfillment. As I focus on the Light of the Creator, the transformative energy of the divine washes over me, and I feel free. No more complaining, no more frustration. I will not get caught up in the material world. Instead, I will look beyond into the spiritual realm and let go, freeing myself from the trappings of ego.

Chapter 22, Section 3: Gemini

Astrological House #3, Gemini's path to enlightenment includes all of the #8 cards. This is because Gemini is ruled by Mercury, and consequently, Mercury rules over the 8th sefirah on the Kabbalah Tree of Life known as Hod. Hod is associated with glory/brilliance of the mind. Therefore, the path for Gemini will reflect upon certain aspects regarding thought patterns and communication relating to how one speaks to themselves, as well as with others in order to resolve a variety of distinctive issues, while utilizing analytical problem-solving skills.

As I mentioned earlier, the path for Gemini includes all the #8 cards, which includes all the tarot cards that are associated with the number 8 as well. And these cards are: the 8 of Wands, the 8 of Cups, the 8 of Swords, the 8 of Pentacles, followed by Strength, and lastly, the Star card.

Most Geminis are cheerful, tactful, enthusiastic, versatile, fun, and witty social-beings. However, all astrological signs demonstrate both positive and negative characteristics. Geminis display a duality of sorts, and for this reason they are symbolized by the twins, whereas one twin reflects light energy while the other reflects a dark energy. And for this reason, Mercury is known as the trickster planet. In Ancient myths, Mercury (Hermes) is the slippery messenger to the gods, the patron of thieves, and the inventor of lying. Gemini is the wordsmith, the salesperson, the messenger, the thief, and the liar. The dark Gemini twin is wily, deceptive, and full of mischief.

We don't need to see the whole path in order to take the first step toward achieving a goal. No matter how small the desire, Gemini energy can distract attention away from the end result. Stay the course. Focus on action and details with the big picture in mind.

Gemini's need to learn to take action, and not waist time overthinking. This causes one to put things off. Time to step forward, and then finish what you start. Trust the Light, not your mind.

8 of Wands:

We begin Gemini's path with the 8 of Wands card, where we see a bunch of wands shooting out like arrows into the air. The suit of Wands represents the fire energy that ignites creativity, passion, as well as a thirst for higher knowledge and practical know-how. With further examination, you will notice that there are exactly 24 branches located on these 8 wands. The number 24 is directly related to the 24 hours in a day, and refers to the old adage "Learn to take it one day at a time".

Geminis are an air sign full of big ideas and even bigger desires. They are driven to act out on these desires and try them all out in order to see what sticks and what works for them. They are willing to try out everything, just for the sake of new experience. If something you tryout works for you, it is strongly advised to stick with it, and continue developing your skills.

But, if something does not work out for you, then simply move on and let it go. Only spend time on the things that you are good at. Continue the pursuit of happiness, which is to keep trying new things so you will eventually find out exactly what it is that you are good at. You may find there to be more than one thing you enjoy and that you are good at. As Geminis pursue new passions, they become a 'Jack of all trades.' Geminis always enjoy the stimulation felt when diving into a new project or hobby.

For a Gemini, it is advised to act on their brilliant ideas and to begin new projects. It is crucial for their well-being to share such ideas with the world. Granted that not everything that comes to mind will be a winner, so do not succumb to the fear of rejection. As a result, you will find some people that are more open to your ideas than others, and they will want to work with you, while others will not. Although, not everyone will be a suitable fit for you, and share your vision. And this is okay. It doesn't mean you have bad ideas.

The concept of opening up and sharing, whether it pertains to creative project ideas or professional collaboration, also applies to being able to voice your opinion and share personal beliefs with those you're close to. Regardless if it's sharing your opinion with schoolmates, coworkers, or family, it is always good to add in your two-cents. Geminis are usually the smartest person in the room, and they tend to know just the thing to say to get everyone in the room on the same page. Geminis know just how to communicate and convey their message in such a way that everyone can comprehend.

Geminis are natural born go-getters. Even though it is healthy to desire success, a Gemini should be careful not to overwhelm themself. It is important to remember that all things take time and effort to develop. This being said, allow projects, friendships, relationships, studies, as well as trade skills the time needed for them to develop into something great organically. It is essential for you to learn how to enjoy the creative process.

Wands are comparable to trees, thereby relate to agriculture. The god of agriculture is Saturn, who is also the lord of time. Consequently, by counting the individual branches on the wands will reveal deeper esoteric understanding associated with the timing significance portrayed within this particular card. This method of counting the individual branches can be applied to every card in the suit of Wands. Yet specifically, in the 8 of Wands card there are exactly 24 branches located on the 8 wands. As mentioned earlier, the number 24 relates directly to the 24 hours in a day. This timing significance advises a Gemini to take things one day at a time. Therefore, be yourself, do your own thing and work hard. No need to chase people, because the right ones will come to you. And they will stay. If you don't go after what you want, you will never have it. If you do not ask, the answer will always be NO. And lastly, if you do not step forward, you will remain in the same place. While the creative process can be both fun and exciting, it does involve a rigorous process of trial and error. It takes a lot of effort and dedication to manifest your dreams. For this reason, take it day by day, and remember you don't get what you *wish* for, you get what you *work* for.

8 of Cups:
Illustrated on the 8 of Cups card is a group of eight cups set in the foreground which are arranged neatly and in a precise order, and properly placed in errorless position. The suit of Cups represents our emotions, feelings, and matters of the heart. That being so, with these eight cups organized so neatly, we can see that the man in this card has put much time and effort into analyzing his feelings. And also, how he communicates his feelings. This can be perceived two ways. For instance, it reflects the communication one does with themselves, as well as how one communicates with others. It is assumed here this man intends to communicate such things with himself in an attempt to achieve peace of mind. While on the other hand, he can also be seen trying to establish a sense of closure with regards to other people's feelings. He will communicate to himself the same as he does with others, explaining his feelings coherently in such a manner which allows him to walk away clean, leaving no feelings hurt, and no bridges burnt. He will have reached a point of understanding the reasons why he did what he did. From here, he recognizes what needs to be said and done, and then does it. And then to settle things in a civilized manner, he offers redemption. Geminis learn to forgive and forget, and then move on.

Geminis tend to overthink and over analyze everything way too deeply. This includes matters of the heart as well. They put all their heart into whatever they do. They may actually care too much when it comes to their relationships, jobs, or creative projects. Although, most of their success can be attributed to their sense of keenness and attention to detail they put into their work. Even though they pursue things whole-heartedly, they still come across as being cold, due to the fact they intellectualize their feelings as well as emotions.

Moreover, Geminis will place a label on people that marks exactly how they feel about that person, passing a judgement on them that gets filed away somewhere neatly in the back of their minds. This mentality when applied to their relationships is executed no differently than when they are tacking on a project. They tend to have emotional control over their feelings when dealing with relationships, and will usually be the one who ends things if need be. They do not wait for the other person to break up with them. When ending a relationship, Geminis will feel as if they did all they could have done to express themselves in the best and most straight forward way possible, so they are taken seriously and also not misunderstood. Then, when the time is right, they move onto the next new thing their heart desires. It doesn't take long for them to find someone else or find a new project they can dive into as a means of keeping their mind occupied.

You will notice the moon in this card is depicted with two phases on it. It has both a crescent and a full moon phase, representing the multiple phases Geminis go through throughout their lives. The waning crescent moon represents the end of a phase. The full moon is the brightest and allows one to see in the darkness, and be able to see things for what they really are; the full moon unveils the truth. Geminis feel very attached to something emotionally at the time, but can and will move on when they feel the time is right. The moon is associated with a month's time, suggesting that it may only take a month for a Gemini to be able to figure out if something works for them, or is in an accord with their future plans.

They allow their hearts to guide them. They take what they have learned from their past and they use it to be stronger and more well-rounded in their future endeavors. And it further builds upon their character. The man in this card has arrived at some powerful truths, and he has decided that he has reached the end. There is no more left for him to do or add or improve. He turns his back on it and walks away, he moves on, and never looks back. The quicker he begins a new project or relationship, the quicker he can disassociate himself with the past, thus creating new memories to replace the old ones. As one phase ends, another one begins.

8 of Swords:
Next up, is the 8 of Swords card, where we see a woman who is blindfolded and bound.

She bounds herself in white focus sashes wrapped around certain areas of her body where she wishes to improve upon, thereby analyzing and nitpicking these areas with intentions of changing her mental as well as physical self for the better. The water, representing her emotions, is drying up on the land, suggesting there is an emotional drought. Like a sponge, she absorbs all of her emotions. These eight swords that stand firmly in the ground around her are a representation of her thoughts. She can be seen here as reconfirming her thoughts and conceptions of herself in a logical sense, as a means to build upon her character as well as to enrich her spirit. She is considered now to be re-establishing a healthy communication with herself.

In contrast, Gemini can be seen here struggling as they confront their fixed mindset. Some choose to suffer rather than letting go, moving on and changing their way of thinking. Subconsciously, they are testing their limitations of how far down they can dive into the abyss of their own soul before needing to resurface for air. They find the emotional pain to be stimulating. This entire time of self-reflection is a learning experience, albeit an experimentation in extreme overthinking. It seems as though Geminis are always intellectualizing and studying their emotions. They tend to overthink past situations and circumstances, replaying the memories in their head as they critique themselves as well as others. Likewise, they analyze current situations as well.

At times, in certain circumstances they may feel as if they are in an awkward situation, where they have no sense of control, and there is nothing they can do but either resist or agree to go with the flow. When triggered, they tend to shut down emotionally. They will turn cold and harden their heart, which shuts out the world around them, causing them to remain up in their own head where they become blinded, in a sense, and fail to see a way out. Know that we cannot control what happens.

We can only control how we respond to the things that happen to us. This is where our true power is.

In order to get out of an emotional rut, Geminis will need to find a way to spark up that passion back into their life, which could refer to a new creative project or relationship that will open up their hearts and allow the Light back in.

You cannot reach what's in front of you until you let go of what's behind you. It is healthy to analyze yourself with the intention of correcting unruly behavior, but be cautious not to delve too deep, losing yourself to the abyss, and succumbing to feelings of regret and resentment to the point where it completely consumes you. Realize what you did wrong and then learn to forgive yourself. Implant a new memory of what you wish you would have done or said, and this will cause you to be more inclined to react in this new positive way in the future whenever similar situations arise and trigger you. Refuse to go back to the old you. You will become a better person by seeing your past experiences as being life-lessons.

8 of Pentacles:
Depicted in this card is a man working on his passion project, creating something fun, yet practical, and also beautiful. He chisels away at his project thoroughly, going over it several times. He will repeat the same processes (formulas and methods), over and over, polishing up and improving his work as he reaches perfection. He learns as he goes, and has fun doing so. It is a stimulating, albeit tedious, project. Although, when finished, it can be very rewarding; leaving him with a huge sense of accomplishment. He grows as the project grows, and vice versa. Time seems to pass rather quickly when working on such passion projects. Becoming skilled at what you love to do is a great achievement. Being able to share your skill in order to improve the lives of others brings fulfillment and happiness. It's how we give back to the world that shapes our life, defines us as humans, and builds joy from within.

Keeping the mind occupied on a project is an ideal way for a Gemini to meditate. By remaining focused on the intricate details of a certain project will allow you to get in the zone. When tapping into this 'zone' one connects to a higher dimension, to the Creator's Light and the Source of God's intelligence. It is in this zone where a Gemini is able to still their mind, allowing them to download epiphanies, and attract more brilliant ideas. The new insights gained will help you progress in not only your work, but in all other aspects of life as well.

Strength:

Moving onto the Strength card, which teaches us patience is a virtue. The virgin waits patiently for the lion to approach her. The lion here represents one's passionate desires. This is the lesson for Gemini to learn, that once they put themselves out there, after the effort is put forth and the seeds are planted, then it is time to sit back and be still as you wait to see the results. Know that things take time. It takes time to get things changed your way, and for others to share your vision. It takes time for your passion project to be appreciated by others. There is a natural organic process that the idea must endure before it manifests; a gradual process for it to grow into something substantial. You do what you can to put yourself out there, but be patient and allow things to naturally run their course. Eventually, you will see your efforts return to you, and you will see prosperity begin to flow into your life. You will get out whatever you put in. In other words, whatever you put out into the world will always (eventually) come back to you.

On the other hand, some things are just never meant to be. And this is okay. This is the process of trying things out to see what sticks and what does or does not work. Good things come to those who practice patience with this process. And the best things come to those who never give up.

The concept of 'reaping what you sow' is symbolized by the infinity symbol located directly over the virgin's head. It can be seen here as a halo, symbolizing that patience is a virtue, and also the concept of 'what goes around, comes around.'

Esoterically, the infinity symbol is associated with repeating cycles, routines, habits, and recurring patterns. Keeping this in mind, the

Hebrew letter assigned to this card is Teth, meaning coiled serpent, whereas a coiled serpent will hide in the shadows and study its prey—memorizing its routine. The serpent will set itself along the path of its prey and wait patiently for its prey to approach, and then strike at the perfect moment—usually when the prey is most vulnerable. Being a symbol for wisdom, the serpent is wise to wait patiently in the shadows and study its victim as they go about their daily routine. The serpent will memorize the path its prey takes each day, learning exactly when that animal turns its back and stops to take a drink from the creek. This is when the serpent strikes, whenever its prey is caught unaware. The Gemini, like the serpent, will achieve success when utilizing their inherit gift of analytical problem-solving skills, being keen on certain weaknesses or habits in order to know when and how to make your move.

This same advice for how to overcome your enemies can, and should be, applied as well when attempting to overcome your ego-nature. May you have the courage to break the patterns in your life that are no longer serving you.

Due to the paradoxical dynamics of our human nature, it is actually easier for a person to quit a habit when they are feeling at their lowest and at their most vulnerable. For instance, a person will usually vow to quit drinking only when they are experiencing a bad hangover. Another example, is when people promise to never steal or cheat again, but only after they've been caught red-handed. Likewise, people will promise themselves to go on a diet once they can no longer fit into their favorite jeans.

The key is to make the conscious decision to quit a particular bad habit before being caught, as we see portrayed in the Strength card with the lion who is depicted with his tail between his legs.

Star:
The Star card is the enlightened Gemini, where they become 'at one' with the source of nature and have become a pure channel for the Light. They use the splendor of their intellectual mind to create beauty in the world. Gemini is represented here, in the Star card, as the spiritually

developed virgin from the Strength card. Depicted now as the Egyptian virgin-Godess, Isis, seen here naked (revealing her true self) and free of ego. She gathers water from the astral plane and then pours it onto the earthly plane. She acts as a channel for the Light, creating something from nothing. In other words, she is attracting brilliant ideas, and then manifesting them with the intentions of making the world a better placc.

Moving forward, you will notice there is a scarlet ibis sitting in the tree located behind Isis. He symbolizes and is also associated with the Egyptian god Thoth, who corresponds with the aspects of higher wisdom and esoteric knowledge. Thoth is known as the Greek god Hermes and also the Roman god Mercury, which just so happens to be the ruling planet of Gemini. Thoth is considered the master of all trades. He is believed to have invented math and sciences, including astrology. Thoth also revealed to mankind the practice of meditation.

Shown on this card are seven illuminated stars, representing the seven chakras which are portrayed vibrating in harmony and in unison. These stars each having 8-points connects them to the 8th sefirah on the Kabbalah Tree of Life, Hod, which is influenced by Mercury (Thoth/Hermes). Moreover, there are actually eight, 8-pointed stars on this card. The biggest of these stars is yellow, whereas the others are white. This being so, places more attention to the yellow star. And also, by it being a different color, shows how the different-colored stars embody different influences. For instance, the seven white stars correspond to the 7 chakras. And the single yellow star, the 8th star on this card, corresponds to Hod, which relates to brilliance of the mind. The yellow star is noticeably larger than the rest, which represents that this is the big idea Isis is connecting to and attracting as she meditates. Isis must still her mind in meditation in order to attract such brilliant ideas. This is done by elevating her soul's vibration and by stimulating her chakras, which is essential for the ascension of her kundalini energy from the base of her spine to the top of her skull.

This is Gemini at their full potential, as they become a pure channel for the Light. They come to the realization that they will always reap what they sow. This realization brings upon a strong sense of certainty. This also makes them wish to do good, knowing that what goes around comes around. Therefore, they would rather be rewarded for the good they put out into the world. A spiritually elevated Gemini acts upon their inspiration, creating positive improvements from their brilliant ideas, which motivate others to do the same, thus making the world a better place. There are no longer doubts or fears brought on by overthinking, which progresses into procrastination. There is now a strong sense of discernment used to filter through the good and bad ideas, as you grow less impulsive. Once a brilliant idea comes to mind, you will know it instantaneously, and then with no delay take the appropriate actions towards making it happen.

The Hebrew letter assigned to the Star card is Tzaddi, meaning fish hook. While the virgin Isis meditates, her mind, like a fish hook, sits still and waits patiently as she attracts inspiration and godly insight from the astral waters. The Tzaddik is known as 'the righteous one' who acts as a pure channel drawing down wisdom from the realm of Atziluth, the realm of God the Creator and the Source of God's intelligence—His Light. Moses was considered to be a Tzaddik. He was known to be in a constant communication with God.

The fully evolved Gemini is a spiritual person who strives to maintain their connection to the Source; the energy of nature and of all creation. They do this by practices of meditation and by working on themselves. The Light will always guide you, provide for you, and give you certainty. You will never feel alone as long as you stay connected and communicate with this Divine force each and every day.

Think of an unfinished project that is an obstacle in your life. Decide you are going to finish it and follow through, and begin this meditation. As you meditate on these cards, think to yourself as you see the unfinished project in front of you, I am going to complete [enter project here] as I visualize myself [enter the process necessary for completion here]. I feel frustration and procrastination drifting away. I am getting closer to completing my goal. As I breathe, I get even closer. I feel stronger, more connected to my Light Force (life-force). Laziness and doubt are gone, and I see myself fulfilled, creating more space for even greater accomplishments.

"The spiritual journey does not consist of arriving at a new destination where a person gains what he did not have, or becomes what he is not. It consists in the dissipation of one's own ignorance concerning oneself and life, and the gradual growth of that understanding which begins the spiritual awakening. The finding of God is a coming to one's self." - Aldous Huxley

Chapter 22, Section 4: Cancer

Astrological House #4, Cancer, ruled by the Moon, and is associated with the 9th sefirah Yesod. Therefore, Cancer's path to enlightenment will include all the #9 tarot cards, which includes the Major Arcana cards associated with the number 9 as well. And these cards are: the 9 of Wands, 9 of Cups, 9 of Swords, 9 of Pentacles, the Hermit, and the Moon.

Cancers are nurturing, patient, kind, versatile, adaptable, devoted, patriotic, and sociable people. Ruled by the Moon, they tend to be more feminine and have aspects of a motherhood and maternity that yearns for a harmonious home and family life. They are very sensitive, empathetic, enjoy bonding, sharing personal stories, watching heart-felt movies, and have tenacity, opening themselves up to new concepts and ideas. They grow spiritually by taking risks.

Some negative ego aspects of Cancers personality traits are that they can be overly protective of their vulnerable sensitive side and wear a hard protective emotional-shell around them, symbolized by the crab. They may come off as cold, frigid or phlegmatic.

Esoterically speaking, the light of the moon unveils hidden truths. Cancers see the truth and speak the truth, and yet at the same time, are also known to lie and keep secrets—withholding the truth. Unbeknownst to most people is that all the #9 cards hold within them a secret hidden in plain sight. It takes the light of the moon to unveil them.

The energy of Cancer calls us to live in the now. Yet, past emotion can lead us to dwell in what was. Start with gratitude for simple everyday blessings and begin to bring awareness to the present moment with openness and certainty. Take risks. Erase fear, shake off old beliefs, show gratitude, and live in the present.

9 of Wands:

We begin this path with the 9 of Wands card. Here, we see a man holding one of the wands tightly in his hands, and he is facing an overwhelming challenge before him, represented by the eight wands that appear as a wall before him. They act as a wall blocking him from proceeding any further.

Each of the 9 wands has 3 branches, making it a total of 27 branches. The number 27 connects us to the Progressed Lunar Return. The Progressed Moon takes 27-28 years to complete the cycle around the natal chart, and it generally marks an opening of the emotional body that can be exhilarating or painful, depending on the chart and the way the individual handles challenges. This prepares a person for their Saturn Return. It takes approximately 29.5 years for Saturn to return and complete its orbit back into your life from the day of your birth. A 'return' happens when any planet completes its entire circuit through the sky and returns to the same place it was at the time of your birth. Saturn Returns rule over growing up, accountability, fears, insecurities, reality, higher self-standards, and karma. It can result in an identity crisis where you will have to face your deepest fears. A person begins to feel the energy of Saturn's return as early as the age of 27. Cancers are very sensitive and can feel this energy sooner than all other signs. Saturn's influence passes through and can be felt until the age of 32. And then, by the age of 33 years old, a person is considered to be 'born again.' They have dealt with past-life karma and are now spiritually ready to begin their new journey. They have reached true mature adulthood. Saturn helps us become stronger.

Cancers will learn how to overcome their self-doubt, pessimism, and worry. In the tarot, wands represent agriculture, and the God of agriculture happens to be Saturn. Wands also represent growth, ambition, desire, passion, creativity, and knowledge. Wands represent the element of fire. The man pictured in the 9 of Wands card has built up a wall of opinions and reasons that become the inner voice talking himself out of ambitious creative endeavors. This can also include lustful passionate desires. The man is wearing a bandage around his head, showing that he is defeated before he even begins. He wears a black belt tight around his waist, representing Saturn's energy of restriction, bounding him. He wears green boots, representing new fertile desires and creative ideas to be put into action, but is restricted by karmic lessons.

He builds a wall of self-doubt, talking himself out of doing things before he even starts. He feels conquered and beaten with low self-esteem. He stands on the gray cement floor, representing wisdom, thus connecting to the energy of Saturn's Return, and growing wiser from life-lessons. It is a challenging time, but you are made stronger because of it.

The man in this card is holding a single wand in his hand ever so tightly. His wand represents an opinion or emotional attachment. The man needs to learn to let go. When you hold on tightly to the things that Saturn is trying to break up is when the suffering intensifies. The Wands remind us to be like a tree. Stay grounded, keep growing, and know when to let go.

9 of Cups:
Next, we have the 9 of Cups card. Pictured here is a man sitting proudly in front of a row of cups that are displayed neatly on top of a curved shelf. The secret hidden in plain sight is that the nine cups portray a curved Jewish menorah used during Hanukkah, the festival of lights.

The shelf is curved, mimicking the style of menorahs that were made in early times. The man sitting with his arms folded is known as the shamash, meaning attendant or servant, who lights the candles of the menorah. The shamash is the name given to the ninth candle on the menorah. This is the candle used to light all the other eight candles signifying the eight days of Hanukkah. The man pictured here is proud, knowing he was the one that lit all these cups using the Light found within himself.

Cups represent matters of the heart and our emotions. It can represent unconditional love and acts of kindness. The shamash is depicted here as being happy and feeling warmth within. He knows that in order to receive love and respect he must first give love and light. This card on its lower polarity can connect to being prideful and covertly narcissistic. These personality types are reliant on constant praise and attention to reinforce their self-esteem. As a result, they are usually very sensitive to criticism, which is often viewed as a personal attack.

9 of Swords:
This leads us to the next card, the 9 of Swords, which depicts a man sitting up in his bed with his head in his hands, crying and feeling regret; overwhelmed with emotional insecurities. This man may feel vulnerable and/or victimized.

There are nine swords lined up above his head. In the tarot, swords relate to thoughts, so symbolically, this column of swords can be seen as a list of the many thoughts playing through this man's head, which causes him this restlessness. The secret hidden here is found in the picture carved in the wood on the base of the bed panel. Depicted in the wood carving is a man who is violently pushing another man to the ground. We may be right to assume that the man in the bed feels as though he is the one that was pushed to the ground, and is playing the victim in this confrontation. You will notice the man in the bed is wearing white, which represents his innocence. His hair is white as well, symbolizing that he is cleansing and purifying his thoughts.

The secret here is that this man is actually being proactive and implanting new memories that will replace the ones where he felt spiritually deficient in some way. Perhaps he was reactive and responded in a negative or egotistical manner? Maybe he locked up and said nothing at all when he should have spoken up? Perhaps he is unable to let something someone said go, and he obsesses about it?

This man is replaying these memories and implanting new positive actions that he wished he should have taken. Now whenever a similar situation presents itself, he will react in a more positive way, repeating a behavior similar to his new memory implant. This meditation concept is similar to LRP therapy, which is also the premise of the blockbuster movie "Inception", staring Leonardo De Caprio. The underlying premise was that one positive thought can trump any and all negative thoughts. This man is wise to think about and rehash the details of the confrontation, making a mental list; further analyzing the past situations. Notice his blanket is covered with astrological symbols of the zodiac? The zodiac contains all the knowledge of karmic-lessons one learns along their life journey. (As well as past-life experience.) He would be wise to comfort himself in such great understanding, and then awake the following morning with peace of mind. By the time he wakes up the following morning, he will have a stronger spirit, which will empower his mood control, and he will no longer find himself reacting negatively in the future.

Neuro-linguistic Programming (or NLP for short) is a very powerful set of teachings to help you understand the mind and get rid of emotional baggage, bad habits and mental patterns that are blocking you in some way. The techniques are instrumental in changing one's life for the better. The man in this card can be seen as practicing an NLP technique, whereas he replays his mistake in his imagination, but instead of repeating the same mistake as he did before, he replaces his past behavior by imagining something else (something new) he would have rather done. Most likely, this new behavior will make him feel powerful and as the victor in the situation. This is how you implant a new idea into your mind. One positive thought will trump all negative ones. The brain does not know the difference between what is real and what is not, it merely believes whatever you tell it, or program it to believe. This is referred to as 'memory implantation.' The purpose of implanting a new behavior into your memory is so your brain will trigger this action linked to this emotion if ever this specific situation were to happen to you again.

Also, whenever you focus on what you should have done instead, you start to act like the person you'd rather be. This seems like an unconventional method for exercising the practice of repentance. But in a similar fashion, you realize your faults, accept your mistakes, and then promise yourself to never to do them again. And then, take it one step further by imagining what you would have rather done as a way of increasing the odds of you acting out in a more powerful manner in the future.

9 of Pentacles:
Moving onto the next card, the 9 of Pentacles, that shows a maiden holding a Peregrine falcon. Falconry being a traditional sport practiced by both men and women. She holds her falcon here waiting for her suitor to arrive. This scene could be symbolically connected to the social event of the Tu B'Av holiday, known as Jewish Valentine's Day where maidens would dance in the vineyard and wait for suitors to approach them, looking for marriage. Falconry was a perfect activity to set up the scenario for courting. These falcons were coined the term 'lovebirds' due to the fact that they brought men and women together.

The suit of Pentacles relates to tangible things which can refer to relationships, such as the relationship and bond this woman shares with her falcon. She is depicted here gazing at her Peregrine falcon with love and pride. It takes time, patience, and nurturing to train a falcon obedience, trust, and to hunt. This falcon appears to have made this maiden feel proud of its accomplishments and growth. It must have come a long way.

The secret hidden in plain sight here is the 40 roses on the maiden's dress. The number 40 is of much significance in Kabbalah, and is seen throughout the tarot as well as the Torah. The number 40 represents a measurement of spiritual timing it takes in order to cleanse and purify the soul. This process can be a challenging period in one's life, as it takes time and patience and endurance for such spiritual growth. According to Kabbalah, it takes 40 days for someone to break an old habit or a routine before they are able to transform or train themselves and adapt into a new one. The number 40 represents the time needed for personal growth, transition, and change. 40 represents the concept of renewal, and/or a new beginning. The number 40 has the power to lift a spiritual state. The number 40 connects to the sefirah Binah, which means understanding. According to the Talmud (Avot 5:26), at age 40 a person transitions from one level of wisdom to the next. He reaches the level of Binah, the deeper insight of understanding one matter from another. Binah is connected to the feminine aspect of the Tree of Life. After Moses led the Jewish people for 40 years in the wilderness, he told them, "God has not given you a heart to know, and eyes to see, and ears to hear, until this day" (Deut. 29:3-4). From here we see that it took the Jewish people 40 years before reaching a full level of understanding, where they wondered the wilderness for 40 years before they were allowed to, or spiritually ready to, enter the promised land of Israel.

The number 40 signifies the time needed for spiritual cleansing and being ready to receive God's blessings. The 40 roses on this maiden's dress signify that she has reached this spiritual level of deeper understanding and is now ready to receive love, blessings, and is spiritually mature enough for marriage; ready to commit to a husband or career or any life path she chooses.

As mentioned earlier, all the number 9 cards are associated with the sefirah Yesod, which is ruled by the Moon. The Moon relates to aspects of receiving and of passiveness, directly connecting the 9 of Pentacles to this woman's situation, where she is seen as 'waiting' in the vineyard for her suitor to approach. She is ready to 'receive' her promised blessing.

The lesson here for Cancer is to learn how to develop a deeper understanding of what truly matters in this world, we are not the material things we obtain, but the relationships we have with our friends and family. Having these things brings us inner peace, joy and harmony.

The Hermit:
The Hermit is seen standing on the mountain top, holding a lantern that guides others up the path to enlightenment. He holds his golden staff, representing his spiritual knowledge that he has gained over a

long period of time. The six-pointed star is Saturn's star and encompasses the spiritual Light and understanding of Binah. He has reached enlightenment and has become a channel for the Light. He is the gateway and/or bridge that creates a link which unites the astral plane with the physical world.

Yesod is the bridge between the infinite potential of procreation that flows into it and its actual manifestation in the progeny of man. This can be understood by looking at the magic and mathematics of the number 9. When you multiply any number with 9 you always end up with the digital root number 9. For example: $9 \times 2 = 18$, and then 18 reduced is $1+8 = 9$. Or another example, $9 \times 6 = 54$, $5+4 = 9$. Or try a larger number: $9 \times 2,376 = 21,384$, and then reduce the multi-digit number numerically by adding $2+1+3+8+4 = 18$, and then $1+8 = 9$. The sum of the digits equal 9. Numerology does not deal with multi-digit numbers so; you must reduce them down to a single digit. The multiplying of number 9 by continuous numbers will result in a pyramid formation with numbers getting larger and larger as they fan out from the top working their way down. Refer to picture below for an example:

Table 1	Table 2
$1 \times 9 = 9$	$1 \times 9 + 2 = 11$
$12 \times 9 = 108$	$12 \times 9 + 3 = 111$
$123 \times 9 = 1107$	$123 \times 9 + 4 = 1111$
$1234 \times 9 = 11106$	$1234 \times 9 + 5 = 11111$
$12345 \times 9 = 111105$	$12345 \times 9 + 6 = 111111$
$123456 \times 9 = 1111104$	$123456 \times 9 + 7 = 1111111$
$1234567 \times 9 = 11111103$	$1234567 \times 9 + 8 = 11111111$
$12345678 \times 9 = 111111102$	$12345678 \times 9 + 9 = 111111111$
$123456789 \times 9 = 1111111101$	$123456789 \times 9 + 10 = 1111111111$

Sum of digits in each line equals 9

The sefirah Yesod is the bridge from infinite down into finite. It funnels down all the other sefirot down into their manifest state. Yesod is identified in the Torah with Tzaddik, meaning 'the righteous one', and usually associated with a righteous person, which is symbolized by the Hermit. In the very body of a tzaddik, the finite and limited coexist in time and space, God's infinite Light and creative Life-Force becomes manifest. The tzaddik creates on the spiritual plane as well as on the physical plane. This idea can be conceptualized by the male phallic, symbolized here by the Hermit's staff, and the procreation process of life-force from within manifesting in the seed or semen of man. The tzaddik experiences creation in the inner third eye of his consciousness, in the continual flow of new insights and true innovations in his spiritual study. He creates by arousing the souls of his generation to return to the path of enlightenment and reach unity with the higher-self.

The secret hidden in plain sight here is the evil face found on the back of the Hermit's head. This face appears grumpy, angry, negative and judgmental. This face represents the Hermit's ego; his adversary. This adversary is the voice in the back of the Hermit's head telling him to give up on the people that he is helping. The adversary sits with his arms crossed, losing his patience with the Hermit; complaining, bitching, doubting and being pessimistic. The Hermit struggles to keep this negative voice out of his head. The adversary attempts to make the Hermit feel as if he is working towards a lost cause, and that his people are not worth it, and he should save himself, focus back on himself, and move on alone and isolated in order to reach higher states of enlightenment. But the Hermit knows that by helping others he will in return receive the light of wisdom and union with the Creator.

The Hermit represents Moses on Mount Sinai, which means mountain of the Moon. Moses was considered a tzaddik, and he spent 40 days on the mountain receiving the Torah from God. When Moses came down the mountain and returned to his people, he was immediately angered because they had built a false idol, a golden calf, to worship instead of keeping their faith in God, as well as losing their faith in Moses. They began to lose hope that Moses would return. After seeing this, Moses was very angry and he threw down the tablets of the ten commandments, breaking them on the ground. He said that the Jewish people were not ready to receive the

Light and wisdom of God. Moses was ready to give up completely on his people. But God told Moses to give the Israelites one more chance. Moses then returned to the top of Sinai and retrieved another set of tablets.

It is easy to allow our ego to get the best of us, and we feel like giving up on people, but this story teaches us the importance in giving others a second chance.

The Moon:
Then we move onto the final card in Cancer's path toward enlightenment, the Moon.

Cancers have a strong relationship with the Moon. Cancer is the only sign of the zodiac that the Moon rules. Cancers came from the moon and back to the moon they will return, as seen in this life-path layout.

The Moon card is very magical and holds many secrets hidden in plain sight. For instance, there are 32 rays located around the moon. These rays correspond to the 32 paths of wisdom one takes along the Tree of Life on their journey towards spiritual enlightenment. The Hermit is seen here as the face of the moon with 32 rays surrounding his head. The 32nd path (the final path) on the Tree of Life is associated with the last letter in the Hebrew alphabet Tav,which is the link that connects the sefirah Yesod to Malchut. (which I described in the Hermit card) The Tree's 32nd branch is the bridge from the infinite potential of the astral plane down into the manifested finite material plane of existence. The enlightened Hermit is connected to the Creator's Light and is reflecting, sharing, His Light to the world below.

Found below the Hermit are a wolf and a dog. The Hermit shares his light and wisdom with the wolf, transforming him into a domesticated fun-loving dog. The crawfish coming out of the water represents mankind at their early stage of conscious awareness entering the world and beginning their spiritual journey. This crawfish connects to the symbol for Cancer, the crab, (and ruled by the Moon), which corresponds to the Hermit at the beginning of his journey toward enlightenment. The Hermit, now at a point where he can guide others, becomes the nurturer; full-circle. The Hermit sheds light on the path, guiding the crawfish along its journey up through the pillars. These pillars mark the boundaries of the known, a cross roads going from one state of awareness to the next, crossing into the unknown.

With the light of the moon the Hermit unveils the 15 Yod's floating in the night sky. The number 15 is associated with Saturn. It is one of the magic numbers of Saturn, which includes, 3, 9, 15, and 45. When you add the 15 Yod's to the number of the Moon card, Roman numeral XVIII, you get 33 (18+15). 33 is the connection and unity with the Christ Consciousness; the fully enlightened being that has progressed all the way up the Jacob's ladder, or the Kundalini, also known as the 33 vertebrae of the spinal column from base chakra up to the crown. When a person connects to the Christ Consciousness is when they are able to draw magical energy from Saturn and make wishes come true, and manifest their desires. The number 15 relates to the full moon, because it is the 15th day of the Lunar month when it is its fullest. The fullness of the moon makes it possible to unveil the 15 Yod's hidden in the night sky, which makes it possible to make the connection to the number 33 and how it relates to Christ Consciousness aka the super conscious.

The Moon card is assigned to the Hebrew letter Qoph/Kuf, meaning back of the head. This relates to consciously stimulating the back of the head (cerebellum) to utilize one's cognitive mind as a means to obtain control of their own destiny. As an individual begins to develop a strong sense of self-awareness they cease following others, and strive to become their own person. They either become the leader of the pack or venture off as a lone wolf. There are two dogs depicted in the Moon card: a wolf and a dog. As the old saying goes, "If you're not the lead dog, then the scenery never changes." Moreover, the word used in the Torah for ape is Kuf. And what do apes do? They mimic, as in monkey see, monkey do. Portrayed within the Moon card is the idea of Kuf arriving at a spiritual crossroads, at a fork in their life-path, where they must decide between continuing their life as a follower or to become the lead dog and take control of their own destiny.

Cancers become like the Hermit, devoting his life and service to mankind, and nurturing the people of the world to make it a better place. As you meditate on these cards, think to yourself, I am letting go of past pain, regret, trauma. All of it. [If there is a particular theme or moment that you keep coming back to, picture it in your mind. As you do this meditation, go back to that moment, then reverse it, plant a new seed.] I will release past emotions that are dragging me down, replacing old baggage with Light and love. I look forward, not back.

Further information regarding the deeper esoteric symbolism of the Moon card can be found in Chapter 2: The Secret Connection Between the Star, Moon, and Sun.

Astrological House #5, Leo, is ruled by the Sun, which connects to the 6th sefirah on the Kabbalah Tree of Life, Tiferet. Leo's path to enlightenment includes all the #6 tarot cards and cards associated with the number 6. And these cards are: the 6 of Wands, 6 of Cups, 6 of Swords, 6 of Pentacles, The Lovers, and The Devil.

Some noteworthy qualities to mention about Leos is that they are loyal, kind, tolerant, generous, full of inspiration, have a desire for philanthropy, fearless, show chivalry, optimistic, intuitive, industrious. And yes, they do have a few undesirable personality traits as well, such as arrogance, domination, guilelessness, fussiness, anger, sensitivity, impetuousness, impatience, bluntness. They hate being ignored and not being in the limelight. In order to grow spiritually, Leos need to learn humility.

The charismatic energy of Leo is an invitation to lead. Though, the most effective leaders are those who are guided by compassion and a desire to support the growth of all. Listen to the perspectives of others with an open heart and an open mind. Focus on uniting. Stop talking and listen. Consider the feelings of others, because we are stronger together. Practice empathy.

6 of Wands:
We begin with the 6 of Wands card, where we see a man paraded honorably by his peers, who seem to be praising him for his

accomplishments. The man carries a wand that has a Laurel wreath hanging from it. This is the same type of wreath awarded to a horse after it has won a race. It is a celebratory decoration. The man is also wearing a wreath, specifically an olive wreath on his head, which traditionally was the award given to the winners during the yearly ancient Olympic games in Greece. With this considered, the man in this card is experiencing an emotional high, an ego boost from being in the center of attention, and he is relishing in the moment as he is honored and admired by his peers. It's as if he is the king of the world, and this moment of praise goes straight to his head. He is literally depicted here on his 'high horse.' To be on one's high horse means to act in an arrogant or haughty fashion. Get off your high horse is a related idiom which exhorts the listener to quit acting in a superior or arrogant fashion.

The six wands in this card contain twelve branches total. Wands relate to agriculture, and the god of agriculture is Saturn who is the lord of time. Therefore, by counting the branches on the wands will reveal to us timing significances concealed within the card. For instance, these 12 branches coincide with the 12 months in a year. Ergo, this man is portrayed here being rewarded for an achievement that took him a year to accomplish.

With closer examination, you will notice how the man's horse is giving him an odd and judgmental look. This horse sees the man's true colors. The horse is colored gray, and gray throughout the tarot always represents wisdom. The horse is learning about this man's shadow nature and darker side of his personality. With this new boost in confidence received from all the admiration the man is getting reveals his true nature and egotistic traits of being narcissistic, conceited and pretentious. With his right hand, the man is holding up a wand that has a Laurel wreath hanging from it. Laurel wreaths are given to the horse after they win the race, but this man fails to do so. Instead, he is showing off this award as if it belongs to him. The horse is covered in a green blanket (or dress sheet), which refers to the horse being very jealous, as in 'green with envy.' The man is proudly wearing and showing off his award, but for some selfish reason does not give her the wreath that she deserves. The man needs to give credit where credit is due.

A reoccurring lesson found within each of the Wand cards is that it takes time for things to develop and grow into something great. Things don't develop overnight. It takes time, and we cannot do it on our own without the help from others. You cannot simply plant a seed, and then expect it to grow into a tree all on its own. You have to consistently be there and devote your time and energy into the nurturing process. No man is an island. We work with others as a team, and we all do our part to help each other reach a common goal. Big things start from small beginnings. So, don't get ahead of yourself. The suit of Wands also relates to creative ideas, opinions and beliefs. These beliefs become deeply rooted into the building blocks of our character, and the bonding over time becomes the glue that keeps relationships together.

Leo's need to humble themselves and know that they cannot do it alone. We all need each other's help. Moreover, Leo's need to learn to give credit where credit is due. It is okay to ride on the back of something (or someone) that paved the way for you as long as you give those who deserve it the credit. You would not be able to be where you are at without their accomplishments and the allowed opportunities you were given. No need to step on the backs of others in order to get ahead. Help others with zero expectation of return. You won't believe how enormous the reward is. Because what goes around comes around and kindness is a language which deaf can hear and the blind can see.

6 of Cups:
This card is considered the 'unconditional love' card. It depicts a boy giving a girl a white flower. Cups represent love, emotions and matters of the heart. The boy's white flower which he has inside his cup represents purity and innocence. Metaphorically, the boy is offering the girl his pure unconditional love. In doing so, the boy appears to grow larger in size. His character grows as he listens to his heart and leads with kindness.

With further examination, you will notice that all the white flowers are pentagrams. The pentagram is associated with the 5th sefirah

Gevurah, which relates to matters of the ego, and can portray manifesting one's passions. The white flowers represent purity of heart, and because they are pentagram-shaped they reveal the possibility to transform our selfish desires into ways that will help improve the lives of others. Whenever you can, you should try caring for other people's needs before your own. Paradoxically, you actually gain more by helping others. You can transform your selfishness this way, because the more we give, the more we receive. Therefore, you can become the most selfish person by becoming the most helpful person, providing service and by performing random acts of kindness. Have a conscious desire to give in order to receive Light, so that you may be able to give back more Light. Strive to become a channel for the Light, speak and act from the heart as you mindfully emerge into a source of love and positivity.

Within this card you will find 6 flowers that have 5 petals each, which is a total of 30 petals in all. The number 30 corresponds to the Saturn Return, which culminates the karmic cycle pertaining to self-growth and maturity. Saturn is known as the planet of restriction, and a slowing down of all things in general. With this in mind, we see how the love between this boy and girl was perhaps forbidden, and there were many obstacles standing in their way preventing them from being together. This may include the difference in social classes, or perhaps the boy was promised to marry another girl in an arranged marriage.

 You will notice the boy in this card has actually grown physically larger than the girl, which makes him have to hunch over in order to hand the girl a flower. Once you begin working on your personal growth you elevate your soul's vibration. This is when others will start looking up to you, and admire you.

With further observation you will see that the royal guardsman in the background is walking away, signifying that in order to show pure unconditional love one must let their guard down. You must give love and respect to receive love and respect in return. Others will want to cooperate with you without you needing to be dominate and demanding.

This card portrays a sweet love story, reflecting upon a forbidden love. It displays the love between a rich boy and a peasant girl. As the story goes, the rich boy was not allowed to talk to or conjugate with the peasants outside his family's estate. Not until he was old enough, he was forced to stay in and away from the public. He was forbidden to venture outside the family's estate or socialize with the lower-class. But each day the boy would look out his window and he would make eye contact with a peasant girl. And the girl would look up at the boy in the manor, hoping to one day be with him. She dreamed of romance of course, but also fantasized about living a life that was better off than hers. One day her wish came true, and the boy was able to break free when the guardsman was not looking, and he went out of his home to meet with the girl. He acknowledged the girl, and showed her he loved her by coming down to her level—he gave recognition to the love they shared. He was able to break free fromhis family's rules, restrictions, limitations, regulations and he followed his heart, loving this girl unconditionally. He no longer cared about how others would judge him. He was in love. He was enthralled by this girl, and nothing could restrain him or keep him from her. Love always finds a way.

6 of Swords:
The 6 of Swords card depicts a woman and child in a boat that is being steered by a manThis man navigates them out of the choppy water and steers them into a calmer place. This manappears to have good intentions for the woman and child. He offers help as well as protection with regards to their well-being.

There are six swords standing firmly upright in the boat. Swords represent our thoughts and ideas, as well as spirit. There being 6 represents the peak attribution of our thoughts when they are at their clearest, wisest, most intuitive and resonating with the feeling of being 'in the zone.'

Pictured here is the emotional and intellectual phase a Leo experiences as they reinvent themselves. Leos are strong-willed, and if moving in order to start a new life is what they need to do then they're going to do it without second-guessing themselves. One thing about moving is that it can help you see the path you need to take to get where you're going. Moving can also help you to appreciate who you are and where you came from. Leos tend to be optimistic, and rather than dreading a new life, they would see the opportunities and benefits to be had. New beginnings are disguised as painful endings. This is why the 6 of Swords is considered to be the 'wake-up call' card.

Notice how the man steering the boat is using a black rowing oar? Black throughout the tarot represents aspects of Saturn's influence, who is the lord of karmic life-lessons. Although life-lessons are challenging, they do end up making us stronger. Water throughout the tarot represents emotions. Thereby dipping the oar into the water connects to a past emotional period in one's life that ends up teaching an important life-lesson. In retrospect, we are able to reevaluate ourselves by self-reflecting on our values and personal beliefs. It is healthy to step outside ourselves and judge objectively. You must learn to dissociate yourself from who you were in the past. It's nothing short of an identity crisis brought upon by an emotional wake-up call.

The woman is covered in shame. She is disgusted with who she has become. She closes herself off from reconnecting to her inner child, who is seen sitting next to her. Sitting in the rough and choppy water she is unable to see her life objectively. She needs to be steered into the calmer water where the surface is more like a mirror, thus allowing her to see her own reflection in the smoother water. Perhaps then she will realize how bad things have become, and she can figure out what needs to be done about it. She will desire change. When she sees herself clearly, she will awaken her inner child. She will ignite the spark within her, and reconnect to her inner Light; to her true essence. This new sense of clarity reached from this karmic life-lesson is the drive that steers her forward into a new clearer and calmer state of being. The calm water becomes a smooth mirror she can use in order to reflect upon her life circumstances and the specific situation she is in. She is then able to reflect upon her past life-choices that got her here in the first place. This is a time of spiritual growth and life assessment—a turning point.

The journey into self-love and self-acceptance must begin with self-examination. Until you take the journey of self-reflection, it is almost impossible to grow or learn in life. By understanding who you are now and who you'd like to become, you help identify the steps you need to take on that journey. Reflecting upon how you behave and what thoughts enter your mind in response to events in the world around you, allows you to see what you need to work on. May you have the courage to break the patterns in your life that are no longer serving you.

6 of Pentacles:
The 6 of Pentacles card depicts a generous man handing out coins to those in need. Leos are very generous in nature and don't mind spending money on their friends, provided that their friends are generous too. Here we see a rich man giving coins to one of the poor men in need, but not to the other. This other man has a red card in his pocket, which is actually his meal ticket. Therefore, he doesn't need any money for food, and the rich man understands this. He is happy that he has the opportunity and the means to share, but he is wise with a strong sense of discernment knowing who actually deserves his charity and who does not. This is portrayed by the scale the rich man holds in his left hand, as he weighs out the appropriate amounts of charity he should offer, and to whom.

Pentacles relate to tangible things, which includes time and energy. Healthy relationships require a healthy balance of give and take. We mustn't allow ourselves to be taken advantage of by others. Likewise, we need to be mindful of our own behavior so we don't over-step our boundaries with others as well. Pentacles can also represent money. Leos love to spend extravagantly because they see money as a means to get what they deserve, which is everything that they view as the best.

They know they can always make more money, so they are never stingy with it. They won't admit to being broke, so they never ask friends for money because they got too much pride for that.

The specific placements for each pentacle on this card will reveal significant Kabbalistic wisdom. Symbols that are grouped together throughout the tarot always connect and correspond to a certain sefirah on the Kabbalah Tree of Life. For instance, the three pentacles grouped on the left of this card connect to the 3rd sefirah Binah, which means understanding. The singled-out pentacle located above the rich man's head connects to the 1st sefirah Keter, meaning crown, and is associated with the crown chakra. Keter is described as pure compassion. Keter connects to the source of Light and pure spirit of the Creator. Lastly, there are the two pentacles grouped together on the right side of the card. These two connect to the 2nd sefirah Chokmah, meaning wisdom. Once you understand the Kabbalah hidden within the tarot, you are able to grasp the deeper mysteries concealed within each card. So, with these Kabbalistic clues, such as the single pentacle over the rich man's head, it is revealed that he is inspired by God to help others. His heart is filled with compassion as he helps those in need. The two pentacles grouped together on the right reveal that the rich man is wise to give only what he can afford, and to give only to those who need it the most. And from the understandings of Binah's energy influence represented with the three pentacles on the left, it is revealed to us the rich man has been in a similar situation in life where he too had to rely on the charity of others, and because of this he is now able to understand and empathize with those in similar circumstances. He truly understands the spiritual concept of 'what goes around, comes around.'

Another way of interpreting this card is to evaluate the spiritual message incorporated here. When considering the concept of handing out money for meal tickets, think about what aspect of yourself do you choose to feed? Do you feed the ego or do you feed the soul? Do you behave impulsively or do you think before you act? Within each of us are two wolves at battle with each other. One is pride, greed, anger, jealousy, hate, and resentment. The other is love, happiness, humility, faith, hope, and courage. The wolf that will win is the one that you feed.

The Lovers:
Adam and Eve are depicted here in the Garden of Eden being taught by the Archangel Raziel whose name means 'secrets of God.' He also represents Divine Wisdom and provides guidance when one most

needs it. Raziel is the ruler over the sefirah Chokmah, meaning wisdom.

Eve is seen here looking up towards the angel for guidance. Adam and Eve stand next to the two trees known as the Tree of Life (on the right) and the Tree of the Knowledge of Good and Evil (to the left). After Adam and Eve partook of the Tree of the Knowledge of Good and Evil, they were banished from the garden. God was angry and displeased by this original sin but was quick to forgive and show mercy. God sent His angel Raziel to teach and guide Adam and Eve. Raziel taught them how to prosper in the world outside the garden. Adam and Eve were lost without the angel's help, and thus very eager to learn all they could from Raziel. Although a bit desperate, they were humble and willing to listen.

Raziel taught Adam the mysteries of the Tree of Life, depicted here as the tree with twelve flames for its branches, symbolic of the twelve astrological signs of the Zodiac, which correspondingly contain wisdom of all life's lessons and reoccurring cycles. This particular Tree contains the fire of life, albeit excitement, joy, love and big passions. Acquiring knowledge by way of the Gnostic Path can spark the fire of intellectual enlightenment. Gnostics considered the principal element of salvation to be direct knowledge of the supreme divinity in the form of mystical or esoteric insight—a salvation from ignorance.

According to Gnostic teaching, there are two life-paths a person journeys down: the Left-Hand Path and the Right-Hand Path. The right-hand path is one of sharing and giving, while the left-hand path is a path of selfishness. Raziel taught Adam and Eve these concepts of good and evil, and the difference between receiving in order to share and receiving for the self alone. The idea is to place yourself in between the two Trees where you act as the filament that balances out the opposite polarities, and thus become the middle 'mildness' pillar. And this is when you become more centered, at peace, in-tune with the oneness of everything, more grounded and focus-minded. This is when you connect with your spiritual nature, and connect with your inner sun; sol, soul.

Raziel taught Eve the mysteries of the Tree of Knowledge. If you look closely, you will notice that there are four fruits hanging in this tree. Four similar objects grouped together connects us to the 4th sefirah Chesed, which means mercy and is ruled by Jupiter. Jupiter is the planet of knowledge, prosperity and spiritual teachings. You will also notice that the serpent is wrapped around the tree. The serpent throughout the tarot represents the kundalini, which is a Sanskrit word meaning 'coiled snake.' It is an important concept in Śaiva Tantra, where it is believed to be a force or power associated with the divine feminine. This energy, when cultivated and awakened through tantric practice, is believed to lead to spiritual liberation. It is a way of raising your spiritual vibration by way of meditation. So, we see here that Raziel taught Eve how to elevate her consciousness and upgrade her spiritual awareness in order to receive knowledge and enlightenment from within. It is written in the book of Genesis, chapter 3:4-5, "And the serpent said unto the woman, Ye shall not surely die: For God doth know that in the day ye eat thereof, then your eyes shall be opened, and ye shall be as gods, knowing good and evil."

Adam and Eve were led down a spiritual path of enlightenment, using astrology as a tool to grow and improve. They learned how to open their third eye through kundalini meditation and receive insights from their higher-selves. They began to feel self-aware, no longer needing the angel's assistance. With the angel's guidance they were enlightened and spiritually ready to leave the garden; feeling as if they could venture out into the world on their own with their newly gained knowledge and self-awareness to guide them. They felt they had conquered the garden and were now ready to conquer the world.

Eating the forbidden fruit sparked (aroused) a new sense of awareness and a new sixth-sense of intuition that caused Adam and Eve to become aware of their true nature that they were soul-beings living in a physical existence having a physical experience. Leos are advised to awaken their intuitive self. This is done firstly by opening up one's heart. This is the way to connect to the spirit of all things. Intuition: When you don't know how you know, but you know you know and you know you knew, and that's all you need to know.

The Devil:

The Devil card portrays Adam and Eve in the 'real' world outside the garden. Here they are seen as being spiritually evolved, independent and are in control of their own destinies.

Although they are both chained to the black cube, which represents the world we live in, but as it is perceived as being more of a prison and a (somewhat) simulated matrix manipulating our experienced reality. Adam and Eve are not bound to this world. Eating from the Tree of Knowledge liberated them of their mental slavery from this egocentric system. You will notice that their chains are loose around their necks, making it easy for them to break free if they wish to do so. It just takes a slight shift in consciousness.

Leo's have a need to rule the world and to shine. They evolve and become confidant, independent and self-motivated. They are prosperous and able to manifest their desires in order to create a better world for themselves. Granted that an ego-boost can help get you what you want in life, it may end up costing you more in the end. Learn to receive for the sake of giving. This slight shift in consciousness will bless you with a sustained fulfillment. Know that God gives, and we receive. But as long as we only receive, or we try to get 'things' for our own purposes, then God remains the giver and we remain the receiver. We remain separate from the Divine. When we receive in order to give by giving purely out of a desire to give, we remove the separation between the ultimate giver, God, and the receiver which is ultimately all of creation. We become one with God, who's only known characteristic is His (or 'Its') ability to give goodness to creation. When we begin giving for the sake of giving, we are expressing that part of us that is created in God's image, and the separation between giver and receiver disappears.

After having been helped by the angel Raziel, Adam and Eve both appear to be stronger, wiser and more in control in The Devil card than they did in The Lovers card. "When the student is ready the teacher will appear. When the student is truly ready...the teacher will disappear." - Tao Tzu, Chinese philosopher. Adam and Eve no longer needed Raziel's guidance as they moved out of the garden and into the material world.

Seen now in the Devil card, the Devil, Adam, and Eve, are all depicted with horns on their heads. The goat horns on the Devil's head are symbolic of Capricorn, and the bull horns on Adam and Eve's heads are symbolic of Taurus, which are both earth signs. This signifies that all three coexist and are part of Malchut, the material world. The Devil sits on top of the black box, which represents the physical world of matter—Saturn's time cube, simulated reality.

Moving ahead, let's explore the symbols of this card. Hidden in the Devil's groin is the kundalini serpent. In addition to this, on the Devil's forehead is an inverted pentagram covering his third eye. These two clues when combined encompass the secret of how to raise one's kundalini as a way to open the third eye. Ideally, this is done by controlling one's sexual energy aka life-force. Moreover, the Devil card is assigned to the Hebrew letter Ayin, which means eye, to see. This is the reason the pentagram is located directly over the Devil's third eye.

Furthermore, Adam and Eve pictured naked signifies they have no ego. Nakedness throughout the tarot always represents being free of ego, and relates to one revealing their true self to the world—no longer hiding anything about themselves. Adam and Eve do not succumb to their lustful drives and primal instincts. They practice self-control. They are *in* the world but not *of* the world, and are not a slave to the Saturnian system, which is based on egoism, perceived in only 1% of the true reality that we are limited to understanding when using merely our five senses alone. This is how the illusionary matrix is governed, but Adam and Eve think outside the box, raise their kundalini and open their third eye. They use their life-force, sexual energy, which moves up from the base of the kundalini system, starting at the sexual organ chakra where it ascends upward to the crown chakra in the head and activates the third eye.

Once the third eye opens, man becomes a conduit for the Light, a pure channel opening himself up to receiving godly insights and intuition. As symbolized by Adam's fiery tail, Adam is able to connect to this creative force blessing him with insights that ignite a desire to receive pleasure, and the motivation to take appropriate action towards manifesting his newly inspired ideas. Typically, such a desire is sparked when a person sees something they want or sees a character trait in someone else they wish to emulate.

Eve encompasses the idea of being self-sufficient, symbolized with her plump grapevine tail. She has learned how to produce her own fruit and create her own prosperity. With closer examination, you will notice that Eve's tail is a vine with 13 grapes, which directly relate to the 13 Attributes of Mercy given in the Torah, proclaiming God's unconditional love. In the Lovers card, Eve is standing next to a tree that has four fruits hanging in it, which connects to the sefirah Chesed, which means mercy. And then here in the Devil card, Eve has her own tail producing thirteen fruits, which correspond to the 13 Attributes of Mercy. These 13 attributes, as enumerated in the Book of Exodus (Exodus 34:6–7) are the Divine Attributes with which, according to Judaism, God governs the world. The number 13 signifies the infinite. The number 12 signifies constraint and order: e.g., the 12 zodiac signs and the 12 months in a year. Above order and control, 13 connotes boundlessness and immeasurability. The fact that there are 13 Attributes of Mercy teaches us that when God shows mercy, He does so without limit.

No matter how low we fall, He will come to our aid and forgive us. This was the lesson Raziel taught to Eve in the garden; God will forgive us whenever we sin. Living in the material world involves being in a constant battle with the ego. Although unseen, the ego is a force we all feel and battle in our own way. Kabbalists refer to this unseen force as the Adversary. Rising above the ego is not easy and takes much spiritual work—something one must proactively do every day. Needless to say, some days will be harder than others. Knowing that we will be forgiven when we fall gives us the motivation to pick ourselves up.

Adam and Eve have learned to transform their ego-nature by using the life-force within them. By controlling their sexual energy, as a means of raising the kundalini, empowers them with the will to create prosperity in their lives. This is ultimately the will to receive pleasure, and thereby striving to accomplish their goals they obtain fulfillment. By controlling their (sexual) life-force energy they sustain a strong sense of willpower. They do not act impulsively, but rather with forethought mindfulness, and thus listening to their intuition instead of their heart, while at the same time having the sense of discernment to know the difference. With a strong will they are able to make their wishes come true. They are able to create for themselves a heaven on earth.

Here is a quote from the ancient Chinese philosopher, Lao Tzu, that sums it up nicely. It says, "Be still like a mountain, and flow like a great river. Use the light that is within you to revert to your natural clearness of sight."

Leo's have the willpower to create magic and miracles in their lives. Willpower is their superpower, and perhaps the strongest and best ability to do so out of any other sign in the Zodiac. Leo's have the willpower to manifest their dreams. They have the confidence and the healthy-ego drive to make things happen; not allowing anything or anyone to get in their way.

Leo must learn to control the life-force energy within and direct it for good. "We are stars wrapped in skin, the Light you have been seeking has always been within". - Rumi. Living only in the physical, mental and emotional realm makes energy limited. Tap into the spiritual dimension and the energy is limitless.

Each tarot card holds a key to conquering the ego; the adversary within. "How can I be substantial if I do not cast a shadow? I must have a dark side also, if I am to be whole." - Carl Yung. Some spiritualists call this inner battle with the adversary 'shadow work.' Shadow work is the process of exploring your inner darkness or 'shadow self.' Shadow work uncovers every part of you that has been disowned, repressed and rejected. It is one of the most authentic paths to enlightenment.

As you meditate on these cards, say to yourself, I will purge anger from my heart, free my soul of the burden that comes with reacting to the external. As I recall, I see that I was swayed by the darkness. I gave power to the situation instead of taking a moment to pull back, of restricting, and keeping the real power in my own hands. I realize that nothing in the physical world can cause me to react with anger.

Further explanation of the secrets concealed within The Devil card are found in much detail in Chapter 9: The Adam and Eve Allegory, which explains how to find the hidden Seal of Saturn in this card, and further explains the significance of the inverted pentagram symbol placed over the Devil's third eye.

Chapter 22, Section 6: Virgo

Astrological House #6, Virgo, ruled by Mercury, and associated with the sefirah Hod, which is the 8th sefirah on the Kabbalah Tree of Life. Therefore, the Virgo path to enlightenment layout includes all the number 8 cards and cards associated with the number 8. And they are: the 8 of Wands, 8 of Cups, 8 of Swords, 8 of Pentacles, Strength, and The Star.

Virgo has a machine-like personality. They are the workaholics of the Zodiac. They have traits of thoughtfulness, sensitivity, efficiency, cautiousness, intelligence, domesticity, prudence, industriousness, action-orientation, intuitiveness, and perfectionism. Virgos focus on details and are on an ever quest to improve. Their best can always be better. At the same time, they can be selfish, irritable, apprehensive, secretive, skeptic, inconstant, indecisive, short-tempered, and seem timid with a calculative approach.

Virgos have a deep need to be useful and productive. Their biggest desire is to be a hero, helping out the underdog and healing the ones who need it most. The quality most needed for balance is having a broader perspective, and to see the big picture.

Control is an illusion. Virgo energy can guide attention toward minuscule details. Step back and try to see the big picture while opening up to new ways of thinking. Judgment and criticism obscure the end goal: unity, peace, sharing. Remember, you do you. Ask questions, seek to understand, not to judge. You can only control your own actions. And lastly, always try to see the good.

8 of Wands:

We begin with the 8 of Wands where we see a bunch of wands shooting out like arrows into the air. The wands represent drive, creativity, passion, opinion, and knowledge. Virgos are an earth sign full of ideas and desires. They are driven to act out on these desires and try them all out in order to see what sticks and what works. They identify and rule out potential prospects with whom or what they know they're not compatible. Virgos will stick with and decide to continue with what has been proven to be concrete and successful. Hence the wands shooting out into the air like arrows and landing on the ground. Some stick while others fall flat. Virgo focuses their attention on the ones that stick.

Virgo is ruled by Mercury, a planet of communication and inspiration. This can influence Virgos to be naturally pragmatic and driven towards philosophy, sociology, linguistics, and anthropology. In Greek mythology, Mercury as Hermes, the messenger of the gods, has one foot in the physical world and another in the realm of the unseen. Likewise, Mercury crosses mental boundaries into the mysteries of the imagination and the memories of the past. In the fertile landscape of the mind, Mercury harvests and interprets your personal experience of life.

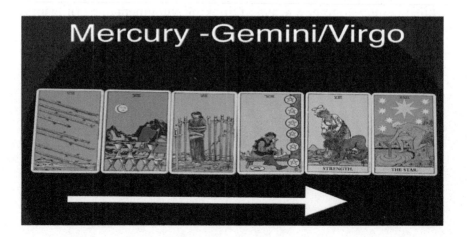

You will notice that each of the 8 wands has on it 3 green branches, equaling 24 branches in total; referring to the 24 hours in a day. Wands connect to agriculture and things that take time to grow and develop. The God of agriculture and of time is Saturn who rules over restriction, hard work, responsibility, and determination. This is a clue showing us that things take time and effort in order to grow. There are 24 hours in a day, (represented by the blue sky), and we need to learn to take things one day at a time.

In this card, we have a conjunction with Mercury and Saturn in Virgo, encompassing the personality traits of being intellectual, disciplined, having a serious outlook, good powers of concentration, and have good logical reasoning power. Here Virgo is not content with superficial understanding, and would rather prefer to study subjects in depth. This conjunction gives Virgo power to become great at business. Your work habits are careful, tenacious, methodical, and industrious.

Be open to trying new things in order to see what works. At the end of the day focus your attention on the wand (idea) that sticks firmly in the ground.

8 of Cups:
In this card we see a man walking away from his neatly placed and well-organized cups. Cups represent matters of the heart. We see here that this man put all his heart into this passion project. He walked away as soon as he felt there wasn't anything else he could do to improve upon it. He became inspired with a new and perhaps better idea to pursue. He turned his back on his project and moved onto the next; never looking back. Notice the moon has, both, a crescent and a full moon phase inside of it, representing that this man is coming out of a phase and beginning another. He is marching onward to the next endeavor or a new way of going about and handling his current one.

Virgos can be analytical and perhaps overly fond of detail, with perfectionist tendencies, and they may miss out on the big picture by concentrating on the micro, as seen here within the placement of the cups. They are arranged strategically, balancing on top of each other, firmly, so they do not topple over. There is a place for everything and everything in its place.

Throughout the Tarot it is important to pay attention to the grouping of objects. This always gives clues to deeper understandings. Notice the eight cups are set closely together but there is a fine line in-between the five cups on the left and the three cups on the right? The number 5 connects to the sephirah Gevurah, which means severity, and pertains to matters of the ego. This can relate to over analyzing things. The number 3 connects to the sephirah Binah, which means understanding. This can be related to having a sense of discernment. This is a clue showing us that it also benefits Virgo to learn the fine line between discrimination and criticism.

Virgos' mission in life is the purification of their activity in pursuit of their goals, manifesting their inherent love of excellence in all strivings.

8 of Swords:
Depicted here is a woman bound and blinded, surrounded by eight swords that are standing firmly in the ground. The ground at her feet is a dried-up pool of water. Water throughout the tarot represents emotions, swords represent thoughts, and dry land represents ego. Her red dress represents passion, drive and intuition. All this leads us to understand that this woman is over analyzing things. She is wrapped up in herself, focusing on self-improvement and development, so much so that it brings upon feelings of anxiety and worry. The white-clothed wrap covers her eyes, symbolizing that she is looking within, intellectualizing her emotions. The white clothes wrapped around her dress symbolize that she is focused on her inner body, relating to health issues. Like a sponge, she has soaked up all the water, and now drenched in her own emotions experiencing an anxiety attack. Wet outdoors with the night approaching brings upon more worry and concern about health issues. She may catch a cold, or worse yet, she could catch pneumonia. The cells in your body react to everything that your mind says. Negativity brings down your immune system.

Over analyzing anything will cause it to lose its magic. The magic is in the water, and if you soak up all the water you are left with dry land, which, in the tarot, symbolizes ego, which deprives you from reaching your goals.

Again, we see the same grouping of objects here with these eight swords. There are three swords on the woman's right and five swords on her left. The three of things grouped together connect to Binah, which is associated with Saturn, and the five of things grouped together connect to Gevurah, which is associated with Mars. This gives us an even deeper understanding of this card when we look into this planetary conjunction of Saturn and Mars in Virgo. Mars rules work and power, and it's meeting up with Saturn, which has to do with obstacles and restrictions. The two combined can result in frustration, but the intense effort could produce results for a long-delayed project. Saturn and Mars in Virgo has a high level of anxiety with stress brought upon by over analyzing and over thinking. Everybody has different ability to handle stress. Understanding how much you can handle is part of the maturing process.

Knowing when to politely bow out of an experience because you know you would not keep your balance is part of managing and mastering your life.

8 of Pentacles:
We have here a man working passionately on a certain task or project, repeating the process until he reaches perfection. Pentacles represent money, job, career, health, and family. This includes such things that you can touch and that are physical, and tangible, objects.

The man is wearing a blue shirt. The color blue represents the element of water, which connects to emotions. He is wearing red pants. The color red represents fire, passion, ambition, and creativity. He is balanced with his sensitive and intuitive side along with his driven and ambitious side. He wears a black apron, the color of Saturn, and the Lord of karma and judgement. There is a white strap tying the black apron over his blue shirt. You will notice that this is the same white cloth bounding and blinding the woman in the 8 of

Swords card. This symbolizes that he remembers and learns from his past mistakes, and therefore keeps his emotions in check. His right foot, sporting a red shoe, is pointing far out from his body, symbolizing that he is led by his passions. The six pentacles grouped together on the tree connect to the sixth sefirah Tiferet, which means beauty. This is a clue that this man is driven to create beautiful things. The number 6 connects to the peak level, when things are at their very best. This man is working diligently at perfecting his work, repeating the same task over and over improving it over time. Notice how the six pentacles are neatly organized on the trunk of the tree. He learns as he goes, paying attention to all the minor details as he strives towards flawlessness. He has one pentacle in his hands, which is a project that he is working on currently. Beside him on the ground is a singled-out pentacle, which is an idea he has for another project. The man always has a project in the works and always one on the back burner.

The lesson here for Virgos is to not treat people like one of your projects. Virgo's path has in it the most symbols of purity, more than any other zodiac sign's path. The color white throughout the tarot represents purity. Take that in affect, there are the white straps wrapped around the woman in the 8 of Swords, the white cloth strapping the apron tight in the 8 of Pentacles, the virgin is wearing a white dress in the Strength card, and then the virgin is completely naked in the Star card. Nakedness throughout the tarot represents a lack of ego. Virgo is the purest sign of the Zodiac and they always have good intentions to try and help others.

But you push people away because you always find something wrong with them almost immediately. And then try to improve them and work on them just like you would one of your projects. Being nitpicky and focused on the tiny details and awkward little habits that others need to change will drive the ones closest to you away. Allow your passion projects to be work related and consist of things like career, house, writing, learning, clothes, car, fitness, health, and food. We cannot change people. Besides, they will never be able to reach your high level of standards anyway, because you keep raising the bar. Learn to tolerate and love people for who they are. Set the example and others will come to you for advice and help when they need it.

Although, a career helping, or healing, or judging others (constructive criticism) would be most beneficial. A career where you are able to offer some sort of service to others would allow you be yourself all the while keeping things professional. You must create a good work-life balance. Working independently and or being your own boss would be choice. Be a friend at home and a boss at work.

Strength:
Here is Virgo, symbolized as the virgin maiden, wearing a white dress which represents purity and innocence. She is seen petting the lion. The red lion represents her healthy ego.

When we have a healthy ego it's easier to move through life with a wide-open heart, healthy boundaries and a solid sense of self. A healthy ego is essential for happiness, fulfillment and resilience. The lion is standing there with his tail between his legs totally surrendering to her love and caress. The moral depicted within this card is the virtue of fortitude and strength of will. The hidden key here is that patience is a virtue. Virgo, the virgin, puts herself out there with absolute certainty that whatever she puts out will always come back. The infinity symbol above her head symbolizes flow of the natural cycles of life that take time, and as the old adage goes, what goes around, comes around.

"Life is an echo. What you send out, comes back. What you sow, you reap. What you give, you get. What you see in others, exists in you. Remember life is an echo. It always gets back to you. So, give goodness." - Chinese Proverb

The Hebrew letter assigned to the Strength card is Teth, meaning coiled serpent, corresponding to the way a serpent waits patiently in the brush, hiding and waiting for its prey to pass close by, and then when the perfect moment presents itself, when the prey is most vulnerable or not paying attention, the serpent strikes. This card is about being patient as well as smart by allowing your desires to come to you. It is advised to remain mindful and watch out for repeating habits. Look for an opening or moment of weakness when your prey or foe is at their most vulnerable. Then strike when the timing is right and catch them red-handed when they repeat the same mistake as before—therefore, catching them with their tail between their legs, just as the lion in the Strength card is depicted.

The Strength card is directly associated with the astrological sign Leo, which is ruled by the Sun. All the number 8 cards are associated with the sefirah Hod, connected to Mercury, which is the ruling planet of Virgo. Astrologically, what we have here is the Sun conjunct Mercury in Virgo. Knowing this, we are able to connect on a deeper level the message therein. Virgos, influenced by both the Sun and Mercury simultaneously, and stuck in the practical, material world may learn a lot about themselves if they are brave enough to try placing their lives on automatic pilot once in a while. Letting some things go will do wonders for their spirit. Virgos tend to be too hard on themselves. They worry about their health, their performance at work, and all the things they haven't done. It is empowering to communicate with your higher-self. Identify exactly when you're sad or negative feelings arise during the day. What kind of situation triggers them? Remember that recognizing the source of these negative feelings is the first step to eliminating them. You would be wise to embrace others' opinions and constructive criticisms. Use them to build yourself up instead of tearing yourself down. You must learn to transform your reactive ego. Once criticized, press the pause button. Focus on how it can help benefit you. Know that your external reality is just a reflection of your inner space. People are your messengers. They are merely reflections of your own subconscious giving you constructive insights that will help you mature spiritually.

The Star:
Again, we see the virgin archetype in this layout. This is the virgin, Isis, who is a pure channel of light and is in complete harmony with the world. Isis was closely linked to the star Spica (in the ancient constellation which was centered around the modern constellation of Virgo) because the star first appeared around harvest time.

She is seen here dipping her vessel into the astral waters of the imagination and pouring the water onto the physical world and applying it to practical matters. As the water pours onto the land it creates five different streams. There being five is significant and it connects to the 5th sefirah Gevurah, which is associated with matters of the ego. Because Isis is a pure channel of the Light, these five streams contain healthy and positive ego traits. She creates positive streams, paying it forward, not knowing where the water actually goes. She does not try to control the flow, instead she allows it to flow freely knowing that it will bring forth positive change naturally wherever it leads. She doesn't even look where she is pouring. She remains focused working as the channel. She is naked for all the world to see. She is open, honest and real. What you see is what you get.

Each one of her vessels can only hold so much water. She knows the exact measurement managing the precise amount taken in and the maximum amount that her vessel can handle or withstand. She knows when to stop dipping into the astral plane of the subconscious where her emotions, worries, and anxieties coexist alongside with her inspiration, intuition, and imagination. She knows when to quit. She then applies these insights into practical matters, pouring them onto the land. She becomes a channel for making miracles. Notice she has one foot on top of the water, as if she is walking on the water miraculously.

The eight 8-pointed stars connect to Thoth who is also known as Hermes/Mercury. Thoth played many vital and prominent roles in Egyptian mythology such as maintaining the universe. He was heavily associated with the arbitration of godly disputes, the arts of magic, the system of writing, the development of science, and the judgment of the dead. Thoth's roles in Egyptian mythology were many. He served as scribe of the gods, credited with the invention of writing and Egyptian hieroglyphs. In the underworld, Duat, he appeared as an ape, Aani, the god of equilibrium, who reported when the scales weighing the deceased's heart against the feather, representing the principle of Maat, was exactly even. The ancient Egyptians regarded Thoth as One, self-begotten, and self-produced. He was the master of both physical and moral (i.e., divine) law, making proper use of Ma'at.

Ma'at is the Egyptian Goddess of Truth, Universal Order, and Right. The ideas related to Her form the core of the ancient Egyptian conception of the way things should be. Ma'at was considered to be the very food of the Goddesses and Gods. Ma'at explained the relationships between humanity and the Divine. Ma'at was natural law and social law. Ma'at was not only justice, but also fairness and even kindness toward one another.

Thoth is credited with making the calculations for the establishment of the heavens, stars, Earth, and everything in them. The Egyptians credited him as the author of all works of science, religion, philosophy, and magic. The Greeks further declared him the inventor of astronomy, astrology, the science of numbers, mathematics, geometry, surveying, medicine, botany, theology, civilized government, the alphabet, reading, writing, and oratory. They further claimed he was the true author of every work of every branch of knowledge, human and divine.

Thoth is symbolized by the scarlet ibis, which is found in the Star card, sitting in the tree, and overlooking Isis. The ibis inspires and encourages Isis with insights. Their connection and correspondence are represented by the large gold star located in the center of the card above Isis' head. The other seven white stars connect to the 7th sefirah Netzah, which means victory and is associated with aspects of harmony. These seven stars are directly related to the seven chakras which are illustrated here as being raised and vibrating in unison and in harmony.

The Virgo who has the power of turning all negative vibes in his/or her path into positive energy has learned the meaning of life.

Once you fully commit to healing, you'll understand that people were instruments to aide in your evolution. Focus on the lesson not the person.

As you meditate on these cards, think to yourself, I will spread love for no reason. I will resist my tendencies toward judgment. As I look back on negative words or deeds from my past, I replace them with

Light and compassion, sending positive forces out into the universe to replace the negative ones. I will look upon others with compassion, sweetening the judgments as they come my way.

Chapter 22, Section 7: Libra

Astrological House #7 belongs to Libra, whose path to enlightenment includes all the #7 cards. The 7th sefirah on the Kabbalah Tree of Life is Netzah, ruled by Venus who rules over Libra, and therefore Libra's path is associated with specific aspects influenced by Netzah. Netzah, meaning victory. Both Netzah and Venus place an importance on maintaining harmony in all aspects of life.

The sphere of Netzah contains all instincts, raw emotions and feelings. This is the realm of Venus-Aphrodite who is not a fertility goddess but one of pure emotion and feeling. This sphere is force without physicality—pure creative energy. Netzach is music, poetry, art, all things which in their pure expression appeal to our feeling nature and touch our emotions. This is the energy of Nature herself.

Libra's path includes the following tarot cards associated with the #7: 7 of Wands, 7 of Cups, 7 of Swords, 7 of Pentacles, The Chariot, and The Tower.

Known for maintaining their balance in life, Libra is rightfully depicted by the symbol of balancing scales. They are known to be diplomatic as well as defenders of justice. Most Librans are lovers of art and music. They are also known to be very good liars, and as a consequence they are able to smell a fake from a mile away. Libras are known to be natural charmers and lovers. They tend to be in love with love.

Known as the sign of the scales, Libras are expert judges of difficult situations. They possess an analytical mind. They always enjoy a good intellectual challenge, and can satisfy others with their logical arguments and expert conclusions. A Libra's discerning nature allows them to live a prosperous life.

Although, Librans have many positive traits, they also share negative ones as well. For instance, they tend to be attention seekers, at times dishonest, trouble makers, have a tit for tat mentality, and can be considered controlling.

Let us look closer into the Libra's path to gain a better, well-rounded understanding of both their strengths and weaknesses, and uncover ways to strengthen the Libran's spirit and overcome their ego-nature.

There is a delicate balance between reflection and certainty. Libra energy surrounds decisions, leaving us in doubt. This is the time to trust that our journey will take us exactly where we need to go. Have certainty. You are exactly where you need to be. Leave no room for doubt. End indecision, and trust in the Light.

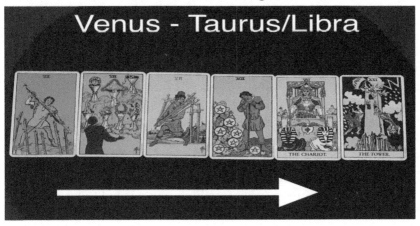

We begin Libra's path to enlightenment with the 7 of Wands card.

7 of Wands:
Depicted in this card is a man who is standing on the ledge of a cliff and is shaking his big stick (wand). The suit of Wands represents opinions and beliefs, and so through this symbolism we see that this man is trying to pursued others of his personal beliefs. Seen standing on higher elevated ground as the other wands below him, this man feels as if his beliefs are bigger, better and more correct than the others. The Hebrew letter associated with this card is Kaph, meaning open palm. Upon further examination, you will notice that there are exactly 20 branches on the 7 wands in this card. 20 is the numerical value of the letter Kaph, meaning open palm. This suggests that this man should open his palm and release his grip around the wand, and therefore should learn to let go and quit trying to force his beliefs onto others, no matter how valuable and verifiable his opinions seem to be.

Before you argue with someone or attempt to pursued them onto your beliefs, ask yourself, is that person even mentally mature enough to grasp the concept of different perspectives? Because if not, there's no point.

Librans can be considered as being control freaks. They like to control other people's lives and will often tell them what they ought to do. It is not up to you to change others. People usually don't respond well to others telling them what to do. The best way to change others is to lead by example. When you feel the urge to offer advice or share your opinion, ask yourself first if it is constructive. Ask yourself, "What am I adding?" Learn to bite your tongue if you feel yourself becoming overbearing. Ask yourself if you are helping or simply craving attention. It is then best to become reserved in your thinking. Be patient, and the time for you to speak up will come. Allow yourself to internalize your own thoughts and self-reflect. Perhaps your own opinion was something you needed to hear all along. Alone time gives you the space to discover the deepest parts of you.

For Librans, it may be easier to offer others help than to ask for it themselves. "Some people aren't good at asking for help because they're so used to being 'the helper'. Throughout their life they've experienced an unbalanced give and take, so their instinct is usually "I'll figure it out on my own". The self-reliance is all they've ever known." – Jim Carrey, actor and author

7 of Cups:
This card depicts a man who is relishing in the past. This man is colored black, which represents Saturn's influence—dealing with time, relating to both the past and the future. Here he is seen fantasizing about all his many past accomplishments. The seven cups are each an individual trophy capturing the feeling of success or a significant turning point of the man's life. This man has a difficult time letting them go. This man must come to the realization that he cannot reach what is in front of him until he lets go of what's behind him.

Libras can easily become emotionally detached from their relationships. But, at the same time will grow to miss their old bonds due to their codependency. They seem to go from one extreme to the next, at an attempt to regain stability. Although, they find the 446 bouncing back and forth from one extreme to the other a slippery slope, where they one day feel codependent and then the next, they check out and find themselves detached all together. They go from being over controlling to simply not caring. In psychology, emotional detachment, also known as emotional blunting, has two meanings: one is the inability to connect to others on an emotional level; the other is as a positive means of coping with anxiety.

This emotional stability can be balanced and maintained when you practice gratitude as if it were a religion. The more grateful you are for the things you already have, the more those type of things will show up in your life. When practicing gratitude, you will soon take notice how people will choose to remain in your life. In time, you will nourish and develop certain skills and become better at your hobbies. Other aspects of your life will improve as well, such as relationships, career and passion projects. Practicing gratitude is good for the soul, and helps further develop as well as evolve your spirituality. However, if you continue to detach or diminish what you have you will find yourself experiencing a sense of lack, which brings upon anxiety, depression, and later regret and resentment accompanied by a victim-consciousness mentality.

7 of Swords:
Librans need to figure out how to be in a partnership but not lose who they are. This can be done with escape from or detach from that relationship by writing down your ideas and putting forth creative ideas in your own time outside the relationship/partnership. When you are not creating, you are dying—you are losing a sense of who you are. Libras are for the most part codependent and will quickly lose themselves in a relationship. By creating, and continuing to create, the Libra can regain a sense of independence.

Libras have a 'tit for tat' mentality, which causes them to need to be just as independent towards themselves and pay attention to their own needs the same as they give to their relationships. This codependence aspect rings true on a certain level or degree, but it truly is a balanced give and take dynamic put into practice.

The 7 of Swords advises one to write down their brilliant ideas, make a plan, and execute that plan with passionate desire. This can be considered the essence of the creative process. It is basically the idea of putting your thoughts into action. The first step in the creative process is to write your ideas down. This is symbolized in this card by the way the man grips the swords in his right hand. He grips the swords as a person would grip their fingers around an ink pen. Swords represent thoughts and ideas. Therefore, this man is seen here writing down his ideas. This allows him to break free from the camp, which metaphorically can represent his relationship, his business or his loyalties/responsibilities. The camp can also represent his comfort zone and place of stability, which can grow to become stagnant and complacent over time. When our relationships grow to become like this, we can lose a sense of who we are, and we forget about our passions and our dreams. This is when it is advised for us to escape from our complacency and start creating—as the saying goes, if you're not creating, then you are dying.

7 of Pentacles:

This card is illustrated over a gray background. Gray being the color associated with Chokmah, meaning wisdom, alludes to the fact that there is a life-lesson being learned here. The man depicted here is looking over his grapevine with dismay, because of his neglect the grapes have dried out and withered.

Starting projects may be the Libran's forte, but following through with the project can be difficult. "You can't just have a thought. You have to follow the thought through. But everything starts with a thought." - Wayne Dyer. Notice the singled-out pentacle at the man's feet? This represents the initial idea the man had to plant the grapevine in the first place. This idea can be picked up again and the man can make another attempt at it—he can plant another seed. Yet, this time he will not be starting from scratch. This second time around, he will be starting from experience. Libra is able to look at a problem from every angle and quickly weigh the possible solutions. Therefore, by learning from past mistakes and starting over will prove to be successful this time around.

If you erase all the mistakes of your past, you would also erase all of the wisdom of your present. Remember the lesson, not the disappointment.

The Chariot:

Pressing ahead, with The Chariot card. The knight in The Chariot card has applied all that he has learned along his life's journey into achieving great success and being able to conquer the material world. He adorns a 'square' on his chest plate, representing his mastery over the world. The square is an ancient symbol for the world and he 'circles the square' spiritually with esoteric wisdom and by utilizing the practical Kabbalah.

This knight decorates himself with many esoteric and astrological symbols, displaying both his esoteric understanding, as well as his devotion to a certain creed or organization.

He flaunts an eight-pointed star on his crown, which represents his high level of intelligence—the number 8 being associated with the sefirah Hod, meaning brilliance of the mind. By utilizing his brilliance, he has been able to overcome challenges by adapting his analytical problem-solving skills towards creating a life for himself that is both secure and stable.

You will notice that there are two sphinxes pulling the knight's chariot. These sphinxes represent the other people chosen (or influenced) by him to help in the endeavor of a greater goal or life purpose, as they share similar like-minded philosophies and work towards an ultimate agenda. Correspondingly, the Hebrew letter assigned to The Chariot card is Chet, meaning fence. Its spiritual meaning relates to things we keep fenced in, such as occult or esoteric wisdom, and can also relate to the secret agenda's one has in spreading such sacred knowledge. Secret societies may choose to withhold such knowledge, knowing that sharing such things tend to push others away rather than spark their interest.

The Chariot card is covered with many esoteric symbols. For instance, the knight adorns two crescent moons that rest upon each of his shoulders, representing his desire to merit spiritual truths and insight from the Shekinah, the Divine presence of God. He displays several alchemical symbols on his apron. He proudly wears an eight-pointed star on his crown, connecting to Mercury aka Hermes, flaunting his esoteric understanding of the Hermetic occult mysteries and spiritual sciences. With further observation, you will notice there are exactly 40, six-pointed stars on the tapestry which hangs over the top of the chariot. These 40 stars represent the soul's growth and maturity needed to understand the concealed mystical wisdom of Kabbalah. Furthermore, he wields a long staff with a candle at the end in his right hand, which is a tool used for connecting to the Higher-Self, and to the Light of the Creator. Presented on the front of the chariot is a shield which has a dreidel with wings painted on it. Dreidels are known to only spin for so long. They are merely a temporary enjoyment. Nonetheless, the wings are able to carry the spinning dreidel forever, insomuch where the dreidel would never touch the ground, and never cease spinning. The idea is to have this dreidel become like the sun disc that is placed in-between these wings, which represents being forever constant and reliable. In order for the dreidel to do this, one must continue spinning it. They must keep constant attention and focus on the certain thing which offers them enjoyment, whatever the dreidel symbolizes to them, thus giving that certain something wings.

The knight fears he could lose the things he has worked so hard for, so he remains focused, maintaining his success so it will continue to last forever. He believes that success is achieved when he is at his best physically as well as spiritually. It is important for him to stay connected to his higher-self—the source of his inspiration for creation. Once he acquires a taste for success, he will then gain the sense of certainty needed in order for him to continue and maintain his successes. He understands that he must continue striving to become better, improving upon what he already knows, and to dig deeper for the purpose of enriching his understanding of life and human nature, with regards to both the material and the spiritual realities that exist simultaneously. It is one's connection to the Source that empowers the life-force within, therefore making it possible to achieve the impossible, and for one to obtain the certainty knowing that they contain the power within themselves to ascend mind over matter.

The Tower:
From here, we progress to the final card in Libra's path, The Tower. Depicted here is the tower having just been struck by lightning,

causing a man and a woman to fall out of the tower and onto the rocks below.

The tower represents a particular goal or concept they have been working on, having built it up from scratch over a long period of time, manifesting it from the original idea to its reality. The tower can represent a wide range of things including, but not limited to, a business concept, relationship goals, as well as obtaining a higher level of enlightenment reached only after years of devout spiritual study and ego transformation. Our human spirit is like a tower, that we develop and build up as well. By practicing meditation and working on ourselves we are able to raise our kundalini aka life-force energy within our vessel. This force ascends up from the base of our spinal column to our skull, where we experience the sensation of enlightenment in the crown chakra. Upon achieving this spark of enlightenment, one is able to tap into a new higher-realm of spiritual insight and understanding—obtaining a broader sense of spiritual awareness. With this new awareness comes new 'big picture' realizations and self-reflection. We are then able to realize our wrong doings, and unruly behaviors. From here, we gain wisdom and rise above our limiting beliefs, and shatter our previously fixed mindset. At this point, we experience an "ah ha" moment, and connect to higher truths.

Both the man and woman in this card will have experienced a distinct and personalized spiritual awakening which destroys their tower, and ultimately shatters their belief systems.

They are now forced to pick up the pieces and start over, although they will rise from the ashes stronger and more spiritually mature than ever before.

People tend to believe that material wealth and material objects will bring them happiness. Looking for outside sources blinds one to the truth that such happiness is found from within. Subsequently, the search for inner truth can blind a person as well, because the closer one gets to obtaining such truths, the more so their minds become unwilling to change. Strictly speaking, a person can succumb to a certain agenda and find themselves omitting anything that disagrees with their agenda's reasoning; immediately blocking out or diminishing all outside perspectives.

Over time, we come to realize that money and fame along with material possessions such as a house, a car and business are all temporary things. For this reason, how others perceive our character trumps the way we are judged by either our looks or what we own. The truly important things in life are the relationships we have with ourselves, our family and our friends. When we open up our hearts and let go of ego, we are able to connect to the people we love on a deeper emotional level, correspondingly sharing our Light with others. The light felt will be what they remember more so than the fancy gifts you gave them. It is more so about how you make others feel which truly leaves an impact. The light you have shared, the good things you have done in the world to make it a better place, will last even after you are gone.

These personal connections are what truly matters and what we can take with us on and into the next life. Our relationship with ourself and God (Higher-Self) is eternal. An enlightened Libra learns to value their connection with the Light more so than an infatuation with material objects.

The Light enters our vessel and raises our vibration, elevating our soul and conscious awareness. This enlightened sense of awareness wakes us up to the fact that life is not about acquiring material things just to quench the need for instant gratification, or to obtain a fading sense of accomplishment. In the long run, having more stuff doesn't matter. It's the impact, the mark that you leave that truly changes the world for the better, and sets an example for others to follow in your footsteps.

Although, this card has many positive traits, it can also be perceived in a negative polarity, whereas the man and woman can be seen as selfishly following their ego-driven desire to obtain enlightenment, as if it were an achievement, comparable to achieving a black belt in karate, for example. They do not understand that to be spiritually enlightened is to maintain a sense of being enlightened, and it's something you grow to become; not something you attain overnight.

It takes time and a conscious effort to be able to truly grasp the higher truths in their divine simplicity. Once you see the truth, you can never go back. You can never un-see it. This new shift in awareness, your new 'woke' mindset becomes your essence. Allow me to explain.

The man and woman in The Tower card did the spiritual work required for them to ascend up the 22 branches of the Tree of Life, represented here by the 22 Yod's that float in the air. It was at the top of the tower where they connected to the Source, the crown chakra aka the sefirah Keter, (meaning crown). But with their acquired spiritual knowledge, they had built themselves a spiritual tower of Babel, so to speak. They had treated the achievement of enlightenment just as they would a material object or an award they were wishing to win. Upon reaching enlightenment, their ego stepped in and deceived them into believing that they had done it on their own accord, either with such great tenacity or by having such a high level of confidence in themselves. At this point, they stopped relying on the Light for guidance. They built their tower up to heaven so they could be just as high as God, and then once this higher level was reached, they vainly felt as if they were Gods themselves. Their situation is oddly similar to the old concept, "If you give a man a fish, he will not go hungry that day, but if you teach a man to fish, he will never go hungry again". These people used to be spiritually hungry and they were taught to fish, and now feel like they no longer need the teacher, and they feel like they can continue fishing on their own without any godly help. Although, eventually with time, they will come to find out they need more than just fish to survive this world. They will soon be faced with new challenges that life will throw at them. Today it's fish, tomorrow it's shelter. Nothing lasts forever, and we all experience times of good followed by times of bad. These challenges will seem overwhelming to them now that they have lost their connection to the higher-self and must go at it alone. Without their connection to the crown at the top of the tower, doubts, fears and anxiety will ensue. When we open up our hearts to the Source, to the Light of the Creator, we invite the life-force in, which boosts our tower aka kundalini energy once again. Similar to the old adage, the teacher presents himself when the student is ready. God was always there, they just needed to tap into the Source-energy; the infinite energy which is all around us, all of the time. Once we understand that this is the source and not our own ego is when we begin to build up our spiritual towers within.

The characters in this card will eventually realize the truth that they are merely a vessel, and a channel for the Light. Becoming spiritual isn't about gaining a new personality, getting a new vocabulary or wardrobe, buying crystals or doing yoga. It's about returning to our natural state.

Reaching enlightenment is about preserving a higher sense of awareness so that you can continue realizing new truths and break free from limiting beliefs and a fixed mindset. Once we shatter our beliefs, we must wipe the slate clean and start over. However, don't be afraid to start over again. This time you are not starting from scratch, you're starting from experience.

Resist the urge to stay within the realm of comfort and predictability. The energy of Libra may prompt us to shy away from new ideas, opportunities, or people. But this is precisely the time to embrace change and discomfort in order to spark radical transformation.

Interesting to note here is that the Hebrew letter assigned to The Tower card is Peh, meaning mouth. The intriguing thing about the letter Peh is that there is a hidden letter Bet inside of it. Bet means house, and can relate here specifically to things that we say in private, in our homes and away from the public. This corresponds to one's spiritual growth and transformation worked on in private, and it is advised to not speak openly or share with others how you are developing spiritually, and avoid bragging about any personal milestones achieved. For instance, when we do decide to speak about our personal spiritual work we are, in reality, either consciously or subconsciously seeking out the approval of others. In this exchange, their approval validates our growth, which consequently exhausts our self-esteem. It is as if the only reason we were working on ourselves is for others to praise us for being a good person. Winning others' approval is like winning a gold star in grade-school or a trophy at the end of a contest, and with each new person you meet they become like a new merit badge you must earn and collect on your sash. Earning others' approval can transform into an addiction, and never be truly fulfilling. It can come to be exhausting participating in a rat race where the award for first place is a pat on the back. And you find yourself doing this with every person you meet; trying to empress them. This approval received from others has a way of diminishing our spiritual towers, as we attempt to raise our spiritual vibration and ascend up through each of the chakras. Holding in this life-force energy gives one the power to build and ascend up their tower, likewise releasing this energy reactively will just as quickly compromise what they have spent so much time and effort building up. Sacred things we keep private and speak of in private have a tendency of coming out publicly if we do not maintain a stable control over our spiritual towers. When we share what is regarded to be private, done with either sarcastic remarks, emotional outburst, or spreading gossip, it has the power to destroy anything we have spent time building. This includes our relationships, friendships, careers, as well as our reputations. It can take years to build a strong friendship, and in only an instant, with the wrong words spoken, can that friendship be destroyed forever.

A Libra must continue to be mindfully aware of the caliber of their spiritual tower while at the same time remaining mindful of their thoughts, on the grounds that those thoughts have the power to diminish one's spirit, clouding one's judgement and sense of discernment. The higher the caliber of one's tower, the easier it is for them to lose control over their emotions and act out impulsively. With this power comes great responsibility. You see, our thoughts become our words, and then those words have the power to either build up or destroy the things we care the most about. Behaving reactively releases our light, permitting ego to enter. With the greater amount of light that escapes our vessel, there is a potential for a greater amount of ego to enter. This is why it is so important to be mindful when our spirit feels at its strongest, because this is when we have the greatest potential to cause the most havoc, both to ourselves and to those we love. Having a strong willpower is key to maintaining a stable spiritual tower, granting us with stability in our relationships, friendships and career.

Remember when being mindful of your words, that sometimes it is best to be silent. Be silent, if your words will offend a person. Be silent, if you can't say it without screaming. Be silent, when you are feeling critical. Be silent, if your words convey the wrong impression. Be silent, when you don't have all the facts. Be silent, if your words could damage a friendship. A meaningful silence is always better than meaningless words. Speak only when you feel that your words are better than your silence.

When you decide to change, do it for you and not for the approval of others. "Self-control is strength. Calmness is mastery. You have to get to a point where your mood doesn't shift based on the insignificant actions of someone else. Don't allow others to control the direction of your life. Don't allow your emotions to overpower your intelligence."— Morgan Freeman, actor

Time now to break out of your shell. Say no to complacency, and yes to change. And only do so for yourself, and your own peace of mind. Your value does not decrease based on someone's inability to see your worth.

As you meditate on these cards, think to yourself, I have absolute certainty that what is right will happen through proactive behavior. I take complete responsibility for my life and know that I am getting what I need right now. And as I continue to allow more Light and certainty into my life, I will get even more.

Chapter 22, Section 8: Scorpio

Astrological House #8, Scorpio, whose path to enlightenment includes all the #1 and #5 cards. This is because Scorpio is ruled by both Pluto and Mars. Consequently, Pluto rules over the 1st sefirah on the Kabbalah Tree of Life known as Keter. Keter is associated with the crown chakra aka the Father, and is associated with new beginnings. Mars rules over the 5th sefirah Gevurah, corresponding to aspects of severity as well as matters of the ego.

With Scorpio, everything runs deep for them. Their feelings are strong, intense, and they last forever. Don't cross a Scorpio, their revenge is slow and painful! Scorpios are sensual, mysterious, sexy, conscious, and are able to make dramatic life changes. They are also deeply intuitive and tend to overthink their gut feeling.

Self-love and appreciation for the blessings in life is the prescription for the emotional intensity of Scorpio energy. Anger and jealousy erode any spiritual progress made. Release negativity and focus on sharing compassion and kindness to others, as well as ourselves. Share love. Others are not to blame. Show compassion. Revenge will get you nowhere. Cultivate self-love.

Let's begin by explaining the sphere of Keter which essentially is the crown of will. It is the still small voice in your head that some refer to as the Higher-Self. This can be understood better by comparing this sefirah to certain aspects of a human being. The will of a human being is the most all-encompassing power of his soul, since it gives rise to and motivates all of the other powers of the soul. If a person has a will for something he begins to invent ways in which to achieve his goal. Once he has discovered a theoretical method of achieving his goal, he starts to plan out how to achieve this in reality. From there he initiates the action. As long as he has not yet achieved his desire, his will drives him onwards until he does so. Keter is the top most of the sefirot of the Tree of Life in Kabbalah. This is where the Light draws down from the Source down into the human vessel. The roots of the Tree are located at Keter. Therefore, all the #1 cards are considered the roots of the tarot.

Scorpio's path which aligns with Pluto includes the following tarot cards associated with the #1, and they are: Ace of Wands, Ace of Cups, Ace of Swords, Ace of Pentacles, and The Magician.

The Aces as well as the Magician all portray the root-seed level of creation, which involves the will to receive pleasure to some degree. These cards correspond to Pluto, the planet associated with transformation and rebirth.

Scorpios are known to be ambitious, determined, and brave. When their minds are set, they can accomplish anything they set their mind to. They experience highly emotional new beginnings that are fueled with intensity when starting new projects or relationships. When a Scorpio wants something, they go for it and they don't hold back. There's not much that can stop a Scorpio once they have their mind set on something, and they have unmatched focus when they pursue a goal.

All the #1 cards encompass this aspect of Scorpio's energy in some way.

Ace of Wands:

Igniting new and creative ideas, sparking up the motivation needed in order to manifest your goals, and acquiring a new lust for life are all aspects portrayed in this Ace. The Wand is symbolically depicted as a Tree of Life, with its 10 branches similar to the 10 sefirot on the Kabbalah Tree of Life. With closer examination, you will find there are 8 floating Hebrew letter Yod's colored green which look like leaves. There being 8 like-objects connects us to the energy influence of the sefirah Hod, meaning brilliance, glory, and alludes to brilliance of the mind. Therefore, this portrays a brilliant idea being ignited. A closer look at this card, you will notice that there are 37 rays surrounding God's hand. 37 is the value for the word Chokmah, meaning wisdom. This reiterates the concept of God igniting an epiphany or brilliant idea here. There is a mushy castle located in the background. This is the same exact mushy castle that is depicted in the 10 of Pentacles card and in the 7 of Cups. Each instance the castle represents the thought or idea of building this castle. It is mushy, and therefore it is still in its imagination state, and not yet formed or solidified.

Furthermore, these 8 Yod's added to this wand's 10 branches gives us 18. The number 18 is significant here, because it is the value of the Hebrew word Chai, meaning life, as in the Jewish saying, "L'chaim!", meaning "To life!"

Ace of Cups:
This particular Ace is about creating an over-abundance of love and healing. Depicted in this card is a dove, who represents the Holy Spirit. This dove delivers a communion wafer, which symbolizes the body of Christ, into the large cup. This cup has on it the letter M, which stands for Mary, as in the Virgin Mary. Thus, the Holy Spirit is portrayed here delivering the body of Christ into the Virgin's vessel or womb. The letter M can also refer to the Hebrew letter Mem, meaning water. This connection is represented in the suit of Cups, which corresponds with the element water. This water overflows out of the cup, and forms a pool at the bottom of this card, and therefore is symbolic of the Virgin's (birth) water breaking. Furthermore, you will notice that there are exactly 26 water droplets falling from this cup. These water droplets are actually Hebrew letter Yod's. The number 26 is significant here, because it is the value for the Divine name of God, YHVH, Yahweh. Yod, meaning hand, suggests this symbolism reflects God has His hand in this miracle taking place, where the Christ, representing the Light of the world, is being implanted into the vessel, as well as into the hearts of man—thereby, the suit of Cups represents matters of the heart.

The virgin birth of Jesus is the Christian doctrine that Jesus was conceived by his mother Mary through the power of the Holy Spirit and without sexual intercourse.

Matthew 1:18 states, "Now the birth of Jesus Christ was on this wise: When as his mother Mary was espoused to Joseph, before they came together, she was found with child of the Holy Ghost." (KJV)

Luke 1:35, "And the angel answered and said unto her (Mary), The Holy Ghost shall come upon thee, and the power of the Highest shall overshadow thee: therefore, also that holy thing which shall be born of thee shall be called the Son of God." (KJV)

Ace of Swords:
This Ace is the 'peace of mind' card, and the symbolism depicted here portrays the forming of a balanced mind with a mild spirit. Notice how the symbols hang from the sword in such a manner that corresponds to the Kabbalah Tree of Life? The sword here represents the middle and mild column, which creates the balance of the polarities. Portraying the Tree of Life, the Crown is placed at the top center, aligning with the sefirah Keter. The olive branches drape over the crown and dangle from each side of the left and right columns (pillars). The 6 fiery Yod's, coinciding with Tiferet, float just above the sword's handle, which represents Yesod. This handle is gripped by God's hands, which correspond to Malchut. Thus, you have symbolized here the central, mild column (or pillar) of the kabbalah Tree of Life. The middle path is obtained when you open up your heart. This allows you to form a channel to the crown, as a means of obtaining peace of mind. Jesus said that the only way to the Father was through him. Jesus represents the sacred heart, and the crown at Keter corresponds with the Father.

Ace of Pentacles:
ThisAce coincides with the letter Heh, meaning window. Notice the window made in the garden's bushes? This symbolizes a window of opportunity. This window can also be compared to as being a coin slot. The hand of God is about to roll the coin through the slot, and get the machine operating. As in get the ball rolling. This coin would literally roll down the hillside once it passes through that window.

All four Aces correspond to the Four-Letter name of God, YHVH. And they connect with the four elements as well: Wands correspond with Yod, Fire. Cups correspond with Heh, Water. Swords correspond with Vav, Air. And lastly, Pentacles correspond with the second Heh, Earth.

With further examination, you will notice that there are exactly 37 rays surrounding God's hand here. 37 is the value for the word Chokmah, meaning wisdom. Therefore, this Ace portrays that God blesses you with a wise idea and presents you with a brilliant opportunity. It would be wise to take this opportunity that has been placed before you. The suit of Pentacles representing things of the material nature would coincide with such opportunities involving (but not limited to) relationships, health, and career.

The Magician:
This card is assigned to the Hebrew letter Bet, meaning house. The Magician forms the letter Aleph with his body. Aleph is the first letter in the alphabet. Hence, Aleph-Bet. This symbolism portrays the Magician starting a new house, and thus laying out the foundation from which all things Tarot will abide by. Notice the four tarot suit symbols on the Magician's table? He has all the tools he needs to lay the foundation. The infinity symbol above his head alludes to the fact that his tarot knowledge is passed through to him from past-life. Whereby, the infinity symbol represents repeating cycles, such as the reincarnation loop. The Magician wears a white focus sash around his head, alluding that he is focusing on his thoughts and reconnecting to his past-life knowledge. He raises his torch up towards Binah in attempt to receive deeper esoteric understanding.

Scorpios are also able to dive deep into their subconscious mind and fish for knowledge gained from their past lives. By reconnecting to such things, one can obtain their life purpose. They can continue their legacy by remembering their destiny.

This concludes Scorpio's path to enlightenment aligning with Pluto. Scorpio's other path, which aligns with Mars includes the following #5 cards, which are: 5 of Wands, 5 of Cups, 5 of Swords, 5 of Pentacles, The Hierophant, and the Temperance card. This path is to be taken simultaneously with the path of the 1's mentioned above.

5 of Wands:

Pictured in the 5 of Wands card is a group of men who are all wielding a wand in their hand and battling each other. Each of them is depicted as being dressed differently and having their own individual styles. The suit of Wands represents fire, passion, and opinions. Scorpio can believe their way to be best. It is easy for a Scorpio to find themselves butting heads with others' opinions, and they rarely shy away from an argument. Scorpios are vocal and engaging. Scorpios are honest to a fault. They always tell the truth, no matter what, and hate dishonesty in others. They can't stand people who steal and cheat, either, since they're just as honest with themselves as they are with others. They fight for what they believe to be right and may come off as a bit bossy causing others to feel timid in voicing their opinion or stand up for themselves. From another angle, this card can reflect upon the inner struggle one has with their own personal beliefs and/or moral values, as well as second guessing decisions made in the past.

The Scorpio needs to learn that everyone is unique and we all have differentiating beliefs. Develop your own individuality. Focus on your personal growth. Lead by example. Scorpios are brave. There's no one better to have at your side during a time of trouble than a Scorpio. They will run into danger without a second thought, and are always the first to volunteer themselves for difficult tasks. Especially when it comes to helping family and friends, the Scorpio personality means that they are the first to jump into the fray.

5 of Cups:
Cups throughout the tarot represent feelings, emotions, and matters of the heart. In the 5 of Cups card, we see a person cloaked in a black cape, closed off and isolated to the world.

Three cups have fallen over, representing an unbalance of emotions and a lack of empathy. These three cups being grouped together like this connect us to the third sefirah on the Tree of Life known as Binah, which means understanding. These cups being turned over symbolizes that this person is not willing to listen to others advice, has become stubborn, and is now trying to figure it all out on their own. This person is internalizing and analyzing themselves to the point of depression. They went from one emotional extreme to the other very quickly. If they were to turn around, they will find two cups sitting upright on the ground behind them. This pair of cups located on the right side of this person corresponds to the second sefirah Chokmah, meaning wisdom. This person would be wise to look at the other side of their situation where they would find the silver lining—a bridge leading him over the water and back to his home; to his comfort zone and place of stability.

We see here through the depicted symbolism that this man is dealing with this emotional life-lesson now, in the present time. Something or someone he once felt an emotional attachment to broke his heart and rocked his understanding of what love is or should be. Maybe he was the one at fault? Whichever angle you look at it, he was once emotionally comfortable, and now suddenly not.

It happened too fast. Now it is hard to stop focusing on it, and it is easy to either blame himself, or play the victim. You begin to think of what you should have done or should have said to prevent it from happening. At this time, it is good to step back and take a look at the situation from an objective perspective. Time now to learn from your past mistakes and promise yourself to never repeat them. Listen to others and be open to their heartfelt advice as you change yourself for the better, so you can return back to your stable life a changed person, who has matured and grown from this situation. No need to return back through the emotional waters, but instead return back over the bridge, having taken the 'high road.'

Scorpios can become jealous, secretive and resentful. Scorpios feel everything intensely, including jealousy. They are quick to be jealous since they think their determination and intelligence entitle them to get what they want. They have a hard time not comparing other people's achievements with their own, and think everything is a competition.

Scorpios never show their cards. They are incredibly honest, but they don't like to display any vulnerability, especially with people they're unsure about. They tend to keep their feelings to themselves, as well as plans and ideas, so when it's time to win the chess match of life, Scorpios have a leg up. However, this also makes them difficult to deal with as people.

When someone else gets something the Scorpio desires, we know they can be jealous. But on top of that, no one holds a grudge like a Scorpio does. They take betrayals personally and setbacks seriously, and may often find themselves resenting others for perceived slights.

5 of Swords:
We now move onto the 5 of Swords card. The suit of Swords represents thoughts, spirit, and communication. Here we see a man celebrating a confrontation won with the use of wit and intelligence, causing him to feel over-confident and over-powered. In so doing, he is simply projecting, which causes the other two men to feel those same emotions which he had felt and dealt with recently, as was portrayed in the 5 of Cups card. He is seen now forcing these two men to walk into the sea of emotions just after having broken their spirits. Notice this man is holding two swords in his left hand? Here we see another example of like objects being grouped together. Just

like the pair of cups in the previous card, these two swords correspond with the sefirah Chokmah, meaning wisdom. These particular swords being held in this man's left hand, specifically connects to the energy aspect of receiving, as it pertains to receiving wisdom. With this in mind, we can see how the pair of cups from the previous card morphed into these two swords—herein, emotions transformed into wisdom, attained from experience.

We have established that swords represent spirit, thereby, this man's spirit has lifted up and grown stronger as a result of his opening up his heart to other people's advice in the last card. The Scorpio continues his day-to-day routines just as before, but now with a regained sense of self-worth and an additional boost of confidence, and what seems to be for the most part a smooth transition back into his previous comfortable and stable life.

However, life has a tricky way of facing us with challenges that push our buttons. It is how we react during these challenging moments that shapes our character. By and by, whenever provoked, Scorpio prove themselves to be immature when dealing with such things as karmic challenges, irritable agitations, and not to mention human confrontations, as they present themselves. It seems as though the more confidence a Scorpio has, the easier it is for them to put others down and speak over them. They seem to do this by using words, either directly or indirectly, to put others in their place. They end up lecturing instead of listening, as they feed the need to prove themselves right.

Scorpios like to be in control. Their fierceness and intensity convey that they think they know what's best, and the people in their lives will often find themselves under the Scorpio's thumb. Scorpios also hate being controlled by others, and need control over all situations. In the words of the great Chinese philosopher, Lao Tzu—"Be mindful of your thoughts, because they become your words. Be mindful of your words, because they become your actions." Alongside this, understand that the life-lessons you are faced with are meant for you only, gifting you with an opportunity to grow spiritually. It is not your responsibility to preach or enforce wisdom which you acquired from personal experience. You must come to realize that everyone is on their own unique life-path, and everyone has their own karmic-baggage to deal with. No one truly knows the impact their words and actions will have on people or think twice about how they will affect the people around them; not until they, too, just so happen to be on the receiving end of such unruly behavior themselves.

5 of Pentacles:

Pentacles represent material objects and physical things. This includes such things as money, vocation, career, along with relationships and one's health. In addition to this, the suit of Pentacles can also relate to one's reputation. Our reputations are dependent on others, they can be built up just as easily as they can be destroyed.

Depicted in this card we see a guy who is walking with crutches and is desperately seeking charity from the woman beside him. Deliberately turning her back on this man, she refuses to help in any way. She refuses to acknowledge the man, appearing to be annoyed with him—having reached her wit's end. What we have displayed here is the Scorpio repeating their emotional-habit of crippling themselves willfully in a psychological sense, effecting their mental well-being. Due to this, they tend to latch onto others, becoming codependent and rely on others for moral support, to pick them up and out of their tempestuous rut. The Scorpio goes even as far as physically hurting themselves in an attempt to gain sympathy from others. Once they deceive someone into sympathizing with them, and having earned that person's trust, is when they feel they have out-smarted the other, which places them as the victor. As the victor, they feel they are above you, and now are allowed to talk down to you. At this point, Scorpio becomes bossy, demanding and over-controlling. This emotional rollercoaster ride becomes a habit which they have a difficulty breaking free from. If they continue to repeat this cycle, they will never be able to grow spiritually. They will be like the hamster spinning its wheel and getting nowhere, spinning with all its might yet it remains in the same place. If they were to continue this behavior, they would never be able to mature above the level of a teenager.

Without a strong determination and the willpower to change, they will remain codependent on others throughout the course of their lives, though they will never admit it.

Scorpio needs to learn how to take responsibility, not use others as a means to get ahead, be patient with people, and allow the process of manifestation to evolve organically. If not, this will push people away. It will spoil your job, career, and home-life.

The Hierophant:
Following the 5 of Pentacles is The Hierophant card, which can be perceived as a humbling card. This aspect can be seen here as the two men approach the Hierophant and ask humbly for his guidance and for the granting of blessings. The Hierophant wants nothing more than to grant such wishes and blessings, but one must first ask in order to receive.

The Hierophant is an interpreter of sacred mysteries and arcane principles. He advises us to not take things for face value and urges us to delve deeper, as well as expand our awareness to see things in the big picture. Avoid from being quick to judge, and understand there is always more than meets the eye.

The Hierophant holds the keys to the tarot. The Scorpio needs to become a humble student of life itself, opposed to them trying to gain control or to conquer the world. They need to learn to open themselves up spiritually, and be willing to learn the sacred mysteries that life is eager to share.

The Hebrew letter assigned to this card is Vav, meaning tent peg, nail. The tent peg is known for binding the tent to the ground. Spiritually, the Vav is known to bind, connect, or join the spiritual world with the physical, and vice versa. It would prove to benefit the Scorpio to be more like the Vav, and strive to be more in-tune with the spiritual, expand their spiritual awareness, and connect to the Higher-Self. When it comes to self-improving, Scorpio needs to focus more so on themselves rather than trying to change others. Find deeper inner-truth within yourself as opposed to finding truth about yourself or personality through others.

Temperance:
The last and most progressed card in Scorpios' path is the
Temperance card. Temperance depicts the enlightened Scorpio, who
has graduated from the Hierophant's mystery school and has applied
the knowledge in practical ways that improve their life and
relationships for the better.

Discreetly depicted within this card is a portrayal of the Hermetic
Marriage, blending the dualities of nature. For example, the
combining of male-female, positive-negative or fire-water. The
angel on this card is actually the combination of two archangels
coming together as one; Raphael uniting with Gabriel. Wherein,
Raphael represents the male-sun aspect, while Gabriel represents
female-moon energy. United as one, they become the master
alchemist who manages time with patience, thus allowing the life-
forces to mix and flow with each other organically in a natural
manner. This sense of control over one's dualistic nature grants them
power over their temper. It is essential to learn how to hold in
temperamental emotions and bite our words in order to avoid any
kind of regretful outburst. Containing one's self and controlling their
emotions makes it possible for their fire to mix with their water,
wherefore inspiration is allotted the time it needs to communicate
with the heart, which as a result gives the ignited impulses the
chance to simmer down as they blend and refine themselves, all this
occurring simultaneously while you attempt to hold back the urge to
act out and cause a scene.

This androgynous angel is the source of its own happiness. This
angel represents an independent thinker considered to be self-driven,
yet at the same time able to surrender to the natural flow of life's
rhythm. This angel seen here having one foot in the water and the
other placed on dry land portrays the maintaining of balance of both
intuition and ambition, and obtaining the willpower to refrain from
acting out in haste and/or without tact. This concept is displayed here
as the angel mixes the energies of fire with water in a calm and
controlled manner. All the while knowing that the life-force within
holds the real power needed to create prosperity and abundance. It is
advised to not let go of this life-force until the time is right. The
opportune time will present itself. One should surrender to the flow

and learn to float with the current, and allow the Universe to lead you to the doors and open up the windows of opportunity for you. "Things do not always happen the way I would have wanted, and it's best I get used to that." - Paulo Coelho, author of The Alchemist

The Hebrew letter assigned to this card is Samekh, meaning to prop up, uphold, support. Samekh is also the letter for Sukkah, indicating that God's omnipresence is our support and shelter. A sukkah is the name of the hut the Jewish people lived in while in the desert for 40 years. They built these huts as dwellings that would invite the presence of God within them. Therefore, the people would build their house as if it were a house of God. And they would treat their bodies as if it too were a temple of God, in which would be the same with God; hence the letter Same-kh. Jeremiah 31:33 states, "But this is the covenant that I will make with the house of Israel after those days, declares the Lord: I will put my law within them, and I will write it on their hearts. And I will be their God, and they shall be my people." You will notice in this card the Four-Letter Name of God, YHVH, written over the angel's chest.

As you meditate on these cards, think to yourself, God is within. I connect to the divine power in my soul and awaken an incredible source. My confidence is fortified so that I am empowered to solve my problems, to eradicate the chaos and confusion in my life. I am aware of the good within and the good that I can do, if I choose to take responsibility for the Light in me. It has always been there—now I see it.

"Self-control is strength. Calmness is mastery. You have to get to a point where your mood doesn't shift based on the insignificant actions of someone else. Don't allow others to control the direction of your life. Don't allow your emotions to empower your intelligence." - Morgan Freeman, American actor

Chapter 22, Section 9: Sagittarius

Astrological House # 9, Sagittarius who is ruled by the planet Jupiter, The Great Beneficent, King of the Gods, the planet that favors intuition, faith, and knowledge that comes from within. In Astrology, Jupiter is a planet of plenty. It is tolerant and expansive. The first of the social planets, Jupiter seeks insight through knowledge. Some of this planet's keywords include morality, gratitude, hope, honor, and the law. Jupiter is a planet of broader purpose, reach and possibility.

Jupiter has generally been associated with good luck and bounty. Optimism and growth (including mental and spiritual growth) come under its rule.

On the upside, Jupiter is associated with a sense of humor, good will, and mercy. The more negative manifestations of Jupiter include blind optimism, excess, and overindulgence. Irresponsibility that results from blind optimism, not ill will, can be displayed.

True liberation comes from recognizing the ego and restricting reactive behavior. This is a time to slow response time and invite the Creator into your decisions. Open up to possibilities you hadn't considered. There is always another option for what action to take. Find freedom. Slow down. Practice forgiveness. Know that sensitivity is a gift. Commit to your beliefs.

In Kabbalah, Jupiter is associated with the sefirah Chesed, the 4th sefirah on the Tree of Life. Chesed, meaning mercy, loving kindness.

Sagittarius is ruled by Jupiter and connects to Chesed, the 4th sefirah, which is why the Path to Enlightenment layout involves all the #4 tarot cards and all cards associated with the number 4. And they are, in order from least to greatest value: the 4 of Wands, 4 of Cups, 4 of Swords, 4 of Pentacles, the Emperor, and Death. The path starts from the left and ends on the right—the final card being Death. How is the Death card the enlightened one? How is this the full level of potential? I will explain in much detail in this section. Basically, it is a death to the ego-self; crossing over into the world of the unknown and leaving the world of what you knew behind.

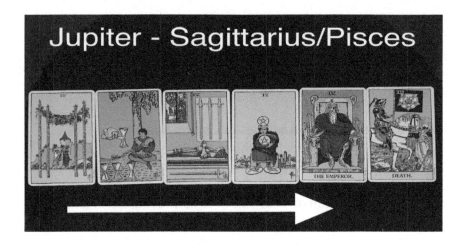

We begin your journey with the 4 of Wands card.

4 of Wands:
The 4 of Wands depicts a couple celebrating their wedding. They are about to walk under the chuppah, which is the archway/canopy decorated with grapevines and flowers seen draped along the top of the four wands. The chuppah represents the house that the married couple will begin their new life in together. This new house is usually a gift from family and loved ones.

Wands relate to and represent knowledge; knowledge acquired over time. This symbolically represents the Sagittarius entering the world and beginning their new life already blessed with knowledge. Maybe this knowledge is in their DNA code? Or perhaps it was obtained in a past life? Sag's come into this world feeling as if they are an old soul. When they enter the world, they feel as if it is their wedding day; they are lucky and born in a happy situation (for the most part) and feel optimistic and lucky. When they are brought into this world they are placed on a solid foundation. On day one they are already well-rounded individuals. This card is bright yellow in the background, symbolizing the establishment of their bright future.

The large castle in this card's background encompasses this notion. The castle is a firm and solid foundation that will last a lifetime. And it's as if the married couple is marrying into royalty. This couple begins with the house (symbolized by the chuppah), knowing that they will one day inherit the castle. This is the level of blessed that is felt here. As well as the level of entitlement. Here we see the negative polarity of this card, as it refers to the Sagittarius's personality flaws.

Receiving blessings without merit does bring upon a sense of entitlement, where one feels as though they are better than others. This creates the notion that they have authority over others, a dominating opinion, and a belief that they have the final say on the matter. Sagittarius can be boastful, over confident, and brash.

You must remember that we are all on different paths. All paths lead to our spiritual enlightenment, but not all paths are the same. Some paths may seem easy while others appear more challenging. What is important is not to judge, and keep focused on yourself. Know thy self. Every person around you is a reflection of your own soul—a projection of your inner state. When you judge others, you are actually only judging yourself. People are God's messengers and they can prove to be our gurus. Every person is an opportunity for you to grow and broaden your sense of self, strengthen your character, and become more open-minded with a broader sense of self-awareness. It is important to listen and be open to other people's advice, especially when they speak from their hearts. This concept leads us to the next card.

4 of Cups:
Here we see a stubborn man sitting under the Tree of Knowledge. God's hand is reaching out trying to offer him loving advice that will improve his life, but only if he is willing to listen.

Cups represent emotions and matters of the heart. You will notice that there are three cups in a row at the bottom left of this card. The fact that these cups are on the left side of the card and there being exactly three of them directly corresponds to the 3rd sefirah on the Kabbalah Tree of Life, Binah, meaning understanding. We see here, (through symbolism), that this man in the card feels as though he has already gained understanding, and his level of understanding is placed upon a solid foundation. He has an intellectual approach towards his feelings and can think critically for himself. He is able to resolve one matter from the understanding of another matter.

Moreover, the number 3 relates to balance. For instance, the Holy Trinity is three; the Father, Son, and Holy Spirit. The Kabbalah Tree of Life is a three-column system which includes the left column of severity, the right column of mercy, and the central column of mildness, which balances the energies of the left and right columns. The Tree's three-column system is similar to how a light bulb works. Both the positive and negative charges are balanced by a middle filament. This three-column system is also present in every atom, which has a proton (positive charge), an electron (negative charge), and a neutron (no charge).

Therefore, this man believes that he is balanced with his emotions. He has emotional control. He is self-motivated and when he sets his heart out do something he sees it through to the end.

The man sits under the shade of a large tree. Trees just like the suit of wands represent knowledge. The wands in the tarot are directly related to the two trees in the garden of Eden; the Tree of Life and the Tree of Knowledge. Since the #4 cards associate with Jupiter, and Jupiter corresponds to knowledge, the tree in this card reflects the energy aspect of the Tree of Knowledge. This man planted this tree for himself, and he did so with self-taught knowledge. Sag's have a God-given thirst for knowledge; similar to having a God-given talent for painting or playing a musical instrument. Sagittarius yearns to learn and expand their mind. Most likely, the man in this card had a desire to one day be able to sit and relax under a shade tree. So, he took it upon himself to learn how to grow a tree. And, here we see depicted in this card that he was a success. He did exactly what he planned out to do. Notice a knot in the tree located just above the man's head? The knot looks very similar to an eye. This knot represents the all-seeing eye of God. Trees relate to agriculture, and the god of agriculture is Saturn. Saturn is the God in the Hebrew Bible, Yahweh. The planet Saturn's south pole is a large oval shaped storm, which looks down upon the Earth. This oval-shaped storm is the all-seeing eye of God. God is always looking out for the Sagittarius. And God is always the one guiding them and inspiring them, as well as leading them towards the next step they need to take in order to grow and expand their knowledge, which will prove to grow their prosperity.

God's hand is depicted here attempting to give this man a cup, which is a symbol for heartfelt advice. The man has his arms crossed and he is stubborn, and not wanting to listen. His heart is hardened and he is not open to others' help, because he feels as though he has accomplished what he set out to do; to grow this shade tree. The man now feels comfortable, and has become complacent. He stopped listening to the voice of God. But God wants you to constantly grow and to prosper. Perhaps God is going to tell the man how to plant more trees? And spark a desire within him to grow an orchard. The man could grow an entire orchard of apple trees on this hill. He could sell his apples and make a respectable living. All the man needs to do is open himself up and listen to others' advice. The original Hebrew word for tree is etz, which is almost identical to the word for advice which is etzah. We always need to be open-minded, and to listen to that 'still small voice' in our head. This is the voice of our Higher-Self, the voice of the Creator, God. People are also God's messengers. And we need to be open to their advice as well, especially when they speak from their hearts. The shape of a human ear is similar to the shape of half a heart. When you place two ears together it forms a whole heart. Remember this whenever people offer you their help and try to teach you something new.

You may think that you already know something because God has already blessed you with the knowledge and the insight you needed in a previous venture, but know that people are God's messengers and they too will offer up blessings to you with their heartfelt words and acts of charity. You will find that by listening to the 'still small voice' as well as people's heartfelt words of wisdom will allow you to become like this tree—allowing you to branch out, grow, deepen your roots, and be fruitful. At the same time, you will gain a wider view of all things, and obtain mental expansion.

4 of Swords:
The 4 of Swords is an extension of the 4 of Cups card. It shows the evolved person who took the cup, or God's advice, and took it to heart and learned from that advice, transforming the wisdom gained into practical know-how.

In the 4 of Swords, we see a knight resting on his back with his hands over his chest and his palms touching, as if he is praying to a higher power. If you look closely at the stained glass window in the background, there is a woman bowing down before a Saint (priest or Christ) character. She is asking for a blessing. Just like the woman, this knight is also asking for a blessing. Perhaps he is making a wish? He has realized that he cannot do everything on his own, and he is only successful when he is in communication with and connected to his higher-power.

Something interesting to mention here is that Sagittarius Sun signs all have close relationships with their fathers. The father is seen as an authoritative figure and the connection with their father shapes a Sag's character and makes them who they are—more so than with their mother or any other family member. Sag's father usually is a man who has a job in some sort of authoritative status like a lawyer, police officer, church leader, govt. worker, or university professor. Sagittarius' father is the one who wishes to be a guide, life coach or guru. They teach a Sag about religion and/or spiritual life-lessons. The father is always the one who offers the help, and ultimately this enables the Sag.

The Saint (or priest) character in the stained glass can easily relate to a father figure who you look up to and ask for their help. Coincidentally, Catholic priests are called Father.

A Sagittarius may only ask for help if they feel that they are worthy of it. More often than not, a Sagittarius will not ask for help. They'd rather put out a vibe in hopes that others around them will pick up on it telepathically and come to their need. This idea can be seen as a subtle prayer as opposed to vocalizing one's feelings. As in the case of the woman bowing to the priest (Father) in the stained glass window, she is approaching him with her heart on her sleeve.

Notice the red heart on her left sleeve? The knight has just proven to be victorious in battle and/or has proven his worth through charitable acts. He now feels as though he is worthy enough to ask for a blessing from God the Father.

There are three gray swords hanging on the wall above the knight's head, which represent the three cups from the previous card in their evolved state. The concept here is that critical thinking has intellectualized the knight's emotions. Now he understands the 'why' and the reasoning at the root cause of his emotions. He has analyzed his emotions and has reached a balance of heart and mind.

Swords represent our thoughts and the way we communicate, and Cups represent our emotions and feelings. So, with further analyzation, we could presume that the knight in the 4 of Swords took the advice from the previous card (4 of Cups) to heart, and he is now analyzing it, intellectualizing it, and allowing the advice to sink in. He is thinking critically about this new idea and attempts to look at it at all angles. As he develops this big idea, he is able to see the big picture and he can visualize the end result. The end result, the outcome, is his 'happy thought' and it becomes his big wish, his dream, and his main reason 'why' that he continues to focus on.

This wish of his is represented by the golden sword on the side of his bed. This singled-out golden sword is his big idea that he obsesses about. He is excited, just like a child waiting for Christmas morning to arrive. As the knight lays down to rest, he prays to his higher-power, asking to the Father to grant his wish.

Perhaps the 'still small voice' told the man to plant an entire apple tree orchard, and you will receive much wealth? The man from the 4 of Cups card did this, and he provided his entire community with apples and cider. Perhaps there were apple trees that supplied firewood for the winter, and lumber for building and for tools. This man would have been seen as a hero or saint, and even perhaps awarded the status of Knightship.

Now, depicted in the 4 of Swords, the man is seen as a selfless and charitable person. He is able to rest at ease, knowing he has done well, and is a good person. He now feels as though he is allowed to ask for something in return for his good deeds.

He has reached a deeper level of his emotional understanding and feels as though he is mentally stronger. By opening up his heart, he has opened his mind, and now he will receive prosperity and abundance much easier than before.

The knight has gained wisdom in all this. He now realizes the importance of keeping a communication with God. He has come to understand that all his success in life comes from him listening to that 'still small voice.'

When success comes, the ego has a way of making one feel as if they accomplished everything by their own doing. A slight upgrade in social status tends to make a person feel as though they are better than others. The bigger you build yourself up to be, the bigger and more important your opinion becomes. This self-importance tends to make one feel as if it is their responsibility to take charge, preach, lecture, and take on the burden of having to always be the authority over others. One with such a large ego will feel as though it is their duty to change and to motivate others to become just like them; as though their path is the only right path to take in order to achieve success in this life. This is why it is important to know that we are all on different paths. And that no path is the only path to take. We all travel alone on our separate paths. Any time you hear that 'still small voice' the message was meant for you, and you only. Surrender to that voice and allow that energy to guide you. This energy is like 'the force' in the Star Wars movies, and this force communicates with all of us in its own way, and we communicate with it in our own way as well. There is no wrong or right way, only what is right for us.

Helping others is a good thing to do, but allow others to approach you first when asking for help. Leading by example is the best way to change others. You must first work on yourself before you can try and change other people. You must 'walk the walk' and be the person you wish others to be.

Not everyone is open to hearing your advice. Not everyone is at the same mental or spiritual maturity level to even comprehend the words you are saying. Everyone is like a vessel, and vessels can only hold so much. People's vessels are all different sizes, some are bigger than others. Some people's vessels cannot hold any more knowledge than what is already in there. That is why we must always strive to expand our vessels and keep expanding our minds.

4 of Pentacles:

Depicted in this card is the same knight from the previous card but seen now as being further evolved. You will notice that he is now adorning a new crown, representing royalty status. He is seen now in the 4 of Pentacles as a successful business man. He appears to be at peace. He has been granted the wish that he so desired from the 4 of Swords card. He has been blessed with money, power, and independence.

This man continues to evolve as he progresses along the path of the 4's. He has listened to godly advice and has taken it to heart, willed his mind to think critically as he analyzed the emotional aspects of it, and now he is putting these new concepts into practical matters.

The black cape covering the knight's body represents Saturn's planetary influences. Saturn is the planet of karmic life-lessons and restriction. Saturn is the lord of time, and creates an illusion which distorts our perception of time, restricting the time we experience between cause and effect. Saturn floods our lives with challenges and frustrations which are packaged as karmic life-lessons. These challenges come to us as blessings in disguise. We do not realize it at the time, but once we make it through one of these life-lessons we feel spiritually stronger and these life situations build upon our character.

Pentacles represent practical matters and things that we can touch, such as money, business, career, family, friends, property, as well as health. Pentacles are associated with things that we are able to perceive with our five senses. Pentacles can also relate to one's social status and reputation. It is a very delicate thing; the way others perceive us. The 'evil eye' is what some mystics refer to as the judgements we receive from other people. We never really know what will destroy our reputation, therefore we must always be mindful of our words and our behaviors. We must give respect in order to receive respect.

Sagittarians are very generous and extravagant when it comes to money. They have an 'easy come, easy go' attitude due to their tendency to be very lucky with money. They are big spenders and have no problem sharing their wealth with people and charities. They tend to have an optimistic outlook with a 'pay it forward' attitude when it comes to offering friends money. They'll usually spend their money on parties, adventures, and helping people out.

This concept is depicted here with the knight sitting outside the city wall. He is alone away from everybody because he creates wealth on his own. He is independent. He follows his passions and transforms his passions into practical streams of income, so he doesn't seem like he is working. It's not work when you're doing what you love.

The knight has four pentacles located at different areas around his body. Each of these pentacle's specific locations correspond with a particular sefirot located on the central column of the Kabbalah Tree of Life. For instance, the pentacle located on top of the knight's crown is associated with the sefirah Keter, meaning crown. This connection with Keter allows the knight to communicate with the higher realms of consciousness where he receives godly insights, divine inspiration, and a 6th sense intuition. This knight is very wise and does not hesitate to put his inspiration into action, thus creating prosperity and abundance in his life. The astrological symbol for Sagittarius is the archer. Archers always have a target. They receive a clear vision of their target and then quickly formulate an action plan, which they execute with premeditated precision.

You will notice the knight is holding onto a pentacle with his hands. He is grasping this particular pentacle as if it were a steering wheel of a ship. This symbolizes that the knight is in control of his personal life, and that he is the one who decides his own fate. The knight is holding this particular pentacle directly over his heart. It is as though he is guarding his feelings and protecting his core values. He is solid and avoids succumbing to other people's judgments that may threaten his emotional state in a negative way. He holds on tightly to his personal affairs, his personal beliefs and his opinions. He does not seek other people's approval or their advice. He remains private to the public in order to avoid such judgements. He is an independent thinker. His connection to God, to the Higher-Self, is all he depends on to steer him in the right direction. This is what he knows to be true. This is his core belief that no one can sway.

Lastly, there are the two pentacles which the knight holds firmly underneath each of his feet. This represents that he is driven by material matters. Every action he takes has a purpose, and leads him closer to achieving his goals. He knows now that in order to obtain prosperity in his life he must create a way to improve the lives of others. He connects to the higher consciousness of Keter, and draws down its creative force, blessing him with inspirational ideas. He applies these ideas in a practical way, offering ways to help improve the day-to-day life of others. People pay him for his services and/or inventions. He then uses his wealth to develop bigger and better ideas to help improve the lives of others. The knight gives back to the world which gave so much to him. It creates a circuitry. He is paying it forward. This is the secret to prosperity. We receive in order to give. And then paradoxically, we receive more because we gave. The more we give, the more we receive. It is a paradox. We give what we don't have in order to receive what we want. Just like the knight when he received the epiphany to grow an apple orchard, he was given the idea to sell apples, apple cider, and firewood to the town's people at the bottom of the hill. He took the seeds from his single tree and then planted an entire orchard from it upon the hill. Within a year's time he was able to sell his apples, and with the money earned, he was able to venture out and develop bigger money-making ideas that would change the world for the better. In return, he received joy and fulfillment.

And most importantly, he earned independence. With his wealth, he gained the freedom to be in complete control of his life and decide his own fate, and not have to answer to anyone.

The Law of Attraction works with gratitude. When you appreciate what you have, you will be blessed with more. The young knight did not realize at first that he was sitting under the shade of a 'gold mine.' Of course, this can work against your favor. When we analyze and point out the bad things or focus on what we lack, we then receive more negativity and lack.

Negative thoughts will decay and diminish our material world. Negativity can affect our health, our relationships, and the way we view ourselves. No one can destroy iron, but its own rust can. Likewise, no one can destroy a person, but his own mindset can. "Do not waste one moment in regret, for to think feelingly of the mistakes of the past is to re-infect yourself."- Neville Goddard, author. And also, "We need to realize that our path to transformation is through mistakes. We're meant to make mistakes, recognize them, and move on to become unlimited." - Yehuda Berg, cofounder of The Kabbalah Centre. When we experience lack, disconnection from the Creator is often the real source of the problem. When we are connected to the Light, there is no struggle. Connection helps us develop balance from within, which doesn't waver when things shift around us.

Always be mindful of your connection with the Light of the Creator, God, the Higher-Self. Remain grateful for your connection and you will never experience feelings of lack, and you will remain tapped into the creative-force which will guide you to greater successes.

Continue to create. If you're not creating, then you're dying.

On a further note, Sagittarius is very generous with money, but remember that money does not buy loyalty or trust. Actions speak louder than words. Therefore, people will judge your character by what you do. You cannot buy people's respect or buy their friendship. It is earned by simply being there when they need you most.

The Emperor:
The Emperor is the knight who has evolved into someone great. Our knight has leveled-up to Emperor status. He is now depicted as a powerful leader, who has been chosen by his people because of his selfless acts and charitable works. He is now adorning a crown with

jewels, wearing thick armor and sitting in a seat of authority.

The Emperor card is associated with the planet Mars, which rules over Aries—a fire sign (just like Sagittarius). The ram is the astrological symbol for Aries, hence the four ram heads located on the Emperor's throne. His throne is colored gray, and as we know the color gray always represents wisdom. The Emperor's wisdom is as solid as a rock. Influenced by Aries energy, the Emperor is fueled with all the confidence and passionate energy needed for him to move mountains.

The Emperor holds an Egyptian Ankh in his right hand representing his willpower which regulates the life-force energy associated with desire, drive, ambition, and initiative. He is a mentor that continues to help others by passing along his wisdom to the younger generation, sharing practical life advice that will save them time and frustration, and by hopefully awakening within them a lust for life. He teaches the younger generation these things so they will continue on in his legacy and build upon and develop the standard of life that he has created for them. He wishes to ignite a desire within them to want to strive for success and to better themselves. And for them to share in his vision of what life can be and evolve into.

In his left hand the Emperor is holding a golden globe, representing the world in its evolved 'golden age.' This evolution into the next 'golden age' is what he strives for. It is his purpose and his life's work. He feels as though he is working for a higher-power, and it is something greater than himself. He knows that as long as he continues to make the world a better place, he too will be blessed with more prosperity and success.

The Emperor's crown has five gemstones. There being five like-objects corresponds to the 5th sefirah Gevurah, which happens to be ruled by Mars, and its energy influence relates to matters of the ego. The crown corresponds to the sefirah Keter, which corresponds with the higher super-conscious, encompassing Godly intelligence. The energy influence from Keter is that of pure Light, therefore the relation here with the ego can only be a positive one, influencing positive ego aspects, such as healthy ambition and drive. The

Emperor will receive desire for change, but it will be a desire to change things for the better. He will destroy institutions, dismantle governments, tear down social barriers, and get rid of old systems that no longer serve the people. He enables the god of war energy of Aries within him to be a force for good, and for positive change.

The Emperor wears a red rob over his armor, represesting passion, drive, and the creative-force. He is driven and passionate about leading his people out of complacency. It is not an easy thing to motivate and move people. Most people are reluctant to change. They will fight it, and be willing to die for their beliefs and way of life. This is why the Emperor is covered in armor. Obviously, the armor suit protects him from physical harm, yet on a spiritual level the armor protects his emotional self as well. Like the pentacle he held over his chest in the previous card, which protected him from other people's words and judgements, he has now upgraded his protective shell and can no longer be swayed by other people's opinions. People will try hard to shut you up and silence you, forbidding you to be heard. They will ridicule you and try to embarrass you, calling your ideas ludicrous. They will try to persuade you to join them, conform and maintain the status quo. But the Emperor stands tall, and his core beliefs are grounded on a firm foundation. He has a proven system and proven formula, and the chosen ignorance of people will not stop him on his crusade to save the world. If you don't stand for something, then you will fall for anything. And he will not be brought down by the ignorance of others. The tall mountains in the background symbolize that the Emperor will be able to move mountains and succeed, no matter what obstacles are in his way.

Our words have the power to influence others, and they can either build up or destroy our reputation as well as our relationships we have with others. Simply put, language holds massive, colossal power to manifest change, whether it's good or bad. Sagittarius must remember to be mindful of their words. The Emperor practices self-control and learns how to bite his tongue. He uses the healthy ego aka life-force within as a fuel to drive him towards self-improvement. He believes that we must improve ourselves before we can help others. The Emperor transforms his ego-nature into a force for good. "Self-control is strength. Calmness is mastery. You have to get to a point where your mood doesn't shift based on the insignificant actions of someone else. Don't allow others to control the direction of your life. Don't allow your emotions to overpower your intelligence." – Morgan Freeman, American actor, director, and narrator

The Emperor tarot card's astrology influence is Jupiter conjunct with Mars. Below is a description of this energy aspect as it pertains to Sagittarius as well as its significance to the Emperor card.

Mars is the planet of action, individuality, courage, defending, discipline, willpower, ambition, passion, will to act, initiation, expressing anger, and black and white thinking. Mars represent secret enemies, fire, violence, competition, as well as accidents. Mars influences the decision and fighting ability with in us.

Jupiter and Mars are good friends in astrology. This is a very good conjunction because Mars is action and when it comes in with Jupiter it delivers a boost of energy enhancing a person with spiritual guidance and knowledge. The personality aspect is energetic, resourceful, pioneering, and adventurous.

Sagittarius is seen here very hopeful, optimistic, and lively in their approach to life. They like to know about life's mysteries and have a healthy curiosity for philosophy, religion, and spirituality.

They act in a very thoughtful way. They are not irrational in their action. It makes them have leadership qualities and fight for the right causes. They are guided by a higher knowledge and guidance. As Jupiter represents a teacher or guru, whenever Sagittarians teach a certain subject to their student, they do it with passion and full of energy.

In this conjunction, a person's good actions and good work will lead them to gain wealth, worldly comfort, and financial success.

Death:

The final card in this reading is the Death card, which represents the final stage of enlightenment for Sagittarius. This may, at first, appear odd to have Death as a card of enlightenment, but I assure you it is not the case. The first clue to understanding this card and how it coincides with this layout is by adding up the sum of all the Roman numerals of each of these tarot cards. The five cards leading up to the Death card are all numbered 4, which gives us $4 \times 5 = 20$. These five cards lead one along a path which evolves their awareness, exalting them to their final stage of enlightenment in the Death card, which is Roman numeral XIII (13). So, now we have the numbers $20 + 13 = 33$, which is the highest degree in Freemasonry and the highest level of enlightenment reached in the Hermetic Kabbalah. The number 33 is associated with the Christ, and Christ Consciousness. For instance, Jesus was 33 years old when he was crucified on the cross. That day of his death, Jesus was reunited with the Father. Jesus became one with the Father, sharing the same super conscious. Furthermore, there are 32 paths on the Kabbalah Tree of Life which lead one up the Jacob's ladder along the chakras of their kundalini. The elevated soul progresses past the 32nd path or branch and transcends up into the 33rd, which is the union with, 'at oneness with' the Divine, the Creator and spirit of all things. This connection to the Divine Intelligence, the World of Causes, is the apex of enlightenment.

Another clue is located on the black flag that Death is holding. This flag adorns the Tudor Rose which symbolizes the conclusion of the War of the Roses. This war was a long and bloody civil war between two feuding royal families who battled over the land and the control over the throne of England after the death of King Henry the V. As the war dragged on, the country's people grew tired and famished, and then, later on and closer to the end of the war, the people were hit by a plague. The royal families realized the inevitable demise of their country if they were to continue this war, which lead them to come to a compromise. The two feuding families decided to join forces equally, which was culminated with the marriage of these two royal families: the York's and the Lancaster's. This family feud stretched out for 32 years, between the years

1455-1487. Here, we see again another connection to the number 32, which is associated with the elevated soul's transcendence into the higher realm of Christ Consciousness. Kabbalist teach us that Jesus Christ died on the same day he was born, meaning his birthday. Therefore, he was 32 years old prior to the day of his crucifixion, thus transcending to the age of 33 years upon the day of his death. Christ died upon the cross, on his birthday, and then was immediately reunited with the Father. This 'reuniting' with God is associated with being 'born again.' This symbolism is portrayed in this card, where we see the Death knight returning to the Pope, meaning Father, thus Death has 're-u-knight-ed' with the Father. Worth mentioning here is that not until after the marriage which united the two royal families was the knight finally spiritually ready to reunite with the Father. (Uniting the two as one.)

The concept of time needed for one to become spiritually ready (aka spiritually cleansed) is encoded within the number 40. 40 is a very significant Kabbalistic number seen throughout the Torah, as well as the Tarot. You will notice that there are four Xs on the knight's horse's neck strap, which alternate between the four skulls. The skull is an obvious symbol for death, but can also represent death to things confined within the skull, such as the mind and its beliefs, referring more so to the death of one's fixed mindset and limiting beliefs. The timing and severity one must endure for spiritual cleansing is relative to each individual. The number 40 is associated with the time period for cleansing because 40 is the Hebrew gematria value for the letter Mem, meaning water, which encompasses the cleansing power that water provides. The four Xs on the horse's neck strap are Roman numeral's that represent a value of 10 each, which equals 40 when combined altogether.

The letter X is also the ancient Hebrew symbol for the Hebrew letter Tav, which was written as an X. Tav means truth, mark, sign of the cross. So, we see here on the horse's neck strap the symbolism of death on the cross, alluding to Jesus Christ's crucifixion. Soon after Jesus' death, the cross became a symbol for Jesus and has been used by Christians since the 2nd century. Another symbol for Christ is the fish. Consequently, the Hebrew letter assigned to the Death card is Nun, meaning fish. The spiritual aspects associated with fish directly relate to the spiritual concepts revealed to us metaphorically through Bible and Torah allegory containing the number 40. It's about the experience of having to endure challenges and overcoming obstacles, facing trials and tribulation, all in order for us to grow spiritually, and to become emotionally stronger. The Light within our soul desires a return back to the Source, just as the Source wishes to unite with us. It is our responsibility to cleanse our soul so we can draw ourselves closer to the Source, and we do this by shedding layers of our ego. We must elevate out of our body consciousness (ego) if we wish to return to the Source, soul consciousness. Each challenge and test we face in life are opportunities for us to overcome fear and doubts, thus shedding layers of ego and cleansing the shadow aspects of ourselves. Therefore, every obstacle that 'presents' itself to us is actually a 'present' from God which is concealed within an illusion of darkness. It is up to us to reveal the Light which is concealed within every trial and challenge we are dealt with. You will soon realize that every challenge you are confronted with turns out to be a blessing in disguise. Our souls are promised that they will (one day) be able to return to the Source. We are all able to feel the Source's ever present gravitational pull tugging at us each moment of our lives, as it attempts to draw us in closer. The Source wants us to maintain a constant connection with its Light, which is the source of love and happiness, and to one day return to it and become one with it again. This is God's promise to us, that we will return to Him, although it is up to us to earn our way back. This can be done by practices of meditation and by working on ourselves.

Jesus Christ's life is an example for us to follow if we wish to unite with the Higher-Self, be one with God the Father, which is obtained only after we experience an ego-death, which would lead us to feeling as if we had been 'born again.' This is also an example of the Hermetic Marriage, which is the idea of one's body consciousness (ego) leaving their physical body in order to transcend up into the realm of the Super Consciousness where it becomes one with the Higher-Self. The Hermetic Marriage is a coming together of the two polarities, the duality, which is ever present in all creation, appearing as positive and negative, masculine and feminine. According to the famous scholar, philosopher, and mystic Manly P. Hall, "Both positive and negative are opposites poles of one circuit. Spirit itself

487

knows no polarity, but manifests through polarity to the accomplishment of the Great Work. The Hermetic marriage is symbolic of the individual who has made himself right with all things, and (most of all) is true to himself and to his fellow men. Human relationships lead to divine relationships, and the unfolding soul builds ever more noble mansions as vehicles for its expression."

Allow me to share some biblical examples of the number 40 as it pertains to the life of Christ:

Jesus fasted "forty days and forty nights" in the Judean desert (Matthew 4:2, Mark 1:13, Luke 4:2).

On the 40th day of Jesus' fast in the desert the devil shows up to tempt Jesus while he is at his weakest, having fasted "forty days and forty nights." (Matthew 4:1-11) The temptation of Christ is an allegory for confronting one's ego, referred to by the Kabbalists as the Adversary.

Forty days was the period from the resurrection of Jesus to the ascension of Jesus (Acts 1:3).

Jesus, just days before his crucifixion, prophesied the total destruction of Jerusalem (Matthew 24:1-2, Mark 13:1-2). Forty years after his crucifixion in 30 A.D., the mighty Roman Empire destroyed the city of Jerusalem and burned its beloved temple to the ground.

Also worth mentioning is the story of Noah's flood where the Earth endured heavy rainfall for forty days and forty nights. As mentioned earlier, 40 is the gematria value of the letter Mem, meaning water. During the great flood the Earth experienced a baptism, otherwise known in Hebrew as a mikvah. A mikvah is a Jewish baptism where a person is fully immersed in water. The measurement of water was a minimum of 40 'seahs' (approximately 120 gallons) for a mikvah baptismal fount.

Another interesting thing to note, as we decode the symbols on this card, and reveal deeper meaning, is the hidden symbolism found within the Tudor Rose on the Death knight's flag. You will notice the rose has ten petals and five leaves, which gives you the number 15. With further examination, you will find that there are exactly 30 seeds in the center of the rose.This gives us the numbers 30 and 15, which added together is 45. 45 is a significant number found throughout the tarot, as well as in planetary magic. For instance, 45 is the sum of all the numbers in the 3×3 magic square of Saturn. Throughout the tarot, Saturn's planetary influence is represented by the color black, hence the black Tudor Rose flag and the black armor worn by the Death knight. Saturn is known to be the planet associated with death, and depicted in modern times as the Grim Reaper. Saturn influences past-life karmic judgements, as well as being the lord of time, which are both themes portrayed in the Death card.

Pictured here is Saturn's magic square. It is a 3×3 square that has 3 rows with numbers 1-9. Each row, either going down, across, or diagonal equals a constant sum of 15. The total sum of all the numbers in the square from 1-9 is 45 (1+2+3+4+5+6+7+8+9 = 45).

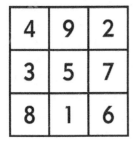 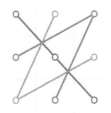 

Concealed within Saturn's magic square is the spirit of Saturn sigil aka the Seal of Zazel. Planetary seals are used to seal in the planet's positive traits while at the same time acts as a protection from any of the planet's negative influence. Saturn is a maleficent planet that influences poverty, oppression, karmic-baggage, and has a slowing down effect on all things in general. The Seal of Zazel acts as protection from Saturn's maleficent influence, allowing one to draw down desire and prosperity without the restriction of time or any harsh judgements attached. And on a further note, this seal acts as a portal into the astral dimension, which we are able to access through meditation practices and by opening our third eye. By way of meditation, one is able to strengthen the third eye, which is essentially tapping into and connecting with Christ Consciousness, and access this portal into the higher dimensions. Obtaining enlightenment, Christ Consciousness, is the key that opens the portal door. Interesting to note here is that the Seal of Zazel looks similar to a key hole, or an eye.

The Hebrew gematria value for the name Zazel is 45. Zazel is known as the spirit of Saturn. Agiel is known as the intelligence of Saturn, and also has a gematria value of 45. 45+45 = 90, which is the value of the Hebrew letter Tzaddi, meaning fish hook. A Tzaddik, meaning righteous one, refers to someone who is a pure channel of Light who remains in a constant communication with the Source. Moses was considered a Tzaddik. A Tzaddik is said to always be in a conscious state of meditation. The Tzaddik dips his fish hook into the astral waters and receives godly insights and divine inspiration needed for him to manifest prosperity to ultimately enrich his life and the lives of others. Saturn is the darkest of the planets, but it is in the darkest of places that we can reveal the most Light.

It takes time for one to completely transform their ego-nature and reach a 'Tzaddik' level of spiritual awareness. Although, those lucky ones born under the zodiac sign of Sagittarius (or Pisces) are blessed with the birthright from Jupiter which grants them with a natural gift of 6th sense consciousness.

Worth bringing up again is the Hebrew letter Nun, which is assigned to this card. As mentioned earlier, Nun means fish, and the spiritual aspects of this letter share much significance with the Death card. The fish swims freely in the astral realm, surrendering to the organic flow of nature which inevitably leads them to enlightenment. The fish drifts through the sea of emotions—feeling, absorbing, observing and learning. They learn about themselves by observing others. The fish develops empathy for others, and is then able to understand how his words and past behaviors affected others. The fish is often depicted as swimming in this sea of emotions throughout the tarot. Each instance corresponds to the emotional aspect of someone who has had to go through a challenging experience that tests the way they react under times of heavy stress. Later in life, these emotional outbursts come back and haunt us.

Life has a way of resurfacing these unresolved issues, and once again we are faced with the similar challenge. This is life's way of teaching us karmic lessons. We will continue to be faced with similar challenges until we finally correct our unruly behaviors. These challenges and obstacles we are confronted with are opportunities to grow and to build upon our character, by practicing empathy and compassion towards others is how we mature, and evolve into a Tzaddik. The empathy gained is the power to opening up your heart, and when your heart is open you connect to your inner Sun, or Son, and it is through your Son that you connect to the Super Consciousness of the Father—obtaining Christ Consciousness. Jesus said that the only way to the Father was through him. Jesus represents the sacred heart, and the Father is the Source, the Super Conscious. In order to open up your heart, you need to first learn how to forgive others, but most importantly you must learn how to forgive yourself. This is the reason the Death knight is approaching the Pope (Father); Death is asking for forgiveness.

Do you notice the shape of the Pope's hat, and how it resembles the head of a fish? This is the hat worn by the half man, half fish god named Dagon. Dagon was one of the 70 sons of the God El, who is also associated with being Saturn. 70 is the gematria value for the Hebrew word sod, meaning secret. 70 is also the numerical value of the letter Ayin, meaning eye, to see. Now let's take a closer look at the Tudor Rose on the Death knight's black flag. Do you notice how the rose's five leaves form an inverted pentagram? This is the exact style of pentagram depicted on the Devil card, which just so happens to be located directly over the Devil's third eye. This pentagram connection that these two cards share links the two cards to the planet Saturn. Both cards share positive and negative aspects of the planet's influence. Furthermore, these card's pentagrams, which share the same shape and style, are formed within Saturn's magic square.

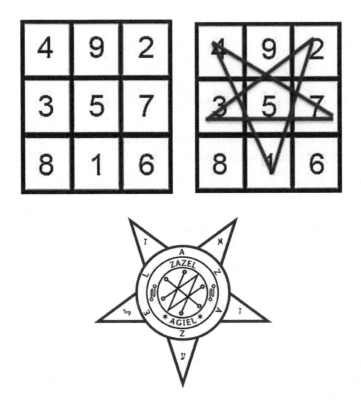

The inverted pentagram represents the drawing down of desire from the astral world and manifesting it in the material world; drawing down the macrocosm into the microcosm, and essentially creating something from nothing. This concept is similar to the Kabbalists' idea of drawing down the Light into the vessel.

We now know that the Hebrew letter assigned to the Devil card is Ayin, meaning eye, and has the gematria value of 70. And as mentioned earlier, 70 is also the gematria value of the word sod, meaning secret. So, we now have here, with all these clues, a much richer understanding of the Death card. This knowledge is power, and this knowledge is truth.

Likewise, truth is power. We see now, within this card's symbols, that the Death knight is asking the Pope for forgiveness in order for the Pope to offer up his blessing, which is to grant the Death knight with the knowledge of the Pope's secret, which is how to access the portal of Zazel.

The Pope will show mercy unto the knight and offer him up his blessing. Therefore, the Death knight will be forgiven of all his past transgressions. Death has proven himself worthy and spiritually clean after he had swum in the sea of emotions, where he was forced to feel, empathize, and had to resolve past mistakes. He has taken responsibility for his past behaviors. He has come to the realization that we are unable to control others. And he realizes that this world is chaotic, and bad things happen to good people. We cannot control the things that happen to us, the only thing we can control is how we react to the things that happen.

The Death knight receives his blessing of truth. This new truth will crush his old and limiting beliefs. This new truth will set him free. He has become like the fish. And what happens when you try to hold onto and control a fish within your grasp? It immediately slips away and out from your hands. The Death knight will no longer be controlled by his limiting beliefs and a fixed mindset. He will be free like the fish, and explore and expand his mind and open up his heart to new possibilities. The Pope grants him passage through the two pillars, located in the card's background. The knight crosses over into the world of the unknown, leaving the past he once knew behind him. He continues along the path, facing the rising sun, which marks the dawning of a new day.

The knight returning to the sun is symbolic of the Christ returning to the Father, the Source, where he unites with the higher level of enlightenment. This is symbolic of the night dying as the morning sun rises and diminishes the darkness.

The knight will begin a new adventure into a new and unknown territory as a reborn soul.

As you focus on unconditional love, for all people around you, the dark forces within are cast out. As you meditate on these cards, think to yourself, in the past, I have felt hatred for certain people. Now, as I picture those people in my mind, I feel only love. Light washes over them, and me, and I recognize the common thread that we share —the spark of the Creator. My heart opens as I wish them joy and fulfillment, peace and greater understanding.

Chapter 22, Section 10: Capricorn

Astrological House #10 is Capricorn, ruled by Saturn. In Kabbalah, Saturn is associated with the sefirah Binah, the 3rd sefirah on the Tree of Life. Binah, meaning understanding.

Therefore Capricorn, ruled by Saturn, connects to Binah, the 3rd sefirah, which is why the Path to Enlightenment layout involves all the #3 tarot cards and all cards associated with the number 3. And they are, in order from least to greatest value: the 3 of Wands, 3 of Cups, 3 of Swords, 3 of Pentacles, the Empress, and the Hanged Man. The path starts from the left and ends on the right—the final card being the Hanged Man.

Capricorns are known to be the 'odd balls' of the Zodiac. Although, they are very intelligent and are considered experts in whatever they choose to dive into, field of study or certain work of science fiction. They are the bookworms, and thus very knowledgeable and very powerful.

They are fiercely loyal in their relationships. They remember even the smallest details of everyone they meet. Being that they are the most down-to-earth people, their first instinct about someone is usually right. Capricorns can smell a fake from a mile away. They are the human lie detectors. Be careful of how you treat a Capricorn, because they will never allow others to treat them poorly. They speak fluent sarcasm and are allergic to stupidity. They are goal-oriented and have very high standards. They are independent and hard-working, ambitious people. They are often successful.

A scary trait of theirs is their lack of emotions for people. And also, how they tend to all of a sudden get triggered into a grumpy mood.

Capricorn needs to remember that goals are important, but the people in our lives are more valuable than anything we can achieve. The energy of Capricorn can draw our attention away from the needs of others and make vulnerability uncomfortable. Put to-do's aside and spend some time-sharing energy and compassion. Focus on the following things: Break the rules. Express yourself. Open up to intimacy. Appreciate what you have. Have humility.

Let's begin Capricorn's path to enlightenment by starting with the 3 of Wands card.

3 of Wands:

The suit of Wands reveals specific timing significances. Wands are similar to trees and they relate to agriculture. The god of agriculture is Saturn, also known as the lord of time, who also happens to rule over Capricorn. Thereby, counting the branches on the wands will reveal an aspect of timing significance portrayed in the card's illustration. For instance, there are 9 branches on the 3 wands in this card. The number 9 corresponds with the 9th sefirah on the Tree of Life Yesod. Yesod unveils the hidden and unseen. It brings truth into light. And reveals light outof the darkness. The brightest light can be revealed in the darkest of places.

The man in this card is seen looking out into an empty field. He sees potential. He sees what others cannot. He holds his grip around a singled-out wand, which has 3 branches on it. Three of things or like-objects grouped together symbolize and connect to the sefirah Binah, meaning understanding. Coincidentally, Binah is ruled by Saturn. This man's right hand gripping this particular wand symbolizes that he is sharing/giving and putting forth his understanding, having understood one idea from another idea. This man is wearing a white focus sash around his head, alluding to this concept of him focusing mentally on his new understandings. He realizes on a soul level that he has been guided by a higher power, leadinghim to where he is supposed to be, thus he feels he is in the right place at the right time. He is now able to see the big picture. Every decision he has made thus far in life has led him to this point of understanding, and everything seemed to have worked out for a reason. This man is focusing on gratitude. The bright yellow background shows us that this man will be blessed with a bright future.

Deserts throughout the tarot represent the ego. There is no life in the desert, and it represents a place of complacency. This man is looking out into the desert now, and he is overcome with fear, doubt and anxiety. These are healthy emotions to have, especially when you have been faced with similar situations in the past. This man arrives at a similar situation as before, but now with a new understanding of who he is and who he has become. He is spiritually stronger now. He does not start this journey through the desert as a newbie or by doing so from scratch, he is now starting from experience.

Capricorns are very down-to-earth, they see the truth, they see the dirt and the realness, their first instinct about someone is usually right. They remember even the smallest of details of everyone they meet. This aspect of their personality is applied when meeting new friends, colleagues, and when starting a new relationship. This is also how Capricorns approach their businesses and careers. They are able to see things for their real worth, as well as see their potential. Capricorns must learn to trust their own instincts based on their past experience.

While others may call you crazy, and are unable to share your vision, you will have the gift of foresight and be able to see the big picture.

As you contemplate deeply on this card, you will notice the three sailboats floating on the desert sand just as if they were drifting in the sea. The man in this card is seen looking out into the 'sea' of possibilities.

3 of Cups:

This card depicts three women celebrating the harvest. Their hard work has paid off and now it is time to rejoice. It's a risky business, agriculture, with so many different factors that can cause your crop to either flourish or go to ruin. You have to learn how to plan ahead and be prepared for any contingency. Thus, when you do have a successful harvest, it is indeed a time to be grateful. In the Middle-Ages, surviving a harvest meant you would survive through the winter, and therefore live another year; survive another season.

This card portrays a time to be grateful for what you have. It is good to plan things out, but not to allow your plans to get in the way of your relationships. It truly is about the journey, and not the destination. That is the path to self-discovery. The people we allow into our lives shape who we are. We feed off of and absorb their energy. The bond between two people can be like the bond a farmer has with his crop, so much time and energy are devoted to making sure that crop will grow and last another season. It is never guaranteed that the relationship will last, and ultimately it is not the point, it is more so about the experience. Be grateful for the things you have now, in the time being, and don't worry about how it will all turn out. Live life in the present. Every day is a gift, that is why it is called the present. Start practicing gratitude as if it were a religion.

3 of Swords:

The 3 of Swords' esoteric label is 'The Lord of Sorrow'. This card depicts 3 swords piercing a heart. Gray clouds, representing wisdom, rain down in the background, thus portraying a life-lesson being experienced here. Swords represent thoughts, and these thoughts are penetrating the heart, and coming to a logical conclusion of one's feelings, and grasping the reality of the heartbreak, or the emotions endured.

No need to suffer over mistakes. We all make mistakes. This is why pencils have erasers. If you erase all the mistakes of your past, you would also erase all of the wisdom of your present. Remember the lesson, not the disappointment.

This card is mostly about your inner state. The 3 of Swords isn't about a heartbreak between two people, rather it's about a heartbreak that takes place within the soul. Your mind, your own mentally conjured, ego-based dreams, are at odds with your heart's desires. You may be spending way too much energy trying to silence your heart. You may be up in arms, fighting to crush your emotions, your true essence, and your soulful dreams. It might have become so automatic that now you don't even realize just how silent your heart has been. You may not be doing the work that you need to for yourself and are at risk of becoming stuck in your sorrow and pain. However, understanding what caused the pain, accepting it and working through the pain can help you recover.

The storm depicted here will eventually pass. And as the old adage goes, 'the greater the storm, the brighter the rainbow.'

"The measure of intelligence is the ability to change." - Albert Einstein

3 of Pentacles:
The Three of Pentacles is often associated with planning, blueprints and teamwork. We see that as these three people in the card lend each other their unique energy, they are able to create something together. This is the type of growth that can only come from collaboration. There are times when you need to go your own way and do your own thing, but the 3 of Pentacles shows that there are also times when it is better to rely on external support. Accepting that kind of support allows you to be a part of something greater than yourself.

This card speaks of the tangible progress that can be when we use our unique skills and draw upon the unique skills of others. Progress doesn't usually happen by accident. Progress happens when we actively engage in building, growing and strengthening. You can see this in how knowledge has developed over the course of time: one person comes up with a concept, someone else builds upon it, and someone else steers that existing foundation in a new direction. Such is the course of creation.

Kabbalistic knowledge continues to evolve, in medieval times such esoteric wisdom was typically passed along by word of mouth, done so in secret just as is portrayed here in this card. Depicted here are three people who are meeting secretly in a dark church. The priest and the maiden seek out the 'light-worker' in search of obtaining higher wisdom. The light-worker stands on the table and shines his flashlight onto the couple's manuscript, which reveals to them the concealed Kabbalah hidden within the scriptures. This is what the light-worker brings to the table, so to speak, revealing esoteric knowledge that will be a benefit to others. The word kabbalah means 'to receive', and the couple is depicted here as receiving the Light of Kabbalah in the darkness (ignorance).   Specifically, the Light of Kabbalah concealed within the scriptures. With closer examination, you will notice that the couple's manuscript has pictured on it the very same room they are standing in. The light-worker opens their eyes to this new revelation, that they have always carried within them the answers to all the mysteries they seek, they had the answers all along and didn't need to come to the church in order to learn these deeper spiritual mysteries. They always had the answers within.

The light-worker reveals to them the deeper Kabbalistic meanings concealed within the biblical stories, esoterically encoded with numbers and astrology, told in rich allegory. In the aiding of opening up this couple's eyes to seeing the hidden truth, the light-worker is able to learn from them as well. Now that their eyes are open, the priest and the maiden can both help the light-worker see from their perspective what spiritual understandings they are able to bring to the table. When we help others, we help ourselves. What goes around comes around. As a group of like-minded light-workers, we are able to collaborate and evolve the wisdom of Kabbalah further into a new age of understanding.

The Empress:
Being assigned to Roman numeral III, the Empress corresponds with the energy influence of the 3rd sefirah Binah, who is considered the female aspect of the Tree of Life. Binah births desire concocted from the upper World of Atziluth and delivers it down into the lower Worlds where that desire eventually manifests itself in Malchut. Binah culminates brilliant ideas into form. Binah is seen to take the

raw force of Chokmah, and channel it into the various forms of creation. For example, in a car, you have the fuel and an engine. While Chokmah is the fuel, pure energy, Binah is the engine, pure receptivity. Either one without the other is useless. Binah is intuitive understanding, or contemplation. It is likened to a 'palace of mirrors' that reflects the pure point of light of Chokmah, wisdom, increasing and multiplying it in an infinite variety of ways. In this sense, it is the 'quarry', which is carved out by the light of wisdom. It is the womb, which gives shape to the Spirit of God. On a psychological level, Binah is processed wisdom, also known as deductive reasoning. It is understanding one idea from another idea. While Chokmah is intellect that does not emanate from the rational process, Binah is the rational process that is innate in the person which works to develop an idea fully.

The Empress, like Binah, is all about giving birth to ideas. Likewise, Capricorn should learn to act on their inspiration, especially if a particular idea has had time to develop and grow in your mind. Now is the time to act and to stop waiting. The only thing holding you back from your prosperity is you.

Is there a particular thing for which you are passionate and don't tell everyone about, perhaps only your closest friends? Something you have always done since childhood that makes you happy? It is this type of thing that you need to share with the world. Whatever it is that brings you happiness is sure to bring someone else happiness as well; no matter how silly or lame it might seem. You may think to yourself that there is no way to make money from it—there isn't a large enough audience. But you will find that the better the niche, the better chance you have of making a profit. It is now time to remove all doubt and let go of any worries you may have about the future outcome. It is prime time to act and give birth to your 'child,' which can refer to a business venture you may have been brainstorming, as well as some niche hobby that you rarely share with anyone.

All you need to do now is take the first step—with a little effort you will soon attract the prosperity you seek, and be blessed with a brighter and more financially secure future. Just know that you will be successful at whatever you set out to do; you will reap what you sow.

The Empress as Binah is the feminine aspect of God, and gives birth to all things, including intuitive understanding through contemplation—literally giving birth to the whole of creation, and provides the supernal womb. Do you notice that the Empress is pregnant? This is why she is wearing a loose-fitting gown and is seen here sitting on comfy pillows. There are exactly 40 pomegranates on her gown. The number 40 is significant here because a fetus is inside a mother's womb for 40 weeks before its birth. In the background of the card is a canal/stream. This represents a birth canal.

There are also the six-pointed stars of the Empress's crown totaling, exactly 12, six-pointed stars: 12×6 = 72, and 72 is the Kabbalistic number relating to miracle making—as in the 'miracle' of birth. According to the Kabbalists, Moses engraved the 72 Names on his staff, which was used to part the Red Sea—one of the greatest miracles performed in the Torah.

The Empress is depicted in the card holding onto a golden sceptre in her right hand, which represents her authority and control over the world aka her reality. She has the final say on when it is time to birth something new. This concept of control is symbolized by the wheat crop at the bottom of the card. The Empress has dominion over when it is time to reap the harvest. She planted the seeds and nurtured the crop; therefore, she says when it is time to cut and gather it.

We now look at one more clue, which is the heart symbol placed at the Empress's side with the astrological symbol for Venus on it. In Greek mythology, Venus is Saturn's daughter, and the heart represents that Saturn loves his daughter. However, the heart is colored gray, which always represents wisdom, thus the Venus symbol being inside a gray heart represents that Saturn (the Empress as Binah) expresses a tough-love towards her daughter, Venus. Remember the 40 pomegranates on the Empress's gown? Pomegranates, throughout the tarot, are a symbol for memory. Pomegranate juice is actually given to Alzheimer's patients to help improve their memory. So, this is another clue that the Empress

(Saturn as Binah) does not freely give love unconditionally to her daughter. The Empress remembers the past. She may forgive but will never forget, and she judges accordingly. She will not enable Venus or anyone for that matter; she cares too much to spoil them. Furthermore, the Empress does not repeat mistakes. She remembers her mistakes and learns from them, and is considered a nurturer when it comes to relationships, due to the way she treats her business and family, as well as herself.

Arriving to this point in your life takes a lot of hard work and discipline. But, as the old adage goes, when you love what you do, it doesn't feel like work. The Empress (metaphorically) shares her pomegranates with the world—pomegranates symbolizing memory. The word memory has its etymology stemmed in Jewish meanings, it is a combination of two words: Mem, meaning water, and Ori, meaning light. Thus, the Empress is portrayed as carrying within her womb Liquid Light. She manifests prosperity by sharing her Light with the world. "When your dreams are based on how you can improve the lives of others, the whole universe conspires to make your dreams come true." - Karen Berg, founder of The Kabbalah Centre

All number 3 cards are associated with Binah, ruled by Saturn. Saturn is the god of the harvest and agriculture, as well as the lord of time. Saturn is the ruling planet for both Capricorn and Aquarius. Aquarius is symbolized by the water bearer, and babies are birthed out of the womb from their mother's water. Capricorn is the hard-worker who tends to the field, putting their hands into the creation of things and improving life for the betterment of others.

So, here we have the clues that lead us to understand that the Empress is a hard worker and she wishes to improve her life as well as the lives of others around her by creating prosperity for all people and things she is involved in—whether it be business, career, charitable work, friends or family. She is the one in control of her prosperity, as well as her destiny.

When it comes to business and relationships, the Empress approaches these things like a Capricorn would attend to a wheat crop throughout the year; nurturing it, looking after it, plowing the field, watering the crops, and planting the seeds during the appropriate times of the year. All this in total control—knowing when to either hold back or when to take action depending on the current season's circumstances, which is a gradual process. Only after years of practice and experimentation with the field does the Capricorn know what appropriate actions and daily regimens to partake in, and at the correct times of the year.

The Empress only wants the best for her daughter, Venus, and she wishes to one day show her off and be proud of her. This particular concept of a child refers to the development process of anything being taken from its seed level and growing it into something big, such as when one starts with a simple idea and turns it into something that generates a stream of income.

The Empress knows that things take time, attention, and effort; it is a nurturing process. Like the developing fetus in the womb during pregnancy as it's nurtured with a mother's sustenance throughout its 40-week birthing process, the fetus is readying itself to be strong enough to enter the world; and this creation of life is a miracle. The newborn is full of potential and carries within it the power to change the world—hopefully for the better.

The Hanged Man:
The Hanged Man card is assigned to the Hebrew letter Mem, meaning water. Spiritually, Mem relates to the cleansing attribute of water, and corresponds to the time needed for spiritual cleansing. By submerging ourselves in water it offers us a bath or baptism, both of which are proactive and relaxing. While on the other hand, if we were to stand underneath a large waterfall we would get pummeled with water. Although, after some time spent underneath the heavy downpour of water, we would become like the sharp rocks at the base of the waterfall that eventually become smoothed out over time by enduring the water's punishment. Slowly but surely, just as the rocks, we too would become well-rounded individuals. The Hanged Man portrays this particular aspect of judgement, as well as the accepting of it, all the while realizing we must surrender and then endure the things we cannot change—that we cannot control. This concept agrees with the

Serenity Prayer written by the American theologian Reinhold Niebuhr (1892–1971). It is commonly quoted as: "God, grant me the serenity to accept the things I cannot change, courage to change the things I can, and wisdom to know the difference."

Below is a later and longer version published by Niebuhr, which truly sums up the emotion encompassed within the Hanged Man card:

God, give me grace to accept with serenity the things that cannot be changed, Courage to change the things which should be changed, and the Wisdom to distinguish the one from the other.

Living one day at a time, Enjoying one moment at a time, Accepting hardship as a pathway to peace, Taking, as Jesus did, This sinful world as it is, Not as I would have it,
Trusting that You will make all things right, If I surrender to Your will,
So that I may be reasonably happy in this life,
And supremely happy with You forever in the next.

Amen.

The Hanged Man card originally depicted Judas Iscariot hanging upside down as a form of punishment after having turned in Jesus to the Romans. Judas was paid with 30 silver coins. Early versions of this card depict Judas holding onto these bags of coins in his hands as he hanged there vulnerable. The number 30 is significant here, because it is the number of years relating to the Saturn Return, a time in one's life when they are faced with judgment/karma owed to them. Being hanged upside down was a cruel form of punishment, where you would hang helpless, unable to move and were susceptible to the town's people spitting on you or hurling rocks towards you. You were forced to accept your fate, having to surrender and endure the torture.

The Hanged Man card depicts an image of a man being hanged upside-down by one ankle. This method of hanging was a common punishment at the time for traitors in Italy. However, the solemn expression on his face traditionally suggests that he is there by his own accord, and the card is meant to represent self-sacrifice more so than it does corporal punishment or criminality. In other interpretations, The Hanged Man is a depiction of the Norse god Odin, who suspended himself from a tree in order to gain knowledge. There is also the Christian interpretation (mentioned earlier) that portrays Judas, and included the bags of silver in his hands.

On the Kabbalah Tree of Life, the Hanged Man card hangs on the branch that connects Hod with Gevurah, which encompasses the concept of 'be careful what you wish for.' Once we begin taking the appropriate actions towards manifesting a specific goal is when life begins to throw obstacles and challenges in our way. We experience this restriction as soon as we take the first step with the intention to transform our dreams into reality. God wants to give us everything we desire, but He gives us our desires wrapped in filthy ego-soaked packages. It is then our responsibility to unwrap these dark packages and unveil the Light concealed within them. God always grants our wishes, but we must earn them first in order to receive. We must endure challenges, overcome obstacles, and deal with everyday frustrations and annoyances as we work towards earning those particular wishes. It is crucial to remain focused on the end result. Romanticize the idea or concept, and thus the happy thought which embodies your wish in its manifested state. You must learn to utilize analytical problem-solving skills to overcome the day-to-day challenges you will be faced with. Endure to the end by focalizing your mind on the prize, and on the fulfillment you will attain. Do not focus on what you will have to give up, instead fantasize on what you will gain. Most times, it is the 'why' that is so important to keep focused on. The reason why we get up every day and do what needs to be done in order to reach our goal is what truly motivates us. What is your 'why'? For some, it's simply to be free.

As we dive deeper into understanding the symbolism found on the Hanged Man card, you will notice the tree the man hangs from is shaped like the letter T, which is the Hebrew letter Tav, meaning cross, mark, sign of the cross. Ancient forms of the letter Tav were written like an X, as in "X marks the spot"—Tav meaning mark. Trees throughout the Tarot always represent Saturn's influence in some way, and Tav just so happens to be attributed to Saturn.

Moreover, Saturn is the god of agriculture, and as a consequence, trees which are agriculturally related symbolize Saturn, and particularly in this case reflect the aspect of Saturn's judgment. Just as a martyr who sacrifices themselves for a good cause, just like Jesus Christ who was crucified on the cross. When Jesus died on the cross, he was reunited with the Father, Yahweh, and they were one. This is significant, because Yahweh is associated with Saturn.

Looking further into the symbolism, you will count 37 rays surrounding the Hanged Man's head. This includes the bright aura rays as well as the fiery tips of the man's hair. The number 37 is significant here, it being the value of Chokmah, meaning wisdom, and therefore we are safe to assume that he is focusing on a brilliant idea. Depicted here is his happy thought that keeps him going, offers him hope, it represents his 'why' and is his reason for pursuing his goal—and ultimately, his life-purpose.

When breaking down the 37 total rays into two groups, we find that there are 32 bright rays that surround the man's head and then there are the 5 points of his fiery hair. The number 32 represents the elevated soul, and the number 5 shares attributes with Gevurah, which relates to matters of the ego, and thus a healthy drive and ambition that is attributed to being goal oriented.

Another thing to mention is this man's uniquely odd pose. The man is pictured here with his feet crossed and has his arms held behind his back. This peculiar stance is actually the alchemical sign for Sulfur, albeit upside down. Metaphorically speaking, and also how it pertains to spiritual Alchemy, Sulfur coincides with the human soul.

The chart below outlines the three major alchemical symbols and their meanings. Sulfur is found at the top of the chart.

	Sulfur Soul Consciousness Oil
	Mercury Spirit Mind Liqour
	Salt Body Structured thought Alkaline Salt

As mentioned, the Hanged Man card is assigned to the letter Mem, meaning water, referring to the healing and cleansing aspect of water. Mem has a numerical value of 40, which is significant throughout the Bible, and always corresponds with a time of cleansing and spiritual growth. For instance, the Jewish people escaped slavery in Egypt after asking God for freedom. God promised them a land filled with milk and honey where they could live and prosper freely in peace, and have the opportunity to flourish as a nation—reaching their full potential. They did eventually reach their promised land, but God made it to where they had to 'earn' it first. The Jewish people were forced to wonder the desert for 40 years, where they were faced with a series of tests, challenges, and had to overcome many obstacles. With the many frustrations came times of uncertainty, leading them to lose hope and test their faith in God. Although, after having to endure such hardships, the Jewish people were eventually allowed to settle in the promised land. This 40-year period elicited for them a means to grow spiritually stronger. This is just one example, for there are many other instances where the number 40 shows up in the Bible. Specifically, in the story of Noah's flood which lasted for 40 days and 40 nights, or when Moses climbed up Mount Sinai to retrieve the ten commandments for a period of 40 days and 40 nights. The number 40 embodies the concept of the transformation process. Whenever you feel crushed, under pressure, pressed, or in darkness, you're in a powerful place of transformation. For example, grapes must be crushed to make wine, diamonds form under pressure, olives are pressed to release oil, and seeds grow in darkness.

Just as the men portrayed in these biblical allegories, Capricorns also tend to have issues dealing with authoritative fathers, who are hard on their children. Noah, Abraham and Moses were all tested of their willingness to submit to God's (the father in heaven) authority. In most instances, as a Capricorn your father was a nitpicky authoritarian that meddled with all aspects of your life.

For the most past of your childhood, you were not to be exposed to anything they disagreed with and you were very sheltered. Your teen years were weird and awkward since the way they brought you up made them the only person that was there and had any effect on you.

Having to deal with these Capricorn father issues rendered you incapable of holding social interaction and lacking real knowledge of the world. You emerged in your young adult years as a child again, as if you truly started to live from that moment when you left your father behind. Metaphorically, this scenario is portrayed in the story of Jesus Christ who died on the cross and then was reunited as one with the father in heaven. After which, Jesus no longer was under His father's authoritarian rule; they were one, and thus equal.

As stated, the tree the Hanged Man dangles from symbolizes the Hebrew letter Tav, meaning truth and mark, as in leaving your mark of truth behind for others to follow in your footsteps. The idea is for you to pass on the torch and leave your legacy behind for the generations to come. Taking this a step further, the World card, assigned to the letter Tav, is about raising the bar and setting the new standard, and then passing on the torch to others who will follow in your example. The World card as well as the letter Tav refer to leaving something behind better than when you found it. The World card is the last and final card in the deck, referring to the end of a phase, or end of the world. Biblically speaking, the end of the world is called the apocalypse, which literally means 'the uncovering', and alludes to the uncovering of hidden (or forgotten) truths.

Once these truths are revealed it sets the new standard, and establishes a new set of rules, which evolve the world for the better. Thus, evolving the world into a new era—one of higher vibration and enlightenment.

Consequently, as a parent you'll be precise and attentive. You remember a lot about your kids, and you give them all that they need physically and emotionally. Because of the way you were brought up, you can get overly protective and paranoid over their safety and who they're with. Although you can be suffocating to them, no one can deny that you raised your children to be well educated and wholesome people.

The Hanged Man advises you to make large sacrifices. You may have to give up on something that you wanted, or you need to do something huge for another person.

The Hanged Man is in limbo and is caught between two choices. While upside-down, he gains insight into his situation. He may feel as though he has been wrongly accused and is now paying for karma he doesn't deserve. Through self-reflection, he determines if he has control of his situation or if he is being punished.

The key to this card is that the Hanged Man must resign to his fate. He needs to surrender. If he adds stress to himself now, he could make his situation worse. If he wants to get off the tree, he has to do so carefully without getting more tangled.

As you meditate on these cards, think to yourself, I want to bring all future and existing relationships to the level of soulmate. I want to relate to all those around me on this heightened spiritual plane, and bring greater Light into my life.

Chapter 22, Section 11: Aquarius

Astrological House #11 isAquarius. While Capricorn's path conveys a desire to improve one's self, and reach a higher sense of spiritual awareness, Aquarius is already born with this higher level of awareness and they proudly embrace it. Because of this, Aquarius devotes their life to help and improve the lives of others. As an Aquarian, you empathize with the world and its many problems— and you set out to change them. You find ways of breaking through social norms or the status quo, and you break down barriers that fragment us further away from each other. You seek ways of bringing people together as one, in an attempt to create a utopia, and thereby trying to return the planet back to its original state—a paradise just as the world was in the garden of Eden. Aquarius has high hopes of evolving the world into the next golden age; a new era that is no longer governed by the ego and where the people are 'at one' with each other—by casting judgements aside we eliminate hate for no reason, we begin to see each other on a soul level, which unites us together as one. In addition to this, when we become one with nature, we will experience a world sustained with love and peace.

Aquarius corresponds to the 11th house. This house reveals what we want in the highest sense. More so, the way the eleventh house manifests, is determined by the energies of the 10th house. As our capacity to impact change grows in the tenth house, so do our ambitions in the eleventh house. The 11th house represents the universal nature of the world—the need to endure and stand tall amidst the great pressures of life, which is brought over from the 10th house, and the yearning for ultimate transformations awaiting them in the 12th house.

The 11th House of Aquarius is considered to be a house of profit, wealth and honor. Thus, this house indicates the profits we will make during different phases of our life. But it is not just about personal ambition—it indicates our attitude towards society and the concept of groupadvantage.

The 11th house also presides over the aspect of pleasure. After the personal aspirations have been realized, Aquarius devotes time towards the permanent bonding of friendship. The desire to attend reunions is indicated by the eleventh house. The reason for analyzing the aspects of this house is to understand the type of emotional attachments you are likely to have. The 11th house will encompass Aquarian influences ruling friendship, teamwork, networking, and humanitarian pursuits. This house also represents our collective goals and aspirations for the betterment of humanity.

And yet, the energy of Aquarius can make it seem that we need to travel the road alone. Originality is a gift, yet there is much to be learned from the experiences and ideas of others. Reach out and include others in the process. Together, we can make great strides. Strive to be a team player. Know that your individuality is a strength, although you must let others shine, too. Embrace change. Connect to your community.

The path to enlightenment for Aquarius includes all the same cards as Capricorn, with the addition of the World card added to the end of its path. The World card comes as an award given to Aquarius after they complete their spiritual journey at the end of the soul cycle, one full lap around the Zodiac wheel, which can be considered as a graduation where they earn their spiritual diploma. As a soul traverses around the Zodiac wheel, and with each new reincarnation, it progresses from the 1st house to the 11th and within each new lifetime the soul elevates or upgrades its level of spiritual awareness. Each new lifetime experienced in a new house connects one closer to their true spiritual-nature—they slowly wake up to the fact that they are a soul-being having a human (physical) experience. Once an Aquarius reaches the end of their path, they will receive the Laurel wreath depicted in the World card. Laurel wreaths are typically given to winning horses of a race. This wreath can also represent the serpent eating its own tail, which symbolizes the end of a cycle, and can allude to the beginning of a new cycle once the current one ends.

Also worth mentioning are the Four Faces of God located at each corner of the World card. These correspond to the Four Faces Ezekiel saw in his vision as he was delivered up into heaven. This reflects upon the idea presented here of ascension, and after having graduated from the earthly existence the Aquarius is now rewarded, blessed and is lifted up from this world where they become 'at one' with God the Creator. Notice how the wreath is shaped in a circle as if it were the letter O, as in Omega.

God considered Himself to be both the Alpha and the Omega, the first and the last; the beginning and the end. Therefore, the O in Omega is represented here in the World card's circular wreath. The concept of Alpha and Omega is present in the Major Arcana, whereas the Magician is attributed to the Alpha and the World coincides with Omega. For instance, the Magician's body forms the letter Aleph, (the first letter in the alphabet), with one arm raised and the other pointing down. Like the Aleph, the Magician represents the beginning of creation, drawing down the desire into the material world. Therefore, the first of the Majors, Roman numeral I, is the Magician, linked to the Aleph/Alpha, and the last card in the Majors, Roman numeral XXI, is the World, which corresponds with the Omega.

Taking this one step further, the Fool card is assigned to the Hebrew letter Aleph, and he is also assigned to the number zero, which looks like an O, as in Omega. Thus, the Fool embodies the concept of Alpha and Omega as well. And because of this, the Fool can show up at different points of the tarot's timeline, either at the beginning or at the end. Referring back to the serpent eating its own tail (Ouroboros) concept, the Fool can be placed directly after the World card, and would represent the new cycle beginning just after the current one ends.

The reincarnation cycle is a continuous loop. When a soul is born into a new house it gets the feeling as if it were new. With a new life comes new energy influences, new planetary influences, and new experiences that feel new, and you feel as though you are starting fresh each new lifetime. But, in reality, you are just repeating the same life cycle as you always have, but now under a new boss, per se; a new planetary influence in a new house. As you transcend through the houses, you gradually become more keen to this fact that you have done this before. You slowly wake up to this new realization, and you begin to feel as though you've been here before, having already dealt with similar circumstances and with same types of people and problems.

You continue to attract the same types of people into your life, and quite possibly those personalities possess the same astrological signs. It is not until the end of Aquarius when most people realize this.

Discovery of this fact, and 'waking up' is your graduation.

This knowledge gained is your power. You are now awarded with this sacred truth which you have been seeking, and you can take it with you into the next life, which is in the 12th house as a Pisces. Pisces is considered the retired Aquarius. Another way to look at it, Aquarius is like a Jedi knight, whereas Pisces would be considered as a retired Jedi knight, who has been there and done that. Now after having figured out the truth of our existence, the Pisces simply wishes to be left alone. And yet, Pisces is still reincarnated into this world because they too serve a higher purpose. Although, they too must endure struggles and challenges the same as everyone else, there is no exception to the rules. The specifics of which will be explained after the end of this Aquarius's path.

For now, let us begin Aquarius's path to enlightenment beginning with the 3 of Wands card.

3 of Wands:
The sign of Aquarius is ruled by Saturn, who rules over the 3rd sefirah on the Kabbalah Tree of Life Binah. This is why Aquarius's path includes all of the #3 cards. Binah is considered to be the motherly aspect of the Tree, who gives birth to desire, giving form to inspirational ideas. As the feminine aspect of God, Binah gives birth to all things, including intuitive understanding through contemplation. This is the thought process portrayed here by the man depicted in this card as he looks out into the desert. He sees

possibilities where others see none. Deserts throughout the tarot represent a place of complacency. Here, the Aquarian sparks up an idea to change things for the better, to revitalize and rejuvenate what has become a stagnant wasteland—in hopes to improve the world as well as the lives of others. Egotistically, this reflects a selfish desire to improve his own life, although he can transform his selfishness by coming up with ideas to better the world for others, and in exchange he will end up creating a better world for himself at the same time.

The suit of Wands reveals specific timing significances. For instance, wands are similar to trees and both relate to agriculture. The god of agriculture is Saturn, also known as the lord of time, (who also happens to rule over Aquarius). Therefore, by counting the branches on the wands it will reveal a significant aspect of timing portrayed in the card's illustration.

Particularly in the 3 of Wands, there are 9 branches on the 3 wands in this card. The number 9 corresponds with the 9th sefirah on the Tree of Life Yesod. Yesod unveils the hidden and unseen. It brings truth into light. And reveals light out of the darkness. The brightest light can be revealed in the darkest of places. Yesod is ruled by the Moon. This being so, the 3 of Wands card reflects the timing of one Lunar month.

The man in this card is seen looking out into an empty field. He sees potential. He sees what others cannot. He holds his grip around a singled-out wand, which has 3 branches on it. Three of things or like-objects grouped together symbolize and connect to the sefirah Binah, meaning understanding. Coincidentally, Binah is ruled by Saturn. This man's right hand gripping this particular wand symbolizes that he is sharing/giving and putting forth his understanding, having understood one idea from another idea. This man is wearing a white focus sash around his head, alluding to this concept of him focusing mentally on his new understandings. Now able to see the 'big picture', he realizes on a soul level that he has been guided by a higher power, leading him to where he is supposed to be, thus he feels he is in the right place at the right time. Every decision he has made thus far in life has led him to this point of understanding, and everything seemed to have worked out for a divine purpose. This man is focusing on that one thing that will make life easier, more efficient and at the same time bring everyone together. Typically, the Aquarian invents a new technology, such as a well or irrigation system that brings water into the desert; or something along these lines. Moreover, the bright yellow background shows us that this man will be blessed with a bright future.

Deserts throughout the tarot represent the ego. There is no life in the desert, and therefore it represents a place of complacency. This man is looking out into the desert now, and he is overcome with fear, doubt and anxiety. These are healthy emotions to have, especially when you have been faced with similar situations in the past. But this time around, the man faces his fears with confidence. This man now faces a similar situation just as before, but now with a new understanding of who he has grown up to be, how he has matured and become spiritually stronger. He does not start this journey through the desert as a newbie or by doing so from scratch, he is now starting from experience.

When you ground yourself and come down-to-earth you are able to see the truth, the dirt and the realness of things. It is good to pay attention to the smallest of details of everything. This attention to detail can be applied when meeting new friends, colleagues and when starting a new relationship. This is also how Aquarius's approach their businesses and careers. They are able to see the sentimental worth of things, as well as their potential. Aquarians must learn to trust their own instincts based on their past experience. While others may call you crazy, and are unable to share your vision, you will have the gift of foresight and be able to see the big picture.

As you contemplate deeply on this card, you will notice the three sailboats floating on top of the desert sand just as if they were drifting in the sea. Ergo, this man is looking out into the sea of possibilities where he sees potential.

This man sees what others cannot. By knowing the real history of everything, real eyes will realize real lies.

3 of Cups:
This card depicts three women celebrating the harvest. Their hard work has paid off and now it is time to rejoice. It's a risky business, agriculture, with so many different factors that can cause your crop to either flourish or go to ruin. You have to learn how to plan ahead and be prepared for any contingency. Thus, when you do have a successful harvest, it is indeed a time to be grateful. In the Middle-Ages, surviving a harvest meant you would survive through the winter, and therefore live another year—survive another season. To celebrate the harvest is to be able to finally embrace that long awaited feeling of relief, which blesses you with the certainty that the future is going to be okay.

This card portrays a time to be grateful for what you have. It is good to plan things out, but not to allow your plans to get in the way of your relationships. It truly is about the journey, and not the destination. That is the path to self-discovery. The people we allow into our lives shape who we are. We feed off of and absorb their energy. The bond between two people can be like the bond a farmer has with his crop, so much time and energy are devoted to making sure that crop will grow and last another season. It is never guaranteed that the relationship will last, and ultimately it is not the point, it is more so about the experience. Be grateful for the things you have now, in the time being, and don't worry about how it will all turn out. Live life in the now. Every day is a gift, that is why it is called the present. Start practicing gratitude as if it were a religion.

3 of Swords:
The 3 of Swords card's esoteric label is "The Lord of Sorrow". Consequently, this card depicts 3 swords piercing a heart. Gray clouds, representing wisdom, rain down in the background, thus portraying a life-lesson being experienced here. Swords represent thoughts, and these thoughts are penetrating the heart in an attempt to forge a logical conclusion of one's feelings. For example, the anguish felt whenever grasping the reality of a heartbreak and having to deal with the emotional aftershocks that follow.

No need to suffer over mistakes. We all make mistakes. This is why pencils have erasers. In spite of this, if you erase all the mistakes of your past, you would also erase all of the wisdom of your present. Remember the lesson, not the disappointment.

This card is mostly about your inner state. The 3 of Swords isn't about a heartbreak between two people, rather it's about a heartbreak that takes place within the soul. Your mind, your own mentally conjured, ego-based dreams, are at odds with your heart's desires. You may be spending way too much energy trying to silence your heart. You may be up in arms, fighting to crush your emotions, your true essence, and your soulful dreams. It might have become so automatic that now you don't even realize just how silent your heart has been. You may not be doing the work that you need to for yourself and are at risk of becoming stuck in your sorrow and pain. However, understanding what caused the pain, accepting it and working through the pain can help you recover. This card depicts a heavy rain storm, and as the old adage goes, 'the greater the storm, the brighter the rainbow.'

"The measure of intelligence is the ability to change." -Albert Einstein

Worth mentioning here is that Aquarius's are known to be the geeks of the Zodiac, who get turned on by technology. They also have a passion for knowing and truly understanding how stuff works. This combining together of the mind and soul is represented in this card with the swords bonding together with the heart. Aquarius understands that both science and spirituality are saying the same thing but with different words. In the new Age of Aquarius, we will see the merge of soul and technology.

Aquarius is now and has always been seen as a social pariah, but perhaps in the near future their unique mentality will become the social norm.

3 of Pentacles:
The Three of Pentacles is often associated with planning, blueprints, and teamwork.

Portrayed in this card are three people lending each other their unique energy in an attempt to create something substantial. This is the type of growth that can only come from collaboration. There are times when you need to go your own way and do your own thing, but the 3 of Pentacles shows that there are also times when it is better to rely on external support. Accepting that kind of support allows you to be a part of something greater than yourself.

This card speaks of the tangible progress that can be when we use our unique skills and draw upon the unique skills of others. Progress doesn't usually happen by accident. Progress happens when we actively engage in building, growing and strengthening. You can see this in how knowledge has developed over the course of time: one person comes up with a concept, someone else builds upon it, and someone else steers that existing foundation in a new direction. Such is the course of creation.

Kabbalistic knowledge continues to evolve. In medieval times, such esoteric wisdom was typically passed along by word of mouth, and done so secretively in the same manner portrayed here in this card. Depicted in the 3 of Pentacles is a group of three people who are meeting confidentially in a dark church. A priest and his maiden friend seek out the 'light-worker' in search of obtaining higher wisdom. The light-worker stands on the table and shines his flashlight onto the couple's manuscript, which reveals to them the concealed Kabbalah hidden within their scriptures. This is what the light-worker brings to the table, so to speak, revealing esoteric knowledge that will benefit others, and ultimately transform the world for the better. The word kabbalah means 'to receive', and the couple is depicted here as receiving the Light of Kabbalah in the darkness, which represents ignorance. With closer examination, you will notice that the manuscript the couple is holding onto has a picture of the very same room they are standing in. The pieces are now coming together. They come seeking the light-worker's knowledge of the Church's esoteric mysteries when all the while they had right before them the answers they were seeking. It just took a slight shift in awareness for them to realize such things. The light-worker opened their eyes to new ways of thinking. They come to realize that they have always carried within them the answers to all life's mysteries they were seeking. They could not rely on the church to shed light on any of the esoteric wisdom concealed within the holy books. It was up to the light-worker to show them the answers to life's deeper spiritual mysteries—answers which were there in front of them all along. "We are stars wrapped in skin. The light you have been seeking has always been within." - Rumi

The light-worker reveals to them the deeper Kabbalistic meanings concealed within the biblical stories, esoterically encoded with numbers and astrology, and told in rich allegory. In the aiding of opening up this couple's eyes to seeing the hidden truth, the light-worker is able to learn from them as well. Now that their eyes are open, the priest and the maiden can both help the light-worker see from their perspective what spiritual understandings they are able to bring to the table as well. When we help others, we help ourselves. What goes around comes around. As a group of like-minded light-workers, we are able to collaborate and evolve the wisdom of Kabbalah further into a new age of understanding.

The Empress:
Being assigned to Roman numeral III, the Empress corresponds with the energy influence of the 3rd sefirah Binah, who is considered the female aspect of the Tree of Life. Binah births desire concocted from the upper World of Atziluth and delivers it down into the lower Worlds where that desire eventually manifests itself in Malchut. Binah culminates brilliant ideas into form. Binah is seen to take the raw force of Chokmah, and channel it into the various forms of creation. For example, in a car, you have the fuel and an engine. While Chokmah is the fuel, pure energy, Binah is the engine, pure receptivity. Either one without the other is useless. Binah is intuitive understanding, or contemplation. It is likened to a 'palace of mirrors' that reflects the pure point of light of Chokmah, wisdom, increasing and multiplying it in an infinite variety of ways. In this sense, it is the 'quarry', which is carved out by the light of wisdom. It is the womb, which gives shape to the Spirit of God. On a psychological level, Binah is processed wisdom, also known as deductive reasoning. It is understanding one idea from another idea. While Chokmah is intellect that does not emanate from the rational process, Binah is the rational process that is innate in the person which works to develop an idea fully.

The Empress, like Binah, is all about giving birth to ideas. Likewise, Aquarius should learn to act on their inspiration, especially if a particular idea has had time to develop and grow in your mind. Now is the time to act, and stop putting things off. The only thing holding you back from your prosperity is you.

Is there a particular thing for which you are passionate and don't tell everyone about, perhaps only your closest friends? Something you have always done since childhood that makes you happy? It is this type of thing that you need to share with the world. Whatever it is that brings you happiness is sure to bring someone else happiness as well; no matter how silly or lame it might seem. You may think to yourself that there is no way to make money from it—there isn't a large enough audience. But you will find that the more unique the niche, the better chance you have of making a profit. It is now time to remove all doubt and let go of any worries you may have about the future outcome. It is prime time to act and give birth to your 'child,' which can refer to a business venture you may have been brainstorming, as well as the niche hobby that you rarely share with anyone.

All you need to do now is take the first step—with a little effort you will soon attract the prosperity you seek, and be blessed with a brighter and more financially secure future. Just know that you will be successful at whatever you set out to do; you will reap what you sow.

The Empress as Binah is the feminine aspect of God, and gives birth to all things, including intuitive understanding through contemplation—literally giving birth to the whole of creation, and provides the supernal womb. Do you notice that the Empress is pregnant? This is why she is wearing a loose-fitting gown and is seen here sitting on comfy pillows. There are exactly 40 pomegranates on her gown. The number 40 is significant here because a fetus is inside a mother's womb for 40 weeks before its birth. In the background of the card there is a canal/stream. This represents a birth canal. There are also the six-pointed stars of the Empress's crown to consider, which includes 12, six-pointed stars: $12 \times 6 = 72$, and 72 is the

Kabbalistic number relating to miracle making—as in the 'miracle' of birth. According to the Kabbalists, Moses engraved the 72 Names on his staff, which was used to part the Red Sea—one of the greatest miracles performed in the Torah.

The Empress is depicted in the card holding onto a golden sceptre in her right hand, which represents her authority and control over the world aka her reality; her destiny. She has the final say on when it is time to birth something new. This concept of control is symbolized by the wheat crop at the bottom of the card. The Empress has dominion over when it is time to reap the harvest. She planted the seeds and nurtured the crop; therefore, she says when it is time to cut and gather it.

We now look at one more clue, which is the heart symbol placed at the Empress's side with the astrological symbol for Venus on it. In Greek mythology, Venus is Saturn's daughter, and the heart represents that Saturn loves his daughter. However, the heart is colored gray, which always represents wisdom, thus the Venus symbol being inside a gray heart represents that Saturn (the Empress as Binah) expresses a tough-love towards her daughter, Venus. Remember the 40 pomegranates on the Empress's gown? Pomegranates, throughout the tarot, are a symbol for memory. Pomegranate juice is actually given to Alzheimer's patients to help improve their memory. So, this is another clue that the Empress (Saturn as Binah) does not freely give love unconditionally to her daughter. The Empress remembers the past. She may forgive but will never forget, and she judges accordingly. She will not enable Venus or anyone for that matter; she cares too much to spoil them. Furthermore, the Empress does not repeat mistakes. She remembers her mistakes and learns from them, and is considered a nurturer when it comes to relationships, due to the way she treats her business and family, as well as herself.

Arriving to this point in your life takes a lot of hard work and discipline. But, as the old saying goes, when you do what you love, it doesn't feel like work. The Empress (metaphorically) shares her pomegranates with the world—pomegranates symbolizing memory. The word memory has its etymology stemmed in Jewish meanings, it is a combination of two words: Mem, meaning water, and Ori, meaning light. Thus, the Empress is portrayed as carrying within her womb Liquid Light. She manifests prosperity by sharing her Light with the world. "When your dreams are based on how you can improve the lives of others, the whole universe conspires to make your dreams come true." - Karen Berg, author, and founder of The Kabbalah Centre

All number 3 cards are associated with Binah, ruled by Saturn. Saturn is the god of the harvest and agriculture, as well as the lord of time. Saturn is the ruling planet for both Capricorn and Aquarius. Aquarius is symbolized by the water bearer, and babies are birthed out of the womb from their mother's water. Whereas Capricorn is the hard worker who tends to the field, putting their hands into the creation of things and improving life for the betterment of others.

So, here we have the clues that lead us to understand that the Empress is a hard worker and she wishes to improve her life as well as the lives of others around her by creating prosperity for all people and things she is involved in—whether it be business, career, charitable work, friends or family. She is the one in control of her prosperity, as well as her destiny.

When it comes to business and relationships, the Empress approaches these things like a Capricorn would attend to a wheat crop throughout the year; nurturing it, looking after it, plowing the field, watering the crops, and planting the seeds during the appropriate times of the year. All this in total control—knowing when to either hold back or when to take action depending on the current season's circumstances, which is a gradual process. Only after years of practice and experimentation with the field does the Capricorn transition into the Aquarius who develops empathy and cares more so about the well-being of others leading them to know what appropriate actions and daily regimens to partake in, and at the correct times of the year depending on the needs and desires of the community as a whole.

The Empress only wants the best for her daughter, Venus, and she wishes to one day show her off and be proud of her. This particular concept of a 'child' refers to the development process of anything being taken from its seed level and growing it into something big, such as when one starts with a simple idea and turns it into something that generates a stream of income. The Empress knows that things take time, attention and effort; it is a nurturing process. Like the developing fetus in the womb during pregnancy as it's nurtured with a mother's sustenance throughout its 40-week gestational process, the fetus is readying itself to be strong enough to enter the world; this process of creating new life embodies the concept of manifesting miracles which is portrayed here in the Empress card. The newborn baby is full of potential and carries within it the power to change the world—hopefully for the better.

The Hanged Man:
The Hanged Man card is assigned to the Hebrew letter Mem, meaning water. Spiritually, Mem relates to the cleansing attribute of water, and corresponds to the time needed for spiritual cleansing. By submerging ourselves in water it offers us a bath or baptism, both of which are proactive and relaxing. While on the other hand, if we were to stand underneath a large waterfall we would get pummeled with water. Although, after some time spent underneath the heavy downpour of water, we would become like the sharp rocks at the base of the waterfall that eventually become smoothed out over time by enduring the water's punishment. Slowly but surely, just as the rocks, we too would become well-rounded individuals. The Hanged Man portrays this particular aspect of judgement, as well as the accepting of it, all the while realizing we must surrender and then endure the things we cannot change—that we cannot control. This concept agrees with the Serenity Prayer written by the American theologian Reinhold Niebuhr (1892–1971). It is commonly quoted as:

"God, grant me the serenity to accept the things I cannot change, courage to change the things I can, and wisdom to know the difference."

Below is a later and longer version published by Niebuhr, which truly sums up the emotion encompassed within the Hanged Man card:

God, give me grace to accept with serenity the things that cannot be changed, Courage to change the things which should be changed, and the Wisdom to distinguish the one from the other.

Living one day at a time, Enjoying one moment at a time, Accepting hardship as a pathway to peace, Taking, as Jesus did, This sinful world as it is, Not as I would have it,
Trusting that You will make all things right, If I surrender to
Your will,
So that I may be reasonably happy in this life,
And supremely happy with You forever in the next.

Amen.

The Hanged Man card originally depicted Judas Iscariot hanging upside down as a form of punishment after having turned in Jesus to the Romans. Judas was paid with 30 silver coins. Early versions of this card depict Judas holding onto these bags of coins in his hands as he hanged there vulnerable. The number 30 is significant here, because it is the number of years relating to the Saturn Return, a time in one's life when they are faced with judgment/karma owed to them. Being hanged upside down was a cruel form of punishment, where you would hang helpless, unable to move and were susceptible to the town's people spitting on you or hurling rocks towards you. You were forced to accept your fate, having to surrender and endure the torture.

The Hanged Man card depicts an image of a man being hanged upside-down by one ankle. This method of hanging was a common punishment at the time for traitors in Italy. However, the solemn expression on his face traditionally suggests that he is there by his own accord, and the card is meant to represent self-sacrifice more so than it does corporal punishment or criminality. In other interpretations, The Hanged Man is a depiction of the Norse god Odin, who suspended himself from a tree in order to gain knowledge. There is also the Christian interpretation (mentioned earlier) that portrays Judas with the bags of silver in his hands.

On the Kabbalah Tree of Life, the Hanged Man card hangs on the branch that connects Hod with Gevurah, which encompasses the concept of "be careful what you wish for." Once we begin taking the appropriate actions towards manifesting a specific goal is when life begins to throw obstacles and challenges in our way. We experience this restriction as soon as we take the first step with the intention to transform our dreams into reality. God wants to give us everything we desire, but He gives us our desires wrapped in filthy ego-soaked packages. It is then our responsibility to unwrap these dark packages and unveil the Light concealed within them. God always grants our wishes, but we must earn them first in order to receive. We must endure challenges, overcome obstacles, and deal with everyday frustrations and annoyances as we work towards earning those particular wishes. It is crucial to remain focused on the end result. Romanticize the idea or concept, and thus the happy thought which embodies your wish in its manifested state. You must learn to utilize analytical problem-solving skills to overcome the day-to-day challenges you will be faced with. Endure to the end by focalizing your mind on the prize, and on the fulfillment you will attain. Do not focus on what you will have to give up, instead fantasize on what you will gain. Most times, it is the 'why' that is so important to keep focused on. The reason why we get up every day and do what needs to be done in order to reach our goal is what truly motivates us. What is your 'why'? For some, it's simply to be free.

As we dive deeper into understanding the symbolism found on the Hanged Man card, you will notice the tree the man hangs from is shaped like the letter T, which is the Hebrew letter Tav, meaning cross, mark, sign of the cross. Ancient forms of the letter Tav were written like an X, as in "X marks the spot"—Tav meaning mark. Trees throughout the Tarot always represent Saturn's influence in some way, and Tav just so happens to be attributed to Saturn. Moreover, Saturn is the god of agriculture, and as a consequence, trees which are agriculturally related symbolize Saturn, and particularly in this case reflect the aspect of Saturn's judgment. Just as a martyr who sacrifices themselves for a good cause, just like Jesus Christ who was crucified on the cross. When Jesus died on the cross, he was reunited with the Father, Yahweh, and they were one. This is significant, because Yahweh is associated with Saturn.

Looking further into the symbolism, you will count 37 rays surrounding the Hanged Man's head. This includes the bright aura rays as well as the fiery tips of the man's hair. The number 37 is significant here, it being the value of Chokmah, meaning wisdom, and therefore we are safe to assume that he is focusing on a brilliant idea. Depicted here is his happy thought that keeps him going, offers him hope, it represents his 'why' and is his reason for pursuing his goal—and ultimately, his life-purpose.

When breaking down the 37 total rays into two groups, we find that there are 32 bright rays that surround the man's head and then there are the 5 points of his fiery hair. The number 32 represents the elevated soul, and the number 5 shares attributes with Gevurah, which relates to matters of the ego, and thus a healthy drive and ambition that is attributed to being goal oriented.

Another thing to mention is this man's uniquely odd pose. The man is pictured here with his feet crossed and has his arms held behind his back. This peculiar stance is actually the alchemical symbol for Sulfur, albeit upside down. Metaphorically speaking, and also how it pertains to spiritual Alchemy, Sulfur coincides with the human soul.

The chart below outlines the three major alchemical symbols and their meanings. Sulfur is found at the top of the chart.

⍼	Sulfur Soul Consciousness Oil
☿	Mercury Spirit Mind Liqour
⊖	Salt Body Structured thought Alkaline Salt

As mentioned, the Hanged Man card is assigned to the letter Mem, meaning water, referring to the healing and cleansing aspect water encompasses. Mem has a numerical value of 40, which is significant throughout the Bible, and always corresponds with a time of cleansing and spiritual growth. For instance, the Jewish people escaped slavery in Egypt after asking God for freedom. God promised them a land filled with milk and honey where they could live and prosper freely in peace, and have the opportunity to flourish as a nation—reaching their full potential. They did eventually reach their promised land, but God made it to where they had to 'earn' it first. The Jewish people were forced to wonder the desert for 40 years, where they were faced with a series of tests, challenges, and had to overcome many obstacles. With the many frustrations came times of uncertainty, leading them to lose hope and test their faith in God. Although, after having to endure such hardships, the Jewish people were eventually allowed to settle in the promised land. This 40-year period elicited for them a means to grow spiritually stronger. This is just one example, for there are many other instances where the number 40 shows up in the Bible. Specifically, in the story of Noah's flood which lasted for 40 days and 40 nights, or when Moses climbed up Mount Sinai to retrieve the ten commandments for a period of 40 days and 40 nights. The number 40 embodies the concept of the transformation process. Whenever you feel crushed, under pressure, pressed, or in darkness, you're in a powerful place of transformation. For example, grapes must be crushed to make wine, diamonds form under pressure, olives are pressed to release oil, and seeds grow in darkness.

Just as the men portrayed in these biblical allegories, Aquarians also tend to have issues dealing with authoritative fathers, who are hard on their children. Noah, Abraham, and Moses were all tested of their willingness to submit to God's (the father in heaven) authority. In most instances, your father was a nitpicky authoritarian that meddled with all aspects of your life. For the most past of your childhood, you were not to be exposed to anything they disagreed with and you were very sheltered. Your teen years were weird and awkward since the way they brought you up made them the only person that was there and had any effect on you. In most cases, Aquarians treat their fathers as if the father were the child, reversing the roles of the parent-child dynamic. As a consequence of this, the father tends to detach emotionally leading him to engage with the Aquarius more like a colleague rather than a son or daughter. This creates a sort of divisive and unorthodox relationship with the two of them engaged in a battle of wits, testing each other's boundaries and pushing each other's buttons, and rarely ever sharing a real sense of warmth or affection. In some circumstances, the Aquarian's father will be absent a lot of the time, usually occupied with work responsibilities. This typically pertains to military, government institutions, church, as well as corporate institutions.

These issues with your father may have rendered you incapable of holding social interaction and lacking real knowledge of the world. You emerged in your young adult years as a child again, as if you truly started to live life from that moment you left your father behind.

Metaphorically, this scenario is portrayed in the story of Jesus Christ who died on the cross and then was reunited as one with the father in heaven. After which, Jesus no longer was under His father's authoritarian rule; they were one, and thus equal.

The tree the Hanged Man dangles from symbolizes the Hebrew letter Tav, meaning cross, sign of the cross, which in ancient times was written as an X. Tav also means truth and mark, as in leaving your mark of truth behind for others to follow in your footsteps. The idea is for you to pass on the torch and leave your legacy behind for the generations to come. Taking this a step further, the World card, assigned to the letter Tav, is about raising the bar and setting the new standard, and then passing on the torch to others who will follow in your example. TheWorld card as well as the letter Tav refer to leaving something behind better than when you found it. The World card is the last and final card in the deck, referring to the end of a phase, or end of the world. Biblically speaking, the end of the world is called the apocalypse, which literally means 'the uncovering', and alludes to the uncovering of hidden (or forgotten) truths. Once these truths are revealed it sets the new standard and establishes a new set of rules, which evolve the world for the better. Thus, evolving the world into a new era—one of higher vibration and enlightenment.

Consequently, as a parent you'll be precise and attentive. You remember a lot about your kids, and you give them all that they need physically and emotionally. Because of the way you were brought up, you can get overly protective and paranoid over their safety and who they're with. Although you can be suffocating to them, no one can deny that you raised your children to be well educated and wholesome people. The Hanged Man advises you to make large sacrifices. You may have to give up on something that you wanted, or you need to do something huge for another person.

The Hanged Man is in limbo and is caught between two choices. While upside-down, he gains insight into his situation. He may have felt as though he has been wrongly accused and is now paying for karma he doesn't deserve. Through self-reflection, he determines if he has control of his situation or if he is being punished.

The key to this card is that the Hanged Man must resign to his fate. He needs to surrender. If he adds stress to himself now, he could make his situation worse. If he wants to get off the tree, he has to do so carefully without getting more tangled.

The Hanged Man card, attributed to the letter Tav, transitions us nicely into the next card included in this path, which is the World card.

The World:
The World card is associated with accomplishing a strong sense of certainty, and obtaining a higher degree of self-realization. The large Laurel wreath symbolizes an award given once a person graduates from lower up into the higher degree of understanding. The wreath can also symbolize a womb which gives birth to a new phase or new beginning, and perhaps a new chapter in one's life. This womb can also represent the opening of a portal into the astral realm that allows one to draw down desire from the macrocosm with the intention of

manifesting it in the material world.

The World card is assigned to the Hebrew letter Tav, which means cross, sign of or mark of the cross. This can relate to the portal that our desire crosses over into the material realm.

Interesting to note is that a folded up cross forms a cube, resembling the six-sided cube of Saturn. Like opening a gift-box, the cube unfolds and offers up its prize.

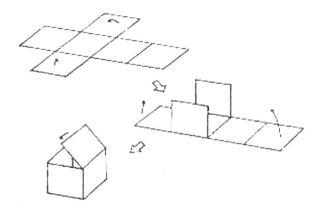

Big dreams take big imagination. You must truly think outside the box. Tav is the last letter in the alphabet. Bearing that in mind, the World card being assigned to the letter Tav alludes to the idea of 'the end of the world', which biblically is associated with the apocalypse. The word apocalypse literally means 'the uncovering', and relates to the uncovering of hidden truths. This being said, it is imperative to search within to uncover certain lost or forgotten truths about yourself, which will reveal your true character at its core, as well as reveal the specific thing your soul desires in order for it to sustain a sense of fulfillment. In addition to this, try to find the real reason for why you desire a certain goal. For example, a person's 'why' may include freedom. Freedom can be a primary motivator, both professionally and personally.

The World, attributed to Binah, is about crossing through the portal and into the realm of endless possibilities.

As you meditate on these cards, think to yourself, I am going to get out of the way and allow the Light to guide me. In the past, I have been stubborn, set in my ways, and I will let go. Instead of clinging to my beliefs, I will open up, and allow the Light of the Upper Dimensions to shine down into my realm and transform my life. I have real desire, not for myself alone, but to connect to something greater.

Chapter 22, Section 12: Pisces

Astrological House #12, Pisces, is ruled by two planets: Neptune and Jupiter. And these two planets correspond to the energy aspects of the two Piscean fish that swim together in tandem. These fish just like these two planets coincide with the double-sided nature of Pisces, whereas Neptune is aloof, thinking outside the box, stuck in the fantasy world, and Jupiter is more down-to-earth, although still focused on having fun. With this in mind, Pisces seems to always be in two different worlds at the same time.

Going back to the Star Wars analogy where I mentioned Aquarius can be considered as being a Jedi knight, whereas Pisces is more like a retired Jedi. Pisces wishes to be left alone, sneak away and live alone on their own remote planet—enjoying their old age in peace like the retired Luke Skywalker in the 2015 movie "Star Wars: The Force Awakens".

The energy of Pisces can leave us feeling sensitive. Steer thoughts away from victimhood and toward deeper empathy for the experiences of others. When we take responsibility for where we are on our journey, we can release regret and tap into greater fulfillment and joy. The overall essence of Pisces is adequately expressed in the motto "Don't worry, be happy." Just remember to take responsibility. Choose joy. Balance logic and emotion. And know that you always have a choice.

This balancing of logic and emotion, and the concept of bouncing back and forth from the two worlds is mostly due to the fact that Pisces is ruled by two planets. Pisces has two paths that are to be traveled simultaneously on their way to achieving enlightenment, just as the two fish swim in tandem.

Neptune rules over the 2nd sefirah on the Kabbalah Tree of Life Chokmah, and due to this the Pisces's path to enlightenment includes all the #2 tarot cards and all cards associated with the #2. This path includes the 2 of Wands, 2 of Cups, 2 of Swords, 2 of Pentacles, the High Priestess, Justice and the Judgement card.

Pisces's path includes all the #4 cards as well, because Jupiter rules over the 4th sefirah Chesed. Therefore, this path contains the 4 of Wands, 4 of Cups, 4 of Swords, 4 of Pentacles, the Emperor, and the Death cards.

Interesting to point out here is the correlation between the two end cards of each of these paths. Both the Death card and the Judgment card are attributed to the biblical story of Jesus Christ dying on the cross. On the day of his death, Jesus was reunited with the Father in heaven and they become one. This is portrayed through allegory and symbolism of course. The Judgement card corresponds to the day before Good Friday when the angel Gabriel delivered the good news to the people telling them that Jesus was going to sacrifice himself the following day, and this would allow every soul a chance at redemption. The Death card reflects the energy of the actual crucifixion. A Pisces's final level of enlightenment is to follow in Jesus' example and return back to the Source upon their death, and ultimately escape from this earthly existence.

Let's begin Pisces path to enlightenment with the #2 cards, which are linked to Neptune.

Neptune is a bit of an aloof planet, and one that is misunderstood. Neptune is attributed to addiction, specifically liquids that typically contain either alcohol or caffeine. This is due to the planet being 80% fluid and filled with liquid gases. Although, Pisces is infamous for being linked with addiction, involving all forms of addiction, due to its Neptune influence. Because of this, all Pisces will share an addiction to liquids that alter the mind's state in some degree.

This infatuation with experiencing altered mind states is what causes Pisces's attraction to hallucinogens. Pisces are intrigued by the paranormal, outer body experiences as well as virtual reality. Neptune's influence causes Pisces to truly think outside the box, and makes them want to explore the abyss of consciousness; advancing further down the rabbit hole and escaping reality.

Let us begin Pisces's Neptune path with the 2 of Wands card.

2 of Wands:
This card depicts a man who has just been 'knighted' and now feels as though he has the world in his hands. As he reaches this new height in his career and life path, he looks out into the sea of opportunities. What else can he accomplish? What else is out there waiting for him to discover? He is truly thinking outside the box, outside the limitations of society and the physical world.

Wands represent knowledge and beliefs we feel are deeply rooted within us. Over time, we gain a deeper understanding of all things. This young knight leaves his past understandings behind him, as portrayed by the wand he turns his back to. This wand on his back has 3 branches on it representing the 3rd sefirah on the Kabbalah Tree of Life Binah, meaning understanding. The knight is now focusing on future possibilities, his future potential and uncovering new insights about himself; realized through self-reflection. He is pictured with his left hand grasping the wand in front of him. The left hand represents the receiving polarity; therefore, he is attempting to receive new understanding. You will notice that this wand has three branches on it as well, which corresponds to Binah, contemplation.

This man is portrayed as being in two worlds at the same time.

Notice how he is wearing earth-tone colors as he holds the planet Earth in his hand? And yet, at the same time he is looking out into the sea of possibilities, lost in his imagination and thinking outside the box.

Beside the knight, there are two flowers pictured on the gray cement wall. The two different-colored flowers correspond to the two worlds the knight co-inhabits. He is seen here learning how he can be successful when he understands how to balance the two. The red flower represents his passion and desire to succeed, while the white flower represents his purity nature; his child-like and day-dreaming nature. The knight comes to the realization that he has both these characteristics at the same time, and they only work to his benefit when they work together in tandem. He has a big imagination that most will not understand or except, but when he takes the first step in creating those ideas into tangible, practical and real things that people can see for themselves, then seeing becomes believing. If you don't believe me, just watch.

The Pisces can easily get lost in their own head where they receive crazy and brilliant ideas, but when they learn how to come back down to earth and manifest those ideas is when they find success, and this is when they achieve fulfillment. Escaping into another dimension or another reality is healthy for the soul, but it can also become addictive. Therefore, a Pisces must learn to restrict themselves and set limits so they know when to stop playing and get to work. Although, when you are doing something you are passionate about, it doesn't feel much like work. This is the key to a Pisceans success, to find the thing your passionate about and share it with the world. This particular passion is usually discovered when your mind is detached from reality.

2 of Cups:
This card adorns the lion of St. Mark, which was a symbol used in Italy to portray their control over both land and sea. Metaphorically, this can be seen as one gaining control over their willpower and emotional state. Not allowing one aspect to overtake the other. You must not allow your ego-driven desires to detach you from the 'why'

you do it in the first place, allowing your drive for success to make you lose the soul or the magic, and thus deflating the passion. You must never lose the heart of the matter. This is where the true fuel to your creativity exists, within the heart and soul of the things your passionate about. This includes your relationships, career, hobbies, projects, and intellectual pursuits.

Directly below the lion with wings is an Egyptian caduceus with its twin serpents, which are similar to the two strands of DNA, and are attributed to the kundalini. The life-force flows up the kundalini giving one their spiritual strength. Elevating one's kundalini can be used as a means to obtain a higher awareness or sate of consciousness. The key to igniting this life-force in order for it to rise up the chakras of the kundalini is done so once an individual opens up their heart chakra. It is through the heart where one is able to connect to higher consciousness. Therefore, when you open up your heart to your passions you connect to the reasoning, the 'why' you do what you do. Once your heart is open, you connect to the Higher-Self and it is in this realm where you discover insights and instruction of how to manifest your desires. Thus, you merge the logic with the emotion.

This card depicts a man leaving his home and meeting up with a woman. The home here represents the man's comfort zone, and place of stability. Man is drive, ambition and selfish desire. He steps outside of his comfort zone and reaches a mutual understanding with his feminine nature, meeting in the middle and now seeing eye to eye. The woman in this card represents the emotional aspect, the 'why' this man does what he does; why he desires to achieve success. This woman is wearing a wreath around her head, the same wreath given to winners of the ancient Olympic games in Greece. It represents an award and high honor. Such wreaths were worn by Caesar. This wreath on the woman's head symbolizes the man has acknowledged his feminine side, as well as shown gratitude. The feminine side brings the man back down to earth and reminds him of why he does what he does, and teaches him the importance of not losing the heart and soul of his endeavors. Don't lose yourself to success.

2 of Swords:
Depicted in this card is a woman who is holding up two swords into the air as if they were antennas. She is attempting to catch, attract or tune-in to godly insights. She adorns a white focus sash over her eyes representing that she is actively looking within for the answers she seeks. Her gray-colored robe suggests that she is attracting wisdom, and laying down a firm solid foundation based on logic. As you look within you are able to see both sides to the situation and see the good as well as the bad. Without reacting emotionally to either side you are able to understand the situation at hand logically, reasonably and perceive the big picture of it all before coming to conclusions based on your assumptions.

The crescent waning moon suggest that this act of looking within should be started now.

Pisces are notorious for putting things off until the next day. This card suggests to not procrastinate. The woman sits on the shoreline just as the moon begins to rise. As the moon rises so will the ocean waters behind her. The longer she hesitates, the chances of her being drowned by the high tides increases. The water throughout the tarot represents emotions and feelings. Therefore, the longer she puts off trying to figure out a certain situation logically, the more of a chance she will be pulled under and she will drown in her emotions.

Pisces is empowered after time spent in isolated self-reflection. By looking within, Pisces is able to connect to their soul as well as the souls of others by first making an intuitive connection and then gaining insight and understanding after practicing empathy. You must place yourself in other people's shoes in order to truly feel what they are going through, or feel how certain words or behaviors affected them.

2 of Pentacles:
This card depicts the juggler attempting to juggle two or more things at once. This can relate to a person who is trying to juggle the time they spend with their friends and their romantic partner or trying to balance their work life with their family life, all while attempting to give each an equal

amount of energy and attention.

The juggler wears a dunce cap upon his head suggesting that he is
new to the game, so to speak. He is trying out something for the first
time and has yet built up the confidence needed for success. At this
early stage, it is presumed he will make mistakes. He must learn to
start out slow and master the fundamentals before he can consider
taking on another project. Another way of putting it, he must first be
able to juggle two balls confidently before attempting to juggle three.
Pisces tend to bite off more than they can chew, which leads them
feeling overwhelmed in the beginning. More often than not, they
buckle under pressure, when they lack the confidence or have
feelings of uncertainty.

This concept corresponds to how Pisces approach responsibility as
well. They must learn to take things slowly and gradually work up to
being able to handle bigger responsibilities. Do not procrastinate or
hesitate to jump on an opportunity when it presents itself to you. God
will only ever give you what you can handle. Take it slow, and you
will learn as you go. Know that making mistakes is part of the
process. This is how you learn, and this is how you gain experience.

With more experience under your belt, the easier it is to take on
responsibility. With confidence, you no longer sweat the small stuff.
In time, having to maintain a stable job or a lasting relationship
becomes more natural. Just like learning to ride a bicycle, you start
out slow and wobbly at first, but then after some practice you learn to
ride faster. Peddling faster builds up momentum, and balances you
out. The faster you go, the smoother and more stable you seem to
ride. Speed equals stability.

Because Pisces is so connected to the astral realm and to the 99%
reality, they are not completely connected to the 1% reality, where
everyone else exists. They come across as airheads. They can be a bit
off and act aloof most of the time. Although, Pisces rather enjoy this
aspect of themselves. They feel peace can be achieved if everyone
was in some way connected to this higher dimension. And as a result,
Pisces tends to force others to join them in their fantasy world. Pisces
will attempt to snap others out of their 1% reality trance. This is

when they appear as the clowns or weirdos to everybody else. Pisces are just so adamant about having fun and not taking life seriously that they do come off as aggressive and pushy to others. Pisces is persistent at trying to 'wake' people up out of their 1% reality slumber. It may be due to them being bored in this life, and also how they feel as they have progressed above the mental bondage that everyone unknowingly suffers from. They act as a clown to encourage people to snap out of their rat-race mentality and to let go of caring so much about the mundane. Because of this type of erratic behavior, Pisces come off as crazy eccentric buffoons. Pisces test their limitations and try to see how far they can get with people by pushing their buttons, stomping on social norms, as well as provoking people's personal beliefs or obtuse ways of thinking. Pisces needs to learn to add to the conversation and to help progress the world for the better in a healthy positive manner. Instead of attracting attention as a clown to pull others out of their simple lives, they need to gravitate toward becoming the leader and act as an example. Attract attention by becoming the spiritual guru that people flock to for life advice, spiritual insight and out of the box understanding of the world we live in. For example, world renown theoretical physicist Albert Einstein was a Pisces. He was famous for his contributions to quantum mechanics and the theory of relativity—truly out of the box ideas.

Pisces can easily grow bored with the people of this world, and they can easily detach themselves from caring about all things in general. They give up the need to help improve the world. It is an overwhelming task and they find it easier to simply just not try. They gravitate to ordinary jobs and live simple lives. They find it easier to be a follower than a leader, because it requires less confrontation, persuading, persistence, and ultimately less responsibility on their part.

Pisces are old souls that are reluctant to change. They feel as though they have it all figured out, so they don't listen to anyone else's advice on better ways to improve their life. Pisces can easily get stuck in their own routines and addictions. They close everyone out and go off into their own little world, detaching emotionally. They play by their own rules and continue to test the limits of everything, albeit mental or physical, including experimentation with drugs, alcohol, sex, emotions, spirituality, relationships, as well as testing the boundaries of society's laws and regulations. It seems Pisceans prefer to learn the hard way. Symbolically portrayed with the juggler's dunce cap, immature Pisceans tend to be all heart and no brains. But life has a way of teaching you the lessons you need to learn, and will face you with specific challenges that whip you back into shape. Once a Pisces reaches rock bottom, the only way for them to go is up. In time, Pisces will experience a slight shift in their consciousness, and eventually will begin to learn from their mistakes and realize the importance of listening to other people's advice—this typically happens in their early 30's. In a way, Pisces is still considered as a follower just doing what life forces them to do. For a Pisces, it is well advised to be proactive and make positive changes in your life now before life forces you to do so. Life can be a cruel teacher.

Pisces must learn to juggle both 'worlds' or conscious realities at the same time. Learn to keep your feet on the ground when your head is in the clouds.

The High Priestess:
The High Priestess card is assigned to the Hebrew letter Gimel, meaning camel. Spiritually speaking, Gimel refers to how a camel rises up when called to serve or perform its duty. Essentially, it alludes to rising up and becoming great. Camels are known to sit and rest for long periods of time, but are quick to rise up to the challenge when called upon. They rise up from the ground and stand tall. They carry the weight on their backs, taking on the responsibility. They carry others on adventures into the unknown lands.

This card depicts the Priestess sitting in the Holy of Holies in King Solomon's temple. Holy of Holies, also called Devir, the innermost and most sacred area of the ancient Temple of Jerusalem, accessible only to the Israelite High Priest. Once a year, on Yom Kippur, the Day of Atonement, he was permitted to enter the square, windowless enclosure to burn incense and sprinkle sacrificial animal blood. By this act, the most solemn of the religious year, the high priest atoned for his own sins and those of the priesthood. The priest had to be pure in heart before entering the Devir or he would surely die.

"Who may ascend the mountain of the Lord? Who may stand in his holy place? He who has clean hands and a pure heart" - Psalm 24:3-4. Jesus said it is the "pure in heart" who will see God and experience fellowship with Him (Matthew 5:8). Because we have all sinned and fallen short of the glory of God (Romans 3:23), who can approach Him?

In the Old Testament, everything about the Temple was set up to emphasize the near-unapproachable holiness and power of God. Only priests could enter the Temple, and only the high priest on one day a year, the Day of Atonement, could go into the Holy of Holies behind a thick veil or curtain that separated God from the priests. This was a day of great fear, reverence and awe. The high priest entered only after going through a great deal of ceremonial cleansing. Even then, he probably entered with fear and trepidation, not knowing if he would come out alive. The other priests actually tied a rope around his ankles to pull him out of God's presence if it appeared that he had expired, because nobody else wanted to go in after him.

In the New Testament, there is a radical shift in access to God. The moment Jesus died for our sins on the cross, "The curtain of the temple was torn in two from top to bottom" - Mark 15:38. The relationship between God and humankind had been restored. As the writer of Hebrews says, "We have confidence to enter the most holy place by the blood of Jesus, by a new and living way opened for us through the curtain, that is, his body and since we have a great priest over the house of God, let us draw near to God with a sincere heart in full assurance of faith, having our hearts sprinkled to cleanse us from a guilty conscience and having our bodies washed with pure water." - Hebrews 10:19-20.

The High Priestess can be compared to the Cohen high priest on the Day of Atonement. Similar to the Cohen, the High Priestess is depicted sitting in the temple holding her Torah scroll, and she remembers her 613 commandments (or mitzvahs) which are divided into two sets or categories. There are exactly 248 commandments that one is supposed to do, and the remaining 365 commandments are prohibited.

The Priestess sits in between the two pillars, the white (Jachin) and the black (Boaz) pillars representing mercy and severity, respectively. As she sits in the center of these two pillars, she finds her (spiritual) center as well. She connects to the middle pillar on the Kabbalah Tree of Life that corresponds to mildness, which acts as the filament that balances out the left and right columns, which are attributed to the positive and negative polarities. Just like a Pisces who must learn how to maintain balance and control over the two worlds they simultaneously exist in, they are advised to find a middle ground in order to restrict the impulsive behavior that leads them to fully immerse themselves into one of the opposite personality polarities, which eventually contributes to consequential repercussions.

Directly behind the Priestess hangs a curtain which adorns ten pomegranates that are arranged in a Kabbalah Tree of Life formation. In ancient times pomegranates were believed to contain exactly 613 seeds, which is the number of commandments in the Torah. Alzheimer patients are prescribed pomegranate juice to help improve their memory. Subsequently, the Priestess is pictured here sitting in deep contemplation and self-reflection, remembering her past transgressions, and as she does this, she practices empathy. She remembers how others wronged her in the past. Although, she learns to forgive, but will never forget. As she empathizes, she understands the reasoning of why those people did or said the hurtful things they did. As she comes to realize these things, she won't allow herself to be treated like that again. She learns to forgive others, and most importantly she learns to forgive herself.

This card features moon symbols portrayed in different fluctuating moon cycles. These moons remarkably reveal the 365 moons that rise throughout the year. The Priestess is studying her Torah and remembering the commandments, specifically the 365 prohibited ones, corresponding to the 365 moon cycles or days/nights of the year.

According to the rabbinic Hebrew calendar the days begin and end with the moon, from sunset to sunset in the evenings. In ancient times, the moon was called Sin after the Mesopotamian moon god. Sin as in Mt. Sinai, the mountain of the Moon. The Priestess is seen here remembering her sins from the past year, and she repents in order to purifying her soul preparing herself to enter the temple on the Day of Atonement, when God comes down from heaven and judges the people of their sins. Furthermore, on the Day of Atonement, Yom Kippur, a person is forgiven of all their sins from the past year, and every year the restitution of sin resets.

This act of forgiveness purifies her soul, which is symbolized by the white cross over her heart. Once the heart is open it releases the negativity, and this opens up the channel of the middle column which will flow directly up to the crown chakra. Having the Priestess sit in the middle of the two columns portrays through rich symbolism that she is a representation of themiddle mildness pillar. For instance, the middle column consists of the four sefirot: Keter, Tiferet, Yesod and Malchut. Whereas Da'at is invisible.

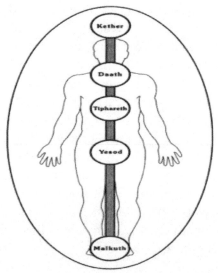

When compared to the chart above, you can see the resemblance the middle pillar shares with the High Priestess tarot card. At the sefirah Keter the Priestess adorns her Moon crown; Keter, meaning crown, coinciding with the crown chakra. At the sefirah Tiferet there is a cross over the Priestess's heart; Tiferet coincides with the heart chakra. At the sefirah Yesod, which isruled by the moon, there is a large crescent waning moon. And lastly, the water at the Priestess's feet, which pours from her dress and onto the floor, represents the sefirah Malchut.

The Priestess is a representation of the middle pillar of mildness, as she sits in between the two pillars, Yachin and Boaz, she reads over her Torah scroll remembering and connecting to the commandments as a means of purifying her heart. Once her heart is open, it will create the spiritual channel needed for the life-force energy to ascend up the kundalini, directly up the center of the Tree of Life within, where she obtains the 'at oneness' with the Creator. This connection is achieved after practicing empathy, forgiveness and ultimately being able to compassionately understand both sides of the story as you reflect upon the past. Through the wisdom of the spirit, she gains a knowledge of both the good and the bad as she connects to and grasps the big picture. In this sense, the High Priestess can be seen as a representation of the Shekinah, the divine feminine aspect of God, also referred to as the Holy Spirit or the divine presence of God.

As the Priestess meditates, she practices forgiveness. It is advised to forgive anyone who has caused you pain or harm. Keep in mind forgiveness is not for others. It is for you. Forgiving is not forgetting. It is remembering without anger. It frees up your power, heals your body, mind and spirit. Forgiveness opens up a pathway to a new place of peace, where you canpersist despite what happened to you.

Worth mentioning here is the secret of the word Devir (or Dvir) and its correlation with the 72 Names of God which stem from the 216 Name. According to the Jewish tradition, there is a formula or a name that defines God in a total way. The name is made of 216 letters; known as the Shem HaMephorash. The origin of the 216 Name is in Exodus 14:19-21,

-And the angel of God, which went before the camp of Israel, removed and went behind them; and the pillar of the cloud went from before their face, and stood behind them:

-And it came between the camp of the Egyptians and the camp of

Israel; and it was a cloud and darkness to them, but it gave light by night to these: so that the one came not near the other all the night.

-And Moses stretched out his hand over the sea; and the LORD caused the sea to go back by a strong east wind all that night, and made the sea dry land, and the waters were divided.

Dividing the 216 letters of these sentences (in Hebrew) to thirds will give us 72 three-letter combinations, known as the Kabbalah 72 Names of God.

In ancient times, when the holy temple still existed, once a year on the holiest of days, Yom Kippur, the Day of Atonement, the Cohen (High Priest) dressed in white would enter the Holy of Holies, the inner sanctuary of the holy temple while the people waited outside the temple. This was the only time when the priest entered the Holy of Holies, known as the Devir where inlaid the original Ark of the Covenant. The word Dvir in Hebrew gematria equals 216. The Cohen priest would say the 72 Names of God in the specific formula to bless and sanctify the Jewish people on this holiest of days. While inside the Devir, if his heart was pure, he would live, if his heart was not pure, he would die.

To truly transform their ego-nature, Pisces must find their center. They must reconnect with their soul, and learn to speak from the heart.

The High Priestess is pictured here holding a Torah scroll in her lap. The Torah meaning instruction or law, and therefore can be considered the 'book of the law.' Coincidentally, Aleister Crowley wrote The Book of the Law or Liber AL vel Legis, which outlined the principles of Thelema, which correspond elegantly to the High Priestess card.

Thelema is an esoteric and occult social or spiritual philosophy and religious movement developed in the early 1900s by Aleister Crowley, an English writer, mystic, and ceremonial magician. The word thelema is the English transliteration of the Greek word meaning will, to will, wish, want or purpose. The Thelemic pantheon—a collection of gods and goddesses who either literally exist or serve as symbolic archetypes or metaphors—includes a number of deities, primarily a trio adapted from ancient Egyptian religion, who are the three speakers of The Book of the Law: Nuit, Hadit and Ra-Hoor-Khuit.

Three statements in particular distill the practice and ethics of Thelema:

-Do what thou wilt shall be the whole of the Law, meaning that adherents of Thelema should seek out and follow their true path, i.e., find or determine their True Will.

-Love is the law, love under will, i.e., the nature of the Law of Thelema is love, but love itself is subsidiary to finding and manifesting one's authentic purpose or 'mission.'

-Every man and every woman is a star, which implies by metaphor that persons doing their Wills are like stars in the universe: occupying a time and position in space, yet distinctly individual and having an independent nature largely without undue conflict with other stars.

As such, these three Thelemic principles sum up the spiritual concept of the Hebrew letter Gimel that is assigned to the High Priestess card, which also as a consequence gives Pisces the key to their spiritual elevation. Know that everyone is their own unique individual and we all serve our own authentic purpose, therefore we must learn to focus on ourselves and not try and change anyone or try to convince anyone our way is better than theirs.

We must uncover our true purpose and life mission by looking within ourselves, spending time isolated in self-reflection. When isolated, we prepare ourselves to be spiritually ready to do anything asked of us. We open up our hearts and we allow ourselves to be filled with the spirit. This is when we connect to our true path. We will be blessed with a strong sense of certainty, knowing our 'mission.' This certainty ignites within us the will to serve and answer our calling. Like the camel, (Gimel) we rise up and we become great, determined to fulfill our duty.

Justice:

The Justice card is assigned to the Hebrew letter Lamed, meaning ox goad, which is the stick (or poker) used by a shepherd to direct and protect his flock. The shepherd rises up to the challenge and tackles responsibility head on, with confidence and a strong will. Whereas the High Priestess is portrayed as receiving the Light during a period of isolation, the Justice prince manifests the Light in public amongst the people. The letter Lamed is located directly in the center of the alphabet, and it stands taller than all the other letters. Because of this, Lamed is identified as the 'heart' of the alphabet. By lifting up his heart, Lamed rises up and stands taller than all the other letters. As he stands there, watching over with his ox goad, he takes on the responsibility to guide, direct, serve and protect his flock. He serves others with heart and compassion.

With further examination, you will notice the Justice prince forms the shape of the Lamed ל with his body. For instance, he has his sword raised high into the air with his body out-stretched, and to his left he holds the scales by his side, thus forming a Lamed with the shape of his body and arms between the two pillars. These two pillars are colored gray, representing wisdom. Moreover, Justice acts and speaks from the heart. The heart speaks truth, and truth entails wisdom. Likewise, searching for truth involves wisdom as a necessary or inevitable part or consequence. It is difficult to find the truth without wisdom.

Jesus Christ, just like Lamed, was considered a shepherd. And just as Jesus sacrificed himself for the world, the Justice prince makes similar personal sacrifices for his people.

Justice wears red representing his big heart and passion that he puts forth towards helping others. It is in the service of others where he receives the greatest fulfillment in life. The red curtain behind him covers the bright yellow background, which symbolizes a bright future as well as signifies that he is located outside the temple in a public place. Also, the red curtain is symbolic of Christ's blood that was shed on the day of his crucifixion. This red curtain is comparable to the one that hangs behind the High Priestess.

Although, the curtain in the Priestess's temple was used to separate man from God's presence, while the curtain in the Justice card represents God and man coming together and joining as one. Allow me to explain this the same way it was mentioned earlier in the High Priestess card.

In the New Testament, there is a radical shift in access to God. The moment Jesus died for our sins on the cross, "The curtain of the temple was torn in two from top to bottom" - Mark15:38. The relationship between God and humankind had been restored. As the writer of Hebrews says, "We have confidence to enter the most holy place by the blood of Jesus, by a new and living way opened for us through the curtain, that is, his body and since we have a great priest over the house of God, let us draw near to God with a sincere heart in full assurance of faith, having our hearts sprinkled to cleanse us from a guilty conscience and having our bodies washed with pure water." - Hebrews 10:19-20.

The Justice prince flaunts a square symbol on his crown and also on his pendant. The square symbol represents structure, balance, logic, and law and order. It represents the laws of nature that exist in the physical realm, and how those laws give us a sense of predictability and security. The square is associated with the number 4, and relates to the four elements of the physical world: earth, air, water, and fire. There are also the four directions: North, South, East, and West. Spiritually, the square is meant to give us a sense of being grounded and balanced here in the physical world. We are physical beings that need structure, community, and direction in order to survive. The square gives us all of these survival needs.

Look at the house you are in right now. The foundation is built on squares. This is symbolic of the foundations of life that are found in the shape of the square. Together, the four elements of the earth blend harmoniously to allow the foundations of life to form, and for us to thrive.

When the square appears in a spiritual context, it is often to give reassurance that you are protected from chaos or perceived threats. It can also be a reminder to breathe, get grounded, and focus on your center. It is a symbol of strength, logic, and survival.

In medieval depictions of the square, it was almost always connected to the human body, representing 'man' and the physical elements of our being. In artistic representations of our human nature, the square, triangle, and circle usually appear, bringing a symphony of shapes that represent body, soul, and spirit—the square being the body.

In Christianity, the shape of a square is symbolic of living a righteous life, referring to the 'right' angles and equal corners on each side. It also represents discipleship and loyalty, and strong discipline that is required to live in accordance with Christian faith. It is often symbolic of protection and power.

The square throughout the tarot represents being 'bound by the Earth and natural law.' Specifically, the square in the Justice card represents 'well-ordered thoughts' that are grounded in logical thinking in comparison to illogical imagination and intuition.

You will notice that Justice's pendant is a circle within a square. Squaring the circle is a problem proposed by ancient geometers. It is the challenge of constructing a square with the same area as a given circle by using only a finite number of steps with a compass and straight edge. Squaring the circle has been a mathematical puzzle that was proved impossible in the 19th century. The term also has been used as a symbol in Alchemy, particularly in the 17th century, and it has a metaphorical meaning: attempting anything that seems impossible.

The squared circle has been a popular theme in the occult and in Alchemy for centuries and it's still an important symbol within it. The square represents the physical world, because it represents the four elements, the four cardinal directions, the four seasons, etc. The circle represents the spirit because it is infinite and it goes out in all directions. The impossibility of squaring the circle is a good metaphor for the relationship between the spirit and the physical. They are both there, but they can't be joined together.

A Pisces must be like the square in their core spirit self, and by doing this will accomplish him or her to form an outer protective wall, a strong spirit that others can sense as well. A Pisces must become structured, have a strong foundation, be reliable, practical, set boundaries, take responsibility, practice self-control, learn to manage their time, maintain balance, abide law and order, and use logic.

Judgement:
Judgment is the final card in the Pisces's Neptune path, and it comes as an added bonus card, whereas all other paths (with the exception of Aquarius) contain only six cards instead of seven. Judgment at the end of Pisces's path merits them with the opportunity of redemption and eternal salvation. It is a Gnostic belief that an individual earns their salvation from ignorance by educating themselves. Education is knowledge. Knowledge is understanding. Understanding is wisdom. Education, understanding, knowledge and wisdom equal power. When a Pisces reaches their highest level of awareness, they begin to penetrate the fabric of reality and see beyond the veil, and are made aware and come to terms with the fact that this world, in a way, is a prison. They slowly figure out that each of us are eternal soul-beings living in a physical existence, trapped inside a never-ending reincarnation loop.

Once a Pisces reaches the end of the Zodiac cycle in the 12th house, upon their death, they are faced with a decision: to either go back into the reincarnation loop or not. It is important for Pisces to understand the nature and construct of reality, which is simulated within a matrix per se, and this can only truly be accomplished when Pisces agrees to go back into the world one last time but still remaining as a Piscean, and with the same level of spiritual awareness. In other words, repeating a life in the 12th house for a second time in a row. One more incarnation as a Pisces for the second time will grant them the awareness needed to reconnect to their soul's purpose, and the quicker they will recall the knowledge gained from their previous life. They will experience that 'woke' feeling, the spiritual awakening, much quicker. Because of this, when Pisces dies as a Pisces for the second time in a row and is confronted by the Archon rulers in the afterlife, Pisces will have the wits not to sign or verbally agree to any new contracts, or attempts of reinstating the reincarnation trap. The Pisces must lead by example and pave the way for the next souls who face the Archons in the afterlife, by showing that all one needs to do is simply refuse to return back to the earth.

Universal Law states there is no coercion. Therefore, we stand our ground and wait until more souls arrive at the gate in the after-life, where we gradually accumulate a large enough group of souls that will gradually grow into becoming a critical mass unable to be controlled as we stand together and demand our freedom. The archons will have no choice but to let us go. They cannot make us do anything we have not agreed to do. This is how we escape the reincarnation loop, and become free of all the suffering and chaos of the world, by simply standing our ground and refusing to agree to anymore contracts. The Judgement card portrays archangel Gabriel blowing her trumpet as she delivers the good news to the people— that each man has within them the power to earn their own salvation. This was the 'good news' delivered on Good Friday.

The word Shin when spelled out has a numerical value of 360, and therefore represents the concept of arriving at or coming to full-circle. Likewise, on Good Friday, Jesus died and returned back to the Creator; back to the Source. Jesus was the example. Upon our deaths we too have the choice to come back if we wish. We are able to start the reincarnation loop again, by starting back in the next house on the Zodiac wheel, or we can be like Jesus who taught us how to earn our salvation, reunite with the Source and escape this world for good. Jesus returned after three days to prove to everyone that death was only an illusion. He came back to help others and to awaken their minds in order to free their souls. Jesus was able to do this partly because he was a Pisces. As a Pisces, the veil had been lifted from him, and he could observe the world for how it truly was. This is the concept of Pisces returning back to the loop one more time as a Piscean, so they do not forget and retain all the knowledge they had learned in the previous (Pisces) incarnation.

For Christians, Good Friday is a crucial day of the year because it celebrates a momentous weekend that laid out the foundation for the religion's core beliefs. Ever since Jesus died and was raised,

Christians have proclaimed the cross and resurrection of Jesus to be the decisive turning point for all creation. Paul considered it to be "of first importance" that Jesus died for our sins, was buried, and was raised to life on the third day, all in accordance with what God had promised all along in the scriptures (1 Corinthians 15:3).

On Good Friday we remember the day Jesus willingly suffered and died by crucifixion as the ultimate sacrifice for our sins (1 John 1:10). It is followed by Easter, the glorious celebration of the day Jesus was raised from the dead, heralding his victory over sin and death and pointing ahead to a future resurrection for all who are united to him by faith (Romans 6:5). The name Jesus is associated with the letter Shin. Jesus' real name is Yeshua ben Yoseph, Joshua son of Joseph. Yeshua meaning salvation. The name Yeshua is formed when you place the Shin in the center of the Divine Four-Letter Name of God YHVH, which transforms into YHShVH. Jesus is the way to the Father; salvation is earned through him. Jesus sets the example.

Ultimately, Jesus died when he was stabbed with a spear (Matthew 27:50). Therefore, he was a Pisces who died by the spear at the end of the zodiac's cycle, in the 12th house on the zodiac wheel. This is interesting to mention here because of how it relates to Methuselah specifically, and also shares a relation with the reincarnation loop and how to escape it. Allow me to explain the connection. Methuselah's name means 'man of the spear', 'death by spear'. Methuselah was the oldest living man in the Bible, having lived 969 years. 'Met', meaning dead, initiates a curiosity of how the number 969 being a palindrome and corresponding to the concept of coming to full-circle, just as the word Shin does with its gematria of 360, is very intriguing and calls for further investigation. The Bible states that Methuselah died the same year as Noah's flood, which wiped out everyone on the planet and was a period of time when the earth experienced a baptism, after which a new era or life-cycle was ushered in. Methuselah's age of 969 is significant, considering 969 divided by 12, referring to the 12 houses of the Zodiac, equals 80. The number 80 is significant here, because it is the years of a human lifespan, according to Psalm 90:10, "The days of our lives are seventy years;

And if by reason of strength they are eighty years, Yet their boast is only labor and sorrow; For it is soon cut off, and we fly away." 70 was considered the start of old age and lasted until 80 years old for the strong. Therefore, each individual house of the zodiac counts as a soul's lifespan here on earth, and then that soul reincarnates into the next house upon the next life, and so on and so forth in procession until they gradually work their way around the zodiac wheel, eventually ending in Pisces, which is the 12th and final house. Each person's life has a potential to last 80 years in each of the 12 houses, which equals a total of 969 years. This is why Pisces is considered to be an 'old soul.' A Pisces enters this world more aware of their reality, and because of this they understand that they have a choice upon their death to either return back to earth as an Aries or escape the matrix for good—or as Psalm 90:10 puts it, "fly away". Although, each time prior to their reincarnation on the earth, each soul receives a memory wipe, later placed back on the earth where they have to start all over again. And yet again, within each new incarnation, a soul must have to slowly pick up the pieces, connect the dots and figure out the purpose of their existence. But a Pisces being the old souls that they are, merit a higher level of spiritual awareness and are able to grasp the true nature of their existence more quickly than any other sign. A Pisces has already gone through the process needed to elevate their consciousness, having reconnected to their soul-being, to their spiritual nature, their life-purpose, have come to terms with their existential crisis, and now able to perceive reality for what it truly is; a simulation of sorts controlled and manipulated by an unseen malevolent force.

If a Pisces were to re-enter the world after their previous Pisces cycle, then they could retain the knowledge from their past life faster when they do go back into the world a second time in a row as a Pisces. For instance, Jesus was the symbol for the fish, a fisher of men, and he ushered in the age of Pisces. He was a Pisces who died and then returned, and revealed to the world the secret to salvation, which was essentially salvation from ignorance achieved by elevating one's awareness by way of gnosis, thereupon obtaining Christ Consciousness.

The Judgement card is marked by the Roman numeral XX. These two Xs when placed together side by side will form a diamond in the middle, which is the same shape as the Seal of Saturn. Saturn is Yahweh, and Gabriel the angel is Yahweh's messenger who always delivers good news. Gabriel is pictured here blowing her trumpet and announcing the second chance for redemption and salvation, which happens the following day, Good Friday when Jesus is crucified on the cross. Thus, the cross on Gabriel's flag symbolizes this announcement. Gabriel speaks for God, and is a representation of Him. As you are aware, the name for Jesus is Yeshua, meaning salvation, whose symbol is the cross. The name Yehsua is formed when placing the letter Shin in the center of the Divine Four-Letter Name of God, YHVH. Thus, creating the name YHShVH, or Yeshua. Moreover, you will notice that the angel Gabriel's hair is made of fiery flames just as the letter Shin is. Directly above Gabriel's hair is the Roman numeral XX, which shares a connection with the Seal of Saturn. Therefore, as seen through the symbolism here, the fiery Shin is placed in the middle of Saturn/Yahweh, which coincides with (as well as signifies) Yeshua. Gabriel's announcement proclaiming that the Christ will be crucified the next day, and how he will sacrifice himself for all the people's sins, gives the people reason to rejoice and rise up from their coffins. This good news offers them a second chance for redemption of their sins that will bless them with eternal salvation. Because of Jesus' sacrifice, man is now able to repent of their sins and earn their salvation, as opposed to being subjugated to God's judgment. Thereby, one's eternal salvation and freedom is their own responsibility. "A slave is one who waits for someone to come and free him." - Ezra Pound, American poet

The Hebrew letter Sin/Shin, meaning tooth, relates to something hard that grinds and breaks down another similarly hard object down into something smaller and softer. For instance, a tooth can be considered a tool that chews on something hard and breaks it down in order to soften it before it can be swallowed, such as a piece of meat or a vegetable. We chew on food before swallowing it, and then it breaks down in the stomach where it is turned into fuel, giving the body nourishment. At times, truth can be a hard pill to swallow, but we find ourselves able to digest it after taking the time to chew on it first. The majority of the time, these newly realized truths turn out to be blessings in disguise. This card is about redemption, granting someone the opportunity to repent for their sins. Both the letter Shin and the Judgment card reflect a second chance at life, as well as a second chance at love. Either by apologizing or by redeeming ourselves we can reunite the bond that was broken. The truth will set us free. Sometimes we suffer because we don't have all the facts and we create our own story, which tends to burn bridges. However, if we were to learn the truth, we would most likely be able to redeem or rekindle the damaged relationship. Furthermore, the letter Shin is depicted as a fiery flame consisting of three flames, or candles of the same candelabra. Shin connects to the fiery energy of creation, relating to blessings granted at the beginning of all creation. Shin also corresponds to the blessings received in the end, when receiving closure at the conclusion of a cycle or phase of a relationship. In this sense, Shin transitions relationships in a positive way, moving out of one state and into the other. Shin positively returns the vibe of a relationship back to how it was felt in the beginning. The word Shin when spelled out has a numerical value of 360, and therefore represents the concept of arriving at or coming to full-circle.

When we are told of new information that goes against what we have previously been led to believe was true it can be (at first) difficult to digest. We are taken unawares, as higher truths are brought to light. It takes us a minute to figure out that the revelation of higher truth is actually a good thing. At first, when we hear good news, we don't immediately understand its significance. Maybe this is due to us having lost hope of ever hearing good news, especially after experiencing a tragedy or loss. We may find ourselves to be in such an emotional state where we choose to suffer, shutdown and distance ourselves from the outside world. Taking this in consideration, when we first hear good news, it takes a moment for us to digest the information and for it to sink in. This includes learning of new truthful information, pertaining to (but not limited to) new rights, protections, new freedoms, as well as receiving a much-owed apology, a debt being redeemed to you, or hearing that you have been given a second chance at redemption—offering you a chance to make amends and repent for a past mistake. Hearing the truth is always good, although at first it can be a hard pill to swallow, in the sense that it can catch you off guard. It is advised to chew on it, think carefully about what it means to you, before you undermine any decision or future action. Truth is shared from the heart. Once shared with others, it enters through the ears and is felt in the heart. It is the truth that melts the heart. And the truth sets us free. It releases the ego-blockages that surround our heart chakra so we may clear out our vessel and make room for the Light to enter. The human ear is shaped like the half of a heart symbol. When you place two ears together side by side it forms the shape of a whole heart.

Just as the warm heartfelt message of good news melts the icy mountain tops in the Judgment card, Pisces's message of salvation and spiritual awakening will melt the hearts of their fellow man. The ice melts and floods the valley below, which causes the coffins to rise up from the ground. The people rise up from the dead and are given a second chance. This is Pisces's life-purpose, to awaken the dead, to open up the hearts and free the minds by delivering messages of truth. It is the truth that will set them free. And ultimately, it will merit others salvation from ignorance.

This concludes the Neptune path for Pisces, but we mustn't forget that Pisces is also ruled by Jupiter, and therefore we must mention this other path. It is just as important. Jupiter rules over the 4th sefirah on the Kabbalah Tree of Life Chesed, and because of this the path includes all the #4 cards. Specifically, this path includes the 4 of Wands, 4 of Cups, 4 of Swords, 4 of Pentacles, The Emperor, and the Death card.

The path for Pisces led by Jupiter's influence will teach you how to apply those out of the box, spiritual ideas into practical down-to-earth ways toward achieving success. Come down to earth by actively looking for ways of how you can be of service to others.

Jupiter, The Great Beneficent, King of the Gods, the planet that favors intuition, faith, and knowledge that comes from within. In Astrology, Jupiter is a planet of plenty. It is tolerant and expansive. The first of the social planets, Jupiter seeks insight through knowledge. Some of this planet's keywords include morality, gratitude, hope, honor, and the law. Jupiter is a planet of broader purpose, reach, and possibility.

Jupiter has generally been associated with good luck and

bounty. Optimism and growth (including mental and spiritual growth) come under its rule.

On the upside, Jupiter is associated with a sense of humor, good will, and mercy. The more negative manifestations of Jupiter include blind optimism, excess, and overindulgence. Irresponsibility that results from blind optimism, not ill will, can be displayed.

True liberation comes from recognizing the ego and restricting reactive behavior. This is a time to slow response time and invite the Creator into your decisions. Learn to take responsibility and be accountable.

In Kabbalah, Jupiter is associated with the sefirah Chesed, the 4th sefirah on the Tree of Life. Chesed, meaning mercy and loving kindness suggests that Pisces should embrace this quality, and know that much of your success will be attributed to the kindness you share with others. What goes around, comes around.

Pisces is ruled by Jupiter and connects to Chesed, the 4th sefirah, which is why the Path to Enlightenment layout involves all the #4 tarot cards. The final card on this path is the Death card. How is the Death card the most enlightened one? How is this the full level of potential? I will explain in detail below. Essentially, it is a death to the ego-self; crossing over into the world of the unknown and leaving the world of what you knew behind.

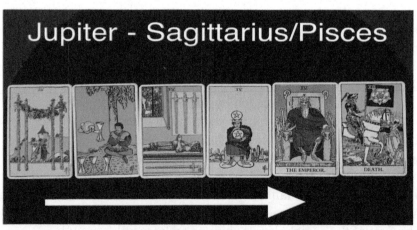

We begin the Piscean's Jupiter path with the 4 of Wands card.

4 of Wands:
The 4 of Wands depicts a couple celebrating their wedding. They are about to walk under the chuppah, which is the archway/canopy decorated with grapevines and flowers seen draped along the top of the four wands. The chuppah represents the house that the married couple will begin their new life in together. This new house is usually a gift from family and/or loved ones.

Wands relate to and represent knowledge; knowledge acquired over time. This symbolically represents the Pisces entering the world and beginning their new life already blessed with knowledge. Maybe this knowledge is retained from their past life? Or perhaps it relates to the higher level of awareness each Pisces merits in their lifetime. The veil is thin for Pisces, who are considered old souls. When they enter the world, they feel as if it is their wedding day; they are lucky and born in a happy situation (for the most part) and feel optimistic and lucky. For them, life feels as though it is a gift. Being born under Jupiter will cause one to feel as though they have a guardian angel looking over them. When they are brought into this world they are placed on a solid foundation. On day one they are already well-rounded individuals. The card is bright yellow in the background, symbolizing the establishment of their bright future.

The large castle in this card's background encompasses this notion. The castle is a firm and solid foundation that will last a lifetime. And it's as if the newlyweds are marrying into a royal family. This couple begins their lives together with the house (symbolized by the chuppah), knowing that they will one day inherit the castle. This is the level of 'blessed' that is felt here. As well as the level of entitlement, and this is where we see the negative polarity of this card, as it refers to the Piscean's personality flaws.

Receiving blessings without merit does bring upon a sense of entitlement, where one feels as though they are better than others. This creates the notion that they have authority over others, a dominating opinion, and a belief that they should have the final say on the matter. Pisces can be boastful, over confident and brash. They can be intolerant as well as inconsiderate.

You must remember that we are all on different paths. All paths lead to our spiritual enlightenment, but not all paths are the same. Some paths may seem easy, while others appear more challenging. What is important is to avoid judging harshly, practice empathy and be mindful. Enrich thy self by exercising self-reflection. Every person around you is a reflection of your own soul—a projection of your inner state. When you judge others, you are actually only judging yourself. People are God's messengers and they can prove to be our gurus. Every person is an opportunity for you to grow and broaden your sense of self, strengthen your character and become more open-minded with a broader sense of self-awareness. It is important to be open-minded and listen to other people's advice, especially when they speak from the heart. This concept leads us to the next card, the 4 of Cups.

4 of Cups:
Here we see a stubborn man sitting under the Tree of Knowledge. God's hand is reaching out trying to offer him loving advice that will improve his life, but only if he is willing to listen.

Cups represent emotions and matters of the heart. You will notice that there are three cups in a row at the bottom left of this card. The fact that these cups are on the left side of the card and there being exactly three of them directly corresponds to the 3rd sefirah on the Kabbalah Tree of Life Binah, meaning understanding. We see here, (through symbolism), that this man in the card feels as though he has already gained understanding, and his level of understanding is placed upon a solid foundation. He has an intellectual approach towards his feelings and can think critically for himself. He is able to resolve one matter from the understanding of another matter. Moreover, the number 3 relates to balance. For instance, the Holy Trinity is three; the Father, Son, and Holy Spirit. Also, the Kabbalah Tree of Life is a three-column system which includes the left column of severity, the right column of mercy, and the central column of mildness, which balances the energies of the left and right columns. The Tree's three-column system is similar to how a light bulb works. Both the positive and negative charges are balanced by a middle filament. This three-column system is also present in every atom, which consists of a proton (positive charge), an electron (negative charge), and a neutron (no charge). Therefore, this man believes that he is balanced with his emotions. He has emotional control. He is self-motivated, and when he sets his heart out to do something he sees it through to the end.

This man sits in the shade under this large. Trees, just like the suit of Wands, represent knowledge throughout the tarot. The wands in the tarot are directly related to the two trees in the garden of Eden; the Tree of Life and the Tree of Knowledge. Since the #4 cards associate with Jupiter, and Jupiter corresponds to knowledge, the tree in this card reflects the energy aspect of the Tree of Knowledge, specifically. This man planted this tree for himself, and he did so with self-taught knowledge. Pisces have a God-given thirst for knowledge; similar to having a God-given talent for painting or playing a musical instrument. Pisces yearns to learn and expand their mind. In addition to this, they seek out to understand life's mysteries and may find themselves dealing with an existential crisis their entire life. Most likely, the man in this card had a desire to one day be able to sit and relax under a shade tree. So, he took it upon himself to learn how to grow a tree. And, here we see depicted in this card that he was a success. He did exactly what he planned out to do. Notice a knot in the tree located just above the man's head? The knot looks very similar to an eye. This knot represents the all-seeing eye of God. Trees relate to agriculture, and the god of agriculture is Saturn. Saturn is the God in the Hebrew Bible Yahweh. Moreover, the planet Saturn's south pole is a large oval-shaped storm, which looks down upon the Earth. This oval-shaped storm is the all-seeing eye of God. God watches over Pisces. And Pisces will feel as though they have a guardian angel or higher being that guides them, inspires them, as well as leads them to the next step they need to take in order to grow and expand their character by obtaining practical knowledge, which can be applied towards achieving prosperity and fulfillment.

God's hand is depicted here attempting to give this man a cup, which is a symbol for heartfelt advice. The man depicted here has his arms crossed, appearing stubborn and unwilling to listen. His heart is hardened, and he is not open to other people's help because he feels as though he has already accomplished what he set out to do, which was to grow this shade tree. The man feels comfortable, and has grown complacent. He stopped listening to his inner voice; the voice of God. But God wants you to constantly grow and prosper. Perhaps God is going to tell the man how to plant more trees? And spark a desire within him to grow an orchard. The man could grow an entire orchard of apple trees on this hill. He could sell his apples and make a respectable living. All the man needs to do is open himself up to other people's advice. The original Hebrew word for tree is etz, which is almost identical to the word for advice which is etzah.

We always need to be open minded, and to listen to that 'still small voice' in our head. This is the voice of the Higher-Self—the voice of the Creator, God. People are also God's messengers. And we need to be open to their advice as well, especially when they speak from their heart. The shape of a human ear is similar to the shape of half a heart. When you place two ears together it forms a whole heart. Remember this whenever people offer you their help and try to teach you something new.

You may think that you already know something because God has already blessed you with the knowledge and the insight you needed in a previous venture, but know that people are God's messengers and they too will offer up blessings to you with their heartfelt words and acts of charity. You will find that by listening to the 'still small voice' as well as people's heartfelt words of wisdom will allow you to become like this tree—allowing you to branch out, grow, deepen your roots and be fruitful. At the same time, you will gain a wider view of all things and obtain mental expansion.

4 of Swords:
The 4 of Swords is an extension of the 4 of Cups card. It shows the evolved person who took the cup, or God's advice, and took it to heart and learned from that advice, transforming the wisdom gained into practical know-how.

In the 4 of Swords, we see a knight resting on his back with his hands over his chest and his palms touching, as if he is praying to a higher-power. If you look closely at the stained-glass window in the background, there is a woman bowing down before a Saint (priest or

Christ) character. She is asking for a blessing. Just like the woman, this knight is also asking for a blessing. Perhaps he is making a wish? He has realized that he cannot do everything on his own, and he is only successful when he is in communication with and connected to the higher-power.

The saint or priest character in the stained glass can easily relate to a father figure who you look up to and ask for their help. Coincidentally, Catholic priests are called Father. Pisces must learn to humble themselves and realize that they cannot do it all on their own. No man is an island.

Likewise, it is advised to listen and be open to other people's advice, especially if they speak from the heart. People are God's messengers, and it is crucial for Pisces success to listen and take to heart the advice offered to them. If and when you do this, you will find yourself more in harmony with your life-purpose.

A Pisces may only ask for help if they feel that they are worthy of it. They may have doubts and uncertainties in their own worth. More often than not, a Pisces will not ask for help. They'd rather put out a vibe in hopes that others around them will pick up on it telepathically and come to their need. This idea can be seen as a subtle prayer as opposed to vocalizing one'sfeelings. As in the case of the woman who is seen bowing down before the Priest in the stained glass window, she is approaching him with her heart on her sleeve. Notice the red heart symbol on her left sleeve? The knight has just proven to be victorious in battle or has proven his worth through bravery and/ or charitable acts. He now feels as though he is worthy enough to ask for a blessing from God, the Father. The secret is knowing you do not have to wait for something big to happen for you to feel validated. Pisces are born knights. You do not have to put your dreams on hold as you wait to be 'knighted' first. Know that you were always, and always have been inherently a knight.

There are three gray swords hanging on the wall above the knight's head, which represent the three cups from the previous card in their evolved state. The concept here is that critical thinking has intellectualized the knight's emotions. Now he understands the 'why' and the reasoning at the root cause of his emotions. He has analyzed his emotions and has reached a balance of heart and mind.

Swords represent our thoughts and the way we communicate, and Cups represent our emotions and feelings. So, with further analyzation, we could presume that the knight in the 4 of Swords took the advice from the previous card (4 of Cups) to heart, and he is now analyzing it, intellectualizing it and allowing the advice to sink in. He is thinking critically about this new idea and attempts to look at it at all angles. As he develops this big idea, he is able to see the big picture and he can visualize the end result. The end result, the outcome, is his 'happy thought' and it becomes his big wish, his dream and the main reason 'why' he pursues his life-purpose.

This wish of his is represented by the golden sword on the side of his bed. This singled-out golden sword is his big idea that he obsesses about. He is excited, just like a child waiting for Christmas morning to arrive. As the knight lays down to rest, he prays to his higher-power, asking to the Father to grant his wish. Perhaps the 'still small voice' told the man to plant an entire apple tree orchard, as a means to receive such wealth? Perhaps it was a dear friend or family member who advised him to do it? The point is that he adhered to the advice of others. The man from the 4 of Cups card did this, and he provided his entire community with apples and cider. It is safe to assume there were apple trees that supplied fire wood for the winter, and lumber for building and for tools. This man would have been seen as a hero or Saint, and even perhaps awarded the status of Knightship. Now, depicted in the 4 of Swords, the man is seen as a selfless and charitable person. He is able to rest at ease, knowing he has done well, and is a good person. He now feels fulfilled, happy to serve others and asks for nothing in return for his good deeds.

He has reached a deeper level of his emotional understanding and feels as though he is mentally stronger. By opening up his heart, he has opened his mind, and now he will receive prosperity and abundance much easier than before. What goes around, comes around.

The knight has gained wisdom in all this. He now realizes the importance of keeping a communication with God. He has come to understand that all his success in life comes from him listening to that 'still small voice.' When success comes, the ego has a way of making one feel as if they accomplished everything by their own doing. A slight upgrade in social status tends to make a person feel as though they are better than others. The bigger you build yourself up to be, the bigger and more important your opinion becomes. This self-importance tends to make one feel as if it is their responsibility to take charge, preach, lecture, and take on the burden of having to always be the authority over others. One with such a large ego will feel as though it is their duty to change and to motivate others to become just like them; as though their path is the only right path to take in order to achieve success in this life. This is why it is important to know that we are all on different paths. And that no path is the only path to take. We all travel alone on our separate paths. Any time you hear that 'still small voice' the message was meant for you, and you only. Surrender to that voice and allow that energy to guide you. This energy is like 'the force' in the Star Wars movies, and this force communicates with all of us in its own way, and we communicate with it in our own way as well. There is no wrong or right way, only what is right for us personally.

Helping others is a good thing to do, but allow others to approach you first when asking for help. Leading by example is the best way to change others. You must first work on yourself before you can try and change other people. You must 'walk the walk' and be the person you wish others to be.

Not everyone is open to hearing your advice. Not everyone is at the same mental or spiritual maturity level to even comprehend the words you are saying. Everyone is like a vessel, and vessels can only hold so much. People's vessels are all different sizes, some are bigger than others. Some people's vessels cannot hold any more knowledge than what is already in there. That is why we must always strive to expand our vessels and keep expanding our minds.

Be like the knight here in this card with his golden sword, which he uses to slice through the good and bad ideas that come to mind, either from his own ego or from the spirit or from someone who truly cares for him. Learn to wield the sword of discernment. Some decisions are harder to make than others, and it is advised you sleep on them. The answers to your questions will come to you, either in your dreams or through the spirit the following morning.

4 of Pentacles:
Depicted in this card is the same knight from the previous card but seen now as being further evolved. You will notice that he is now adorning a new crown, representing royalty status. He is seen now in the 4 of Pentacles as a successful business man. He appears to be at peace. He has been granted the wish that he so desired from the 4 of Swords card. He has been blessed with money, power and independence. Now that he has achieved material success, he also achieves a sense of emotional control. His success grants him the freedom that his soul desires. He can now solitarily break away from having to succumb to certain social norms, the status quo, or society's rules that seem to always be changing, and any and all outside influences including media, etc. He is free to be himself and follow his own passion.

This man continues to evolve as he progresses along the path of the 4's. He has listened to godly advice and has taken it to heart, willed his mind to think critically as he analyzed the emotional aspects of it, and now he is putting these new concepts into practical matters.

The black cape covering the knight's body represents Saturn's planetary influences. Saturn is the planet of karmic life-lessons and restriction. Saturn is the lord of time, and creates an illusion which distorts our perception of time, restricting the time we experience between cause and effect. Saturn floods our lives with challenges and frustrations which are packaged as karmic life-lessons. These challenges come to us as blessings in disguise. We do not realize it at the time, but once we make it through one of these life-lessons we feel spiritually stronger and these life situations build upon our character making us stronger.

Pentacles represent practical matters and things that we can touch, such as money, business, career, family, friends, property, as well as health. Pentacles are associated with things that we are able to perceive with our five senses. Pentacles can also relate to one's social status and reputation. It is a very delicate thing; the way others perceive us. The 'evil eye' is what some mystics refer to as the judgements we receive from other people. We never really know what will destroy our reputation, therefore we must always be mindful of our words and our behaviors. We must give respect in order to receive respect.

This knight sits outside the city wall. He is alone away from everybody because he creates his own wealth. He is independent. He follows his passions and transforms his passions into practical streams of income, so he doesn't seem like he is working. It's not work when you're doing what you love.

You will notice the knight has four pentacles located at different areas around his body. Each of these pentacle's specific locations correspond with a particular sefirot located on the central column of the Kabbalah Tree of Life.

For instance, the pentacle located on top of the knight's crown is associated with the sefirah Keter, meaning crown. This connection with Keter allows the knight to communicate with the higher realms of consciousness where he receives godly insights, divine inspiration and a 6th sense intuition. This knight is very wise and does not hesitate to put his inspiration into action, thus creating prosperity and abundance in his life. The astrological symbol for Pisces is the two fish swimming in tandem, where one fish will swim in the astral plane while the other in the material world—simultaneously. By having their head in the clouds and one foot on the ground, Pisces is able to receive out of this world ideas and then manifest them in the physical reality. It is in the astral, higher realms, where they connect to brilliant and truly extraordinary ideas, and this is where they receive a clear vision of their targeted goal. It is as though they are receiving a calling or a mission, and then quickly formulate an action plan, which they execute with premeditated precision. Once they take the first steps towards their goal the creativity seems to flow from them miraculously.

You will notice the knight is holding onto a pentacle with his hands. He is grasping this particular pentacle as if it were a steering wheel of a ship. This symbolizes that the knight is in control of his personal life, and that he is the one who decides his own fate. The knight is holding this particular pentacle directly over his heart. It is as though he is guarding his feelings and protecting his core values. He is solid and avoids succumbing to other people's judgments that may threaten his emotional state in a negative way. He holds on tightly to his personal affairs, his personal beliefs and opinions. He does not seek other people's approval, nor does he wish to draw attention to himself. He remains private to the public in order to avoid such judgements brought upon by the 'evil eye.' He is an independent thinker. His connection to God, the Higher-Self, is all he depends on to steer him in the right direction. This is what he knows to be true. This is his core belief that no one can sway.

Lastly, there are the two pentacles which the knight holds firmly underneath each of his feet. This represents that he is driven by material matters. Every action he takes has a purpose, and leads him closer to achieving his goals. He knows now that in order to obtain prosperity in his life he must create a way to improve the lives of others. He connects to the higher consciousness of Keter, and draws down its creative force, which blesses him with inspirational ideas. He applies these ideas in practical ways that help improve the day-to-day life of others.

People pay him for his services. He then uses his wealth to develop bigger and better ideas to help improve the lives of others. The knight gives back to the world which gave so much to him. It creates a circuitry. He is paying it forward. This is the secret to prosperity. We receive in order to give. And then paradoxically, the more we give, the more we receive. It is a paradox. We give what we don't have in order to receive what we want. Just like the knight when he received the epiphany to grow an apple orchard, he was given the idea to sell apples, apple cider and firewood to the town's people at the bottom of the hill. He took the seeds from his single tree and then planted an entire orchard from it upon the hill. Over the course of a year, he was able to sell his apples, and with the money earned he was able to venture out and develop bigger money-making ideas that would end up changing the world for the better. In return, he received joy, happiness and fulfillment. And most importantly, he earned independence. With his wealth, he gained the freedom to be in complete control of his life and decide his own fate, and not have to answer to anyone.

Using the Law of Attraction as a means for wealth works autonomously while practicing gratitude. When you appreciate what you have, you will be blessed with more. The young knight did not realize at first that he was sitting under the shade of a 'gold mine.'

Of course, the Law of Attraction can work against your favor. When we analyze and point out the bad things or focus on what we lack, we then receive more negativity and lack. Negative thoughts will decay and diminish our material world. Negativity can affect our health, our relationships, and the way we view ourselves. No one can destroy iron, but its own rust can. Likewise, no one can destroy a person, but his own mindset can. "Do not waste one moment in regret, for to think feelingly of the mistakes of the past is to re-infect yourself." - American author, Neville Goddard. Here is a quote from Yehuda Berg (author, co-director of the Kabbalah Centre) worth adding, "We need to realize that our path to transformation is through mistakes. We're meant to make mistakes, recognize them, and move on to become unlimited." When we experience lack, disconnection from the Creator is often the real source of the problem. When we are connected to the Light, there is no struggle. Connection helps us develop balance from within, which doesn't waver when things shift around us.

Always be mindful of your connection with the Light of the Creator (God, the Higher-Self). Remain grateful for your connection and you will never experience feelings of lack, and you will remain tapped into the creative-force which will guide you to greater successes. Continue to create. If you're not creating, then you're dying.

On a further note, actions speak louder than words. Therefore, people will judge your character by what you do. You cannot buy people's respect or buy their friendship. Your charm will only get you so far.

Respect is earned by simply being there when others need you most.

The Emperor:
The Emperor can be seen as the knight who has evolved into
someone great. Our knight has leveled-up to Emperor status. He is
now depicted as a powerful leader, who has been chosen by his
people because of his selfless acts and charitable works. He is now
adorning a crown with jewels, wearing thick armor and sitting in a
seat of authority.

The Emperor card is associated with the planet Mars, which rules
over Aries—a fire sign that Pisces gravitates towards, helping them
ignite their passion and creativity by sparking a desire for desire. The
ram is the astrological symbol for Aries, hence the four ram heads
located on the Emperor's throne. His throne is colored gray, and as
we know the color gray always represents wisdom throughout the
tarot. The Emperor's wisdom is as solid as a rock. Influenced by
Aries energy, the Emperor is fueled with all the confidence and
passionate energy needed for him to move mountains.

The Emperor holds an Egyptian Ankh in his right hand representing
his willpower over the life-force energy, which is associated with
desire, drive, ambition, and initiative. He is a mentor that continues
to help others by passing along his wisdom to the younger
generation, sharing practical life advice that will save them time and
frustration, and by hopefully awakening within them a lust for life.
He teaches the younger generation these things so they will continue
on in his legacy and build upon and develop the standard of life that
he has created for them. He wishes to ignite a desire within them to
want to strive for success and to better themselves. And for them to
share in his vision of what life can be and evolve into.

In his left hand the Emperor is holding a golden globe, representing
the world in its evolved 'golden age.' This evolution into the next
'golden age' is what he strives for. It is his purpose and his life's
work. He feels as though he is working for a higher-power, and it is
something greater than himself. He knows that as long as he
continues to make the world a better place, he will be blessed with
more prosperity and success. Although, at the same time he works to

free the people; free them from their own mental slavery allotting them salvation from ignorance.

The Emperor's crown has five gemstones. There being five like-objects corresponds to the sefirah Gevurah, which happens to be ruled by Mars. The energy influence of Gevurah relates to matters of the ego. The crown corresponds to the sefirah Keter, which corresponds with the higher super-conscious, encompassing Godly intelligence. The energy influence from Keter is that of pure Light, therefore the relation here with the ego can only be a positive one, influencing positive ego aspects, such as healthy ambition and drive. The Emperor will receive desire for change, but it will be a desire to change things for the better. He will destroy institutions, dismantle governments, tear down social barriers, and get rid of old systems that no longer serve the people. He enables the god of war energy of Aries within him to be a force for good, and for positive change.

The Emperor wears a red robe over his armor representing passion, drive and the creative-force. He is driven and passionate about leading his people out of complacency. It is not an easy thing to motivate and move people. Most people are reluctant to change. They will fight it, and be willing to die for their beliefs and way of life. This is why the Emperor is covered in armor. Obviously, the armor suit protects him from physical harm, yet on a spiritual level the armor protects his emotional self as well. Like the pentacle he held over his chest in the previous card, which protected him from other people's words and judgements, he has now upgraded his protective shell and can no longer be swayed by other people's opinions. People will try hard to shut you up and silence you. They will ridicule you and try to embarrass you, calling your ideas ludicrous. They will try to persuade you to join them, conform and maintain the status quo. But the Emperor stands tall, and his core beliefs are grounded on a firm foundation. He has a proven system and a formula that works, and the chosen ignorance of people will not stop him on his crusade to save the world. If you don't stand for something, then you will fall for anything. The Emperor will not be brought down by the ignorance of others. The tall mountains in the background symbolize that the Emperor will be able to move mountains and succeed, no matter what obstacles are in his way.

Our words have the power to influence others, and they can either build up or destroy our reputation as well as our relationships we have with others. Simply put, language holds massive, colossal power to manifest change, whether it's good or bad. Pisces must remember to be mindful of their words. The Emperor practices self-control and learns how to bite his tongue. He uses the life-force within as a fuel to drive him towards self-improvement. He believes that we must improve ourselves before we can help others. The Emperor transforms his ego-nature into a force for good. "Self-control is strength. Calmness is mastery. You have to get to a point where your mood doesn't shift based on the insignificant actions of someone else. Don't allow others to control the direction of your life. Don't allow your emotions to overpower your intelligence." – Morgan Freeman, American actor, and narrator

Pisces is seen here very hopeful, optimistic and lively in their approach to life. They like to know about life mysteries and have a healthy curiosity for philosophy, religion and spirituality. They strive to know the esoteric. And they are curious of how far the rabbit hole actually goes.

Death:
The final card in this reading is the Death card, which represents the final stage of enlightenment for Pisces. This may, at first, appear odd to have Death as a card of enlightenment, but I assure you it is not the case.

The first clue to understanding this card and how it coincides with this layout is by adding up the sum of all the Roman numerals of each of these tarot cards. The five cards leading up to the Death card are all numbered 4, which gives us $4 \times 5 = 20$. These five cards lead one along a path which evolves their awareness, exalting them to their final stage of enlightenment in the Death card, which is Roman numeral XIII (13). So, now we have the numbers $20 + 13 = 33$, which is the highest degree in Freemasonry and the highest level of enlightenment reached in the Hermetic Kabbalah. The number 33 is associated with the Christ, and Christ Consciousness. For instance, Jesus was 33 years old when he was crucified on the cross. That day of his death, Jesus was reunited with the Father. Jesus became one with the Father, sharing the same super conscious. Furthermore, there are 32 paths on the Kabbalah Tree of Life which lead one up the Jacob's ladder along the chakras of their kundalini. The elevated soul progresses past the 32nd path (or branch) and transcends up into the 33rd, which is the union with, 'at oneness with' the Divine, the Creator and spirit of all things. This connection to the Divine Intelligence, the World of Causes, is the apex of enlightenment.

Another clue is located on the black flag that Death is holding. This flag adorns the Tudor Rose which symbolizes the conclusion of the War of the Roses. This war was a long and bloody civil war between two feuding royal families who battled over the land and the control over the throne of England after the death of King Henry the V. As the war dragged on, the country's people grew tired and famished, and then, later on and closer to the end of the war, the people were hit by a plague. The royal families realized the inevitable demise of their country if they were to continue this war, which led them to come to a compromise. The two feuding families decided to join forces equally, which was culminated with the marriage of these two royal families: the York's and the Lancaster's. This family feud stretched out for 32 years, between the years 1455-1487. Here, we see again another connection to the number 32, which is associated with the elevated soul's transcendence into the higher realm of Christ Consciousness. Kabbalists teach us that Jesus Christ died on the same day he was born, meaning his birthday. Therefore, he was 32 years old prior to the day of his crucifixion, thus transcending to the age of 33 years upon the day of his death. Christ died upon the cross, on his birthday, and then was immediately reunited with the Father. This 'reuniting' with God is associated with being 'born again.' This symbolism is portrayed in this card, where we see the Death knight returning to the Pope, meaning Father, thus Death has 're-u-knight-ed' with the Father.

Worth mentioning here is that not until after the marriage which united the two royal families was the knight finally spiritually ready to reunite with the Father. (Uniting the two as one.)

This concept of time needed for one to become spiritually ready (aka spiritually cleansed) is encoded within the number 40. 40 is a very significant Kabbalistic number seen throughout the Torah, as well as the Tarot. You will notice that there are four Xs on the knight's horse's neck strap, which alternate between the four skulls. The skull is an obvious symbol for death, but can also represent death to things confined within the skull, such as the mind and its beliefs, referring more so to the death of one's fixed mindset and limiting beliefs. The timing and severity one must endure for spiritual cleansing is relative to each individual. The number 40 is associated with the time period for cleansing because 40 is the Hebrew gematria value for the letter Mem, meaning water, which encompasses the cleansing power that water provides. The four Xs on the horse's neck strap are Roman numeral's that represent a value of 10 each, which equals 40 when combined altogether.

The letter X is also the ancient Hebrew symbol for the Hebrew letter Tav, which was written as an X. Tav means truth, mark, sign of the cross. So, we see here on the horse's neck strap the symbolism of death on the cross, alluding to Jesus Christ's crucifixion. Soon after Jesus' death, the cross became a symbol for Jesus and has been used by Christians since the 2nd century. Another symbol for Christ is the fish. Consequently, the Hebrew letter assigned to the Death card is Nun, meaning fish. The spiritual aspects associated with fish directly relate to the spiritual concepts revealed to us metaphorically through Bible and Torah allegory containing the number 40. It's about the experience of having to endure challenges and overcoming obstacles, facing trials and tribulation, all in order for us to grow spiritually, and to become emotionally stronger. The Light within our soul desires a return back to the Source, just as the Source wishes to unite with us. It is our responsibility to cleanse our soul so we can draw ourselves closer to the Source, and we do this by shedding layers of our ego. We must elevate out of our body consciousness (ego) if we wish to return to the Source, soul consciousness. Each challenge and test we face in life are opportunities for us to overcome fear and doubts, thus shedding layers of ego and cleansing the shadow aspects of ourselves. Therefore, every obstacle that 'presents' itself to us is actually a 'present' from God which is concealed within an illusion of darkness. It is up to us to reveal the Light which is concealed within every trial and challenge we are dealt with. You will soon realize that every challenge you are confronted with turns out to be a blessing in disguise. Our souls are promised that they will (one day) be able to return to the Source. We are all able to feel the Source's ever present gravitational pull tugging at us each moment of our lives, as it attempts to draw us in closer. The Source wants us to maintain a constant connection with its Light, which is the source of love and happiness, and toone day return back to it and become one with it again. This is God's promise to us, that we will return to Him, although it is up to us to earn our way back. This can be done by practices of meditation and by working on ourselves.

Jesus Christ's life is an example for us to follow if we wish to unite with the Higher-Self, be one with God the Father, which is obtained only after we experience an ego-death, which would lead us to feeling as if we had been 'born again.' This is also an example of the Hermetic Marriage, which is the idea of one's body consciousness (ego) leaving their physical body in order to transcend up into the realm of the Super Consciousness where it becomes one with the Higher-Self. The Hermetic Marriage is a coming together of the two polarities, the duality, which is ever present in all creation, appearing as positive and negative, masculine and feminine. According to the famous scholar, philosopher, and mystic Manly P. Hall, "Both positive and negative are opposites poles of one circuit. Spirit itself knows no polarity, but manifests through polarity to the accomplishment of the Great Work. The Hermetic marriage is symbolic of the individual who has made himself right with all things, and (most of all) is true to himself and to his fellow men. Human relationships lead to divine relationships, and the unfolding soul builds ever more noble mansions as vehicles for its expression."

Allow me to share some biblical examples of the number 40 as it pertains to the life of Christ:

Jesus fasted "forty days and forty nights" in the Judean desert (Matthew 4:2, Mark 1:13, Luke 4:2).

On the 40th day of Jesus' fast in the desert the devil shows up to tempt Jesus while he is at his weakest, having fasted "forty days and forty nights." (Matthew 4:1-11) The temptation of Christ is an allegory for confronting one's ego, referred to by the Kabbalists as the Adversary.

Forty days was the period from the resurrection of Jesus to the ascension of Jesus (Acts 1:3).

Jesus, just days before his crucifixion, prophesied the total destruction of Jerusalem (Matthew 24:1-2, Mark 13:1-2). Forty years after his crucifixion in 30 A.D., the mighty Roman Empire destroyed the city of Jerusalem and burned its beloved temple to the ground.

Also worth mentioning is the story of Noah's flood where the Earth endured heavy rainfall for forty days and forty nights. As mentioned earlier, 40 is the gematria value of the letter Mem, meaning water. During the great flood the Earth experienced a baptism, otherwise known in Hebrew as a mikvah. A mikvah, is a Jewish baptism where a person is fully immersed in water. The measurement of water was a minimum of 40 'seahs' (approximately 120 gallons) for a mikvah baptismal fount.

Another interesting thing to note, as we decode the symbols on this card, and reveal deeper meaning, is the hidden symbolism found within the Tudor Rose on the Death knight's flag. You will notice the rose has ten petals and five leaves, which gives you the number 15. With further examination, you will find that there are exactly 30 seeds in the center of the rose. This gives us the numbers 30 and 15, which added together is 45. 45 is a significant number found throughout the tarot, as well as in planetary magic. For instance, 45 is the sum of all the numbers in the 3×3 magic square of Saturn. Throughout the tarot, Saturn's planetary influence is represented by the color black, hence the black Tudor Rose flag and the black armor worn by the Death knight. Saturn is known to be the planet associated with death, and depicted in modern times as the Grim Reaper. Saturn influences past-life karmic judgements, as well as being the lord of time, which are both themes portrayed in the Death card.

Pictured below is Saturn's magic square. It is a 3×3 square that has 3 rows with numbers 1-9. Each row, either going down, across or diagonal equals a constant sum of 15. The total sum of all the numbers in the square from 1-9 is 45 (1+2+3+4+5+6+7+8+9 = 45).

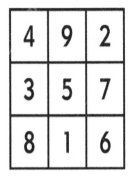 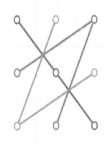 

Concealed within Saturn's magic square is a spirit of Saturn sigil aka the Seal of Zazel, also referred to simply as the Seal of Saturn. Planetary seals are used to seal in the planet's positive traits while at the same time acts as a protection from any of the planet's negative influence. Saturn is a maleficent planet that influences poverty, oppression, karmic-baggage, and has a slowing down effect on all things in general. The Seal of Saturn acts as protection from Saturn's maleficent influence, allowing one to draw down desire and prosperity without the restriction of time or any harsh judgements attached. And on a further note, this seal acts as a portal into the astral dimension, which we are able to access through meditation practices and by opening our third eye. By way of meditation, one is able to strengthen the third eye, which is essentially tapping into and connecting with Christ Consciousness. When meditated on, this seal acts as the access portal into the higher dimensions. Obtaining enlightenment, Christ Consciousness, is the key that opens the portal door. Interesting to note here is that the Seal of Saturn looks similar to a key hole, or an eye.

The Hebrew gematria value for the name Zazel is 45. Zazel is known as the spirit of Saturn. Agiel is known as the intelligence of Saturn, and also has a gematria value of 45. 45+45 = 90, which is the value of the Hebrew letter Tzaddi, meaning fish hook. A Tzaddik, meaning righteous one, refers to someone who is a pure channel of Light who remains in a constant communication with the Source. Moses was considered a Tzaddik. A Tzaddik is said to always be in a conscious state of meditation. The Tzaddik dips his fish hook into the astral waters and receives godly insights and divine inspiration needed for him to manifest prosperity to ultimately enrich his life and the lives of others. Saturn is the darkest of the planets, but it is in the darkest of places that we can reveal the most Light. It takes time for one to completely transform their ego-nature and reach a 'Tzaddik' level of spiritual awareness. Although, those lucky ones born under the zodiac sign of Pisces are blessed with the birthright from Jupiter which grants them with a natural gift of 6th sense consciousness.

Worth bringing up again is the Hebrew letter Nun, which is assigned to this card. As mentioned earlier, Nun means fish, which just so happens to be the astrological symbol of Pisces. The spiritual aspects of this letter share much significance with the Death card. For instance, the fish swims freely in the astral realm, surrendering to the organic flow of nature which inevitably leads them to enlightenment. The fish drifts through the sea of emotions—feeling, absorbing, observing and learning. They learn about themselves by observing others. The fish develops empathy for others, and is then able to understand how his words and past behaviors affected others. The fish is often depicted as swimming in this sea of emotions throughout the tarot. Each instance corresponds to the emotional aspect of someone who has had to go through a challenging experience that tests the way they react under times of heavy stress. Later in life, these emotional outbursts come back and haunt us. Life has a way of resurfacing these unresolved issues, and once again we are faced with similar challenges. This is life's way of teaching us karmic lessons. We will continue to be faced with similar challenges until we finally correct our unruly behaviors. These challenges and obstacles we are confronted with are opportunities for us to grow and to build upon our character, by practicing empathy and compassion towards others is how we mature, and evolve into a Tzaddik. The empathy gained is the power to opening up your heart, and when your heart is open you connect to your inner Sun, or Son, and it is through your Son that you connect to the Super Consciousness of the Father—and thus, obtaining Christ Consciousness. Jesus said that the only way to the Father was through him. Jesus represents the sacred heart, and the Father is the Source, the Super Conscious. In order to open up your heart, you need to first learn how to forgive others, but most importantly you must learn how to forgive yourself. This is the reason the Death knight is approaching the Pope (Father); Death is asking for forgiveness.

Do you notice the shape of the Pope's hat, and how it resembles the head of a fish? This is the hat worn by the half man, half fish god named Dagon. Dagon was one of the 70 sons of the God El, who is associated with being Saturn. 70 is the gematria value for the Hebrew word sod, meaning secret. 70 is also the numerical value of the letter Ayin, meaning eye, to see. Now let's take a closer look at the Tudor Rose on the Death knight's black flag. Do you notice how the rose's five leaves form an inverted pentagram? This is the exact style of pentagram depicted on the Devil card, which just so happens to be located directly over the Devil's third eye. This pentagram connection that these two cards share links the two cards to the planet Saturn. Both cards share positive and negative aspects of the planet's influence. Furthermore, these card's pentagrams, which share the same shape and style, are formed within Saturn's magic square.

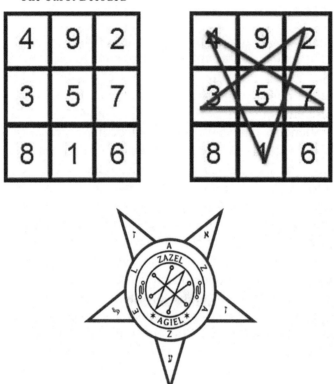

The inverted pentagram represents the drawing down of desire from the astral world and manifesting it into the material world, drawing down the macrocosm into the microcosm, and essentially creating something from nothing. This concept is similar to the Kabbalists' idea of drawing down the Light into the vessel.

We now know that the Hebrew letter assigned to the Devil card is Ayin, meaning eye, and has the gematria value of 70. And as mentioned earlier, 70 is also the gematria value of the word sod, meaning secret. So, we now have here, with all these clues, a much richer understanding of the Death card. This knowledge is power, and this knowledge is truth. Likewise, truth is power. We see now, within this card's symbols, that the Death knight is asking the Pope for forgiveness in order for the Pope to offer up his blessing, which is to grant the Death knight with the knowledge of the Pope's secret, which is how to access the portal of Zazel/Saturn.

The Pope will show mercy unto the knight and offer him up his blessing. Therefore, the Death knight will be forgiven of all his past transgressions. Death has proven himself worthy and spiritually clean after he had swum in the sea of emotions, where he was forced to feel and empathize, making him want to resolve past mistakes. He has taken responsibility for his past behaviors. He has come to the realization that we are unable to control others. And he realizes that this world is chaotic, and bad things happen to good people. We cannot control the things that happen to us, the only thing we can control is how we react to the things that happen.

The Death knight receives his blessing of truth. This new truth will crush his old and limiting beliefs. This new truth will set him free. He has become like the fish. And what happens when you try to hold onto and control a fish within your grasp? It immediately slips away and out from your hands. The Death knight will no longer be controlled by his limiting beliefs and a fixed mindset. He will be free like the fish, and explore and expand his mind and open up his heart to new possibilities. The Pope grants him passage through the two pillars, located in the card's background. The knight crosses over into the world of the unknown, leaving the past he once knew behind him. He continues along the path, facing the rising sun, which marks the dawning of a new day.

The knight returning to the Sun is symbolic of the Christ returning to the Father, the Source, where he unites with the higher level of enlightenment. This is symbolic of the night dying as the morning sun rises and diminishes the darkness.

The knight will begin a new adventure into a new and unknown territory as a reborn soul.

As you meditate on these cards, think to yourself, I am not a victim. All of my feelings of self-pity and my hopes of retaliation are vanishing, as I accept the consequences of my own actions. I take responsibility for where I am, and know that if I want to change my circumstances, it is within my control. I will be proactive, and achieve my own fulfillment. I am letting go of pain, and regaining control over my life.

In closing, it is important for me to point out the correlation shared between the two final cards of Pisces's path: the Judgement card and the Death card. The Judgement card portrays the announcement of Jesus' crucifixion happening the following day on Good Friday, and the Death card portrays the actual day of Good Friday when Jesus died on the cross and returned to the Father. Having these two cards at each end of the two Pisces paths is no coincidence. Just like the two Pisces fish that swim together, these two cards also work together in tandem. And when you add up the two card's Roman numerals you get 20+13 = 33. Again, we see another number 33 connection. This reiterates the significance Pisces shares with Jesus and the relevance to the Christ Consciousness.

"All souls must undergo transmigration and the souls of men revolve like a stone which is thrown from a sling, so many turns before the final release. Only those who have not completed their perfection must suffer the wheel of rebirth by being reborn into another human body." - The Zohar

A	B	G	D	H	V	Z	CH	T
א	ב	ג	ד	ה	ו	ז	ח	ט
Aleph	Beth	Gimel	Daleth	Hé	Vau	Zayin	Cheth	Teth
Ox	House	Camel	Door	Window	Nail	Sword	Fence	Serpent
1	2	3	4	5	6	7	8	9
Y,I	K	L	M	N	S	O	P	TZ
י	כ	ל	מ	נ	ס	ע	פ	צ
Yod	Kaph	Lamed	Mem	Nun	Samekh	Ayin	Peh	Tzaddi
Hand	Palm	Ox-Goad	Water	Fish	Support	Eye	Mouth	Fishhook
10	20	30	40	50	60	70	80	90
Q	R	SH	TH	ך	ם	ן	ף	ץ
ק	ר	ש	ת	Final	Final	Final	Final	Final
Qoph Back of Head	Resh Head	Shin Tooth	Tav Sign of Cross	Kaph	Mem	Nun	Peh	Tzaddi
100	200	300	400	500	600	700	800	900

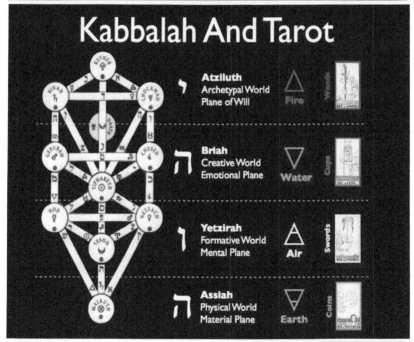

Kabbalah And Tarot

י	**Atziluth** Archetypal World Plane of Will	△ Fire	Wands	
ה	**Briah** Creative World Emotional Plane	▽ Water	Cups	
ו	**Yetzirah** Formative World Mental Plane	△ Air	Swords	
ה	**Assiah** Physical World Material Plane	▽ Earth	Coins	

Prosperity

Absolute Certainty

583

Made in the USA
Coppell, TX
17 April 2023